The Courts And Administration of Law in Nigeria

The Court And Administration of Law in Nigeria

By

Dr. Chief Fidelis Ejike O. Ume,

LL.M., Ph.D. (London), B.L.,

Dip. International & Comparative Air Law, of the Honourable Society of the Middle Temple, Barrister-At-Law, Solicitor and Advocate of the Supreme Court of Nigeria;

The *Ezejiaku* 1,

formerly a Lecturer in Law at The Polytechnic, Wolverhampton, England.

Fourth Dimension Publishing Co., Ltd.

First Published 1989 by
FOURTH DIMENSION PUBLISHING CO., LTD
16 Fifth Avenue, City Layout. PMB. 01164, Enugu, Nigeria.
Tel+234-42-459969. Fax+234-42-456904.
email: fdpbooks@aol.com, fdpbooks@yahoo.com
Web site: http://www.fdpbooks.com.

Reprinted 2002

978-156-281-1

Photoset and printed in Nigeria by
Fourth Dimension Publishers, Enugu.

CONTENTS

It behoves us to keep the law aglow for mankind,
for mankind cannot do without the law.

—Dr Chief Fidelis Ejike O. Ume

Dedication

To Umejiaku family. The lovers of education and progress.

Foreword

It is a truism that it is the administration of law and its application to any particular society that distinguishes law in action from law in theory. So, it has been well said that "the law is nought but as it is administered." The impact of law in any particular society is always proportional to the efficiency and effectiveness of its administration: paradoxically this has not always been recognized.

This is why Dr. Ejike Ume's book on ***The Courts And Administration of law in Nigeria*** has come in to fulfil a very important role in our *corpus juris Nigerianae*. For it has focused attention on an area of our law, the importance of which has not been given a separate and adequate treatment in the past.

The book has covered a very comprehensive field. It sets in its proper historical pattern the development of our administration of law in various courts in Nigeria from 1863 to the stormy period of the Second Republic. The various statutes and constitutions which brought about important changes in the system of administration of law are highlighted, and discussed. Topics such as the reception of English law, judicial attitude to ouster provisions, the place of the judiciary in the body politic, the different stages in our judicial hierarchy particularly the control of inferior courts and tribunals by superior courts by means of prerogative writs, I have all passed through the searchlight of the author's analytical treatment.

Not less attention has been given to the functional aspects of law and its pervading control mechanism over society at large. Fundamental rights, social and economic laws and the highly controversial role of law in the political arena during elections have all been critically examined.

In the book, Dr. Ume has given us the benefit of an interesting combination of high scholastic attainment with his many years of practical experience at the Bar. His academic laurels in London have been well-blended with his diverse court experience in Nigeria. The end result is an enrichment of academic theorizing of classroom law with the practical sobriety of decided cases—a combination of decisions of English and other common law countries with those of Nigerian courts.

Because of its attractive style and wide spectrum covered by its contents, Dr. Ume's book on ***The Courts and Administration of Law in Nigeria*** will surely appeal to a wide reading audience—the lawyer in practice, the law teacher and his student, the social or political scientist and, indeed, all who are interested in knowing about the administration of law in Nigeria. I commend it to each and everyone of them.

P. Nnaemeka-Agu,
Justice of the Supreme Court.

Justice's Chambers, Supreme
Court of Nigeria, Lagos.
March,10 1989.

Preface

The genesis of this work is the thesis presented for my Ph.D. Laws Degree in the Faculty of Law of the University of London while I was at the University College, London in 1967.

This book would have been published earlier than now but had to wait to incorporate as far as feasible, the changes in our constitutional and jurisprudential set-up.

The work deals with the Courts and Administration of Law in Nigeria. It is essentially a study in case-law but relevant constitutional and statutory provisions that have not been subject of judicial interpretation are equally dealt with.

The first chapter after giving the definition of the Courts and the Judiciary goes on to give an account of the judicial and legal institutions that were in existence before the introduction of the British Administration and how they were preserved after. History of the Courts are also dealt with.

Chapter Two then examines the reception of the English law and its application by the Courts.

Chapter Three deals with the Courts under the Nigerian Constitution. Here the various methods of approach in constitutional interpretation as well as the independence of the Judiciary and many decided cases on the subject are considered.

In Chapter Four the judicial interpretation of the Constitution (Suspension and Modification) Decree, promulgated by the Military Government and the events surrounding the Decree, are also considered.

The efforts made by the Courts in preserving the unity in the legal system of the country as well as the constitutional function of the Supreme Court are dealt with in Chapter Five; while Chapter Six deals with the control of inferior tribunals by the High Court.

In Chapter Seven the part being played by the courts in enforcing the Fundamental Rights and Freedoms entrenched in the Constitution is examined. Decisions in other countries have been employed for comparative analysis. Certain important rights deriving from social and economic laws which were not expressly protected in the Constitution but are protected by the Courts and the law are dealt with in Chapter Eight.

Finally, Chapter Nine deals with the role of the Courts in the political arena.

Although I do not claim to have produced a forensic encyclopaedia, it is my fervent hope that this book will provide immense assistance to Judges, Legal Practitioners, Law Teachers, Students of law and other social sciences as well as anybody who wants to know what the law is, the history of our courts, law and legal system generally.

The book will equally be of great assistance to all those who deal in comparative and analytical law as many decisions in many legal systems in different countries of the world and jurisdictions were utilised for purposes of comparison and enrichment of our jurisprudence.

Dr. Chief F. Ejike O. Ume,
Chambers of Dr. Chief Ejike Ume,
Chancery Mansion,
14/15 Enugu Road,
Onitsha, Nigeria

March 16th, 1989.

Acknowledgement

I use this opportunity to express my gratitude to the Management and staff of the Fourth Dimension Publishing Co. Ltd., especially the Managing Director, Engr. Victor U. Nwankwo and the Editorial Manager, Franklin N. Ejiofor for the able, expeditious and efficient way they have handled the publication of this book. I am equally grateful to The Honourable Justice P. Nnaemeka-Agu, Justice of the Supreme Court of Nigeria, who kindly and graciously in his usual able way wrote a dynamic foreword to the book. I also thank The Honourable Justice Chukwudifu Akunne Oputa, Justice of the Supreme Court of Nigeria for his valuable pieces of advice in respect of the reading of the proof.

I must crave the indulgence of my readers for any shortcomings they might encounter in this book. I plead no alibi, the responsibility is entirely mine.

Abbreviations

A.C.	Appeal Cases (Privy Council/House of Lords).
A.&E. or Ad.&E.	Adolphus & Ellis Reports
A. I. R.	All India Law Reports
All. E. R.	All England Reports
All. N. L. R.	All Nigeria Law Reports
App. Cas.	Appeal Cases
B. & S.	Best and Smith Reports
B. Y. I. L.	British Year book of International Law.
Can. Bar. Rev.	Canadian Bar Review
Ch. D.	Chancery Division.
C.L.J.	Cape Law Journal (South Africa).
C.L.R.	Commonwealth Law Reports (Australia).
Cox C.C.	Cox's Criminal Cases Reports
C.P.D.	Common Pleas Reports
C.P.L	Current Legal Problems
C. Rob.	Christofer, Robinson Reports.
Cranch	United States (Supreme Court) Reports.
Cr. App. R.	Criminal Appeal Reports.
D.L.R.	Dominion Law Reports (Canada).
De G.F. & J	De Gex,Fish & Jones Reports.
E.A.	East Africa Law Reports
E.A.L.R	East African Law Reports
E. & B.	Ellis & Blackburn Reports
E.N.L.R.	Eastern Nigeria Law Reports
E.R.	English Reports
E.C.S.L.R.	East Central State Law Reports
E.R.N.L.R.	Eastern Region Nigeria Law Reports
F.S.C.	Federal Supreme Court Reports
Fitzg.	Fitzgibbon Reports
Har. L.R.	Harvard Law Review
Hob.	Hobart Reports
I.C.L.Q.	International and Comparative Law Quarterly.
I.R.	Irish Reports
J.A.L.	Journal of African Law

J.S.C.	Judgments of the Supreme Court (Cyprus).
K.B.	King's Bench.
L.L.R.	Lagos Law Reports
Lew. C.C.	Lewin Criminal Cases Reports
L.R. Ex.	Law Reports, Exchequer
Mer.	Merivale Reports
M.L.J.	Malayan Law Journal
L.T.	Law Times Reports
N.B.J.	Nigerian Bar Journal
N.L.R.	Nigerian Law Reports
N.M.L.R.	Nigerian Monthly Law Reports
N.N.L.R	Northern Nigeria Law Reports
N.R.N.L.R.	Northern Region Nigeria Law Reports
N.W.L.R.	Nigerian Weekly Law Reports
O'M. & H.	O'Malley and Hardcastle Reports.
P.L.D.	Pakistan Supreme Court Reports.
P.L.R.	Pakistan Law Report
P.S.C.R.	Pakistan Supreme Court Reports
S.R.	South African Reports
St. Tr.	State Trials
T.L.R.	Times Law Reports
U.S.	United States (Supreme Court) Reports
W.A.C.A.	West African Court of Appeal Reports
Wall.	Wallace Reports (U.S)
Wheat.	Wheaton Reports (United States Supreme Court)
W.I.R.	West Indias Reports
W.L.R.	Weekly Law Reports
W.N.L.R.	Western Nigeria Law Reports
W.R.N.L.R.	Western Region Nigeria Law Reports
Vent.	Ventris Reports
Y. & C. Ex.	Young Collyer Ex. Reports

Table of Cases

A **Page**

B

D

E

G

H

P

Q

S

T

U

V

W

Y

Z

Table of Statutes

Nigeria

Ordinances of the Settlement of Lagos and Protectorate of Southern Nigeria

Year and Subject	No. Matter		Page
1863	3	Ordinance introducing English Law	83
1863	11	Supreme Court	45, 47, 48
1863	13	Supreme Court	47
1864	1	Supreme Court	47
1964	13	Slave Commission Court	47, 48, 66
1870	7	Courts of Request	48
1876	4	Supreme Court	44, 49, 50, 71, 84, 88, 162
1904		Egba (Jurisdiction of Supreme Court)	53
1908		Yorubaland Jurisdiction	53
1909		Ijebu Ode Jurisdiction	53
1914	6	Supreme Court	62, 84
1914	7	Provincial Courts	63, 65
1915		Jurisdiction of Courts Extension (Protection)	54
1918	5	Native Courts	73
1928	28	Native Courts	74
1933		Supreme Court (Amendment)	65
1933	44	Native Courts	74
1936	16	Native Courts	75
1943	23	Supreme Court	66

Proclamation

1900	4	Protectorate Courts (Northern Nigeria)	60
1900	6	Supreme Court of Southern Nigeria	58, 62
1900	9	Native Court	72
1900	7	Cantonment Courts	61

Nigeria

1946 Edition

Federation of Nigeria and Lagos

1958 edition

1963	ed.Cap.77	Native Authority Law (Elections)	343

Western States

1957	Cap.68	Local Government Law	343, 346
1959	ed.Cap.47	Illiterates Protection Law	295, 296
1959	ed.Cap.78	Moneylenders Law	311
1959	ed.Cap.31	Customary Courts Law	75, 77, 81, 255
1959	Cap.44	High Court Law	67, 97
1959	ed.Cap.70	Local Government Police Law	131
1959	ed.Cap.42	Habeas Corpus Law	203, 204
1959	ed.Cap.78	Moneylenders Law	
1963	No. 3	Administration of Justice (Crown Proceedings) Law 1959. SS.3	188
1960		Parliamentary Electoral Regulations, 1960	366
1963		Constitution of Western Nigeria (Amendment) Law	124, 139, 377

Reports

1860	Brand Report
(1933-4)	Report of the Joint Parliamentary Committee on Indian Constitutional Refor (H.L.6 and H.C. 5 1933-4 216)
1946	Proposals for the Revision of the Constitution of Nigeria, Cmnd. 6599
1957	Reports of the 1957 Nigerian Constitutional Conference Cmnd. 207, 1957
1958	Report of the Constituency Delimitation Commission, Lagos
1958	Report of the Resumed Nigerian Constitutional Conference, Cmnd.469, 1958
1958	Minorities Commission Cmnd.505, 1958

Chapter 1

Historical Background

Introduction

1 *Definition and Historical Background*

The Living Webster Encyclopaedic Dictionary of the English Language, defines Court as a "Place where justice is administered; the person or judges assembled for hearing and deciding causes, as distinguished from the Counsel or jury, any judicial body, civil, military, or ecclesiastical; the sitting of a judicial assembly."[1]

In a *Dictionary of the Social Sciences,* Judiciary was defined thus: "The term judiciary designates a judicial system, comprehending structure and jurisdiction of courts, appointment and tenure of judges and judicial proceedings. In current usage the term judiciary specifically refers to the function of the judge in judicial process."[1a]

In his book,[2] Nwabueze gives a broader definition as follows: "The judiciary refers to the whole body of lawyers who preside at the courts. The term therefore embraces judges of the superior courts and those of the inferior courts - magistrates and district judges."

Judiciary may be defined simply as a system of courts of law and the judges. This definition therefore includes, in this regard, any person duly appointed to preside over a cause or matter. From this point of view, it is intended to adopt a definition which could accommodate the judicial and legal set-ups in Nigeria prior to the establishment of the British Administration and after; that is to say, pre-1849 and after.

Before the arrival of the British and the consequent introduction of the British Administration, there was no one judicial or legal system running throughout the country. The States which now constitute Nigeria (which is a creature of the British) [3] could be broadly grouped into centrally-organised

---

[1] *The Living Webster Encyclopaedic Dictionary of the English Language* 1977, Chicago, U.S.A.

[1a] *"A Dictionary of the Social Sciences"* edited by J. Gould and W.L. Kolb; compiled under the auspices of the United Nations Educational, Scientific and Cultural Organisation, (1964), p.359.

[2] B.O. Nwabueze: *Machinery of Justice in Nigeria* (1963) p.262. The learned author indicated that he excluded lay judges in his definition.

[3] See O.I. Odumosu: *The Nigerian Constitution: History and Development*, (1963) p.5). Vide, also *West Africa* December 22, 1956 Lord Hailey: Native Administration in the British African Territory, Part III, p.1

and non-centrally organised States. Dr. Elias in his book [4] called these "Chiefly" and "Chiefless" societies and to the Chiefly societies he gave the name 'Group A' and the Chiefless 'Group B.' Dr. Elias's grouping was concerned with 'the Nature of African Societies' as a whole.

In the centrally-organised States, there was always a heirarchical administrative and judicial set-up with the Chief or the Oba or Emir at the apex of authority and the village head at the foot of the pyramid. Examples of these states were the Benin (now forming part of the Bendel State of Nigeria), the Yoruba (now consisting the Western States) and the Hausa/Fulani (forming greater part of the Northern States). In these States, a chief was the administrative and judicial head, having final economic and legal control over all the land within his jurisdiction. There could be a delegation of power to some inferior chiefs and headmen in judicial and administration matters. Disputes were usually settled by the village head and appeals usually lay to the Chief or Oba or Emir, as the case may be. Criminal cases invariably went to the Chief either through the village-head or straight to the chief.

Another group were those States without centralised judicial and administrative set-up. Prominent among these were the Igbo (now forming most of the Eastern States and some part of the Bendel State of Nigeria), and the Tiv of the Plateau State. The people were organised in units. The Council of Elders performed judicial and administrative functions. The basic difference between these legal systems and that of the British or English legal system lies in what Montesquieu termed Separation of powers.[5] Both the Council of Elders in non-centrally-organised States and the Chiefs, Obas or Emirs in Centrally-organised States made laws, saw that they were carried out, adjudicated on these and other customary laws and punished the offenders.

We may here examine the judicial and legal systems of these societies and see whether what they had could be called 'law' and whether they had in fact 'judges' and 'courts' who administered the 'law.'

John Austin, the reputed exponent of the analytical theory of law defined law as "a rule laid down for the guidance of an intelligent being by an intelligent being having power over him."[6] This view implies the existence of a political Sovereign whom people in an organised political society are in the habit of obeying on pain of sanction, i.e. punishment. In this light, those Nigerian States, it is submitted, having centrally-organised systems would satisfy Austin's requirement of political sovereignty and the decrees which they issued being 'Commands' and thus 'law properly so-

---

[4] T.O. Elias, *The Nature of African Customary Law* (1956), p.17.

[5] See Sir Ivor Jennings: *The Law and the Constitution* p.283 et seq.

[6] *Lectures on Jurisprudence or the Philosophy of Positive Law* (1885), (5th ed.), Vol. 1 pp.316-7.

called.' But the non-centrally organised States or Societies would not satisfy Austin's requirement. However, Austin would have excluded customary laws of these States as he excluded conventions of the British Constitution and Public International law from his definition of 'law' properly so called. While Austin and those of his school look at law from command theory point of view, the realists, especially the American Realists, would prefer to define law by reference to the Courts.

Thus Mr. Justice O.W. Holmes said: "The prophecies of what the courts will do in fact and nothing more pretentious are what I mean by the law."[7] Gray is even more radical in his reliance upon the courts for his conception of law; he denies the name law even to a statute until it has been used as a basis of decision by the court. Thus he defines law as follows: "The law of a State or of any organised body of men is composed of the rules which the courts - i.e. the judicial organs of that body lay down for the determination of legal rights and duties." [8] Salmond defines law as 'the body of principles recognised and applied by the State in the administration of justice.'[9]

Diamond in his book after doubting whether 'primitive' peoples have law and courts said: 'There are, however, already in the savage societies which do not possess courts, a few rules that are in the direct line of the history of law.'[10] Hoebel has, however, redefined law - steering away from realist complete attachment to the courts and not wholly with Austin and the command theory. Thus he defines law as follows: "A social norm is legal if its neglect or infraction is regularly met, in threat or in fact, by the application of physical force by an individual or group possessing the socially recognised privilege of so acting."[11]

Hoebel's definition comes much nearer in including the legal systems as well as the usual sanctions predominating in different States in Nigeria at the period under consideration. It is submitted that both the centrally-organised States and the non-centrally-organised States had 'courts.' The difference between these courts and the ones established today lies in form. In the final analysis all administered justice, and whether they were Obas, Chiefs or Emirs sitting with their councillors or a council of Elders sitting in a judicial capacity; they constituted a court [11a] and were judges, just as any court in Nigeria today or any other civilized country.

---

[7] O.W. Holmes *"The Path of the Law"* (1897) pp.172-173.

[8] J.C. Gray *"The Mature and Sources of the law"* (2nd ed. 1921) p.82

[9] J. Salmond, *'Jurisprudence'* (1946) p.41.

[10] A.S. Diamond, *'Primitive Law'* (1935) p.191

[11] E.A.Hoebel, *The Law of Primitive Man*, (1954) p.29.

[11a] In *Stroud's Judicial Dictionary* (3rd Ed.) A Court was defined as "a place where justice is judicially administered."

Hartland in his book,[12] considers that Austin's imperative theory is not broad enough to cover the so-called primitive societies and that a new definition of law is needed. He then defined law in this context; "In such communities law is not the act of a sovereign, whether an individual or a body of men: it is the traditional rule of the community; and it is enforced, not by a sanction prescribed ad hoc by the sovereign, but one that is involved in the beliefs and practices of the community."

As we pointed out before, the judges in these Nigerian societies before the establishment of British Administration were the law makers themselves. It must be pointed out equally that most of the laws were customary laws - i.e. having (as Hartland said) evolved from 'the beliefs and practices of the community.' In order words, those customs of the people which had crystallised and became accepted and binding as law.[13] It may then be said that not all customs are laws as such but most of the laws which did not emanate from the direct decrees of the Obas or Chiefs or Emirs and even the Council of Elders are customary. A breach of these laws would attract sanction, i.e. punishment after the determination of the case in a court of a Chief or Emir or Council of Elders. Equally in civil cases, where disputes could not be settled by heads of families or the headman of a village, they were taken to the Chief. Lloyd in his description of the Yoruba customary law and the nature of the traditional Yoruba courts said: "Yoruba society of the Western Region with its Council of Obas and Chiefs sitting in a judicial capacity did in fact have Courts."[14] Obi in his book gave a description of how a dispute could be settled in a traditional Igbo society: The aggrieved would first complain to the head of his family ; who would take up the matter with the head of the family of the other party. A meeting is then arranged. The case may be finished with there and then, but where that was not possible; the case would be transferred to a court composed of the Council of Elders.[15]

In criminal cases, especially in heinous offences, as, incest or murder, the culprit could be apprehended by any member of the community and was taken prisoner. The Elders were usually quickly summoned by the beating of drums. The case was then determined by the Council of Elders in judicial capacity. The culprit was then condemned or acquitted according to evidence (usually given on oath).[16]

---

12 E.S. Hartland, Primitive Law (1924) p.137

13 Cf. D. Lloyd: *Introduction to Jurisprudence* (1965) p.337

14 P.C. Lloyd: *"Yoruba Land Law"* (1962) p.13

15 See S.N.C. Obi: *Igbo Law of Property*, p.27

16 See M.M. Green: *Igbo Village Affairs* pp.99-100 see also ibid p.120 for a description of a judicial trial after a complainant on an appointed day for judging, brought a case before the Council of Elders. See also C.K. Meek: *"Law and Authority in a Nigerian Tribe"* pp.206-213.

In centrally-organised States the Chief or Oba or Emir was always (as we saw before) at the apex of the pyramid of judicial authority. Elias gave a lucid description of a typical court and the seating arrangement as follows: "Sometimes, the judges seating arrangement is casual and unordered; sometimes it is semi-circular, with an inner arc of the senior elders to the front while an outer arc of the junior elders guards the rear, at other times ... it is horseshoe shape, in the centre of which is the chief's dais flanked on either side by his councillors while the other officials sit in a row to the right and left along the parallel but opposite walls of the courtyard."[17]

A marked characteristic of these judicial proceedings whether civil or criminal; whether in the centrally-organised societies or the non-centrally-organised ones, is that the judges in these courts were not usually out for a brutal judgment but amicable settlement and the maintenance or restoration of social equilibrium of the community.[18] In his book,[19] Dr. Allott wrote: "In civil cases in many African societies a chief's or elders' court will try to win the agreement of both sides to his or their proposed decision; often the primary object of the proceedings is to promote peace and restore harmony generally between the opponents, and this may be achieved by the trial of all issues which have arisen between the litigants. The proceedings will not be strictly confined by written pleadings to the particular issue or quarrel that has precipitated the proceedings." Dr. Allott went on, 'a general settlement will be attempted.' It is submitted that even in criminal cases the courts of those days aimed at the restoration of equilibrium generally. This is even implied in Dr. Allott's later statement: "Often the Court sees its role as partly as educative one. It is the task of the judges to remind the parties and the non-participants alike of the basic norms of the society, to get everyone to see what his duty is under the law."[20]

The judicial set-ups of these States continued undisturbed even after the arrival of the British. This was as far back as 1849 when a consul was appointed for the Bights of Benin and Biafra.[21] It has always been the renowned policy of the British not to abolish outright what was existing before their arrival in a foreign territory. They in most cases respected the established laws of the territories, their judiciary and in some cases their methods of administration which were not contrary to natural justice, equity, good conscience. This idea is consonant with what is generally

---

[17] T.O. Elias, *op.cit.* p.238.

[18] Cf. *ibid* p.130.

[19] A.N. Allott: *Essays in African Law* (1960) p.68

[20] Allot, *op.cit.* at 68

[21] Joan Wheare: *The Nigeria Legislative Council* (1949) p.20 also Lord Hailey: *Native Administration in the British African Territories* (1951) p.2

known as 'indirect rule,'[22] The first courts that were established after the arrival of the British were courts of Equity. These were established in 1854 for dealing with local commercial disputes. They were presided over by traders.[23]

The non-abolition of the existing judicial system in these States led to their continued existence up to the present day. Although it must be pointed out that radical changes were brought about by the British Administration. In those areas which were not centrally-organised (most of the Eastern States and the Tiv Division), warrant chiefs were appointed and these supplemented and in most cases took over the judicial functions of the Council of Elders. It may be pointed that ever since the establishment of British Administration the customary law and the native or customary courts have continued to exist side by side with the general laws (i.e English law, received in Lagos in 1874 and the whole Nigeria in 1900, Statutes, Ordinances and decrees). For an example of the judicial metamorphosis among the Igbo we have to refer to Green.[24]

The earliest enactment which recognised and preserved the legal and judicial status quo of these territories was that of 1876. It provided in S.19, "Nothing in this Ordinance shall deprive the Supreme Court of the right to observe and enforce the observance, or shall deprive any person of the benefit, of any law or custom existing in the said Colony or Territories subject to its jurisdiction, such law or custom not being repugnant to natural justice, equity, and good conscience, nor incompatible either directly or by necessary implication with any enactment of the Colonial Legislature existing at the commencement of this Ordinance, or which may afterwards come into operation. Such laws and customs shall be deemed applicable in causes and matters where the parties thereto are natives of the said Colony or territories ..."[25]

This enactment at initial stage was confined to Lagos, but there were similar enactments where the customary laws and courts were preserved and in certain cases modified. To this we shall come later.

2. History of the Courts from the inception of the British Administration to Independence

A *Courts established by the British on English judicial pattern*

---

22 Cf. J. Wheare's idea of 'indirect rule' *op.cit.* at p.22, see also p.12

23 See Lord Hailey: *Native Administration in the British African Territories*, Part III (1951) p.156.

24 Green *op.cit.* at pp.103-108, here the author shows how the elders and 'natural rulers' now preside as judges in Native Court established under the Laws of the Eastern States.

25 Supreme Court Ordinance (No. 4) of 1876

In this survey it is proposed to give account of the courts established by the British as well as those customary courts which were in existence at this period, together with the inevitable changes made to accord with the new order.

As we pointed earlier in the chapter, the only court established prior to 1862 was the Court of Equity which was a commercial court, presided over in turn by traders.[26]

After the conquest of Lagos, a treaty of cession was entered into between King Dosumu and four of his Chiefs and the British Consul at Lagos in 1861. From this date - i.e. 6th August, 1861, Lagos was formally annexed to Great Britain and was created a Colony or 'Settlement' under a Governor in 1862.[27] The lack of judicial and administrative control of state of affairs was adequately brought to light in a report which Consul Brand wrote to the Secretary of State for Foreign Affairs on 9th April, 1860 (- i.e. before the Treaty Cession): It read as follows: "Lagos at present may be said to have no Government; there is no effective protection to property, no mode of enforcing the payment of debts applicable to Europeans; and the wonder is that in such a state of things there are so few disturbances ... this Consulate exercises at present a feeble, irregular and irresponsible jurisdiction over a variety of judicial, police, and even administrative matters ... This jurisdiction has been acquiesced in as a matter of necessity, knowing that the Consulate is the only place where their cases will be heard with impartiality; but, in a large and increasing commercial community there are questions of great importance affecting trade and property frequently arising, which the Consul has not the means, even if he had the authority, of dealing with in a satisfactory manner..."[28] It may be said that this Report had its impact both in accelerating events leading to the formal annexation of Lagos and the establishment of machinery of justice in the Colony. A Police Court was accordingly established in January, 1862.[29] But from the events that followed, this Court did not seem to have been effective, for in 1863 a Supreme Court was set up by Ordinance No. 11 of 9th April, 1863. This enactment was described to be, 'An Ordinance to provide for the better Administration of Justice within the Settlement of Lagos.'[30]

We may here point out that Treaties are always in the realm of International Law but because of many commentaries, including judicial pronouncements about the Treaty of Cession of 1861, we propose to give it

---

26 See Lord Hailey *op.cit.* (Part III) p.148.

27 See A.C. Burns, *History of Nigeria*, p.123. See also Osborn C.J. in The *Attorney-General v Holt & Co. and others* (1910) 2 N.L.R. 1, the historical narrative was reproduced by the Privy Council at p.60

28 Papers Relating to the Occupation of Lagos, 1862, p.4.

29 See J.A. Otonba-Payne: *Table of Principal Events in Yorùba History* (1893) p.12.

30 See, Supreme Court Ordinance, No. 11 of 9th April, 1863.

a brief examination. The Treaty came up for examination in the two well known Nigerian cases, *Oduntan Onisiwo v The Attorney-General* [31] and *The Attorney-General v John Holt & Co. and Others.*[32] The issues in both cases were similar. They centred on the question of the effect of the Treaty of Cession on the acquired rights of individuals prior to the Treaty. We do not at this stage propose to go into the merits of these cases but because the Treaty had been judicially recognised as an "International Agreement,"[33] and because certain doubts had been expressed about the validity, we now propose to examine it accordingly.

Article 1 of the Treaty provided: "In order that the Queen of England may be the better enabled to assist, defend, and protect the inhabitants of Lagos, and to put an end to the slave trade in this and the neighbouring countries, and to prevent the destructive wars so frequently undertaken by Dahomey and others, for the capture of slaves, I Dosumu, do with the consent and advice of my council give, transfer, and by these presents, grant and confirm into the Queen of Great Britain, Her heirs and successors, forever, the Port and Island of Lagos, with all the rights, profits territories and appurtenances whatsoever thereunto belonging ..." Article 2 preserved the judicial powers of King Dosumu by providing as follows: "Dosumu will be allowed the use of the title 'King' in its usual African signification, and will be permitted to decide disputes between natives of Lagos with their consent, subject to appeal to British laws."[34]

The validity of the Treaties entered into between the British and the natives has always been doubted.[35] This fact may be illustrated with the case of *Ole le Njogo and Others v The Attorney-General and Others,* [36] The issue in that case was whether an Agreement made between the natives (i.e. the Chiefs of the Nasai tribe) and the British through His Majesty's Commissioner for the East Africa Protectorate was valid treaty.

That is to say whether the agreement was a valid treaty under international law. The Agreement[37] granted the whole of the Rift Valley 'to be used by the Government for the purpose of European Settlement.' The Court of Appeal for Eastern Africa held that the East African Protectorate was, in relation to the Crown, a foreign country. That the Masai were capable of entering into agreements with the Governor; that such

---

31 (1912) 2 N.L.R. 79.

32 (1910) 2 N.L.R. 1.

33 See Osborne C.J. in *Onisiwo v The A-G., Supra,* at p.81.

34 See *Onisiwo v Att.-Gen.* (1912) 2 N.L.R. at pp.83-4

35 See B.O. Nwabueze: *Constitutional Law of the Nigerian Republic* (1964) pp.9-12.

36 (1913) 5 E.A.L.R. 70.

37 The material position of the Agreement was reproduced in the Report of the case at p.71. See also C. Singh *"The Kenyan Republican Constitution"* (1965) I.C.L.Q. at p.887.

agreements were in fact treaties, claims under which were not cognisable in the Protectorate courts; and that the acts of officers ratified by the Government which were done towards giving effect to such treaties were acts of State.

It follows that the Treaty of Cession of 1861 under which Lagos was ceded to Great Britain was quite valid under International Law. Some maintained that the natives did not understand what they were signing. Others maintained that there was duress. It may be observed that once these natives had interpreters and some educated natives who explained everything to them; the presumption (which is very strong) is that they understood what they were signing and the contents. Duress generally does not affect the validity of an international Agreement especially during that period of international Law,[38] and moreover from the terms of the Treaty it is not easy to discern any element of duress. Article 2 preserved the judicial administrative powers of the King of Lagos - one of the powers which such rulers most cherished.

The Supreme Court - 1863

The *Supreme Court No.11 of 1863*, to which we referred before, was the earliest since the Treaty of Cession of 1861 (supra.) The Ordinance established 'The Supreme Court of Her Majesty's Settlement of Lagos, as a court of jurisdiction, held and presided over by The Chief Magistrate or a duly appointed deputy.' This was a court of record having jurisdiction in civil and criminal cases. All appeals from the Supreme Court lay to the Governor-in-Council.[39] A later Ordinance *No. 13 of 8 September, 1863* substituted for the Supreme Court the title of the 'Chief Magistrate Court.' This Ordinance provided that two assessors should be appointed by the Governor to assist the Chief Magistrate. The name 'Chief Magistrate Court' did not last long for *Ordinance No. 1 of 1864* restored the previous name. This Ordinance established what was described as 'The Supreme Court of Her Majesty's Settlement of Lagos.' A Chief Justice was substituted for the Chief Magistrate as the President of the Court, assisted by two assessors. It was provided that in all civil and criminal cases, the Chief Justice and the two assessors should be 'sole judges and determine all questions as well of fact as of law.' This Supreme Court was also a Court of Probate, granting probate of wills and letters of administration of the effects of deceased persons within the Settlement of Lagos, and exercising the like powers as were by Act of Parliament granted to the Court of Probate in England. The

---

38 See *International Law* by E.A. Stowell (1931) p.403 see also G. Schwarzenberger: *A Manual of International Law* (1960) p.147.

39 See Ordinances of the Settlement of Lagos (1862-74) compiled by Mr. Algernon Montagu. The accuracy of this compilation was referred by Osborne C.J. in *Onisiwo v The A-G.* 2 N.L.R. at p.84.

Court was equally given jurisdiction in bankruptcy over all persons within Lagos who might be 'unable to meet their engagements,'[40]

Commercial or Petty Debt Court

At this time of development of things in this young colony, there was pressing need as was made evident in the Brand Report to the Secretary of State for Foreign Affairs (referred to above), for a Court of justice to adjudicate on commercial transactions. Consequently Ordinance No. 11 of 1863 in S.5 provided: '...that the Court now called the 'Commercial Court' shall be entitled "The Petty Debt Court," and shall take cognisance of cases in which the debts, claims, compensation, or damages demanded, or the matter in dispute, shall not exceed in value the sum of fifty pound sterling.'[41] From the wording of this Section of the Ordinance, it would appear that there was a Commercial Court already in existence before this time but it did not appear to have been established as a court of justice. Appeals from the Petty Debt Court lay to the Supreme Court.

The Court of Requests

The Petty Debt Court, above considered, remained until 1870 when it was abolished by *Ordinance No. 7 of 1870*. This Ordinance instituted 'The Court of Requests Ordinance No. 7 of 1870.' This court was established in Lagos and surrounding districts for virtually the same purpose which animated the establishment of the old - i.e. for speedy recovery of small debts.[42] The Court of Requests in Lagos was composed of the Police Magistrate and the Commissioner of the Court of Requests. In other districts the Court was constituted by the Civil Commandant or District Magistrate of such district and one Commissioner of the Court.

Other Courts

One of the main reasons which gave rise to the bombardment and conquest of Lagos by a British force [43] in 1851, was the need to stop slave trade. Having finally abolished slave trade, the need arose for the establishment of a special Court to deal with problems arising therefrom. Thus *Ordinance No. 13 of 28th October, 1864 established a Slave Commission Court* 'in the Settlement of Lagos for the purpose of protecting liberated Africans, of apprenticing them, and of settling the amount of compensation to be given

---

40 See Ordinances of the Settlement of Lagos compiled by A. Montagu 1862-74 *op.cit.*

41 *ibid.*

42 See Ordinance No. 7 of 1870.

43 See the historical narrative by Osborne C.J. in *A-G. v John Holt 2* N.L.R. reproduced in The Privy Council's judgment at pp.59-60.

to their late owners, being inhabitants of Lagos, or of places the native tribes whereof are in friendly relations with the Government of Lagos.'

It may be observed that in this court could be seen one of the most important roles of the judiciary in caring and protecting the destitutes while at the same time seeing to the payment of slave-owners some compensation for the loss emanating from the liberating of their slaves.[44]

Ordinance No. 2 of 28th June, 1872 established *'The of Divorce and Matrimonial Causes' as a court* of record in Lagos. The Ordinance provided for cases arising from marriages contracted and solemnised within Her Majesty's West African Settlements between persons of whom one at least previously to the marriage had been domiciled there for not less than two years. The court was vested with the power to make a decree of Judicial Separation, Nullity of Marriage or Dissolution of Marriage.

Another in this chain of courts was the *Vice-Admiralty Court*. This was constituted under Vice-Admiralty Courts Act, 1863. The Governor was appointed Vice-Admiral of the Court; The Chief Justice or the Principal Judicial Officer of the Settlement was ex officio Judge, who with the Governor's approval, had power to appoint a Registrar and a Marshal. It was provided that all appointments to the Court should be notified to the Government in the United Kingdom.[45]

Re-Organisation of the Courts Leading to Expansion of the Judicial Set-up

The judicial history of Nigeria could hardly be dealt with in complete isolation from the political and constitutional developments. This could be illustrated by the judicial narrative of Brandford Griffith J. in *Cole v Cole*,[46] (to this case we shall return later). The learned Judge lucidly gave account of the judicial, legal and constitutional developments as follows: "In 1874, the settlement of Lagos was amalgamated with the settlement on the Gold Coast, and the two were erected into a new colony under the title of the Gold Coast Colony. From this date onwards Ordinances were passed for the whole Gold Coast Colony but numerous enactments remained applicable to the Gold Coast ... In 1876 was passed the Supreme Court Ordinance (No. 4 of 1876) establishing a Supreme Court for the newly constituted Gold Coast Colony. By Section 14 of this Ordinance 'The common law, the doctrine of equity, and the statutes of general application which were in force in England at the date when the Colony obtained a local legislature, that is to say, on the *24th day of July, 1874*,'[47] were declared to be in force within the jurisdiction of the Gold Coast Colony."

---

44 C.f. T.O. Elias: *The Nigerian Legal System* p.50.

45 See Olonba-Payne: *Lagos Almanack* (1875). See also T.O. Elias *op.cit.* pp.56-7.

46 (1898); 1 N.L.R. 15 at p.18.

47 Underlining supplied.

As the result of this radical change, a need arose for the establishment of a new and unified court for the new Gold Coast Colony Consequently the Gold Coast Colony legislature passed the Supreme Court Ordinance No. 4 of 1876[48] The existing courts, with the exception of the Vice-Admiralty Court, were in effect abolished and replaced by a single court, i.e the Supreme Court.

The Constitution of the Supreme Court of 1876

S.3 of the Ordinance provided. "There shall be Court of which shall be called the Supreme Court of the Colony of Lagos, and shall constitute the Supreme Court of Judication for the Colony of Lagos and the Territories thereto near or adjacent wherein Her Majesty may at any time before or after the commencement of this Ordinance have acquired power and jurisdiction."[49]

The wording of this particular section was so broad and accommodating for possible judicial expansion (which actually took place), with the result that the Supreme Court constituted a notable landmark in the judicial and legal history of Nigeria. It may be observed that the idea of having a 'Supreme Court under the Republican Constitution, instead of the 'Federal Supreme Court' under the old Constitution, for the whole country, derived from the memory of this renowned 'Supreme Court of Judicature' of unlimited jurisdiction.

The Court consisted of a Chief Justice and such Judge or Judges as the Governor should from time to time appoint by Letters Patent under the Public Seal of the Colony. The Chief Justice and every Judge of the Supreme Court of the Gold Coast Colony were to be Puisne Judges of this Supreme Court of the Colony of Lagos.[50]

Precedence and Powers of Judges

The Chief Justice of the Colony of Lagos was to be the President of the Court, and the Chief Justice of the Supreme Court of the Gold Coast Colony ranked next to him.[51]

The Judges of the Supreme Court were given power to exercise all and any part of the original jurisdiction, Civil and Criminal, vested by this Ordinance in the Court, and to such purpose shall be and form a court.'[52]

---

[48] See Supreme Court Ordinance, 1876 (1901) Vol. 1 Laws of the Colony of Lagos.

[49] S.3 Supreme Court Ordinance, 1876

[50] S.4 *ibid.*

[51] S.5, Supreme Court Ordinance, 1876.

[52] S.6, *ibid.*

The Supreme Court was a Court of Record and in addition was given power to exercise the jurisdiction and powers of the High Court of Admiralty, which are vested in or capable of being exercised by Her Majesty's High Court of Justice in England as constituted by the Supreme Court of Judicature Acts 1873 and 1875.'[53] The foundation for the judicial expansion outside the colony was vividly laid in S.12 of the Ordinance which provided: "The jurisdiction by this Ordinance vested in the Supreme Court shall include all Her Majesty's civil jurisdiction which at the commencement of this Ordinance was, or at any time afterwards may be, exercisable in the aforesaid Territories, near or adjacent to the Colony, for the judicial hearing and determination of matters in difference, or for the administration or control of property and persons and also all Her Majesty's criminal jurisdiction which at the commencement of this Ordinance was, or at any time afterwards may be, there exercisable for the repression or punishment of crimes or offences or for the maintenance of order ..."[54] The Court was given all and singular powers equivalent to the authorities of the Lord High Chancellor of England with liberty to appoint and control guardians of infants and their estates, and such as being of unsound mind and unable to govern themselves and their estates. The Court was also given power to appoint and control guardians and keepers of persons and estates of idiots and lunatics.[55]

The Supreme Court at the early stage of its history handled many cases which were unreported; and in these cases the principle role of the judiciary of maintenance and unholding of law and order was apparent. The country was still in its embryonic stage; the English law was more or less still very new to the large population of the people but the need for upholding justice was imperative.This may be illustrated by the case of *R. v Satomi and others (1882)*.[56] In this case, three people were charged with the murder of a woman. As appeared from evidence, they believed the deceased to be a witch, who had bewitched the son of one of the accused, a woman. The man said to have been bewitched was in fact in a desperate dying condition. There was wide public concern about the trial of these people. The belief generally held was that one was entitled to kill a witch. Even the jury recommended clemency on the ground that the accused were ignorant of English law on the question at issue and that 'when they committed the act they thought that they were doing what was right, just and even

---

53 S.11, *ibid.*

54 S.12, Supreme Court Ordinance.

55 See S.13 *ibid.*

56 This case was reported in J. A. Otonba-Payne's Lagos *Almanack* - (31st May, 1882).

necessary.[57] Despite the ignorance and superstition of this era, it was incumbent on the judiciary to stamp out such cruel and intolerable vendetta. Thus all the accused were found guilty of manslaughter and sentenced to life imprisonment.

Although this decision caused wide resentment which emanated from the ignorance of the people, yet such decision was absolutely essential if rule of law and justice were to be maintained. Even in a very recent case of *Nwiboko Obodo and 6 others v The Queen* [58] decided by Federal Supreme Court of Nigeria in 1958, the Court was called upon to decide a case almost on all fours with *R. v Satomi*. The applicants (i.e the 5 accused persons) were members of a secret society called Odozi Obodo Society. The first applicant was the Chief of the village and he was living at Ishieke. It was shown in evidence that the primary reason for the establishment of the Society was to bring about the security of the area by killing thieves and evil doers. In the case in point, the five were charged with the murder of a woman, who was said to be one of the wives of the first applicant. At a meeting in the second applicant's house the Chief, (i.e. the first applicant) brought the deceased and a man and accused them of killing by poison, his child by another wife. After a 'trial' the woman was condemned and put to death; the killing had been carried out according to the rites of the Odozi Obodo Society - with a brass rod. One of the important issues in this case was mens rea - i.e. did these people know that what they were doing was a crime and not as they thought, for the security of their area? The Court having been satisfied that these men were party to the murder, found them guilty and they were all sentenced to death. These men were later executed. The impact of the decision was great, in view of the fact that the Chief wielded tremendous power in this part of the country. The notorious Odozi Obodo Society was smashed and an end was brought to ignorance, and secret trials of people. Thus the supremacy of the judiciary was restored.

There were other cases[59] decided by the Supreme Court in the earliest period of its history. Among these was a case decided at the Assizes held in Lagos in August, 1877. In this case, six persons were convicted of slave-dealing and sentenced to seven years imprisonment.

With the British jurisdiction being firmly established in the Lagos Settlement and the districts near it, the Supreme Court having by now taken over the functions formerly performed by the earlier courts, the pace was then set for expansion far into the Protectorate. By *Letters Patent of 13th January, 1866*, Lagos was separated from the Gold Coast Colony and created into an independent colony.

---

[57] See *The Lagos Times* of 25th May, 1882, expressing the concern of the people of Lagos and the impact of the judicial supremacy of the new order.

[58] (1959) 4 F.S.C. 1

[59] See J.A. Otonba-Payne's Lagos *Almanack op.cit.* See also Elias op.cit. pp.71-73.

The Government in Lagos was by two *Orders in Council of 1887 and 1901* empowered to exercise whatever power and jurisdiction which had been acquired or might thereafter be acquired in the Protectorate. In pursuance of this, the jurisdiction of Supreme Court of Lagos was extended to the Protectorate. In these areas where the jurisdiction of the Supreme Court was extended the existing judicial and legal systems were allowed to function or re-constituted as statutory native courts (Post). As a result of series of Agreement with the rulers of Yoruba kingdoms, the British influence and authority spread far into the hinterland. An example of these was a treaty signed in 1904 between the Governor acting on behalf of the British Government and the ruler of Egbaland. This was followed by *Egba (Jurisdiction of Supreme Court) Ordinance 1904*.

By the Agreement with the rulers of Egbaland on August 8th, 1904, power was ceded to the British Crown for the repression and punishment of all *indictable offences* committed by all *non-natives* of Egbaland; for the judicial hearing and determination of civil disputes between non-natives of Egbaland or between a native and non-native where the subject matter in dispute was of the value or amount of £50 or more. The Agreement also provided for the establishment of a mixed court, consisting of a British president and two members appointed by the Egba Council. This mixed court dealt with all non-indictable offences committed by non-natives of Egbaland,[60] and in civil cases between non-natives or between a native and non-native where the amount in dispute was less than £50.

The jurisdiction acquired by the Crown under the Agreement with the rulers of Egbaland was by the 1904 Ordinance[61] vested in the Supreme Court of Lagos to be exercised in accordance with the provisions of the Supreme Court Ordinance, 1876.

Similar treaties, as those of Egbaland were signed with Oyo, Ife and Ijebu-Ode. In these the jurisdiction of the Supreme Court at Lagos was extended to reach these new territories.[62]

By the Ibadan and Oyo Jurisdiction of the *Supreme Court Ordinance*, 1904 (later known as *1908 Yorubaland Jurisdiction Ordinance*, and also the *Ijebu-Ode Jurisdiction Ordinance, 1909*, the jurisdiction acquired under the various Agreements in these territories was vested in the Supreme Court at Lagos. The Agreement with the Egbaland provided for a duration of twenty years, but in 1912 an armed riot occurred in Abeokuta; British troops were at the request of the Alake of Abeokuta sent and the disturbance was brought under control. Events in this direction moved faster culminating in a new Agreement in 1914 with the Alake placing Egbaland completely and

---

60 See Annual Report, Southern Nigeria, 1910, p.35. Here the Court was described as "the most perfect compromise between British and native law in all Southern Nigeria."

61 See Egba (Jurisdiction of Supreme Court) Ordinance, 1904.

62 Cf. Elias *The Nigerian Legal System* p.79.

unreservedly under the government of the Protectorate of Nigeria. Finally by the Jurisdiction of the Courts Extension (Protectorate) Ordinance, 1915, the jurisdiction of the Supreme Court was extended to the whole of the Yorubaland (i.e. Western part of Nigeria).

Courts of Equity

The history of the courts which we have been tracing has taken us to the judicial, legal and in certain cases constitutional developments which started from Lagos and expanded to the hinterland, thus covering the whole of Yorubaland; (i.e. the present Federal Capital and what now constitutes the Western States of Nigeria).

We now propose to examine similar developments in the Eastern and certain Western sides of the River Niger and the Delta areas.

It is proposed that by the end of this survey we might have covered the judicial set-up in Southern Nigeria As we pointed out earlier, the first courts of English type that were in existence before the annexation of Lagos in 1861 were courts of Equity.[63] The nature of these courts was appositely described by Dr. Baikie in his work [64] as follows:

> A commercial or mercantile association was, by the exertions of Captain Witt and Others, formed, the members being the chief white and black traders in the place, and the chair is occupied by the white supercargoes in monthly rotation. All disputes are brought before this court, the merits of the opponents are determined, and with the consent of the king, fines are levied on defaulters If anyone refuses to submit to the decision of the court or ignores its jurisdiction, he is tabooed, and no one trades with him. The natives stand in awe of it, and readily pay their debts when threatened with it.

As we pointed out earlier, these courts were presided over by traders (above described by Dr. Baikie as 'supercargoes') in turn, but where the dealings with the natives were concerned they had to depend on the co-operation of a local Chief for giving effect to their decisions.

The earliest court of equity was established at Bonny in 1854. Trading activities gradually extended far into the hinterland following the improvement in means of communication as a result of further exploration of the Niger as a means of transport in 1859. It could be observed here that in contrast to what happened in the Western part of the country, where the expansion of the British administration was mostly by treaties with the Chiefs and Obas, in the Eastern and Delta areas the expansion mostly followed commercial activities of British merchants The Courts of Equity which had by now been established in most commercial centres but they had no authority from the British Government.

---

[63] See Lord Hailey *op.cit.* p.156.

[64] W.B. Baikie, *Narrative of an Exploring Voyage up the Rivers Kwara and Benue in 1854*, p.35

Consequently these areas were in foreign territories. The Chiefs were suspicious of any attempt to convince them to cede their territories.[65] But as events moved faster there was need to protect British subjects in these foreign areas.

Thus a consulate was established at Lokoja, at the junction of the Nigeria and the Benue Rivers, soon after 1867. *In 1872 an Order in council* was passed based on the Foreign Jurisdiction Act 1843. This empowered the Consul for Biafra and Benin to implement any agreement with the Chiefs.[66] This Order in Council followed the gradual climbing down by the Chiefs of the Delta areas who by this time were more compromising. The *Order in Council* was very revealing in showing how jurisdiction in this area was acquired. It was provided that the crown 'hath by sufferance' acquired jurisdiction in Oil Rivers (these areas were called Oil Rivers because they traded mainly on Palm Oil and Palm Kernel). The Consul was empowered to make rules and regulations for pence, order and good government of British subjects and to punish offenders. The Courts of Equity having now been regularized, the Consul was empowered to act as presiding officer.[67]

The Courts were to be composed of British agents and traders carrying on business at the place where the Courts were established. Assessors who were required to assist the Consul in the trial of more important cases were to be drawn from among the members of the Courts. All civil cases between British Subjects in these areas were in the first instance subject to the Consul jurisdiction and only in his absence and with the consent of the parties to the action could the Courts of Equity hear and determine such cases. The sanction of the Consul was very vital to the validity of the decision of the Court Equity in criminal cases. This could be illustrated by an account relating to Courts of Equity given by Smalman Smith C.J. in *Glassie v Leigh*[68] decided by the Supreme Court at Lagos in 1884. This case arose from a decision of the Court of Equity at Brass (in Oil River area). The plaintiff, a British subject had been charged with theft and convicted and imprisoned by a Court of Equity. In the instant case, the plaintiff brought an action against the defendant who had charged him with theft before the Court of Equity. This action was for damages for libel, malicious prosecution and false imprisonment as well as Wrongful Dismissal. The Supreme Court held that the plaintiff was entitled to succeed on issue of False Imprisonment only. The reasoning was that since the

65 See Hutchinson, *Wandering Among the Ethiopians* pp.210-11

66 See Order in Council 1872, Article 1

67 See Article 5 of the Order in Council of 21st February, 1872. See also A.C. Burns, History of Nigeria pp.131-2 and p.136

68 Reports of certain Judgements of the Supreme Court, Vice-Admiralty Court and Full Court of Appeal (1884-92) Lagos: Colonial A.

Consul alone had power to arrest an accused or to entertain a criminal charge, as the Consul was neither present at the trial nor was his sanction ever obtained; the whole proceeding in the Court of Equity was declared illegal. The learned Chief Justice went on:

> It is much to be regretted that Rules and Regulations had not been drawn up for the conduct of these Courts as provided and directed by the Order in Council, 1872, ... or if they have been drawn up that their existence is so little known or their directions so openly ignored. The usurpation of Consular function and duties of so serious a character by private individuals under the aegis of the authority of the Crown might possibly lead to the furthering of private ends or the gratification of private malice under the guise of administering justice.

There is little doubt that the Chief Justice noticed a lot of flaw in the composition of the Courts of Equity which were in fact traders, 'supercargoes' than judges in real sense.[69]

Consular Court

The Order in Council of 1872,[70] as we pointed out earlier empowered Consul or Consuls appointed to the Oil Rivers area to execute and enforce by fine, imprisonment or banishment the observance of any Agreement made or to be made between the Chiefs and the British. Thus the Consul was given power to make rules for peace, order and good government of Her Majesty's subjects being within the said territories. For breaches of rules and regulations in all cases where the penalty was a fine of under £40 or banishment for one calendar month or imprisonment for less than 14 days; the Consul could conduct a summary trial of the case without the assistance of assessors.[71] In civil cases where a suit involved an amount of or more than £100 or £200 the Consul was given power to summon between two and four assessors to his assistance. In such cases, the Consul was to enter in the Minutes of Proceedings all assessors' dissents and the grounds of such dissents.[72] In course of time the Consular Court was established in each Delta area. The Courts were presided over by judicial officers with jurisdiction similar to the first Consular Court, but now included jurisdiction in Probate and Admiralty matters. The Supreme Court in Lagos was made the Court of Appeal for the Consular Courts of what is now known as Niger Coast Protectorate.[73] This appellate provision created

69 See Burns *op.cit.* p.137. Burns gave account of a Court of Equity at Brass which was bullied by the local chiefs into reversing many of its decisions.

70 Article 1.

71 Article 4 of the Order in Council, 1872.

72 Article 8, *ibid.*

73 See Consular Instructions, 1891.

a link which as we shall see, led to establishment of a Supreme Court for the whole of Southern Nigeria.

Courts in Territories under the Royal Niger Company

Before the arrival of Mr. George Goldie Taubman in 1877, there was acute trade rivalry amongst the British firms of West African Company, Central African Company, Miller Brothers and James Pinnock. Mr. Taubman (later,Sir George Goldie) succeeded in amalgamating these British firms to form the United Africa Company, which was three years later re-organised, and incorporated on 12th July, 1882 as the National African Company Limited.[74] As we pointed out earlier, the Oil Rivers Chiefs were at the beginning unwilling to enter into Treaties with the British,[75] but gradually the opposition was dropped and series of treaties were signed between the British Consul and these Chiefs as well as with the Chiefs on the Western side of the River Niger of Asaba. On strength of these treaties the British claim to these territories was internationally recognised in the Berlin Conference of 1885.[76]

Consequently a British Protectorate was proclaimed over the "Niger Districts" in 1885.[77] The National African Company which was virtually in control of these areas was granted a Royal Charter in 1886 and was later known as the Royal Niger Company.[78] In the provision of the Charter the Company was required 'in the administration of justice' to the peoples of these territories to have regard to the customs and laws of the class, or tribe or nation to which the parties respectively belonged. The Company consequently by Regulation No. 6 of 30th July, 1886 promulgated a system for judicial administration. The office of a Supreme Judicial Officer was created. He had power to hear and decide all appeals from the decision of District Agents in all administrative causes 'affecting customs or other revenue questions.' He had also power to hear and decide all civil suits, and also power to try criminal charges preferred by any Executive Authority, or previously investigated by a District Agent in a court of first instance.[79]

In practice, the Company being a trading concern directed most of its attention to the maintenance of customs regulations on the Rivers and trade routes. It became evident that administration of justice would suffer under

---

74 See Lord Hailey, *op.cit.* p.156; see also Payne's Lagos Almanac for 1883 under the date of 12th July, 1882.

75 See Hutchinson *op.cit.* pp.210-11.

76 Hertslet's *Map of Africa by Treaty*, Vol. 1 p.440 (2nd ed.)

77 London Gazette, 5th July, 1885.

78 See A.C. Burns, History of Nigeria, (1948) pp.141-145.

79 See Elias: *The Nigerian Legal System* pp.88-93.

the circumstances. Thus Courts of Justice were established by the Government at Asaba.[80]

Courts in the Colony and Protectorate of Southern Nigeria

With the Berlin Conference of 1885 having internationally recognised the British jurisdiction of this part of West Africa and the charter of the Royal Niger Company having been revoked by the British Government, an *Order in Council dated 27th December, 1899* was made, forming the Protectorate of 'Southern Nigeria.' The area 'comprised of the existing Niger Coast Protectorate together with that portion of the territories of the Royal Niger Company to the South of and including Idah on the Niger River.'[81] This Order in Council of 1899 came into effect on 1st January, 1900. It may be observed that this particular enactment formed a nucleus for the erection of Nigeria into a nation. For at this time all the territories of the Southern Nigeria came under the administrative umbrella of a High Commissioner with power to make laws 'which will be styled Proclamations.' The High Commissioner having been given power to make 'Proclamations' having force of law, the need which arose for the unification of all judicial set-ups was met by the Proclamation of 1900.

The Supreme Court of Southern Nigeria: The High Commissioner, by the 'Supreme Court Proclamation No. 6 of 1900' established the 'Supreme Court of Southern Nigeria as the Supreme Court of Judicature for the whole of the Protectorate of Southern Nigeria.[82] The Supreme Court which served the whole of Southern Nigeria consisted of a Chief Justice and a number of puisne judges. The arrangement which existed in the Supreme Court created in 1876 was followed, whereby the Chief Justices and the judges of the Gold Coast were made ex officio members. The new Supreme Court basically administered justice like the Supreme Court of Lagos of 1876 but because of vast area involved, it created two new courts called *'Niger Courts' and 'Native Councils.'*[83] The Native Council was in fact a court of law presided over by a British officer. Appeals from these courts lay to the Supreme Court.

---

[80] See Lord Hailey *op.cit.* p.157. Asaba is now part of the Bendel State of Nigeria. At that time, an armed constabulary, with British Officers was raised for the protection of peace in the area.

[81] See Order in Council dated 27th December, 1899. The area in question now comprises the whole of the Federal Capital of Lagos, the Western, the Eastern and the Bendel States of Nigeria - (i.e. three of the four Regions of Nigeria - See S.3 of the Constitution of the Federation of Nigeria 1963.

[82] See Supreme Court Proclamation No. 6 of 1900. This enactment following closely the provision of the Supreme Court Ordinance No. 4 of 1876 which established the Supreme Court for 'the colony of Lagos and the protected territories' near Lagos.

[83] See Elias *op.cit.* pp.96-100.

Courts in the Northern Protectorate

The earliest contact between the British and the North was in 1885 when the Royal Niger Company (which was then National African Company) sent an envoy to Sokoto. Treaties were thereafter concluded with a number of Chiefs in the area.[84] The North had by then highly centralised if not autocratic regimes of Emirs and Chiefs. These rulers at the initial stages were not prepared to give up slave trade with the result that the Company was forced in certain occasions to use armed forces against them. By then power of the Company was weakened by the Order in Council, of December, 1899 which while proclaiming the establishment of the Protectorate of Southern Nigeria, revoked the Company's charter.[85]

The first High Commissioner (Colonel Lugard), was appointed and he proved equal to the task. With military power behind him, he quickly suppressed slave raiding and brought the whole area into a system of ordered tranquillity. The next step he took was to adopt a system of native administration under the circumstances. This was consonant with the policy of Indirect Rule which we referred earlier. We may quote from Lord Hailey's work to show the nature of administrative and judicial policy adopted by the British prior to the amalgamation of the Northern and Southern Protectorates in 1914. It ran as follows:

> The policy adopted by the High Commission in respect of the Emirates was expressed in two characteristic statements. On the one hand, the Emirs were given letters of Appointment which made it clear that they were not regarded as possessing sovereign powers, and that they were to obey the laws of Nigeria. The policy of Government was that these Chiefs should govern their people not as independent but dependent Rulers." In the terms subsequently used, their status was to be that of Wakils or Governors, exercising only such jurisdiction as might be conferred on them by law."[86]

This policy led to virtual absence of Courts of justice established by the British on English pattern at the commencement of British Administration in the Northern Region. However, the whole areas were pledged to 'obey the laws' of Nigeria. It follows therefore that they were amenable to the laws of the country; but the establishment of courts by the British was comparatively recent. This was because, with the exception of mainly what are now called the 'Middle Belt' area (especially the Tiv), the Northern areas came under Islamic influences and had already developed a judicial system which the British considered inexpedient to disturb at that time.

---

84 See Sir E. Herslet, *The Map of Africa by Treaty* Vol. 1 1909, pp.128-30. See also Lord Hailey, *op.cit.* Part 3 p.47.

85 See Order in Council of 27th December, 1899.

86 Lord Hailey *Native Administration in the British Africa Territories* 195, Part 3 p.48.

After the revocation of the charter of the Royal Niger Company, and an Order in Council deriving from the Foreign Jurisdiction Act, 1870 was made in 1899.[87] This Order in Council defined the boundary of the territories comprising the new Protectorate of Northern Nigeria.

As we pointed out earlier, the High Commissioner in Southern Nigeria was given power under the Order in Council of 1899 to make 'Proclamations' having force of law.[88] Accordingly the High Commissioner enacted *'The Protectorate Courts Proclamation No. 4 of 1900.'* Under this enactment, (a) a Supreme Court, (b) Provincial Courts and (c) Cantonments Courts were established for the Protectorate of Northern Nigeria.[89]

(a) The Supreme Court of Northern Nigeria: S.4 of the Protectorate Courts Proclamation No. 4 of 1900 provided that 'the Supreme Court of Northern Nigeria should consist of Judges then presiding over the Niger Company's Supreme Court and of such other judge or judges as the High Commissioner might from time to time appoint by Letters Patent under the seal of the Protectorate in accordance with his instructions from the Secretary of State.' The Supreme Court was a Court of Record having appellate jurisdiction as well as supervisory powers. Appeals lay from provincial courts in all suits where all the parties were "non-natives" or where one or more of the parties were non-natives. It was provided that no 'native' had a right of appeal from the decision of the Provincial Court. The law to be applied was, subject to the Proclamation, the English Common Law, the doctrines of Equity and the Statutes of general application which were in force in England on 1st January, 1900.[90] The Court equally had power to order deportation of a felon to any other part of the protectorate or other portion of Her Majesty's Dominions abroad.

(b) Provincial Courts of Northern Nigeria: Northern Nigeria was divided into Provinces and each Province was to have a Court,[91] presided over by a President or by such other person as the High Commissioner may appoint, every such court shall be a court of Record.[92] The Provincial Courts had jurisdiction in all criminal cases including, treason, felonies and offences which might be deemed cognisable by the Court. Where however a proceeding had been wrongly commenced before the court, it was to be

---

87 See Northern Nigeria Order Council, 1899.

88 See Order in Council dated 27th December, 1899.

89 See The Protectorate Courts Proclamation No. 4 of 1900.

90 Cf. S.14 of the Supreme Court Ordinance No. 4 of 1876 where the application of English Common Law, doctrines of Equity and the States of general which were in force on 25th July, 1874 were made applicable for the Supreme Court of Lagos.

91 See Protectorate Courts Proclamation No. 4 of 1900.

92 S.11 *ibid.*

transferred to an appropriate Native Court having jurisdiction.[93] There was no right of appeal from the decision of a Provincial Court.[94]

The Court had jurisdiction in cases involving personal actions of not more than £10. It had power to issue writs of Habeas Corpus and granting of equitable injunctions. There was a right of Appeal in civil cases.

(c) Cantonment Courts of Northern Nigeria: These Courts were constituted under SS.23-33 of the Protectorate Courts Proclamation No. 4 of 1900. But Proclamation No. 7 of 1902 which came into force on 1st April, 1902 replaced these earlier provisions.[95] The Proclamation of 1904 provided that there was to be a Cantonment Magistrate appointed by the High Commissioner. It was provided that there was to be appeal from any order or decision of a Cantonment Magistrate.[96] The judicial powers of the Magistrate were broadly equivalent to those of the District Commissioner under Lagos Supreme Court or of the Commission of the Southern Nigeria Supreme Court. The Court had jurisdiction in civil causes or matters to the value of £5 or less. It had criminal jurisdiction in offences for which the punishment should not exceed 30 days or a fine not exceeding £5.

It may be observed that the main stream of the judicial administration in the Northern Protectorate lay with the native Courts. This was because the system of Alkali Courts which was so well organised that it had taken firm roots to be disturbed.[97] We propose to deal with this judicial set-up when we shall be examining the system of Native courts.

The Judicial Re-organisation following the Amalgamation of Southern and Northern Nigeria in 1914

The amalgamation of Northern and Southern Nigeria was formally completed in 1914 by Sir Frederick Lugard. The work for the amalgamation was in fact started in 1912. Sir Frederick Lugard was appointed Governor of Southern and Northern Nigeria, - and later as Governor-General.[98] The unification of the Southern and Northern provinces into a political entity produced a problem for the unification of the judicial systems which had different historical backgrounds.

Thus, *Supreme Court Ordinance of 1914 which* was described as 'An Ordinance to make provision for the Administration of Justice and to constitute the Supreme Court of Nigeria' was passed. Sir Frederick Lugard

---

93 S.12 *ibid.*

94 S.6 *ibid.*

95 Cantonments Courts Proclamation No. 7 of 1902.

96 S.7 of No. 7, 1902.

97 Cf. Lord Hailey *op.cit.* Part 3 p.80.

98 See J. Wheare *The Nigerian Legislative Council* p.22.

in a Report on the Amalgamation gave account of the judicial structure as follows:

"On amalgamation the Chief Justice and Puisne Judges of Northern and Southern Nigeria were abolished, and a single Chief Justice with four Puisne Judges for Nigeria were appointed, in lieu of the previous seven Judges ... The three Police Magistrates, required for Lagos and Calabar and their relief, are placed under the Chief Justice for administrative purposes."[99]

The Supreme Court of Nigeria, 1914 S.3 of the Supreme Court Ordinance No. 6 of 1914 provided as follows:

> "There shall be a court which shall be called the Supreme Court of Nigeria and shall, under and subject to the terms of this Ordinance, constitute the Supreme Court of judicature for the colony and Protectorate of Nigeria."[100]

The Court was to consist of a Chief Justice and such judges as the Governor shall appoint in accordance with the instructions as he may receive from His Majesty. The Chief Justice and the judges were to hold office during His Majesty's pleasure.[101] The Chief Justice and the every judge of the Supreme Court of the Gold Coast Colony were to be puisne judges of the Supreme Court of Nigeria.[102]

This arrangement was essential because of the lack of personnel during this early stage of the judicial development in Nigeria. The arrangement was such that the Chief Justice of the Gold Coast Colony was ranked next to the Chief Justice of the new Supreme Court of Nigeria who was at the same time appointed the President of the Court. The Judges of the Court were to exercise all and any part of the Original jurisdiction, civil and criminal, vested by the Ordinance.[103] The Supreme Court was to be a superior court of record possessing all powers and authorities, excepting the jurisdiction and powers of the High Court of Admiralty, which were vested in or capable of being exercised by His Majesty's High Court of Justice in England.[104]

It was provided that subject to the terms of the Ordinance that the Common law, the doctrines of Equity and the statutes of general application which were in force in England on the 1st January, 1900, shall be in force

---

99 Sir Lugard's Report on Amalgamation, Commd. 468 of 1920, para. 33.

100 S.3 of the Supreme Court Ordinance No. 6 of 1914 in Laws of Nigeria 1923 Vol. 1 Cap. 3

101 Cf. *Terrell v Secretary of State for the Colonies* 1953 2 Q.B. 482 where it was held that judges held office during Royal pleasure and consequently the Crown had the right to dismiss at pleasure.

102 S.4 of the Supreme Court Ordinance, 1914.

103 S.6, Cf. this section with S.6 of the Supreme Court Ordinance No. 4 of 1876 which set up the original Supreme Court of Lagos.

104 S.12 *ibid.*

within the jurisdiction of the court.[105] Like S.19 of the Supreme Court Ordinance 1876, the enactment of 1914 provided for the observance and enforcement of the native law or custom not being repugnant to natural justice, equity and good conscience nor incompatible either directly or by necessary implication with any local enactment existing at the commencement of the Ordinance.[106]

The extent of the jurisdiction of the court in the Protectorate was so all embracing as to cover almost all the parts of the country [107]

The Governor was given power to appoint 'fit and proper persons to be Commissioners of the Court' who shall within the local limits of the jurisdiction of the court have powers and jurisdictions to issue writs of Summons for the commencement of actions in the Supreme Court. These Commissioners also had powers to administer oaths and take solemn affirmations and declarations.

Every Station Magistrate and District Officer was, within the local limits of the Court to be ex officio a Commissioner of the Court.[108]

The rest of the provisions broadly followed the pattern of the Supreme Court Ordinance of 1876 which we had examined, for example SS.75-77 provided for reconciliation in civil cases and encouragement of settlement some in criminal cases such as common assault.

The new judicial arrangement also brought into existence the set-up of 'The Provincial and Native Courts.

The Provincial Courts in the Protectorate of Nigeria: The Ordinance of 1914 [109] was describea as an Ordnance to make further provision for the administration of Justice and to constitute Provincial Courts in the Protectorate' of Nigeria. Under the Ordinance the Governor was empowered to provide for the division of the Protectorate into provinces, divisions and districts and the boundaries therein.[110] There was to be in each of the Provincces a court which was to be styled the Provincial Court,[111] consisting of the Resident in charge of the province in which the court was situated. Other members of the Court were Residents appointed

---

105 S.14 *ibid* Cf. S.14 of the Supreme Court Ordinance No. 4 of 1876.

106 S.20 *ibid.*

107 See S.22, The areas were described as: (a) "Those parts of the Protectorate lying within a radius of five miles from the Court house at Degema and Calabar and two miles from the Customs House at Buguma and Bakana, (b) 'The townships of Jos, Onitsha, Warri, Sapele, Koko, Forcados, Brutu, Bonny, Opobo, Port Harcourt, Aoa and Oron.' Other places mentioned were Lokoja, Zaria, Kaduna and Kano (all in the North, Abeokuta and Oyo in the West)."

108 S.41 of the Supreme Court Ordinance 1914

109 Ordinance No. 7 of 1914, cited as the Provincial Courts Ordinance - see Laws of Nigeria 1923 Vol. 1 Cap. 4

110 S.3 *ibid.*

111 S.4 *ibid.*

to the province but not in charge thereof; all District Officers and Assistant District Officers of the province and all persons appointed as justices of the peace for each province by the Governor.[112] The Resident was empowered, subject to the Ordinance and any rules of court, to exercise all and any part of the jurisdiction. Civil and criminal vested in a Provincial Court. Equivalent powers were equally conferred on every Commissioner of the Provincial Court.[113] Every Provincial Court was to be a superior Court of record; all civil causes and matters could be commenced and determined in a Provincial Court, and every such court may enquire or, hear and determine all treasons, felonies, misdemeanours and offences of whatsoever description within the jurisdiction of the court.[114] The law to be applied was common law, the doctrine of Equity and the statutes of general application which were in force in England on the 1st January, 1900. Like the provision in the Supreme Court, the Ordinance provided for the observance and enforcement of native law or custom which was not contrary to natural justice, equity and good conscience.[115] The Court could entertain all personal suits of not more than £25 in case of Justices of the Peace, and £50 in case of a District Officer or his Assistant in charge of a division or £100 in case of a Resident not in charge of a province.

The Court also had jurisdiction in all suits between landlord and tenant for the possession of any lands or houses claimed under agreement involving an annual value or rent not exceeding £25 in case of a Justice of Peace, or £50 in case of a District Officer or £100 in a case entertained by a Resident. The Court had power to issue writs of habeas corpus, appoint guardians of infants and to make orders for the custody of infants. It could grant injunctions in any suit instituted before it, and could restrain breaches of contracts or torts.

In criminal cases a Resident not in charge of a province could impose a term of imprisonment not exceeding five years or a fine not exceeding £100, or both, and with or without flogging. A District or Assistant District Officer in charge of a division could impose a term of imprisonment not exceeding two years, or a fine not exceeding £50 or both. Other Commissioners could impose a term not exceeding three months or a fine not exceeding £25 or both with or without flogging.[116]

---

112 S.5 *ibid.*

113 S.6 *ibid.* The Governor was given power to increase the Civil and criminal jurisdiction of the Commissioners by a Specific order, and such Order may be revoked.

114 See S.9 of the Provincial Courts Ordinance 1914.

115 SS.10-11 *ibid.*

116 See S.12 of the Provincial Courts Ordinance

No death sentence or a term of imprisonment exceeding six months or corporal punishment exceeding 12 strokes or a fine exceeding fifty pounds should be carried out unless confirmed by the Governor.[117]

Appeals in civil proceedings were to lie to the Supreme Court from orders or decision of a Provincial Court.[118]

Judicial Development from 1914-54: The judicial regime established after the amalgamation of the Northern and Southern Nigeria continued until 1933. By this time there had been mounting opposition to the Provincial Courts system. This general discontent especially amongst Nigerian lawyers earned sympathetic consideration from Sir Donald Cameron who was the Governor of Nigeria from 1931-1935. The flaws apparent in the composition of the Provincial Courts were more particularly outlined by the new Governor in his address to the Legislative Council in 1933, which ran as follows:

> ... If the judgment of the court is to be the judgment of an officer experienced in the art of sitting and weighing evidence and is to be solely on the evidence which has been laid before him in the case, it does not matter a great deal to me what he is called. Administrative officer or magistrate, or what the court maybe called; it is sufficient that the court is a judicial tribunal and the trial officer judicial officer. But if decision of the court may properly be swayed by political or other non-judicial considerations within the knowledge of the Administrative Officer and is therefore not to be based solely on the evidence which has been led, then, in my judgment, the court has ceased to be a judicial tribunal and the officer has ceased to be a judicial officer.[119]

In this address the Governor was referring to complaints that justice was suffering in the hands of Administrative officers who, not only that they were not lawyers but in certain cases decided issues before them not purely from evidence but from the personal knowledge which they possessed of the locality. The Governor after due consideration provided for the abolition of the Provincial Courts. In the place of Provincial courts were created High Court for the Protectorate, under which were series of Magistrates Courts.[120] The Supreme Court was retained under the new arrangement although the extent of the jurisdiction was reduced. The Supreme Court as well as the new High Courts in the Protectorate possessed unlimited jurisdiction in criminal matters.

Events showed that the re-organisation of the 1933 Ordinance was far from satisfactory. For although the Magistrates' Courts together with the High Courts in the Protectorate took the place of the former much criticised

---

[117] S.17 *ibid.*

[118] S.23 *ibid.*

[119] See Legislative Council Address, 1933, p.25.

[120] See The Supreme Court (Amendment) Ordinance 1933, S.2, in The Laws of Nigeria 1933, p.223.

Provincial Courts, Magistrates' Courts continued to be presided over by Administrative Officers.

The position of things was radically changed in 1943 when a new Ordinance was enacted restoring as far as possible the judicial position of the Supreme Court under the 1914 Ordinance. The preamble made evident the growing need for the unification once more of the Courts in the Protectorate and the Colony of Nigeria, it read as follows:

> Whereas it is expedient to merge the Supreme Court of Nigeria and the High Court of the Protectorate of Nigeria into a single court having jurisdiction throughout the Colony and Protectorate of Nigeria and to establish a Supreme Court of Justice for the Colony and Protectorate of Nigeria... [121]

It may be observed that despite the fact that the idea of trial and error is inherent in any developing judicial or legal system the Ordinance of 1933 appeared to serve no useful purpose in the final analysis. For as was expressly stated in the preamble there was a need for retaining the judicial unity which was brought about by the amalgamation between the Southern and Northern Protectorates of Nigeria.

It was provided that from and after the coming into operation of the Ordinance of 1943 there was to be one Supreme Court of Justice for Nigeria.[122] The Court was to consist of a Chief Justice and such other Judges as the Governor may appoint. The Judges were to be called Senior Puisne Judge, the Second, Third, Fourth and Puisne Judges.[123] The Supreme Court was to be a Superior Court of record, possessing powers and authorities which were vested in or capable of being exercised by His Majesty's High Court of Justice in England. It therefore had jurisdiction for the judicial hearing and determination of matters in difference, or for the administration or control of property and person. It equally had criminal jurisdiction 'for the repression or punishment for crimes or offences or for the maintenance of order.'[124] It was provided that the Supreme Court was to have all the singular powers and authorities of the Lord High Chancellor of England, with liberty to appoint and control guardians of infants and their estates and also keepers of the persons of estates of idiots, lunatics and such as being of unsound mind and are unable to govern themselves and their estates.[125]

As was pointed out above the enactment broadly restored the position created by the 1914 Ordinance, so we do not deem it expedient to re-examine of the provisions. But the position of the Admiralty under this

---

121 See Supreme Court Ordinance No. 23 of 1943 in Laws of Nigeria 1943, pp.A.134-135.

122 S.3, Supreme Court Ordinance No. 23 of 1943.

123 S.4, *ibid.*

124 SS.11 and 12 *ibid.*

125 S.13 of the Supreme Court Ordinance.

enactment requires mention. The Ordinance provided that there was to be a Colonial Court of Admiralty within the meaning of the Colonial Courts of Admiralty Act. 1890. It was to have and exercise Admiralty jurisdiction in accordance with the provisions of the 1890 Act in all matters arising upon the high seas or elsewhere or upon any lake or other navigable inland waters or otherwise relating to ships and shipping.[126] The Supreme Court was to have appellate jurisdiction over Magistrate's Courts. Appeals from the Supreme Court were to lie to the West African court of Appeal and from thence to the Judicial Committee of the Privy Council.

The judicial reform introduced in 1943 continued uninterrupted despite many constitutional changes until 1954. The overpowering demand for a greater regional autonomy made by politicians in the years immediately following the inception of the 1951 Constitution outweighed the plea and desire of many Nigerian lawyers for the maintenance of the judicial *status quo* Eventually in 1954 the judicial system was regionalised.

The Nigeria (Constitution) Order in Council, 1954, created a Federal Supreme Court for Nigeria.[127] The judges of the Court were to a Chief Justice of the Federation, two Federal Justices and such setting Federal Justices as may be appointed. The Court was to be a superior court of record which was to sit in Lagos or any part of Nigeria as the Chief Justice with the approval of the Governor-General should appoint. The Federal Supreme Court was to exercise jurisdiction, exclusive and original in any dispute between the Federation and a Region or between the Regions. It was to have power to issue a writ or order of mandamus or prohibition or an injunction against an officer or authority of the Federation.[128]

Under the Constitution, the Regional Legislatures were empowered to establish their own judicial systems. The Federal Territory of Lagos was also to have its own judicial system.[129] Before the introduction of the Republican Constitution on 1963 the courts established in the Regions on English judicial pattern were the High Court and the Magistrate's Courts. The 1954 Constitution conferred appellate jurisdiction on the Federal Supreme Court from all decisions of the High Courts established in the Regions and Lagos. Where a person was sentenced to death in a Regional High Court appeal to the Federal Supreme Court was to be of right.[130]

With the creation of the Federal Supreme Court, the appellate jurisdiction of the West African Court of Appeal was, as regards cases from

---

126 See S.24 *ibid.*

127 S.13 S.1 1954 No. 114 - The Nigeria (Constitution) Order in Council, 1954

128 S.144, *ibid.*

129 S.142, *ibid.* Having been so empowered, the Regions then established their respective High Courts. See High Court Laws, 1955 of Eastern, Western and Northern Nigeria: No. 20 of 1955, Cap. 44 and Cap. 49 respectively.

130 SS.147, 148 *ibid.*

Nigeria abolished, but appeals from the Federal Supreme Court lay to the Judicial Committee of the Privy Council.

The judicial regime established before independence broadly continued until independence in 1960. The Nigeria (Constitution) Order in Council, 1960 maintained the pattern set up by the 1954 Constitution. But it more particularly spelt out that appeals from the Federal Supreme Court were to be to Her Majesty's Privy Council.[131] It was provided that the Judges of the Federal Supreme Court should include the Chief Justice of each territory.[132] Basically all the powers vested in the Federal Supreme Court by the 1954 Constitution were retained.

The Republican Constitution of 1963 restored the name 'Supreme Court of Nigeria.' We may recall here that since 1914 there has always been the idea of having one 'Supreme Court for the whole of Nigeria. The Supreme Court was to be a Superior Court of record and was to sit in the Federal territory and in such other places in Nigeria as the Chief Justice of Nigeria might appoint.[133] Under the 1963 Constitution the Supreme Court was placed at the apex of the Nigerian systems of Courts and it took the place of the Privy Council and the Federal Supreme Court. Other powers of the Supreme Court were basically the same as those of the displaced Federal Supreme Court. It follows from the arrangement under the Republican Constitution that the Nigeria Supreme Court is the last court of Appeal. It may be observed that in view of the fact that the Supreme Court was given original jurisdiction in certain cases there should have been a judicial set-up which should take the place of the Privy Council as the final Court of Appeal. Such Privy Council should then be performing certain functions which Her Majesty's Privy Council performs in the United Kingdom. The composition of such a Court should include certain judges from the Regions other than the Chief Justices, so that there should be a greater unity of the judicial systems in the country.

One of the new judicial establishments under the 1963 Constitution was the introduction of the Regional Courts of Appeal.[134] Appeals lie from the decisions of the High Court of the Region to the Regional Court of Appeal as of right in final decisions in any civil proceedings before the High Court sitting at first instance, decisions in any civil or criminal proceedings on questions as to whether any of the provisions of Chapter 3 of the Constitution (i.e. provisions dealing with Fundamental Human Rights) of

---

131 S.114 Nigeria (Constitution) Order in Council, 1960 in laws of Nigeria 1960 also S.1, 1652.

132 S.104 *ibid*. The 'territories' in this case meant the Regions, including Lagos.

133 S.111 of the Constitution of the Federation, 1963.

134 See S.56 of the Constitution of the Northern Region.
See S.54 of the Constitution of the Eastern Region.
See S.52 of the Constitution of the Western Region.
See S.52 of the Constitution of the Mid-Western Region.

the Federation had been contravened, decisions in any criminal proceedings in which any person has been sentenced to death by the High Court or in which the High Court has affirmed a sentence of death imposed by some other court, and in any decision involving questions of law alone in any criminal proceedings.[135]

It may be observed that the introduction of Courts of Appeal in the Regions was desirable as they serve to lessen the flow of appeals from all the High Courts of the country to the Supreme Court. With this account we come to the end of the history of the Nigerian Courts established on English judicial pattern. As appeals from the Supreme Court of Nigeria lay to the West African Court of Appeal until 1954, we may therefore give a brief account of the history of the West African Court of Appeal.

B. *The West African Court of Appeal*

The West African Court of Appeal was created by an Order in Council dated 26th February, 1867.[136] The Court consisted of the judges of the Supreme Court of the Settlement of Sierra Leone. A Court of record, it was to have jurisdiction over appeals from the Courts of Civil and Criminal Justice of the Settlements of Gambia, Lagos and the Gold Coast. As was pointed out earlier, Lagos and the Gold Coast were erected into a single Colony of the Gold Coast Colony in 1874. After the dissolution of the union in 1886, the West African Court of Appeal ceased for that time to be a court of Appeal for the Settlements. From thence, appeals from the Supreme Court of Nigeria went directly to the Privy Council. Owing to the mounting demands for the re-establishment of the West African Court of Appeal, an Order in Council[137] to this effect was issued. The necessity for the Court was made evident even in the preamble which read as follows:

> Whereas it is expedient to make further and other provision than that heretofore in force for the hearing and determining of appeals from His Majesty's Supreme Courts of the Colonies of the Gold Coast,Sierra Leone, and the Gambia, and from His Majesty's Chief Commissioners Court of Ashanti ...

The Court was to compose of the Chief Justice of the Gold Coast, who was to be the President, and the Judges of the Supreme Courts of the Colonies.[138] The Court of Appeal was empowered to hear and determine appeals from any of the Courts of the Colonies including reserved questions

---

135 See for example, S.53 of the Western Region Constitution 1963.

136 See the Order in Council - instrument No. 7 of 26th February, 1867. The Order in Council was enacted from the Coast of Africa and Falkland Islands Act, 1843.

137 See Order in Council No. 889 dated 1st November, 1928. It was shown in the preamble that the enactment was made from the British Settlement Act 1887 in respect of the Colonies and the Foreign Jurisdiction Act 1899 in respect of the Protectorates.

138 S.5 of the Order in Council.

questions of law and appeals against conviction. The Court of Appeal was to be duly constituted if it consisted of an uneven number, or not being less than three of the Judges.[139] Although the Judges of the Supreme Court of Nigeria were mentioned in the Order in Council [140] constituting the Court, an Ordinance[141] was passed to bring into effect the regulations and provisions of the Orders in Council. It was provided that appeals were to lie from the Supreme Courts decisions in civil cases to the value of £50 of over or from decree nisi or absolute made by the Supreme Court, and by lease, from interlocutory decisions. Appeals were to lie in criminal cases from the decisions of the Supreme Court or Matine Courts against any conviction on a question of law or fact or a question of mixed law and fact. With leave of the Supreme Court against sentence unless the sentence is fixed by law.

The West African Court of Appeal continued to function until 1954 (as regards Nigeria) when appeals to the Court were stopped, following the introduction of the Federal Supreme Court. From thence appeals from the Federal Supreme Court lay directly to the Privy Council in the United Kingdom. This was consequently brought to an end after the introduction of the Republican Constitution in 1963, and as was pointed out earlier, the Nigerian Supreme Court is now the last Court of Appeal for the whole country.

3. History of the Statutory Native Courts

Early in the chapter we showed the nature of legal systems in the country before the advent of the British Administration. These legal systems flourished even after the arrival of the British because of the renowned policy of the British of not wiping away indigenous or traditional establishments as long as they are not revoltingly intolerable and not contrary to justice, equity or good conscience. Thus the traditional native courts were allowed to function, administering customary laws. As we pointed out at the commencement, these Societies could be broadly divided into centralised and non-centralised States. Those having centralised institutions had Chiefs or Emirs at the apex of the pyramid of authority. These had courts presided over by the Chief and his councillors. At a later stage in the Northern States (after the reception of Islamic laws, the Alkali Courts were presided over by a legally qualified person (i.e. the Alkali). Thus there was an apparent separation of powers. Thus the legislative and judicial powers were vested in the traditional rulers. The Chieftaincy institution in the greater part of the Eastern part of Nigeria, owes its

---

139 S.9 (1) *ibid.*

140 S.5 (2) of the Order in Council of 1928.

141 See West African Court of Appeal Ordinance No. 47 of 1933. This was amended by Ordinance No. 6 of 1938.

existence to the British. The Igbo like the Tiv in the North had no chiefs or purely centralised institutions. There were Council of Elders appointed by the people. These Elders performed legislative (by decrees) and judicial functions. There was no separation of powers equally. The British created in these areas what were called Warrant Chiefs.

These were prominent men in the localities and people who were bold enough to come forward to claim to speak 'for the people.' Having created centralised institutions they never existed and having encouraged them where they already flourished, the British then thought it expedient to bring about a pattern which would be predominating throughout the country, hence the inevitable creation of Statutory native courts.

The Supreme Court Ordinance No. 4 of 1876 which was a landmark in the judicial history of Nigeria was apparently silent on the fate of indigenous courts in Lagos Colony or 'territories subject to its jurisdiction.' It merely provided as follows:

> Nothing in this Ordinance should deprive the Supreme Court of the right to observe and enforce the observance, or shall deprive any person of the benefit, of any law or custom existing in the said Colony, or Territories subject to its jurisdiction, such law or custom not being repugnant to natural justice, equity and good conscience, nor incompatible either directly or by necessary implication with any enactment of the Colonial legislature existing at the commencement of this Ordinance, or which may afterwards come into operation. Such laws and custom shall be deemed applicable in causes and matters where the parties thereto are natives of the said Colony or Territories.[142]

Following this provision in the enactment, the Supreme Court started to take cognisance of the Native or customary laws when and if such cases involving customary laws were brought before it. This could be illustrated by the case of Cole v Cole 1898.[143] In this case, the provision of S.19 (above quoted) was quoted and adequately considered. The point in issue here was inheritance under native or customary law. The plaintiff was the brother of the deceased. The deceased had a lunatic son and left a widow. The plaintiff claimed that under the customary law, he was the rightful heir to the dead brother to the exclusion of the son and the widow. This is true under the customary law, although this right is contingent on the customary heir maintaining the widow and the children of the deceased. In the instant case, the marriage was a Christian marriage which was in fact to be governed by English law.

Brandford Griffith J. held that the customary law of inheritance was inapplicable and thus the plaintiff was not entitled to succeed. He observed: "If the contrary is held, it would be contrary to the principles of justice,

---

142 S.19,Supreme Court Ordinance No. 4 of 1876.

143 (1898) 1 N.L.R. 15.

equity and good conscience."[144] We shall be returning to this case again but it could be observed that with every respect to the learned Judge, the obiter beclouded his decision. For once a marriage is contracted under the customary law it is governed by that law, if otherwise then the customary law is inapplicable. Thus in the case of Christian marriage it is governed by the English law which rules out any application of the customary. As was pointed out above, we shall be revisiting this case when we shall be dealing with co-existence between the general law (i.e. English law, Ordinances, and proclamations and decrees) and the customary. But we have to quote a section of the decision in the judicial Statement of *Rayner C.J.* who although agreeing that native law was inapplicable said: "I think that the respondent is not barred by that provision (i.e. S.19 of the Ordinance) from claiming to have native law applied.[145] It follows that the customary law involved was recognised but could not apply as the marriage was different. From this point of view the decision was quite correct."

It follows that customary law was being applied in the Courts established according to English pattern but the main body of the customary law was left to be administered in the traditional courts. It was not until 1900 that Statutory native courts were introduced. By this time the whole of the Southern part of Nigeria had been proclaimed 'the Protectorate of Southern Nigeria.' The Native Courts Proclamation No. 9 of 1900 was issued 'to provide for the administration of justice in Native Courts.'[146] The proclamation provided for the establishment of two types of courts: (i) *The Minor courts* and (ii) *The Native Councils*.

The Minor courts were to be presided over by a Native Authority. While the Native Councils were to be presided over by a British Officer. It may be observed that the Native Councils were in fact courts of law. It was provided that in the administration of justice in the Minor Courts regard was to be had of any native law or custom 'not opposed to natural morality and humanity.' As we have examined above, S.19 of the Supreme Court Ordinance 1876 had a similar provision with respect to the Supreme Court established in the Colony of Lagos but later its jurisdiction gradually extended to the whole of the Southern Protectorate. The Native Councils were to be under a District Commissioner who was to be the ex officio President. The court was to consist of such persons as the High Commissioner was from time to time to appoint.

The Minor Courts were to have jurisdiction over civil cases where the amount involved did not exceed £25. They were also to o have jurisdiction in land cases where the dispute arose from native tenure or customary

---

144 *Cole v Cole* (1898) 1 N.L.R. at p.22.

145 *ibid* at p.23

146 See Native Courts: 'Proclamation No. 9 of 1900. See also Keay and Richardson: *The Native and Customary Courts of Nigeria* (1966) p.7 et seq.

tenure; and in succession cases if the value of property did not exceed £50. The Minor Courts were to have criminal jurisdiction over offences which were to be described in the rules listed in the Schedule for the guidance of the Court.[147] The Native Councils were given the powers to supervise the Minor Court and were vested with all the powers of the Minor Court including certain mentioned offences.[148] The Native Courts were given jurisdiction over natives only save in any case where non-natives consented to the jurisdiction extending to them. Appeals from Minor Courts lay to the Native Councils.

In the 1906 Native Courts Proclamation[149] account was taken of the need for bringing into the new judicial set-up the original type of judicial administration especially in the Northern Protectorate. Thus three kinds of Courts were established: (i) *The Emir's Court* made up of the Emir and his Council, (ii) *The Alkali Courts* which could sit with or without assessors, (iii) In non-Moslem area a Chief and his Council composed the Court.

With the amalgamation of the Northern and Southern Nigeria in 1914 a single Ordinance was passed for the whole Native Courts in the country. But it was thought desirable to introduce a system which would go a long way to enhance uniformity between the native Courts in the South and the North. Thus the *Native Courts Ordinance No. 5 of 1918* was enacted. A system of our grades of Native Courts, 'A,' 'B,' 'C' and 'D' was introduced to supersede the former system of Minor Courts and Native Councils. The Courts both in the North and the South were to consist as follows: In the Northern Provinces, an Alkali with or without native assistance. In the Southern Provinces, a single native judge or a head Chief with or without minor chiefs or other persons sitting as judges or as assessors with such power as the Resident might vest - and Chiefs or other persons representing the native communities living in the area over which the Court had jurisdiction.[150]

Grade 'A' Native Court was vested with power to entertain all civil and criminal cases including cases involving capital punishment, although no such sentences were to be carried out unless confirmed by the Governor.

Grade 'B' Native Courts: These were empowered to exercise civil jurisdiction over causes or matters to the value not exceeding £50 - (N100) and criminal jurisdiction in cases where the punishment should not exceed

---

147 See S.17 of the Proclamation No. 9 of 1900.

148 The offences were listed in S.20 of the Proclamation.

149 See Native Courts Proclamation No. 1 of 1906.

150 See S.5 of the Native Courts Ordinance No. 5 of 1918. This Ordinance was subsequently amended in 1922.

two years or N50 - (N100) of flogging not exceeding 24 strokes. A subsequent Ordinance[151] increased the value in civil case to £100 - (N200).

Grade 'C' Native Courts: These were given jurisdiction in civil cases involving amounts not exceeding £10 - (N20) and in criminal cases imprisonment of not more than 6 months. The amount in respect of civil jurisdiction was increased to £100 - (N200) by a subsequent Ordinance.[152]

Grade 'D' Native Courts: These types of Courts were the lowest in the grade of Native Courts and were empowered to exercise jurisdiction in civil case involving amounts not exceeding £5 - (N10) and in criminal cases where they were given jurisdiction in cases where a term of imprisonment on conviction should not exceed 3 months.

The history of the ***Native Courts*** continued basically unchanged till 1933 after several allegations were made against many members of the Native Courts especially in the Eastern part of the country.[153]

Much credit for the reform of these native courts should go to the then Acting Governor, Sir Donald Cameron. Under this able man who later became the Governor of Nigeria in 1931, there were series of Ordinances aimed at the general reformation and re-organisation of the Native Courts. The first of these was the *Native Courts Ordinance No. 44 of 1933*. Under this Ordinance, the four grades of the Native Courts continued to function but there was certain reduction in the amount of punishment which some of these courts could impose. Having regard to the financial ability of the people, it was provided that the fines imposed could be paid by instalment. A Native Court Appeal Court was established and the Resident was empowered to appoint the members of the Courts of Appeal. The Resident was given the power to appoint the Court of a Chief Alkali or a Native Court presided over by a Head Chief or composed of not less than three Chiefs or Headmen in a Division.[154] These provisions for the Native Court of Appeal had their origin in the conditions prevailing in the Northern Provinces but their adaptation in the Eastern Provinces was by no means easy.[155] Appeals lay from a Native Court of first instance to a Native Court of Appeal within 30 days, but if there was no Native Court of Appeal or if the warrant so directed, the Appeal was to go to the Final Native Court of Appeal, the Magistrate's Court or the Supreme Court according to the endorsement. Appeal lay to the District Officer where there was no Native Court of Appeal and no right of appeal to other Courts was prescribed.

---

151 Ordinance No. 28 of 1928.

152 Ordinance No. 28 of 1928.

153 See Sessional Paper No. 28 of 1930, A Commission of Enquiry was set up after women riot at Aba in Eastern Nigeria, the Commission found that the riot was a result of "persecution by native Court members..."

154 S.26, Native Courts Ordinance No. 44 of 1933.

155 See Lord Hailey *op.cit.* p.173.

It must be pointed out that the Native Courts Ordinance of 1933 was subsequently amended many times but the structure of the enactment remained.[156] The position of the Native Court thus remained broadly the same until 1943 when certain changes were inevitable following some changes in the structure and composition of some townships in the Northern part of the country. Consequently mixed Courts were established in certain areas. No major changes took place except that before 1943 Native Courts had been established in territories close to the Colony of Lagos known as Colony Districts.[157]

From 1943 no radical changes took place in the history of Native Courts until 1954 when Federalism was introduced in Nigeria. Under the Constitution each Region was empowered to establish its own judicial system.[158] Following this enactment, which was vigorously opposed by lawyers (as regards regionalisation of the Courts), [159] the Native Courts together with other Courts of the judicial system were regionalised and each Region proceeded to establish its own system of Native Courts or Customary Courts as the case may be. The enactment for the Western and Eastern Regions were similarly described as:

> "A Law to provide for the Constitution of Customary Courts and to make further provision for the Administration of Justice."[160] The enactment for the Northern Region was described as: "A Law to provide for the Reconstruction of Native Courts and to make further provision for the Administration of Justice."[161]

We will now examine these Courts in different Regions and see if the original broad pattern which existed before the Federal set-up was introduced still remains, for this enhanced uniformity of the Native Courts under the early British Administration.

Eastern Region (Now Eastern States)

The Minister for Customary Courts and Chieftaincy Affairs was empowered to establish by warrant 'District Courts' which should be Courts of record having jurisdiction over causes and matter in which all the parties belong to a class of persons who had ordinarily been subject to the jurisdiction of customary tribunals, and reside or were within the area of the

---

156 The 1933 Ordinance was amended by Ordinances Nos. 16 of 1936, 8 of 1936, 11 of 1940, 22 of 1942, First Schedule to 23 of 1943, 18 of 1945, 27 of 1948 and 36 of 1948.

157 See Native Courts (Colony) Ordinance 1937.

158 S.142 S.1 1146 of 1954, The Nigeria (Constitution) Order in Council, 1954.

159 See *Daily Times* (Nigeria) January 23, 1953.

160 Cap. 31 of the Laws of the Western Regional Nigeria 1959 Vol. II, and No. 21, Laws of Eastern Region of Nigeria 1956.

161 Cap. 78, Laws of Northern Nigeria, 1963 Vol. II.

jurisdiction of the Court! The warrant was to assign any name to such District Courts as the Minister might deem expedient.[162]

The Minister was also empowered to establish County Courts which were to be Courts of record. These courts were to be Courts of Appeal and were to exercise such powers as might be defined in the warrants establishing such Courts. It must be pointed out that the Native Courts Ordinance No. 44 of 1933 continued to be in force in the Eastern Region.

This is apparent from the provision which empowered the Minister to declare that 'all or any courts established under the Native Courts Ordinance shall be deemed to be District Courts Grade 'A' or 'B' or County Courts established under the present law. The section then went on to provide that the 'jurisdiction conferred on such Courts by the Ordinance shall be deemed to have been conferred on them by the present law.[163] This provisions could be welcomed for it made possible the incorporation of the existing laws and the Native judicial set-up thus avoiding some undue radical change. The Courts established under the 1956 Law were to exercise civil and criminal jurisdiction as listed in the warrants establishing them.[164]

The law to be applied in those Courts was to be the customary law prevailing in the area of which the Courts were empowered to have jurisdiction. So long as such law was not repugnant to natural justice, equity and good conscience nor incompatible either directly or by necessary implication with any Ordinance or Law for the time being in force.[165] As could be recalled from the history of the customary or Native Courts, some of the members were found to be corrupt.[166] For this reason it was found expedient to have a provision expressly prohibiting corrupt practices in these Courts. Thus it was provided that any member of the Native Courts or any officer thereof or servant 'who accepts or claims or obtains or agrees or attempts to accept, claim or obtain for himself or any other person, any gratification for advantage, bribe or reward whatsoever whether money or otherwise... or corruptly showing favour or disfavour to any person, shall be guilty of any offence.' The offence carried a fine of 200 pounds or a penal servitude of a term of a term not exceeding two years.[167]

There was an important provision which took into consideration the cardinal aim of the customary tribunals which were, in existence prior to 1849. This was the amicable settlement of disputes with a view to restoring

---

162 S. 3 No.21 Laws of Eastern Region of Nigeria 1956.

163 See S.II, E.R. No. 21 of 1956, See also the Schedule

164 S. 20 *ibid*, See also the Schedule

165 S.23 *ibid*; c.f. This with S.19 of the Supreme Court Ordinance No.4 of 1876.

166 The Commission of Inquiry set up after the Aba Women Riots reported that the cause was due to "persecution by native courts members and corruption in the native courts" - See Sessional Paper No. 28 of 1930.

167 S.18, E.R. No.21 of 1956.

genéral equilibrium and harmony amongst the people. The section provided that in civil causes or matters a customary court might promote reconciliation among the parties thereto and encourage and facilitate amicable settlement.[168]

Appeals were to lie from the decision or order of a Grade A or B District Court, within 30 days to a County Court; and from thence appeals lay to the Magistrate's Court. From the decisions of the Magistrate's Court appeal further lay to the High Court; provided that there should be no right of appeal to the High Court in civil cases from the decision of the Magistrate's Court without the leave of the High Court where the claim involved could not be above the value of 10 pounds.[169]

In 1966 an Edict was promulgated. This made sweeping changes in the customary courts system in Eastern Nigeria.[170] Under the Edict there was to be one District Court in each area to be specified.

That meant that the division into district courts 'A' and 'B' no longer operated. Each district should be a court of record and exercise original jurisdiction in accordance with the Edict within such territorial limits as may be defined by the warrant, over causes and matters in which all parties belong to a class of person who were ordinarily been subject to the jurisdiction of customary tribunals, and reside or were within the areas of jurisdiction of such district courts.[171] A district court was to consist of a President, and at least two but not more than four other members. For the purpose of discharging its duty of hearing a cause or matter three members should form a quorum, and the President should preside over the court or in his absence the Vice-President, where both were absent or incapacitated the members present might choose one of their numbers to preside over the sitting of the court.[172]

Apart from the simplification of the structure of the customary court system[173] the enactment improved further on the 1956 Law by replacing the County Court with a Customary Court of Appeal whose President was to be a legal practitioner of at least seven years standing

A customary court of appeal shall consist of the President of the Court who shall sit with two assessors in all original causes and matters, whether

---

[168] S.27, *ibid.* C.F. S. 110 of the Supreme Court Ordinance No.4 of 1876 and S.25 of the Western Region Law, Cap. 31.

[169] S.60, *ibid.*

[170] This Edict, a creature of the military government repeals the 1956 Customary Courts Law. See Customary Courts (No.2) Edict, 1966, Eastern Nigerian Gazette No. 65 Vol. 15 of 1st December 1966.

[171] See S. 3. *ibid*

[172] See S. 5, *ibid*

[173] Customary Courts have now been established in many States of the Federation, these exercise their respective jurisdiction in accordance with the enactments establishing them.

criminal or civil, including a land cause or matter. The assessors shall act in an advisory capacity only and shall have no vote in the decision of the court.[174] The law to be administered shall be the customary law prevailing in the area of the jurisdiction of the court or binding between the parties, so far as such customary law is not repugnant to natural justice, equality and good conscience or incompatible either directly or by necessary implication with any law for the time being in force in Eastern Nigeria. Customary court of appeal in addition to its appellate jurisdiction was empowered to exercise in all causes and matters, criminal and civil, original jurisdiction concurrent with the jurisdiction of district courts. Such original jurisdiction was, however, confined to causes and matters transferred from District courts, Magistrate's Courts, or the High Courts.[175] Legal Practitioners, although still barred from appearing in district courts, were entitled to appear in a customary court of appeal. This innovation should be welcomed as it would undoubtedly raise the standard of the customary courts immensely [176]

Western Region (Now Western States and Bendel State)

The Minister was empowered to establish customary courts in the Region subject too the confirmation of such establishments by the Governor.[177] The Customary Courts could sit with or without assessors. The courts were to have jurisdiction 'over all Nigerians' [178] Like the old set-up, the Courts were degraded into Grades 'A', 'B', 'C' and 'D' the laws to be administered by these courts shall not be repugnant to equality, natural justice of good conscience or incompatible either directly or by necessary implication with any written law.[179] The enactment gives customary courts power to try offences against the customary laws notwithstanding that such acts constitute offences also in the criminal code. It may be observed that this is an interesting provision where the customary law was preferred to the code. Although it was provided that the punishment on conviction should not be more than the maximum stipulated in the Criminal Code.[180] Other provisions were basically the same as those we have already

[174] SS. 8-9, *ibid*, Appeal from the decision of a district courts must be lodged within 30 days from the date of the decision.

[175] S. 16, *ibid*

[176] For practice and procedure of the district courts, see Part IV of the Edict, and for Ancillary Powers of the Customary Courts, see Part V. Now new Customary Courts systems have been established in the Eastern States.

[177] S. 3 Cap. 31 Laws of Western Region of Nigeria 1959.

[178] S.17, *ibid.*

[179] S.19 c.f. S.23, E. A. No 21 of 1956 - and S.19, Supreme Court Ordinance No. 4 of 1876.

[180] See S.21 *ibid*

considered while dealing with the Eastern Region. These include provision for reconciliation in civil and criminal cases,[181] provision that the interest and welfare of the child should be the first and paramount consideration in any matter relating to guardianship of children [182] and provisions relating to Appeals.[183]

The Second Schedule to the enactment in Part I listed the offences within *The Criminal jurisdiction of Grade 'A' Courts*, these include, homicide, treason, sedition, child stealing, offences against the revenue of the government, corruption by officials of the government,[184] slave trading, offences against the enactments relating to official secrets, currency notes, coin, posts and telegraphs.

Grade 'A' Courts have unlimited jurisdiction in all civil causes and matters arising under the law administered by the courts provided that they are compatible with the provisions of Section 19 [185]

Grade 'B' Courts were granted unlimited jurisdiction in matrimonial causes and matters between persons married under customary law, this jurisdiction extended to custody of children under customary law, causes and matters relating to inheritance upon intestacy and the administration of interest estates under customary law. The courts were also empowered to exercise unlimited jurisdiction in land matters and other causes and matters, where the debt, demand or damages do not exceed N200. Grade 'B' Courts were equally given powers to exercise jurisdiction over criminal cases where the punishment on conviction will not exceed a penal servitude for one year or a fine of N200. The list of offences corresponds with that of Grade 'A' Courts in certain cases but includes certain offences as witchcraft and juju, conspiracy, defamation, procuration, rape, obtaining goods by false pretences, fraudulent false accounting and corruption of judicial offences.[186] Similar lists for Criminal and civil jurisdictions were provided for the Grade 'C' and 'D' Courts.[187]

It may be observed that some customary courts in the Western States are among the best in the country. These have legally qualified men and there is little doubt that the standard of judicial administration is admirably high. This idea of appointing legally qualified people in the customary courts should be encouraged in all the States.

---

181 SS. 25 and 26 ibid.

182 S.23 *ibid.*

183 SS. 45-50.

184 C.f. S.18 E. R. No 21 of 1956.

185 One of the provisions of the section is that the law to be administered must not be repugnant to natural justice equality and good conscience S.19 (a)

186 See Part II of the Second Schedule, Cap. 31 Laws of the Western Region of Nigeria, 1929.

187 See Parts III and IV *ibid.*

Northern Region (Now Northern States)

Following the authorisation made under the Constitution[188] for the establishment of the Regional Judiciary, the 'Native Courts Law' of the Northern Nigeria was enacted.[189] In this enactment unlike the enactments in Western and Eastern Regions,[190] the Provisional Commissioner was empowered to establish within his province such native Courts as he might deem expedient, subject to the approval of the Minister.[191] Native Courts in the Northern Region are quite peculiar in view of the highly Moslem judicial set-up. It was however, provided that a native court should consist of (a) a chief sitting with such members as are appointed under the Statute. (b) An Alkali (i.e. a person learned in Moslem law) or (c) a president or a Vice-President sitting with members appointed under the Statute. A native court may sit with or without assessors who were to act in an advisory capacity and were not to vote in the decision of the court.[192]

The Courts were to have jurisdiction over persons and classes of persons who had ordinarily been subject to the jurisdiction of native tribunals and all persons residing permanently within the area within the jurisdiction of the Native Authority.[193] These Native Courts were grouped under five grades: Grade 'A', 'A Limited, 'B', 'C' and D'

Grade A Courts were empowered to exercise unlimited jurisdiction in all criminal causes but no death sentence was to be carried out without a confirmation by the Minister. These Courts were given jurisdiction over civil causes arising from matrimonial causes and matters between persons married under native law. Unlimited jurisdiction was conferred on the courts in these cases, custody of children, actions pertaining to debts or damages, matters relating to succession to property and the administration of estates under native law and causes and matters involving the ownership, possession or occupation of land.[194]

Grade 'A Limited' Courts: These Courts were given all the civil and criminal jurisdiction of the Grade 'A' Courts save that they were not empowered to exercise jurisdiction in homicide cases.[195]

---

188 See S.142, The Nigerian (Constitution) Order in Council 1954, S 1 No. 1146 of 1954.

189 See the Laws of Northern Nigeria 1963 Cap. 78.

190 In Eastern and Western Regions, this responsibility was entirely provided to lie with the Minister. It may be observed that this might enhance uniformity.

191 S. 3 ibid

192 S. 5 Native Courts Law, Cp. 78 The Laws of N. N. 1963.

193 See S. 18 *ibid.*

194 See Parts I and II of the Schedule ibid.

195 See Parts I and II *ibid.*

Grade 'B' Courts: The criminal jurisdiction given to this grade of Courts was confined to those offences the punishment on conviction should not exceed three years imprisonment or N300 fine. In civil actions they were given power to exercise jurisdiction in cases where the amount involved could not exceed N400 and N1000 in land and succession cases[196]

Grade 'C' Courts: To these were conferred jurisdiction in criminal causes where the punishment on conviction should not exceed a penal servitude of 18 months or a fine of N60. They were given similar jurisdiction as Grade 'B' Courts in civil matters but the amount was limited to N200 in each case.

Grade 'D' Courts: These were the last in the grade of Native Courts and were empowered to exercise criminal jurisdiction over offences the punishment on conviction should not exceed 9 months imprisonment or N30 fine. Like other grades of Courts they were given power to exercise unlimited jurisdiction in matrimonial causes and matters and suits relating to the custody of children. There were equally empowered to adjudicate on those civil actions where the amount or damages involved could not exceed N100.[197]

The law to be applied in these Courts in civil cases should be native law and custom prevailing in the area of the jurisdiction of the court provided such native law is not repugnant to natural justice, equality and good conscience nor incompatible either directly or by necessary implication with any written law for the time being in force.[198] In criminal cases the native courts should administer the Penal Code Law and the Criminal Procedure Code Law and any subsidiary legislation made thereunder.

Appeal from decisions of Grade 'A' or Grade 'A Limited' native courts or Provincial Courts whether given in Original or appellate capacity were to lie to, (a) the Sharia Court of Appeal (which we shall deal with later) in cases involving questions of Moslem personal law and(b) the High Court of the Region in all other cases[199] Appeals from the decisions of Grades 'B', 'C' or 'D' Native Courts were expressed to lie to the Provincial Court.[200]

---

196 See *ibid.* The jurisdiction in matrimonial causes and custody of children was expressed to be unlimited.

197 See Parts I and II of the Schedule, ibid.

198 S. 23 Native Courts Law Cap. 78 Laws of N. N. 1963 c.f. S. 19 Customary Courts Law Cap. 31 Law of Western Region and S. 23 E. R. No. 21 of 1956, S. 19 Supreme Court Ordinance No 4 of 1876.

199 S. 62 *ibid.*

200 S. 58 All cases in Provincial Court involving Moslem personal law were to be heard and determined by an alkali of the court sitting alone. See S. 61.

The Sharia Court of Appeal

This was created to succeed the Moslem Court of Appeal which was abolished in 1960. The Shariah Court of Appeal consists of a Grand Kadi, Deputy Grand Kadi and two Judges. It was provided that these Judicial Officers were to be appointed by the Governor, 'acting in accordance with the advice of the Premier '[201] Every Judge of the Court was required to have an Alkali or adviser in Moslem law in service of a native authority for at least ten years or hold a certificate showing that he had successfully completed a recognised course in Sharia law. From this point of view, we may recall our observation when dealing with the native customary courts in the Western Region, that there is almost an imperative need for having legally trained men in these courts. The Alkali is a Moslem lawyer and presides in the Moslem (i.e. Alkali) Court. It may be suggested that lawyers trained in English law and having knowledge of customary law should be appointed to preside in native courts in non-Moslem areas. Where these lawyers do not possess a complete knowledge of the native law, they should sit with assessors. If such legally qualified people are appointed, not only will the standard of these courts be raised but also such provisions that no legal practitioner[202] should 'appear or act for or assist' any party before a native court would be unnecessary.

Provincial Courts

Provincial Courts were expressed to be Native Courts and to be established in each Province of Northern Nigeria. This judicial establishment is peculiar to the Northern Nigeria probably because of the vastness of the areas to be administered. Each Provincial Court was given power to exercise jurisdiction at first instance as well as on appeal. The Courts were to consist of an alkali setting with or without assessors. The alkali was to be the President of the Provincial Court sitting with one other member, with or without assessors in the Provinces of Plateau, Benue, Ilorin and Kabba. The Kaduna Capital Territory was deemed to be part of the Zaria Province. It was provided that all alkalai, Presidents and members of Provincial Courts should be called Provincial Court Judges. As we pointed out earlier, appeals from grades 'B,' 'C' or 'D' native court in a Province were to lie to the Provincial Court of the Province in which the native Court is situated.[203] It may be observed that the role of the Provincial Courts is basically the same as those of the Customary Courts of Appeal in the Western and Eastern parts of Nigeria.

---

201 See S.54 of the Constitution of Northern Nigeria, 1963.

202 See S.31, Cap.78, Laws of N.N. 1963 Vol. 11

203 SS. 56-58.

Chapter 2

Reception of English Law and Its Application in Nigerian Courts

It may be said that the English law received or rather inherited in Nigeria form a large part of the Nigerian law; and is freely applied by the Nigerian Courts. For example, in the case of *The Queen v The Governor in Council, Western Nigeria, Ex parte Oyebola*,[1] Duff, J. said: "Our Law on Certiorari Proceedings is based on the English Law." Again, in *The Queen v The Administrator, Western Nigeria, Ex parte Bamgbedu*,[2] Charles, J. went further by stating as follows: "The Jurisdiction of this Court to issue the prerogative writ of habeas corpus and the prerogative orders of mandamus, prohibition and certiorari is a beneficial inheritance from the old Court of King's Bench of England."

In the application of English law the Courts are faced with the task of reconciling possible conflicts between the law received or inherited and the existing indigenous or customary law. Also, the Courts are faced with the controversy arising from the question whether or not there is a time limit with regard to the reception of the law.

The main body of English law was introduced in 1863[3] by one of the earliest enactments. From thence English law and the customary law started to run side by side in the stream of the Nigerian legal system. In most cases the English law so introduced was modifying the indigenous or customary law. However, it became evident that the English law which the Courts were to apply should be defined. This requirement was met by the Supreme Court Ordinance[4] which spelt out the nature of the law to be applied by the Supreme Court. It provided as follows:

> The Common Law, the doctrines of Equity, and the Statutes of general application which were in force in England on *24th day of July, 1874*[5], shall be in force within the jurisdiction of the Court.[6]

---

[1] (1962) W. N. L. R. 360 at p. 364.

[2] (1962) W. N. L. R. 344 at p. 349.

[3] See Ordinance No. 3 of 1863.

[4] No. 4 of 1876.

[5] Emphasis supplied.

[6] S.14, *ibid*, see Laws of the Colony of Lagos (1901) Vol.1.

The territorial jurisdiction of the Supreme Court was expressed to cover the whole of the Colony of Lagos and the territories adjacent to it. It follows, therefore, that English law was 'received' statutorily in Lagos on 24th day of July, 1874. This date is very relevant as we shall see presently.

To ensure the smooth running of the two streams of law, that is to say, the English law now inherited and which from thence became the Nigerian law and the customary law, the Supreme Court was empowered not only to apply the inherited law but also to apply the customary law. Thus Section 19 of the Ordinance[7] provided:

> Nothing in this Ordinance shall deprive the Supreme Court of the right to observe and enforce the observance, or shall deprive any person of the benefit of any law or custom existing in the said Colony (i.e. of Lagos) or territories subject to its jurisdiction, such law or custom not being repugnant to natural justice, equity and good conscience, nor incompatible either directly or by necessary implication with any enactment of the Colonial Legislature existing at the commencement of this Ordinance or which may afterwards come into operation.

It follows, then, that before a customary law was applied it had to pass the tests laid down in the enactment. It may be observed that those aspects of the customary law which dealt with trial by ordeal or burning of a person suspected of witchcraft or cutting off the hand of a thief and such practices as enslaving a person who committed a heinous crime, could not pass the tests laid down.

With the expansion of British authority far into the hinterland, the jurisdiction of the Supreme Court was intended to cover the entire area. After the amalgamation of the Southern and Northern Nigeria in 1914, the Supreme Court Ordinance No. 6 of 1914 provided that the law to be applied in the Supreme Court of Nigeria should include the Common law, the doctrine of Equity, and the Statute of general application which were in force in England on the 1st day of January, 1900.[8]

Since the regionalisation of the judiciary, similar provisions have been incorporated in different laws of the States. Thus in the Interpretation Act 1958, it was provided as follows:

> Subject to the provisions of this section and except insofar as other provision is made by any Federal law, the Common law of England and the doctrines of equity, together

---

Supreme Court Ordinance No. 4 of 1876. It must be pointed out that the Native tribunals were not precluded from adjudicating as before. There were, however, inevitable re-organisations, see Chapter 1 *ante*. The provisions of Section 19 have been adopted in recent enactments; See Section 23 of Northern Nigerian Native Courts Law, Cap. 31 laws of Western Region of Nigeria (1959) Vol. II; and S.23 of the Eastern Nigerian Customary Curts Law, No. 21 of 1956, Laws of Eastern Region of Nigeria, (1956) P.A. 135. The 1956 Law has been repealed by the Customary Courts (No. 2) Edict, 1966. Section 15 of the Edict basically corresponds with S.23 of the 1956 Law. See, The 1966 Edict in Eastern Nigerian Gazette No. 65 Vol. 15, dated 1st December, 1966.

S.14 of the Supreme Court Ordinance, 1914.

> with the Statute of general application that were in force in England on the 1st day of January, 1900 shall be in force in Lagos....[9]

The High Court law of the Eastern Region while reproducing this provision in its S.14 went on to add:

> All Statutes of general application or other Acts of Parliament which apply within the jurisdiction of the Court by reason of this Law or any other written law shall be in force so far only as the limits of the local jurisdiction and local circumstances permit. It shall be lawful for the Court to construe such Statutes or Acts with such verbal alterations, not affecting the substance, as may be necessary to make the same applicable to the proceedings before the Court.[10]

It follows that the 'received' laws were to be applied with due regard to the local circumstances. The provision in respect of the reception of the English law in the Western Region appears to be verbally unique. It reads as follows:

"From and after the commencement of this Law and subject to the provisions of any written law, the Common Law of England and the doctrines of Equity observed by Her Majesty's High Court of Justice in England shall be in force throughout the Region."[11] It is submitted that this provision is much imprecise. There was no reference to any date when the law in England should be applicable. It is essential that the date, 1st January, 1900 or 24th July, 1874, as the case may be, be spelt out for the guidance of the Courts. This view leads us to the controversy[12] emanating from the construction of the wordings of the provisions in the Supreme Court ordinance No. 4 of 1876 and the Supreme Court Ordinance of 1914.[13] The argument involved two issues, to be precise:

(a) Whether the Common law 'received' was the Common law of England or the Common law that had developed in the 'Common law world.'

(b) Whether a specific date as was mentioned, in the enactment, equally referred to 'the Common law' or only to the 'doctrines of

---

[9] S.45 Interpretation Act, 1958 Cap.89.

[10] S.20 The High Court Law E.R. No. 27 of 1955. See also S.28 of the Northern Nigeria High Court Law No. 8 of 1955.

[11] The Law of England (Application) Law Cap.60 Laws of the Western Region of Nigeria 1959, Vol. III.

[12] See Allott; *op.cit.*, pp. 30-33; Park, A.E.W.*The Sources of Nigerian law* pp. 20-23; Daniels, W.C. Ekow, *The Common Law in West Africa*, 1964, pp. 122-123.

[13] The wording of the Statute was as follows: "The Common Law, the doctrine of Equity and the Statute of general application which were in force in England on 24th day of July, 1874, shall be in force within the jurisdiction of the Court." The same wording was adopted in the Ordinance of 1914 which made these aspects of the English law applicable to the whole of Nigeria on 1st January, 1900.

equity' and 'the Statutes of general application.' We may, before going into the merits of these arguments, point out that the *Interpretation Act*, Cap. 89 used the word "together" with the Statutes of general application instead of "and." It may be observed that this verbal alteration which makes no difference in the final analysis was adopted from the dictum of Petrides J. in *Solomon v African Steamship Company Ltd.*[14]

We propose first to deal with the impact of a specific date for the reception of English law. As we have seen, two dates were mentioned in two enactments - 24th July, 1874 for Lagos Colony and 1st January, 1900 for the whole of Nigeria. Park is of the view that there is no limit to the application of the Common law, i.e. that the decisions of English Courts in respect of the Common law continued to bind the Nigerian Courts even after 1st January, 1900. In this view he disagrees with Professor Allott and said that ... "Dr. Allott's reasons, while the declaratory theory of the common law is artificial, it is equally artificial to attempt to freeze the common law at a particular moment."[15] Professor Allott's view is that the pre-1900 decisions of English Courts were binding according to the rules guiding precedents. But the post-1900 decisions were not binding but of great persuasive authority. In support of his argument Park quoted *United African Co. Ltd. v Seka Owoade.*[16]

In this case, it was held that a master was vicariously liable for the fraud perpetrated by his servant in the course of the servant's employment. For this decision the Privy Council relied on the decision of the House of Lords in *Lloyd v Grace, Smith.*[17] Park in his argument concluded:

> Now if Dr. Allott's contention had been correct it would have been incumbent on the Board at least to consider whether the rule they applied did exist before 1900. The fact that they did not do so, is surely conclusive that the limiting date applies only to the English Statutes of general application and not to the common law and the doctrines of equity as well.[18]

We may observe that with due respect, this conclusion is over-simplifying the issue. The Privy Council like any Court of Law can pray in aid any authority, or any judicial decisions including those of the House of Lords to support any decisions. That the Board applied the decision in *Lloyd v Grace, Smith* because the facts in that case were almost on all fours with the instant case did not mean that the Board was *bound* to follow Lloyd's case.

---

14 (1928) 9 N.L.R. 99.

15 Park, *op.cit.*, at p.22.

16 (1955) A.C. 130 (A Nigerian Case).

17 (1912) A.C. 716.

18 Park, *op.cit.* at p. 23.

It was considered a high *persuasive* authority hence it was applied. The argument that the Board would have found it 'incumbent' to consider the decisions before 1900 if there were to be a time limit appears unattractive. The question should have been whether there were more relevant and more authoritative cases than Lloyd's case before 1900? Our view is that there appeared to be none and if there were, the Board would not hesitate to consider them. From this point of view, it is submitted that the Privy Council's application of the principle established in *Lloyd v Grace, Smith* does not mean that there is no time limit for the application of the Common law as expressly stated in the Statute. It follows that there is no cogent reason for saying that 'the limiting date applies only to the English Statutes of general application and not to the Common law and the doctrines of equity as well. The whole question revolves on the construction of this piece of straight-forward enactment. We had already quoted it but it is deemed expedient to repeat it: "The Common law, the doctrines of Equity and ("together with") the Statute of general application which were in force in England on the 1st day of January, 1900." One of the Canons of Statutory Construction is that a literal interpretation should be adopted at the commencement by giving words their usual meaning if there is no real ambiguity, even if hardship results.[19] Another rule is reading the enactment as a whole. It had been argued that "the common law, the doctrines of equity" should be separated from "the Statute of general application" and then apply the date to the Statute of general application only. We find it most difficult to agree with this. For if this view is accepted, then it irresistably follows that "the Common, and the doctrines of Equity" clause will hang in the air - thus producing some startling results. We therefore submit that the clause "which were in force in England on the 1st day of January, 1900" governs the whole provision or enactment. If this view is accepted, then the problem whether the common law was that of England[20] or "the common law world" would be solved. It would then be apparent that the common law intended to be applied was the common law of England. This broad construction will also dispose of the controversy about the time limit (if any). Our view is that to say that there is no time limit will make "1st January, 1900" otiose when applied to the rest of the enactment. Our view as to time is supportable from the American view and practice. A State Constitution provides that "the common law of England .. shall remain in force ...," this is construed as referring to the common law of England as it stood at the time of the adoption of such constitution.[21]

---

19 See *Magor and St. Mellons R.D.C. v Newport Corporation* (1952) A.C. 189. Here rate payers lost a benefit they were clearly intended to enjoy, because of the technical difficulties of interpretation.

20 See Park, *op.cit.*, at p.19; Nwabueze B.O. *Machinery of Justice in Nigeria*, 1963, p.19; Professor Allot, I.C.L.Q. (Supp. No. 10) 1965, p.35

21 *15 Corpus Juris Secundum "Common Law" L.P. 617 (1939 Edn.).*

Although in many cases the judges tend to follow decisions given after the date of the adoption, this, it is submitted, is not because they are bound by the later decisions but because they find it expedient to maintain, as far as possible, the necessary relationship between the mother common law, so to speak, and new. There is, in fact, practical reasons for maintaining a sort of uniformity where necessary between the common law world as whole. But the courts where the common law is expressed to be adopted, e.g. Nigeria on 1st January, 1900, are not, *de jure* bound to follow decisions made after the appointed day, in English Courts but nothing precludes the judges from treating the later decisions as of high persuasive authority. It is felt that there is need to draw a juridical line somewhere to accord with the spirit and letters of the enactments. It therefore follows that all the decisions given on or before the appointed date (i.e. 1st January, 1900) should be binding; but the decisions after that date should be regarded as persuasive and unless local circumstances or enactments provide otherwise, such decisions ought to be followed where necessary.

Having examined the reception of English law in Nigeria we are now to consider the effect of this law on the customary or indigenous law which was in existence prior to the introduction of English law. As was pointed out earlier, *S.19 of the Supreme Court Ordinance No. 4 of 1876*, while providing for the observance and enforcement of 'native law or custom' equally provided that such law or custom should not be contrary to natural justice, equity and good conscience nor incompatible with any existing enactment. The courts had applied this test in many decisions whenever an issue involving customary law has fallen to be decided. Thus in *Ekpenyong Edet v Nyong Essien*[22], the appellant was married to his wife under the native law and custom. His wife left him and went to live with the respondent. Two children were born of the union between the respondent and the wife. It was shown in evidence before the Commissioner of the Provincial Court of Calabar that the appellant had paid dowry (bride-price) for the woman Nyong Edet (his wife) when she was still a child and that subsequently the respondent, having agreed with the girl, when she was of age to marry, obtained the parents' consent, paid the dowry (bride-price) to the parents of the girl and took her as a wife. The appellant claimed the children because his own bride-price paid when the woman was a child had not been refunded to him ere the marriage to the respondent. Under strict customary law, the appellant would have succeeded in his action and would have in fact taken away the two children. For once the bride-price was not returned to him, the woman remained his wife under customary law and he was entitled to the issue irrespective of who was the biological or natural father. But *Carey J.* in the Divisional Court at Calabar held that the appellant was not entitled to succeed, 'as it would be contrary to natural justice,

---

22 (1932) 11 N.L.R. 47.

equity and good conscience' to allow the appellant to claim the children of another man merely because his dowry (bride-price) had not been refunded to him.

There is no doubt that the decision is a right one. For although bride-price is still one of the legalising elements of a customary law marriage[23], the facts of the case reveal certain weakness of the customary law and the courts have found it their primary role not to allow any revolting aspect of the customary law to stand. This attitude of the courts although deriving from statutory provision in respect of the customary law, has been extended even to written Maliki Law. Thus in *Jalo Guri, Adare Birniwa v Hadejia N.A.*[24]. The accused were tried under Moslem law on a murder charge and convicted. The murder was alleged to have been committed in course of "*hiraba*" (highway robbery). Under this law the persons accused of "*hiraba*" were precluded from having the opportunity to exonerate themselves. The provision reads as follows:

> If Maliki Law has seen that those people who cheat others and those who rob other people and the robbers and the like they should not be allowed to bring any reasons to exonerate themselves so long as witnesses are obtained. He should under no circumstances be given opportunity to exonerate himself.[25]

An argument was put forward that the rule was relaxed in this case. But the court observed, "... we are of the view that the relaxation was not of such a nature that we could say that the appellants were given an opportunity to defend themselves."[26] It was equally established that the accused persons had not been identified by two eye-witnesses as required by another section of the Maliki Law. But the primary reason for quashing the convictions was put thus by the Court; "We are of the view that a procedure which does not permit an accused person to put forward his defence is repugnant to natural justice, equity and good conscience."[27]

In certain cases where it appears to the courts that the customary law or any custom would be contrary or incompatible with any enactment they have refused to enforce such laws. Thus in *Re Effiong Okon Ata,*[28] the deceased was slave-born and died intestate. After his emancipation he

---

[23] Bride-price is so essential for a valid customary marriage that the Government of the Eastern Region had to pass a law to regulate the alarming sums paid by young men in order to marry. Some paid up-to £250 - £300. The Statutory amount now is put at the region of £35.

[24] (1959) 4 F.S.C. 44.

[25] Tabsira Vol. 1, p.149.

[26] (1959) 4 F.S.C.R. at p.46.

[27] *ibid.* at p.46. It is also provided by *S.15(2) Moslem Court of Appeal Law* that the court in administering the Maliki Law shall not administer, observe or enforce the observance of, any principle of law which is repugnant to natural justice, equity and good conscience.

[28] (1930) 10 N.L.R. 65.

continued to live on the land of the head of the House. His sister, also a slave-born, applied for letters of administration for the estate of the deceased brother, the head of the House resisted the application on the ground that in spite of the emancipation the deceased had continued to reside on the communal land and therefore remained subject to the Head of the House. *Butler Lloyd J* held that the personality of an emancipated slave remains his and not subject to the Head of the House. The learned Judge then observed that "the effect of the abolition of slavery was to make all persons equal before the law, ... to hold that the mere fact of the slave continuing to reside on the communal property confers any rights whatever on the head of the house in respect of the personal property would be very largely to render nugatory the provisions of the Slave Abolition Ordinance; and to import a native custom to that effect, would be to my mind, contrary to natural justice, in which case by *S.20 Chapter 3* would be improper to apply."[29] It follows that although the head of the house could sustain his claim under customary law, he was no allowed to succeed because that aspect of the customary law was contrary to the *Slave Abolition Ordinance.*[30] The courts have held that slavery itself was repugnant to justice, equity and good conscience. Thus in *Re Kwaku Damptey,*[31] the plaintiff's claim to.administer the estate of the deceased on the ground that he was his blood relation was challenged by the defendant. The defendant contended that the deceased was an *Ahinkwe* who had been "dashed" to his stool. *Ahinkwe* was explained to mean a stool servant, who in the past was an executioner but nowadays only carried an emblem of a Sword before the Chief on occasions and attended him. Kwasi Nuama, gave evidence as the linguist, as to the custom of the *Ashanti*. He said that at the death of an *Ahinkwe*, all the property belonging to the *Ahinkwe* would pass to the Chief. The circuit court of Ashanti held that, according to native custom, the defendant (i.e. the Chief) was entitled to administer the estate.

On appeal to the West African Court of Appeal, it was held that the defendant's claim was based on the fact that the deceased was "dashed" to his Stool. That being so, that that native custom constituted slavery and was repugnant to justice, equity and good conscience

Where the customary law is in keeping with the standard prescribed the courts have always sustained claims made thereunder. Thus in *Majekodunmi v Amodu Tijiani,*[32] the plaintiff was a judgment creditor and attached a property being occupied by the defendant. The property

---

[29] *ibid.* at pp.65-66.

[30] *Cf. Cole v Cole* (1898) 1 N.L.R. 15, where it was held that a claim as to the succession of the property of the deceased under the customary law could not be sustained as the marriage was contracted under English law.

[31] (1930) 1 W.A.C.A. 12 (a case from Ghana).

[32] (1932) 11 N.L.R. 74.

happened to be part of the family (i.e. unpartitioned) property. Under the customary law, the property belonged to all the members of the family and consequently inalienable by any one of them without the consent of all. *Berkeley J.* upholding the customary tenure held that under the customary law, the property was not a separate property of the defendant and therefore could not be legally attached. In another case involving facts similar *Van Der Meulen J.*, held that although the property had originally been acquired by the father of the respondent and claimants under a conveyance according to English Law, yet after the father's death as an intestate, the property vested in the family under native law and custom; that under customary law the individual had no right to alienate his interest without the consent of the family. Therefore, such consent having been withheld, the unliquidated interest of the defendant could not be attached by the plaintiffs in satisfaction of their judgment claim.[33] In another case, *Onisiwo and Ors v Fagbenro & Ors.*,[34] de Comarmond, S.P.J., held that where a piece of land was allotted by the head of a certain family to a person to reside under customary law, any purported alienation on the part of the allottee which amounted to a claim of absolute ownership without the consent of the real owners incurred forfeiture on the part of the allottee. It does not matter that the land had passed from generation to generation; it is no defence that the present holders of the land made a mistake in thinking that their ancestors were absolute owners of the property, inasmuch as they had been in possession for 80 years.[35] But it is not every alienation that would attract forfeiture. The test in every case was laid down by the West African Court of Appeal in Onisiwo and others v Gbamgboye and other[36] as follows:

> The real question is not how the word 'alienation' is used in any judgment is to be interpreted, but what exactly is the Native Law and Custom which applies. The real foundation of behaviour which involves forfeiture is the challenge to the overlord's rights. This is commonly shown by some form of alienation and such alienation may take the form, as in this case, of leasing under claim of ownership. But it is not difficult to imagine cases in which the granting of a lease, e.g., for a short period, would carry with it no challenge to the overlord's right and consequently involve no misbehaviour or forfeiture.

In the determination whether any respect of the customary law satisfies the Statutory conditions for its observance and enforcement, the courts have always had regard to the local circumstances with the result that the standards resorted to are no always foreign provided that, in the opinion of

---

33 *Miller Brothers v Ayani* (1924) 5 N.L.R. 42.

34 (1954) 21 N.L.R. 3.

35 *Ibid.* at p.30. See also Adagun v Fagbole (1932) *11 N.L.R. 110* where it was held that the defendant forfeited to occupy the portion allotted to him under Native Law for granting a mortgage to a third party.

36 (1941) 7 W.A.C.A. 69 at p.70.

the court, they are consonant with justice. This may be illustrated with the decision of the Privy Council in the case of *Dawodu v Danmole*,[37] In this case, a man had four wives and by them got nine children. The property in dispute formed part of the intestate estate of the deceased - i.e. the father of these nine children. The property was in Lagos and here, there is a predominant Yoruba Customary law called *Idi-Igi*. According to this customary law the property should be divided among the children of the deceased in fourths. All the wives had died by then. *Jibowu J.* held that the customary law in question should not be applied as it was repugnant, to justice, equity and god conscience. He also stated that the property should be divided equally amongst the children (i.e. into nine parts) and such a division would agree with "the modem idea," The decision was reversed by the Federal Supreme Court, after calling evidence that established that the customary law was still predominant in Lagos. A further appeal was made to the Judicial Committee of the Privy Council. The Privy Council dismissed the appeal. The Board in their judgment concluded thus:

"In their Lordships' opinion the principles of natural justice, equity and good conscience applicable in a country where polygamy (i.e. polygyny) is generally accepted should not in a matter of this kind be readily equated with those applicable in a community governed by the rule of monogamy. Their Lordships are not therefore satisfied that *Idi-Igi*, proved and found to be still in full force and effect in Lagos, ought not fairly and equitably be applied to the estate of one who left children by his four wives."[38]

It follows that the Courts in their efforts to modify the customary law and make it accord with the changes in modern Nigeria have not indiscriminately swept away those aspects of the law which are in keeping with equity and justice according to the circumstances of the case.

[37] (1958) 3 F.S.C.R. 46, (1962) 1 W.L.R. 1053.

[38] (1962) 1 W.L.R. at p.1060.

Chapter 3

The Courts Under The Nigerian Constitution

1. The Position of the Courts from 1914 to 1963 and After

As we have seen, the erection of the modern Nigeria came to a tangible fruition with the amalgamation of the two separate Governments of the Southern and Northern Nigeria. This great task was formally completed in 1914 by Sir Frederick Lugard who later became the Governor-General, a title peculiar to himself. As a result of this, there was established for the whole country, one Supreme Court.[1]

Equally in the same year, a single Native Courts Ordinance was enacted providing for the establishment of native courts throughout the country.

Following the amalgamation, a larger advisory body called the "Nigeria Council" was set up for the whole of Nigeria. It follows therefore that despite the vastness of the country and the divergence of ethnic grouping the country continued to be governed as a unit. Although there were certain inevitable judicial re-organisation [2] after 1914, the unitary system of judicial administration which was established for the whole country continued undisturbed until 1954. This was the year which saw the regionalisation of judiciary as well as the public service.

Nigeria adopted in 1954, a fully written Federal Constitution, but the concept of federation in Nigerian Constitutional history was much earlier than that date. For Sir Arthur Richards envisaged "a system within which the diverse elements may progress at varying speeds, amicably and smoothly, towards a more closely integrated economic, social and political unity, without sacrificing the principles and ideals inherent in their divergent ways of life." [3] In this dispatch to the Secretary of State, the Governor anticipated that which actually happened in 1954. But it must be pointed out that the actual adoption of a Federal Constitution took place in 1951 but this was more or less partial as the Judiciary and the Public Service were not then regionalised. From the inception of the Federal Constitution in 1951, there followed mounting pressures from politicians for the regionalisation of the Judiciary in particular. Eventually, they had their way. The decision to regionalise the judiciary was strongly opposed by both the Bar and the

---

1 See Supreme Court Ordinance of 1914 (1923 Ed. of Laws of Nigeria).

2 See Chapter 1.

3 See Proposals for the Revision of the Constitution of Nigeria, Comd. 6599.

Bench. The Bar argued that regionalisation "would not be in the interest of the country." The primary reason behind this argument was that the High Court judges might become tools in the hands of politicians; and that differences in the conditions of service offered by the various Regions (which might be unduly competitive) might result in an uneven distribution of competent judges. For the Bench, the mouthpiece was the Chief Justice, Sir John Verity. He argued for the need to maintain the *status quo* because regionalisation of the judiciary might lead to unhealthy divergence in standard of learning, experience and integrity. He stressed the need to avoid the possibility or appearance of political influence in the Courts.[4] Despite all these cogent arguments, the Judiciary as well as the Public Service were brought in line with the regime brought into being in 1951 Thus the Judiciary became a regionalised item under the 1954 Federal Constitution.

Under the *1954 Constitution*, the main relic of unity in the judicial administrative set-up could be found in the establishment of the Federal Supreme Court The 1954 Constitution provided that 'there shall be a Federal Supreme Court for Nigeria.'[5] It may be observed that despite the establishment of this appellate Court, the idea of the regionalisation of the Judiciary is most unsupportable. Although there have been no glaring instances of abuses or misconduct in the judiciary throughout the country; neither have there been political influences especially in the higher segments of the judicial hierarchy, events which led to the break-down of the Federal Parliament itself (a topic to which we shall examine more closely later), exposed the weaknesses of federalism as a concept. From this point of view, Sir Ivor Jennings' aphorism that "nobody would have a federal constitution if he could possibly avoid it" [6] becomes an adage which one will find difficult not to accept. The regionalisation of the judiciary created a situation which made it possible for some to be sceptical about the independence of the lower segments of the judicial system. It has been a widely held view that political machinations found it possible to permeate into the realm of administration of justice in the native or customary courts. In *Ogidi v Commissioner of Police* [7] disturbing allegations were made against certain customary courts and a certain political party in power in the Western Region of Nigeria. In this case, decided by the Federal Supreme Court, the appellant was convicted by a Warri Magistrate's Court on a charge of publishing a seditious publication contrary to S.51(1) (C) of the Criminal Code, Cap. 42. His appeal was dismissed. The case against the appellant was that he sent a telegram to the Minister of Justice, Ibadan;

---

[4] See Memorandum submitted to the Lagos Constitutional Conference in 1954; *West Africa*, 6th February, 1954.

[5] S.138. The Nigerian (Constitution) Order in Council, 1954. S.1 No. 1146, 1954.

[6] Sir Ivor Jennings: *Some Characteristics of the Indian Constitution*, P.55.

[7] (1960) W.R.N.L.R. 201.

Broadcasting, (i.e. the Nigerian Broadcasting Corporation) Ibadan and Lagos, the *West African Pilot*, Lagos and to the Late Chief Festus Okotie-Eboh, Lagos; it was also shown that the appellant caused the text of the telegram to be published in another newspaper called the *Midwest Champion*. The telegram read as follows.

> We strongly suggest abolition customary courts Warri Division or replace Judges in them X since establishment Customary Courts acted deliberately against political opponents of Action Group X Justice denied Nation-Co (National Convention of Nigerian Citizens, N.C.N.C). Supporters charged to Court X Accused sentenced refused bail on Appeal X Customary Courts procedure based on Action Group Doctrine X British Justice not in practice in Courts X Warri Customary Courts are Action Group institutions destined punish Nation-Co supporters X British protected persons nay Warri Citizens not used to this unBritish Justice X unless these Courts abolished we deem them communist institutions X Citizens not safe with Customary Courts still misinterpreted X in Warri X Nation-Co and all Citizens lost confidence and West Regional Government's name and good intention dragged in mud due primitive interpretation of Justice Customary Courts Warri Division X Minister Justice called upon take immediate action abolish or order enquiry.[8]

Brett F.J., delivering the judgement of the Court made this important observation "... We consider that the courts should be slow to attribute a seditious intention to the communication published only to the Minister responsible for redressing the grievance complained of, and we might have taken a different view of the publication which is now in question if it had been communicated only to the minister." The learned Judge went on: "What we are concerned with here is a publication which the appellant caused to appear in one newspaper, and for which he sought further publicity in another newspaper and over the wireless."[9] it follows that what was in issue was the amount of publicity given to the allegation and not the veracity of it. The Court never doubted the truth of the allegation and as the learned Judge pointed out, if the charges against the customary courts were communicated only to the Minister of Justice, the Federal Supreme Court would have taken a different view of the case. The question still remained whether the customary courts victimsed the political opponents of the Government or the party in power. While we do not intend in any way to condone any sweeping allegations against any section of the judiciary, certain measures taken by the military government in the then Western Region showed that the allegations of political influence were not without foundation. For the first step of the military government had to abolish the criminal jurisdiction of the customary courts.[10] The main reason for this was because it was established that 'the customary courts had come to be

[8] *ibid* at p.202

[9] *ibid* at p.203

[10] See *The Guardian 28th January, 1966*, p.13.

used by the party in power as a means of intimidating opposition.' A similar measure was taken in the Northern Region, where before the fall of the Sardauna Administration, there had been consistent allegation of political influences in the administration of justice by the Native Courts. At the inception of the military administration therefore, 'Native Authority Courts were ordered to merge with the judiciary to make them independent of both government and native Authority administration.'[11] We shall return to this issue later when dealing with the independence of the judiciary. But there is little doubt that the dignity and independence of all arms of the judiciary would have been better preserved if the system was not subjected to regionalisation. It might be argued that regionalisation was not the sole cause of the undesirable situation because in the United States the Judiciary is regionalised i.e. each State has its own judiciary. But the position in Nigeria could be seen in a different light. There was no truly national political party with the result that the political parties entrenched themselves in one region or the other and would scarcely brook any opposition or alternative government. This resulted in persecution of political opponents with forces that could make themselves amenable to the party in power. It may be equally observed that the country was not properly divided before the introduction of federalism. For a federal set-up to thrive no one unit should be too large to dominate the rest.[12]

This principle was not observed in Nigerian Federation. The regions were too powerful in such a way as to challenge even the authority of the Federal Government. The Northern region was so vast that the area which constituted the Northern Region was bigger than those constituting the rest of the units of the Federation. As we pointed out earlier, the Native Authority courts were generally regarded as the instrument of oppression against the opponents of the party in power in the Northern Region. Although in most cases these allegations had been exaggerated but they were not totally without foundation. Hence the step towards reform and unification taken by the military governor should be laudable.

Under the 1954 Constitution the Federal Supreme Court which was to be a Superior Court of record was empowered to sit in Lagos and in such other places in Nigeria as the Chief Justice of the Federation might, with the approval of the Governor-General, appoint.[13] The Judiciary having been regionalised, a provision was made in the Constitution for the establishment of the High Courts of Justice in the Regions. Thus Section 142(1) provides:

---

[11] See *West Africa 19th February, 1966*, p.222.

[12] See K.C. Wheare: *Federal Government* 3rd ed. 1953, p.55.

[13] S.136(3) Nigerian (Constitution) Order in Council 1954. S.1. No. 1146 of 1954.

> Subject to the provisions of this section, the Legislature of a Region may, by law enacted under this Order, establish Courts of Justice for that Region, and in particular (without prejudice) to the generality of the foregoing power) establish a High Court of Justice for that Region.

Following this provision, the Regions as well as Lagos proceeded to establish their respective Courts of Justice.[14]

The structure of judicial administration thus established remained unchanged until 1960 when the country was granted Independence. The 1960 Constitution maintained the *status quo* with very minor changes. The Federal Supreme Court was to consist of

(a) the Chief Justice of the Federation,
(b) such number of Federal Justices (not being less than three) as might be prescribed by Parliament; and
(c) the Chief Justice of each territory[15]

The last provision was particularly important as it provided a channel whereby the administration of justice throughout the country could be co-ordinated. The meeting of all the Chief Justices in one Court was essential as that might lead to uniformity of some sort under the circumstances. Like S.44 of the 1954 Constitution, it was provided that the Federal Supreme Court was to have, to the exclusion of any other court, original jurisdiction in any dispute between the Federation and a Region or between Regions if and insofar as such dispute involved any question (whether of law or fact) on which the existence or extent of a legal right depended.[16] The Federal Supreme Court was thus endowed with very wide powers to entertain 'any question (whether of law or fact) in any dispute between the Federation and a Region or between the Regions. To the extent the Federal Supreme Court lived up to the expectation in this regard we shall see when dealing with the case of *Attorney-General of Eastern Nigeria v Attorney-General of the Federation* [17] This case arose out of the census conducted in 1963. There were allegations 'of inflating figures' for political purposes. The first count had already been discarded due to allegations and counter allegations of corrupt practices in some Regions to get very high figures which would mean an increase in the number of representation in the Federal House of

---

[14] See High Court Law 1955, Cap. 44, in Laws of Western Region of Nigeria 1959 Vol. II. See also High Court Law 1955, E.R. No. 27 of 1955, in Laws of Eastern Region of Nigeria 1955; High Court Law 1955 Cap. 49, Laws of Northern Nigeria 1963 Vol. II; High Court Law of Lagos Cap. 80. There were enactments in the Regions in respect of customary or Native courts. - See Native Court Law, 1956 (northern Region), the Customary Courts Law, 1956 (Eastern Region) and the Customary Courts Law, 1957 (Western Region).

[15] S.104, Nigeria (Constitution) Order in Council, 1960, S. 1 No. 1652, 1960.

[16] S. 107 *ibid*

[17] S. C. 231 and 232/1964 (unreported), but see *West Africa* July 4th 1964, p. 751.

Representatives. When, therefore, the figures for 1963 were accepted by the Federal Government, a writ was taken out in the Supreme Court by the Eastern Regional Government, stating that the Federal Government was not entitled to accept or act on the census figures 'because of the manner in which the census was conducted.' It further stated that the census was 'unconstitutional, ultra vires and illegal, and therefore null and void.' It was equally stated that there was a 'wrong assumption of jurisdiction' by the Prime Minister. There was a question as to the legality of the composition of the census board.

The Federal Government put up a counter motion on the ground, it was stated, that the Federal Supreme Court had no jurisdiction to entertain the case. The Federal Supreme Court upholding the Federal Government's contention ruled that it had no jurisdiction. The reason given was that no legal right of the Eastern Region Government had been infringed by the acceptance of the census figures by the Federal Government. We do not propose at this stage to go very far into this case as we shall be examining it in more detail in the later part of this study. But meanwhile we cannot help recalling the Statement of Brett, F. J. in a dissenting opinion in *Akintole v Governor of Western Nigeria and Adegbenro* [18] that the task of the Court in Nigeria remained that of construing a written constitution. There is no doubt that the essence of Federation is the division of powers between the general or central government and the units. But in this respect, census was in the concurrent Legislative List.[19] It is not easy to see how 'no legal rights of the Unit of the Federation could be possibly infringed' by the acceptance of the figures which that unit questioned. At the final analysis, the units constitute the Federation and if any unit of it is not represented in a Federal Parliament that Parliament is, *de jure*, not property constituted. Staggering allegations of corruption were made during the period of the census and it is our view that it should have been the role of the Federal Supreme Court to entertain such test cases in order to expose all corrupt practices which were rearing their heads in our public life. Chief Justice Marshall of the United States would have entertained a case of this nature without any difficulty whatsoever.[20] It is most tempting to conclude that if irregularities and corruption were dauntlessly exposed since we attained our nationhood, the bloody revolution of 15th January 1966 would have been averted. It is a notorious fact that the census issue triggered off political animosity which never abated until 15th January, 1966.

In 1963 Nigeria was declared a Republic, consequently a Republican Constitution was introduced. The Federal set-up created in 1954 basically

---

[18] F. S. C. 187/1962, (1962) W. N. L. R. 185; See also (1962) 11 L. C. L. Q 929 at 934, Now see A.G. Bendel State v. A.G. Federation for (1981) 10 S.C.1.

[19] See Item 4 in the list as provided in the Constitution of the Federation, 1960.

[20] *Marbury v Medison* (1803) 1 Crench 137, we shall deal with this celebrated case more fully later.

remained. Appeals to the Privy Council having been abolished, the Supreme Court became the last Court of Appeal for the country. The word "Federal" was dropped from the name of the court but that entailed no change in its structure since the Judiciary continued to be regionalised. The Regions were empowered to establish Regional Courts of Appeal to which appeals were to lie from the High Court of the Region.[21] Despite the fact that the Judiciary continues to be regionalised it has important role to play In any country, the Judiciary plays the important role on interpreting and applying the law and adjudicating over controversies between individual and individual or between the citizen and the State. In any country with a written constitution, the Judiciary has the additional duty of safeguarding the supremacy of the Constitution by interpreting and applying its provisions and by keeping all authorities of the State within the Constitutional framework. In a country with a Federal set-up, the Judiciary has a more important role, namely to decide controversies between the units of the federation *inter se* as well as between the Central Government and the constituent units. As we pointed out earlier, the essence of federalism is the allocation of powers between the centre and the States. This being so, an arbiter is therefore required to scrutinise laws to see whether they fall within the alloted area and usually this great task is left to the Judiciary.

With the abolition of appeals to the Judicial Committee of the Privy Council, the Nigerian Supreme Court enjoys the top-most position in the judicial hierarchy of the country. Thus it stands at the apex of the Nigerian Judicial system. It is the supreme interpreter and guardian of the Constitution and the ultimate interpreter of the general law of the land and thus maintains a valuable uniformity in the entire judicial system. It follows therefore that in is onerous task the judiciary not only interprets the Constitution but also acts as its protector and guardian by keeping all authorities - legislative, executive, administrative and even quasi-judicial, within the ambit of the Constitution.

An important arm of the judiciary which had been radically affected by the Constitution is the Native or Customary Courts system. The law administered in these courts was largely unwritten. It is provided in the Constitution that no person should be convicted of a criminal offence unless that offence is defined and the penalty therefore prescribed in a written

---

[21] See S. 56 Constitution of Northern Nigeria, S. 45 Constitution of Eastern Nigeria; S. 52 Constitution of Western Nigeria in The Constitution of the Federal Republic of Nigeria (Federal Ministry of Information, Printing Division, Lagos 1963). The 1979 Constitution of the Federal Republic of Nigeria listed the Courts created under the Constitution as: The Supreme Court, The Court of Appeal, The Federal High Court, The States High Courts, The Sharia Court of Appeal of a State and The Customary Court of Appeal of a State.

law.[22] It follows therefore that no conviction will be valid under the constitution unless the act which constitutes an offence is defined in a written law.[23], [23a] and penalty for the offence prescribed therein.

2. *The Independence of the Judiciary*

Independence of the judiciary is absolutely essential in the administration of justice. Thus Dr. A.L. Goodhart wrote:

> It has been recognised as axiomatic that if the judiciary were placed under the authority of either the legislative or the executive branches of the Government then the administration of the law might no longer have that impartiality which is essential if justice is to prevail.[24]

A similar view was expressed by Sir William Holdsworth on the status of the judiciary. He wrote as follows:-

> The judges hold an office to which is annexed the function of guarding the supremacy of the law. It is because they are the holders of an office to which the guardianship of this fundamental constitutional principle is entrusted, that the judiciary forms one of the three great divisions into which the power of the State is divided. The Judiciary has separate and autonomous powers just as truly as the King of Parliament ... The separation of powers in the British Constitution has never been complete. But some of the powers in the constitution were, and still are, so separated that their holders have autonomous powers, that is, powers which they can exercise independently, subject only to the law enacted or unenacted. The judges have powers of this nature because, being entrusted with the maintenance of the supremacy of the law, they are and always have been regarded as a separate and independent part of the constitution. It is true that this view was contested by the Stuart Kings; but the result of the Great Rebellion and the Revolu'ion was to affirm it.[25]

No emphasis can be otiose to show the vital need for the independence of the Judiciary. Those responsible for the administration of justice should not be interfered with in carrying out their great task. They should be placed in such a position that would ensure impartiality which stimulates public confidence in our judicial system. The end of the law being 'social engineering,' this task will be greatly jeopardised in any society where the

---

[22] S.22 (10), the Constitution of the Federation (Government Printer, 1963) Lagos. Now S.33 (12) of the Constitution of the Federal Republic of Nigeria 1979

[23] In *Aoko v. Fagbemi (1961) 1 All N.L.R. 400* a conviction of a woman for adultery (which she admitted) under unwritten customary law was quashed by the High Court.

[23a] The Courts established under the 1979 Constitution are the Supreme Court of Nigeria S. 210; The Court of Appeal, S.217; The Federal High Court, S.228; The High Court of a State, S.234; Sharia Court of Appeal of a State S. 240, Customary Court of Appeal for a State, S.245.

[24] A.L. Goodhuart: *English law and the Moral Law* (Stevens London, 1953), p.60.

[25] Sir W.S. Holdsworth. *His Majesty's Judges (1932), 173 Law Times* 336 at pp.336-337. See also W.R. Lederman: *Independence of the Judiciary (1956) 34 Can. Bar Rev. 769.*

judiciary is not free. The judiciary should be insulated from politics, for one of the most successful politicians of our time, Sir Winston Churchill, said:

> The principle of complete independence of the judiciary from the Executive is the foundation of many things in our island life. It has been widely imitated in varying degrees throughout the free world. It is perhaps one of the deepest gulfs between us and all forms of totalitarian rule ... The British Judiciary, with its traditions and record, is one of the greatest living assets of our race and people and the independence of the judiciary is a part of our message to the ever-growing world which is rising so swiftly around us.[26]

Judicial independence is largely dependent on the type of persons who are called upon to perform the onerous task of judicial administration. This point is very important in our society; for it was very much undesirable for issues leading to the abrogation of criminal jurisdiction in the Customary Courts of the Western Region by the military government to have arisen in our judicial system. People will live in a state of insecurity if they feel that they would not obtain justice in a court of law. Professor Schwartz writing on the quality of the men who should be entrusted with the administration of Justice said:

> ... the quality of justice depends more upon the quality of the men who administer the law than on the content of the law they administer. Unless those appointed to the Bench are competent and upright and free to judge without fear or favour, a judicial system, however sound its structure may be on paper, is bound to function poorly in practice.[27]

In this respect we may recall our observation earlier that careful attention should be given in the method of selection of the judges of our Native or Customary Courts. These Courts should be assimilated wholly into the mainstream of the judicial system. The judges should be legally qualified and where necessary assisted by assessors. It is our submission that men of integrity should be appointed to man our judiciary and only by this will the independence of the judiciary be safeguarded. Sir Kenneth Robertsway writing about the independence of the judiciary in the Commonwealth countries states:

> To the question how the independence of the Judiciary is preserved I suggest a fourfold answer; first, by appropriate machinery for appointment of Judges; secondly, by giving judges security of office; thirdly, by such general acceptance of, and respect for, judicial independence that the members of the Judiciary can rest assured that it is not likely to be challenged and has not continually to be fought for; fourthly by the terms of service of members of the judiciary.[28]

---

[26] Hansard, March 23, 1954, Vol. 525, Cols. 1061, 1063.

[27] B. Schwartz: *American Constitutional Law* (1955), p.130.

[28] See *Changing Law in Developing Countries* edited by J.N.D. Anderson (1963) at p. 63

3. *Appointment of Judges*

As the most methods of judicial appointments in the Commonwealth derive from the British practice, it may serve to quote what Sir Winston Churchill once said in this and other regard when dealing with the judges in a House of Commons Debate. He said:

> There is nothing like them at all in our Island. They are appointed for life. They cannot be dismissed by the executive Government. They cannot be dismissed by the Crown either by Prerogative or on the advice of Ministers. They have to interpret the law according to their learning and conscience. They are distinguishable from great officers of State and other servants of the Executive, high or low, and from the leaders of Commerce and Industry. They are also clearly distinguishable from the holders of less exalted judicial office. Nothing but an Address from both Houses of Parliament, assented to by the Crown, can remove them.[29]

In the United Kingdom, the appointments of High Court Judges are made by the Queen on the advice of the lord Chancellor; but the Lord Chief Justice, the Master of the Rolls, the President of the Probate, Divorce and Admiralty Division, the Lords Justices and the Lords of Appeal in Ordinary are appointed by the Queen on the advice of the Prime Minister. To anybody who is not conversant with British administration of justice the arrangement looks awkward as there appears from superficial analysis that political influence would permeate to interfere with the administration of justice. But this is far from the truth. The position is a bit more complicated from the point of view of separation of powers by the position of the Lord Chancellor. This post, i.e. that of the Lord Chancellor, is politically filled. That is to say, the Lord Chancellor is identified politically with the Party in power. He is a politician with manifest integrity. Constitutional conventions and traditions have ensured recognition of the dual nature of his office and confidence that he could be relied upon that in exercising this dual role he would not allow political consideration to overweigh his judgment.

The United Kingdom practice was not adopted root and branch in the Nigerian Constitution of 1960. Under the Constitution,[30] the Chief Justice of the Federation was to be appointed by the Governor-General, acting in accordance with the advice of the Prime Minister. under the 1979 Constitution the Chief Justice is appointed by the President in his discretion subject to confirmation by the Senate.[30a] The Federal Justices were to be appointed by the Governor-General, acting in accordance with the advice of the Judicial Service Commission of the Federation.[31] Similar provisions were made for the appointment of Judges in the Regions. For example, it

---

[29] House of Commons Debates, March 23, 1954, Col. 1061.

[30] S.105(1) The Nigeria (Constitution) Order in Council, 1960. S.1 No. 1652, 1960.

[30a] S.211(1) The Constitution of the Federal Republic of Nigeria 1979.

[31] S.105(2), *Ibid.*

was provided for the Northern Region that the Chief Justice of the Region was to be appointed by the Governor, acting in accordance with the advice of the Premier. The Judges of the High Court of the Region were to be appointed by the Governor, acting in accordance with the advice of the Judicial Service Commission of the Region.[32] The introduction of the Judicial Service Commission was comparatively new, but it has much that enhances judicial independence.

In the older independent Commonwealth countries the appointments of judges are broadly the same as in the United Kingdom. The Judges of the Supreme Court of Canada and the High Court of Australia are appointed by the Governor-General in Council. In New Zealand and the Province of Canada power of appointment is vested in the Governor-General alone. In some Australian States the power rests with Governors, in others in the Governor in Council; in the State of Victoria, the Governor appoints with the advice of the Executive Council. In India, the Judges of the Supreme Court are appointed by the President. When appointing the Chief Justice of India, the President is required to have consultation with such of the Judges of the Supreme Court and the High Courts as he may deem necessary. In the appointment of other Judges the President is required to consult the Chief Justice of India though he may also consult as he may deem expedient.[33]

It may be observed that as the Indian President is not an Executive President, he acts on the advice of the Cabinet.[34] It follows that there is little or no difference with the Indian system and the older independent Commonwealth countries in his regard. But it seems that there is a clear difference in the appointment of the High Court Judges. The Judges are appointed by the President after consulting the Chief Justice of India and the Governor of the State concerned. In the case of appointment of a Judge other than the Chief Justice of the High Court, such Chief Justice is to be consulted.[35]

In the newer Commonwealth countries constitutions, like the 1960 Nigerian Constitution, the vogue in the appointment of Judges lies with the establishment of the Judicial Service Commissions. In Malawi the Chief Justice was to be appointed by the Governor-General, acting in accordance

---

[32] S.50 of the Northern Region Constitution; see also S.49 of the Western Region and S.49 of the Eastern Region Constitution in S.1. *Ibid.* Under the 1979 Constitution the Chief Judge of a State is appointed by the Governor acting on the advice of the State Judiciary Service Commission, subject to approval by the House of Assembly. That of a High Court Judge is on the recommendation of Judiciary Service Commission of the State - S.23(1) and (2)

[33] See Article 124 (2) of the Indian Constitution.

[34] See M. P. Jain: Indian Constitutional Law, (Bombay), 1962, p. 138

[35] See article 217 of the Indian Constitution

with the advice of the Prime Minister.[36] The Puisne Judges were to be appointed by the Governor-General, acting in accordance with the advice of the Judicial Service Commission.[37] Local conditions brought a change in the pattern as evidenced in the Jamaican Constitution. Here it was provided that the Chief Justice was to be appointed by Governor-General on the recommendation of the Prime Minister after consultation with the Leader of Opposition. The Puisne Judges were to be appointed by the Governor-General acting on the advice of the Judicial Service Commission. In a Presidential regime such as Zambia, the appointment of the Chief Justice rests with the President simpliciter.[38] But the appointment of Justice of Appeal and Puisne Judges were to be made by the President, acting in accordance with the advice of Judicial Service Commission.[39]

The Judicial Service Commission was dispensed within the Nigerian Republican Constitution and the old method which predominates in the United Kingdom and the older Commonwealth countries adopted. S.112 of the Constitution provides:

> The Chief Justice of Nigeria and the Justices of the Supreme Court shall be appointed by the President, acting in accordance with the advice of the Prime Minister, so however that four of the Justices of the Supreme Curt shall be appointed by the President acting on the advice, as respects each of those Justices severally, of the Premier of a different Region.[40] [40a]

It follows that whenever the President had occasion to appoint a Justice of the Supreme Court, he had to act on the advice of the Premier of the Region from which the Judge was to be appointed. The provisions for the appointments of Judges in the Regions follow the pattern set out for the appointment of Judges of the Supreme Court. In the Northern Region the Chief Justice and the judges of the High Court of the Region were to be appointed by the Governor, acting in accordance with the advice of the Premier. The name provisions were made for the Eastern Region, Western Region and the Mid-Western Region.[41] The abolition of the Judicial Service Commission was very unfortunate. It is imperative that the Judiciary is not only insulated but seen to be insulated from any atom of political influence

---

[36] S. 76 The Malawi Independence Order 1964, S. 1 916, 1964.

[37] S. 76 (2) *ibid*

[38] S.99 (1) The Zambia Independence Order, 1964, S.1. 1652, 1964.

[39] S.99 (2), *Ibid.* Now Cf. S.211 of the Constitution of the Federal Republic of Nigeria 1979.

[40] The Constitution of the Federal Republic of Nigeria (Government Printer, Lagos), 1963. In Ghana Judges were appointed by the President alone.

[40a] Under the 1979 both the Federal Judicial Service Commission and the Senate have roles to play in the appointment of the Judges of the Supreme Court - S.211 (2).

[41] See S.51 of the Northern Nigeria Constitution
S.51 of the Eastern Nigeria Constitution and S.49 of the Western Nigeria Constitution.

in every young nation. There is no doubt that Judges would be more independent if they owe their appointment to no politician as such. In this respect we do not have to copy the British practice of the appointment of judges; for here the fight for the independence of the judiciary had been fought and won.[42] The Nigerian Bar Association had in very strong words expressed opposition to the abolition of the Judicial Service Commission. In its annual conference in 1963 the Association passed a resolution which read as follows:

> That in the opinion of the N.B.A. (Nigeria Bar Association) the decision to abolish the Judicial Service Commissions is deplorable and unjustified and we hereby call upon the Governments of the Federation to restore them as soon as possible.[43]

The danger of allowing politicians to have direct hands in the appointment of judges finds expression in the criticism usually levied on the American system where in some States Judges were elected basically on party lines. Thus Professor Mayers writes:

> In 21 of these States the names of the judicial candidates appear together with those of party candidates for non-judicial office, under a party listing, at the regular election. In four additional States, though on the ballot the candidates are listed without party designation, they are nevertheless party candidates, having been named at party primary elections.[44]

In his criticism of this system the author observed that although among the lawyers who engage in active politics, there are many who are sufficiently well qualified for judicial office but he concluded by saying that the unfortunate thing in practice is that it is by no means the best qualified among them are the most likely to be chosen by those who control the party machinery. He cited instances of choice obtained by the 'devious machinations of intraparty cliques,' and went on:

> Even where the history of his designation is entirely honourable, the judge who owes his appointment or nomination to the favour of particular groups or individuals within the party enters upon his office under a load of political debt; and however high-minded he may be, he will find it almost impossible to resist completely the importunities of his creditors for payment through judicial favours - sometimes slight, sometimes not so slight.[45]

While we do not suggest that the above will be the case in Nigeria, but as we pointed out, only very few men of great integrity will take a firm stand

---

[42] See Sir Alfred Denning: *The Road to Justice* (Stevens), 1955, p.10 *et seq.*, especially at p.12. Here the great Judge showed how after the glorious revolution of 1688, the independence of the Judges became a *fait accompli*.

[43] See *The Nigerian Bar Journal* (1964) p.45.

[44] Lewis Mayers: *The American Legal System*. New York, 1955, p.374.

[45] *Ibid*, p.376.

in political cases where a governor who recommended his appointment is a party. Our contention is buttressed by the article which appeared in the Nigerian Daily Times soon after the Army takeover. It reads as follows:

> The Judicial Service Commission should be revived. A contemporary lawyer has written in the Sunday Times that: 'The appearance of a Military Government is a mark of dishonour to the courts established by the constitution. It is presumed that if they had been vigilant enough they would have, by their activities curbed the events which eventually lead to military rule.[46]

We may here recall our observation in respect of the ruling made by the Supreme Court that it had no jurisdiction to entertain a case[47] arising from the census conducted in 1963. The allegations of corruption and dishonesty in 'inflating figures' were made in astonishing magnitude. The legality of the statement by the Prime Minister that his acceptance of the figures was final and should not be disputed by any individual or unit of the Federation was questioned in the writ. All these should not have been allowed to be pushed aside, under the blanket of 'no jurisdiction;' only to brew to the catastrophe which came to a head on January 15, 1966. It is our contention that on the true and fearless construction of the Constitution,[48] the Court would have entertained cases of that nature. But events in Nigeria and the utterances of politicians could make any court tread warily in cases having a political flavour. This may be illustrated by the reactions of the political leaders when an action was taken challenging the legality of the steps taken by the Federal Government for the creation of the Mid-West State. The late Prime Minister said:

> We were dragged to court[49] on the bank inquiry and now we are being dragged to court on the Mid-West. Well, if our courts will allow themselves to be used in the way they are being used on any minor thing, I am afraid people will make a mockery of our courts. ... Personally, I think it is wrong for every small constitutional matter to go to courts, people will soon come to laugh at the court ...[50]

---

[46] See *Daily Times January 26, 1966, p.6, col. 4.*

[47] *A-G for Eastern Nigeria v A-G for the Federation S.C. 231 and 232/1964* (unreported).

[48] See S.114 read together with Item 4 of the Part II of the Schedule to the 1963 Constitution of the Republic of Nigeria.

[49] See *Doherty v Balewa (1961) 1 All N.L.R. 604* in this case the legality of the Commissions and Tribunals of Inquiry Act, 1961 was question. Certain sections of the Act were declared *ultra vires* and void. The Courts have however refused to be cowed by the Executive. Thus in Military Governor Ondo State & Or. v Victor Adegoke Adewunmi (1985) 3 N.L.R. 493, the Court of Appeal declared void Chiefs Edict (Ondo State No.11 of 1984) which purported to oust the jurisdiction of the Courts in Chieftaincy matters as being contrary to S.236 (1) of the 1979 Constitution which vested unlimited jurisdiction in the High Court to hear and determine 'any civil proceedings' touching interest, legal right, obligation *et seq. Cf.* N.K. Adamolekun v The Council of University of Ibadan (1968) N.M.L.R. 253.

[50] See *Daily Express (Nigeria), May 4, 1962.*

A Statement like this, coming as it did from a Prime Minister is unfortunate. The Executive is not to dictate or educate Judiciary on how it can legally and legitimately carry out the function entrusted to it under the Constitution. One finds it difficult to see how grave constitutional issues involved in the cases in point could be described as 'minor' or classed as 'small cnstitutional matter.' The issues are to be left to the Courts to determine and where a case is frivolous or vexatious the courts would not hesitate to throw it out with adequate costs. In the interest of good government, the Judiciary should not declare war on the Executive nor should the Executive cow down the Judiciary from protecting and preserving the supremacy of the law and the fundamental freedoms of man. If the Supreme Court is bullied into silence, then the very idea of the independence of the Judiciary will be meaningless and the rule of law will suffer. The Supreme Court in a State with a written constitution must be dauntless[50a] in carrying out its constitutional role. As Marshall C.J. said: "It is emphatically the province and duty of the judicial department to say what the law is. Those who apply the rule to particular cases must of necessity expound and interpret the rule."[51]

4. *Safeguard for the Independence of Judges during Tenure of Office*

To ensure that the salaries of judges are not subject of debate on the annual estimates, these are charged on the Consolidated Fund. It is also provided that salaries and terms of office of the judges shall not be altered to the disadvantages of the holders after their appointments.[52] In England, Holdsworth summed up the position as to the early remuneration of the judges thus: "From the first they were paid salaries by the Crown which in the course of years were gradually and continuously increased."[53] But it must be pointed out that their salaries were not the only source of income allowed to the judges. They were entitled to share in the fees[54] which the litigants paid, and the Chief Justices in particular enjoyed very valuable patronage, in that they had the disposal of the non-judicial offices of their courts. There was however a gradual change with the result that the seventh paragraph of the third section of the Act of Settlement after dealing with the

---

[50a] The Supreme Court of Nigeria has lived up-to expectation in handling constitutional matters. It declared void decision given by the Court of Appeal contrary to S.258 of the 1979 Constitution; vide Chief Dominic Onuora Ifezue v Livinus Mbadugha (1984) 5 S.C. 79; an appeal done by the author of this work.

[51] *Marbury v Madison (1803) 1 Cranch 137.*

[52] S.133 (3) (4) of the Constitution of the Federation of Nigeria, 1963.

[53] Holdsworth, op. cit., Vol. I, p. 252.

[54] See Buckley v Edwards (1892) A.C. 387 at 392. In this New Zealand Case the Privy Council gave account of the early method of appointment of Judges and their remuneration.

tenure of judges, provided that their salaries were to be "ascertained and established." The need for insulating the judges' salaries from certain influences was made abundantly clear in a legislation passed under George III.[55] The Act was entitled thus: "An act in the former legislation (i.e. the Act of Settlement) relating to the commissions and salaries of judges." The preamble was more illuminating, it read as follows:

> Whereas your Majesty has been graciously pleased to declare from the throne to both houses of Parliament, that you look upon the independence and uprightness of judges, as essential to the impartial administration of justice, as one of the best essential to the rights and liberties of our loving subjects, and as most conducive to the honour of your crown; and in consequence thereof, your Majesty has recommended it to the consideration of your parliament, to make further provision for continuing judges in the enjoyment of their offices during their good behaviour, notwithstanding the demise of your Majesty, or any of your heirs and successors; and your Majesty has also desired your faithful commons, that you be enabled to secure the salaries of judges, during the continuance of their commissions ...

There is no doubt that the view expressed in this preamble had been the guide-light as evidenced in most of the Commonwealth countries' written Constitutions.[56] There is a convention which now appears in certain written constitutions that the conduct of judges shall not be subjected to parliamentary criticism except on a substantive motion.[57] Thus members are not allowed to make reflections on the conduct of the judges during their speeches in the Legislatures. In his work, Todd quoted an illuminating statement of Mr. Gladstone as follows:

> But nothing could be more injurious to the administration of justice than that the House of Commons should take upon itself the duties of a court of review of the proceedings of an ordinary court of law; or of the decisions of a competent legal tribunal - or that it should tamper with the question whether judges are on this or that particular assailable and endeavour to inflict upon them a minor punishment by subjecting their official conduct to hostile criticism.[58]

Equally, judges are immune from legal liability for words spoken and acts done in the exercise of their judicial Functions. Their dignity and integrity are protected by the law relating to contempt of court. The rule applies to all

---

[55] This was Chapter 23 of the first year of George III.

[56] In these Constitutions the salaries of judges are expressed to be 'charged on and paid out of the Consolidated Fund.' By an Act of the 6 Geo.4 Salaries of Puisne Judges were fixed at £5000 p.a. and charged on the Consolidated Fund. It was provided that the Salaries payable to the Chief Justice of Nigeria, Justices of the Supreme Court, the Chief Justice or other Judges of the High Court of Lagos were to be charged on the Consolidated Fund of the Federation. See S.133 (3) of the Constitution. Similar provisions appear on the Constitution of the Regions - See SS.63 (4), 60(4) and 59(4) of the Constitutions of the Northern, Eastern and Western Regions respectively.

[57] *Cf.* Article 121 of the Indian Constitution and Article 127 of the Malaysia Constitution.

[58] Alphons Todd: *Parliamentary Government in England*, (Longmans, London, 1887) Vol. II, p.574.

persons performing judicial functions. Thus in *Onitiri v Ojomo* [59] the plaintiff in the instant case was an accused before the defendant, a magistrate, in a case in which the defendant was charged with a criminal offence. In that case, the plaintiff applied for a transfer of the case from the defendant's court. At the request of the defendant, the plaintiff read out a paragraph of his application for transfer. This reads as follows: "The complainant, Mr. Daniel Adebena is in three distinct secret societies with the said Magistrate and have sworn to help each other and avenge any wrong done to any of them." After reading out these words the plaintiff was informed by the defendant that he had committed a contempt of court. The defendant formulating the charges against the plaintiff said that the words were calculated to lower the authority of the Magistrate. He therefore ordered the plaintiff to be kept in prison pending trial by another Magistrate. The plaintiff was taken to prison after the case was adjourned *sine die* by the defendant. The plaintiff in this case brought action for false imprisonment. In his Statement of defence, the defendant pleaded that he was protected by S.61(1) of the Magistrate's Courts Ordinance now Act, Cap. 122.[60] He stated that at all material times he was acting judicially and that the act or order complained of was done or made by him in the discharge of his official duties as a Magistrate in good faith and in the belief that he had jurisdiction to do the act or make the order complained of.

S.61(1) of the Magistrates' Courts Ordinance reads:

> No Magistrate, justice of the peace or other person acting judicially, shall be liable to be sued in any civil court for any act done or ordered to be done by him in the discharge of his judicial duty whether or not within the limits of his jurisdiction: Provided that he at the time, in good faith, believed himself to have jurisdiction to do or order the act complained of.

Upholding the defendant's preliminary objection based on S.61(1) (above quoted), De Comermond S.P.J. dismissed the action. The learned Judge observed:

> It is clear to me that the law-giver intended that a Magistrate should not be inhibited from his duty, or what he conceives to be his duty, by fear of being sued if he makes a mistake. This to my mind, is a most important provision. It does not mean that a Magistrate can be reckless: for example, if it is pointed out to a Magistrate that he is going to do something outside his jurisdiction and and he says that he does not care, it seems that it would not be difficult to establish that he was not acting in good faith.[61]

---

[59] (1954) 21 N.L.R. 19.

[60] Laws of Nigeria, 1948, Cap. 122.

[61] *Onitiri v Ojomo (1954) 21 N.L.R. at p. 23.* If a judge purported to act judicially, even if he did go outside his jurisdiction in error, he would still be acting judicially: Thus in Anderson v Gorrie (1895) 1 Q.B. 668 at 670 Lord Esher said: "...the question arises whether there can be an action against a judge of a court of Record for doing something within his jurisdiction, but doing it maliciously and

This statutory provision has therefore adequately protected Magistrates and justices of the peace against any civil liability when acting judicially unless it could be proved that such a magistrate or justice of the peace was acting in bad faith. The test in each case is whether the magistrate or justice of peace acted in good faith; this provides a balance which should operate to eradicate any abuse For as De Comermond S.P.J. rightly pointed out, the section of the Ordinance should not be regarded as a Charter for recklessness or for wrongful assumption of jurisdiction of punishing for a criminal contempt by the summary process of attachment or committal

5. *Security of Judicial Tenure*

To ensure the independence of the Judiciary, Judges are not arbitrarily removed. Elaborate provisions are made in the written constitutions prescribing how a judge could be removed. Under the Nigerian Republican Constitution it was provided as follows:

> A person holding or appointed to act in the office of Chief Justice of Nigeria or a Judge of the Supreme Court shall be removed from his office or appointment by the President if - (a) there are presented to be President addresses from both Houses of Parliament praying that that person be so removed for inability to discharge the functions of the office in question (whether arising from infirmity of mind or body or any other cause) or for misbehaviour: and (b) the address from each House bears a certificate which is signed by the person who presided at the meeting of that House at which the motion for the address was passed and which states that no less than two-thirds of all the members of that House voted in favour of the motion; and, except on the revocation in pursuance of S.112 (where an unqualified person was appointed a judge) of this Constitution ... a person holding or appointed to act in such an office shall not be removed from his office or appointment in any other circumstances.[62]

For the Regions there were similar provisions to ensure security of tenure for the Judges appointed to serve in the courts established therein. An example of such provisions reads as follows:

> A person holding or appointed to act in the office of a judge of the High Court of the Region shall be removed from his office or appointment by the Governor if - (a) there are presented to the Governor addresses from both Houses of the Legislature of the

---

contrary to good faith. By common law of England it is the law that no such action will lie. The ground alleged from earliest times as that on which this rule rests is that, if such an action would lie the judges would lose their independence, and that the absolute freedom and independence of the judges is sic necessary for the administration of justice." "It is a principle of our law that no action will lie against a judge of one of the Superior Courts for a judicial act, though it be alleged to have been maliciously and corruptly ... The public are deeply interested in this rule, which existed for their benefit, and was established in order to secure the independence of the judges, and prevent their being harassed by vexatious actions." - Per Crompton J in *Fray v Blackburn (1863) 33 B & S. 576 at 5781; 22 E.R. 217.*

62 S.113 The Constitution of the Federal Republic of Nigeria, 1963; Now vide S.211 (1), (2), (3), (4) and (5) of the 1979 Constitution.

> Region praying that that person be so removed for inability to discharge the functions of the office in question (whether arising from infirmity of mind or body or any other cause) or for misbehaviour; and (b) the address from each House bears a certificate which is signed by the person who presided at the meeting of that House at which the motion for the address was passed and which sates that no less than two-thirds of all the members of that House voted in favour of the motion; and, except on the revocation in pursuance of S.51 of this Constitution ... a person holding or appointed to act in such an office shall not be removed from office or appointment in any other circumstances.[63]

The Constitution was drafted when it appeared that no one party could easily muster such a majority as was required to bring about the dismissal of a judge which they do not like or which stood firm against political influences. But from what followed in the Nigerian political scenes especially in the Regional Assemblies, to pass a resolution in the Regional Assemblies with two-thirds majorities demanding the removal of a judge was as easy as passing a resolution adjourning a sitting for a break. The Houses of Chiefs which were designed to perform the functions similar to that performed by the House of Lords in the United Kingdom - of revising and stopping certain rash and discriminatory or oppressive legislations - have turned out, contrary to every expectation, to be the rubber-stamp of the Regional Assemblies. Under the circumstances, it is suggested that the question whether allegations of inability or misbehaviour have been made out and, if so, whether they justify the removal of a judge should be made determinable by a judicial tribunal.[64] There is every advantage in this from the point of view of seeing that justice is done, by tribunal which can be looked up to determine judicially what constitutes a misbehaviour. It is also suggested that there should be a medical officer in such a tribunal.

In this regard, the provision in the then Southern Rhodesia Constitution deserves close examination. It reads as follows:

> A judge of the High Court may be removed from office by the Governor by order under the public seal only for inability to discharge the functions of his office (whether arising from infirmity of body or mind or any other cause) or for misbehaviour, and shall not be so removed unless the question of the removal of that judge from office has been referred to an independent tribunal and that the tribunal has recommended that the judge be removed from the office for inability as aforesaid or misbehaviour.[65]

---

63 S.52 of the Constitution of the Eastern Region; See also SS.50 and 55 of the Constitutions of the Eastern and Northern Regions respectively.

64 Cf. Article 125 of Malaysia Constitution, here the Judicial Tribunal consists of five members presided over by the Lord President or the Chief Justice.

65 S.54 The Southern Rhodesia (Constitution) Order in Council 1961. Southern Rhodesia is now Zimbabwe.

This provision appears to be ideal and makes judicial tenure in no way dependant directly or indirectly on the executive or the legislature. The process for the removal of the Chief Justice, who was appointed on the advice of the Prime Minister, is more fascinating. It is as follows:

> If the Prime Minister (in the case of the Chief Justice), or the Chief Justice (in the case of any other judge), advises the Governor that the question of removing a judge of the High Court from office for inability as aforesaid or misbehaviour ought to be investigated, then - (a) the Governor shall appoint a tribunal which shall consist of a chairman and no less than two other members selected by the Governor from among persons who have held office as a judge of the High Court tor who hold or held office as a judge of a superior court of the United Kingdom or of any country in which the common law is Roman - Dutch and English is an official language; (b) that tribunal shall inquire into the matter and report on the facts thereof to the Governor whether or not that judge should be removed; (c) if the tribunal recommends that the judge be removed, the Governor shall act as provided in subsection (1) of this section." i.e. get the judge removed from office.[66]

These provisions provide adequate security for the judges and would in no doubt enhance the independence of the judiciary.

There is no doubt that the methods of appointment and removal of judges adopted in the Constitution of the Federal Republic of Nigeria were those predominating in the United Kingdom. But the present stage in the United Kingdom was reached after a long struggle for the independence of the Judiciary with the result that both the judges and the politicians are conscious of the ugly episodes of the past when judges had to fight for their independence and were eventually vindicated by history. The resistance was initiated by a great judge called Sir Edward Coke.

As is well known in English legal history, in Norman times Judges were virtually indistinguishable from Civil Servants. Until the time of William III they were, as a rule, appointed during the King's pleasure and were frequently dismissed for political reasons. This remained so until the Act of Settlement. Coke during the days of King James boldly asserted the independence of the judges. Over this he clashed with the King. Matters came to a head when the King sought to interfere with the decision of the judges on a certain case by telling them not to proceed with it till they had consulted him. Coke while refusing this said: "Obedience to His Majesty's command to stay proceedings would have been delay of justice, contrary to the law and contrary to oaths of the judges." Following this a question was put to all twelve judges thus: "When the King believes his interest is concerned and requires the judges to attend him for their advice, ought they not to stay proceedings till His Majesty has consulted them?" All the judges except Coke answered in the affirmative - "Yes," "Yes," "Yes." But Coke bluntly said: "When that happens, I will do that which it shall be fit for a

66 S.54 (2) *Ibid.*

judge to do."[67] Consequently the King dismissed Coke as a judge but the struggle he initiated endured. After Coke, judges continued to be subservient to the King with the result that when King Charles I imprisoned five men because they would not subscribe money for him, the judges held that if a man was committed by command of the King, he was not to be released by the Courts.[68] In another case when the King sought to levy money to build ships of war without the authority of Parliament, the judges also held that to be lawful.[69] But by this time public opinion had started to gather around the ideal for which Coke stood. This found expression in a case where seven bishops who publicly asserted that the King had no dispensing power were prosecuted for libel; but were acquitted by the jury.[70] The case arose from the fact that when James II wanted to achieve absolute power of the Crown, he removed the twelve judges and replaced them with those he could use and direct as he pleased. These newly appointed judges held that the King had the power to dispense with the laws of the land.

By 1688 events had reached a climax and nothing could stop the glorious revolution. James II fled from the land. After that William Prince of Orange came from Holland to be the King of England, and with his coming people insisted that the judges should be independent. The demand came to fruition with the passing of the Act of Settlement of 1701. The Act for the first time enshrined the concept of security of tenure for the judges and the independence of the judiciary. S.3. of the Act provided:

> (That) Judges' Commission be made *quamdiu se bene gesserint* and their salaries ascertained and established; but upon the address of both Houses of Parliament it may be lawful to remove them.[71]

In a similar enactment in 1875 it was provided that Judges should hold their office during good behaviour, subject to a power of removal by Her Majesty on an address presented to Her Majesty by both Houses of Parliament.[72]

We have now seen the origin of the method of removal of judges through address of both Houses of Parliament. We have equally seen the struggles which led to the enactment. As we pointed out earlier, both the judges and the executive in England or the United Kingdom are eager not to allow history to repeat itself. The independence of the judiciary is firmly established and is generally regarded as *sine qua non* in the upholding of the

---

67 *The Case of Commendams (1616) Hobart 140*

68 *The Five Knights' or Darnel's Case (1627) 3 State Trials*

69 *R.V. Hampden (1637) 3 State Trials 825.*

70 *Trial of the Seven Bishops (1688) 12 State Trials 183.*

71 Act of Settlement, 12 & 13 W.3, C.2.

72 S.5. Supreme Court of Judicature (1873) Amendment Act, 1875.

rule of law. While no adverse reflection is intended, one finds it irresistable to say that our young countries in the Commonwealth should not in this respect copy British practice for the appointment and removal of the judges root and branch but to start with the insulation of the Judiciary from political influences or avenues which could make for such influences. The Judges should be completely free, secure, and owe their appointment to no political party and their dismissals (if any) to no legislature. It is self-evident that in countries with written constitutions many political issues fall to be decided by the courts; with the result that unless the judges feel secure and owe their appointment to no political party directly or indirectly, there will be a tendency of praying on human frailty by threatening a judge with removal if he gives an unwanted decision. In certain instances judges were actually removed after giving unfavourable decisions to the power that be. A classic example of this was the removal of the Chief Justice of the South African Republic by President Kruger, the President of the Republic in 1897.

The disagreement between the Chief Justice Kotze and President Kruger emanated from the judgment given by the majority of the Court in *Brown v Leyds*.[73] The question in this case was whether the sovereign people of the South African Republic had, by the Grondwet [74] limited the legislative capacity of the Volksraad.[75] The Grondwet was not enacted by the Volksraad but was an emanation from the will of the people. The Chief Justice, Sir John Kotze with other judges in the majority decided that the Grondwet of 1858 was a supreme and fundamental law, and that a Volksraad Resolution, not being in the form 'presented' by the Grondwet, was void and that a law, even in the form presented by the Grondwet was not valid if that law was in any way in conflict with the Grondwet (i.e. the Constitution). This decision which was the right one, *de jure*, greatly infuriated President Kruger, who thought he could amend the Constitution in any way he liked by seeing a legislation through the Volksraad. This process of purported amendment was unconstitutional and any amendment which was not in accordance with the Constitution was void. The first move of President Kruger was to write his first threatening letter to Chief Justice Kotze. The letter reads as follows:

> What I wish to speak to you about is that the Court must respect the Volksraad Resolution. I hear that you stated in the *Hess case* that you had changed your opinion expressed in the *case of Doms* and the Court is not bound by a resolution of the Volksraad. How can this be? The law clearly says that all laws and resolutions, published by me, are of force, and cannot be questioned, only the people can in the following year petition against these, and the Volksraad can decide whether it will alter the resolution. You must now tell me that you also think this is so, and

---

73 For an account of this case see *Cape Law Journal* (1898) 15, 94.

74 Grondwet was the Constitution of the land.

75 Volksraad could be interpreted as a legislative Assembly.

> strengthen bond of brotherhood, so that no conflict may arise, otherwise the members and the people will rise against the Court, and I will be in a difficult position. The country may get into great difficulty, rebellion may be occasioned and you must set my mind at ease ...[76]

By the time of this acrimonious disagreement, the Chief Justice had adjourned the Court *sine die* and all that the President was trying to do was to induce him to reverse his opinion and that of the majority of the Court so as to accommodate the unconstitutional and purported amendment of the Constitution. But the Chief Justice knowing that the sanctity of the Constitution and the independence of the judiciary were at stake, like Coke, was resolute and firm. Whereupon the President with a sword drawn for a kill wrote again:

> I always stand for my Judges, but if you reject the resolution of the Volksraad, then I fear for the consequences. I will then be obliged to suspend you.[77]

The President used the word "suspend" only as mere euphemism for he meant dismissal[78] and that he carried out. The Chief Justice dauntlessly retorted:

> A conflict between the Wolksraad and the Court is certainly a serious matter. I do not think lightly of the consequence resulting therefrom, and I do not fear it.[79] The Court never acts hurriedly or precipitately. The Court will do its duty and maintain the Grondwet and other laws. Why should this cause discord? The people are too sensible for that.[80]

The passages above quoted were texts of the correspondence[81] between the President and the Chief Justice. These could not have seen the light of day if the Chief Justice and the other Judges were subservient to the President. It goes without saying that such inducements and threats could be held out and perpetrated on the judges today to obtain one political advantage or the other. But all men of integrity, which the judges should be, should resist all those to the last.

Another instance of direct clash between the Judiciary and the Executive arose after the acquittal in Ghana in 1963, by a Special Court set up by the President to try certain accused persons. These included two Ministers. These men were charged with treason. It was adduced in evidence that the

---

[76] See *Cape Law Journal* (1898) XV at p.91

[77] See *Cape Law Journal* (1898) Xv at p.91

[78] *Ibid*, p.93. This act of the President was equally illegal for judges in the Republic were expressed to be appointed for life. But fury beclouded all reason and wise judgement.

[79] Emphasis supplied.

[80] *Ibid*, p.91.

[81] For the full text of the Chief Justice's letter stressing the need for independence of the Judiciary, See *Ibid* at pp.58-9.

accused had conspired to assassinate the President, Dr. Kwame Nkrumah. Among those charged were Tawia Adamafio, former Minister of Information, Ako Adjei, former Minister of Foreign Affairs, H.N. Cofie-Crabbe, a former Convention People's Party Executive Secretary. The case no doubt had many political implications as evidenced in the defence of some of the accused persons.[82] The Special Court was headed by the Chief Justice of Ghana, Sir Arku Korsha. After a fairly long trial the Court acquitted three of the accused including the two former Ministers but found two guilty of treason and conspiracy to commit treason. They were sentenced to death. Those sentenced to death were Robert B. Otchere, a former United Party M.P. and one Joseph Yaw Manu.

Infuriated by the decision, the President dismissed Sir Arku Korsha as the Chief Justice of Ghana. Consequently Sir Arku Korsha left[83] the Judiciary of Ghana. We shall examine this case in greater detail later in this book. Although Sir Arku Korsha was not dismissed as a judge as such but events leading to his dismissal as the Chief Justice gravely touched and concerned the independence of the judiciary and security of tenure for the judges. The Chief Justice could not have left the judiciary if he had not felt interferred with in the administration of justice and also disgraced by being dismissed as the Chief Justice. The then Acting High Commissioner of Ghana to Nigeria, Mr. J. Owusu-Ansah was reported as saying that "there is a special political relationship between the office of the President and the Chief Justice. It is therefore necessary the President should at no time have reason to doubt the political reliability of the Chief Justice."[84] A statement like this is regrettable. If the statement had been without more, it could be argued to be capable of many interpretations. But when read together with the other statements of Mr. Owusu-Ansah, what he actually meant will apparently emerge. He was reported as saying that the ex-Chief Justice "must have known that the judgment in the treason trial would be fraught with profound political consequences." The statement went on to say that "for some inexplicable reason, the ex-Chief Justice failed to inform the President in advance" before announcing the verdict to enable the Government to take the necessary precautions for the maintenance of law and order. This Mr. Owusu-Ansah described as "a gross dereliction of duty which it would hardly have been in the national interest to gloss over."[85] From the point of view of judicial independence and unswerving integrity, a judge is in no way under a duty to intimate to the head of State the nature of his verdict before it is officially announced in a court of law. As we

---

82 See *West Africa* October 12, 1963, p.1163.

83 Sir Arku Korsha after being dismissed as the Chief Justice resigned as a member of the Ghana Judiciary. See *West Africa* December 21, 1963, p.1443.

84 See *West Africa* January 4, 1964, p.20.

85 *Ibid.*

observed earlier, an irresistable conclusion is reached when the statements are read together, that the President should have no reason to doubt the party political reliability of the Chief Justice. If this is the true meaning of the statement, it is absurd to conceive. On the other hand, it may be argued that once a Chief Justice is appointed by the President, the President would not expect him to declare an open war by giving decisions which are unaccommodating to him. But even on this point, once the Chief Justice is impartial, he should administer justice without any fear of victimisation.

With regard to informing the President in advance and the need to take necessary precautionary measures to maintain law and order after a verdict in a case of this nature, we are of the view that the responsibility should be that of the prosecuting officers who could reasonably anticipate a likely judgement. What under the circumstances should prevent the police from taking the initiative by posting certain police officers around the courts while such important trials are being conducted. The Judges should not in any way disclose their verdicts before they were actually delivered. This would be in accord with judicial independence.

The question which next falls to be considered is whether the non-disclosure of the verdict before it was given was sufficient to dismiss a Chief Justice and to place him in such a disgraceful position that he had no choice than to resign. It is submitted that although the President was empowered to revoke the appointment of the Chief Justice under the Constitution of Ghana,[86] the revocation of the Chief Justice's appointment under the circumstances appears unjustifiable.[86(a)]

6. *Interpretation of the Constitution*

The 1963 Nigerian Constitution like many modern written constitutions, has an express provision making it the supreme law of the land. Any law which is contrary to the Constitution is void. Section one of the Constitution thus provides as follows:

> This Constitution shall have the fore of law throughout Nigeria and, subject to the provisions of section 4 of this Constitution, if any other law (including the constitution of a Region) is inconsistent with this Constitution, this Constitution shall prevail and the other law shall, to the extent of the inconsistency be void.[87]

---

[86] Article 44 (1) of the Constitution of Ghana, 1960 provides that the appointment of a Judge as a Chief Justice may at any time be revoked by the President.

[86(a)] In Nigeria although under 1979 Constitution The Chief Justice is appointed by the President and Chief Judge of a State by the Governor, the Judicial Service Commission advises the Governor while the Senate has to confirm the appointment of the Chief Justice: SS.211 234 of the Constitution. Other judicial appointments are made on the recommendation of the Judicial Service Commission.

[87] S.1 of the Constitution of the Federal Republic of Nigeria, 1963. Section 1 has been modified by a proviso which reads as follows: "Provided this Constitution shall not prevail over a Decree, and nothing in this Constitution shall render any provision of a Decree void to any extent whatsoever."

It follows that the Constitution of Nigeria is placed in a position which makes it the organic law of the land. Being supreme and entertaining no conflict, any law whether written or unwritten which is not in accord with the Constitution will be declared void by the Courts. As Marshall C.J. stated: 'It is emphatically the province and duty of the judicial department to say what the law.' The learned Chief Justice further emphasised: 'Certainly all those who have written constitutions contemplate them as forming the fundamental and paramount law of the nation, and consequently, the theory of every such government must be, that an act of the legislature, repugnant to the Constitution is void.'[88]

> This theory is essentially attached to a written constitution, and is consequently, to be considered by this court as one of the fundamental principles of our society.[89]

It must be pointed out that no act of the government whether executive, judicial or quasi-judicial or legislative, be that at the centre or in a state or region or province, contrary to the Constitution can stand. The Courts being guardian of the of the Constitution should declare such acts illegal, ultra vires and consequently void. It is under the Constitution which is the organic law of the land, that all laws are made and executed; under which all authorities, executive, legislative and judicial derive validity for acts done in carrying out their respective functions. The Constitution therefore provides a measuring rod by which the validity of any act is determined.

Under the Nigerian Constitution, the Courts are endowed with the power to interpret the Constitution.[90] Of these, the Supreme Court, as the highest Court in the land, takes pride of place. The Constitution more particularly spells out this function as follows:

See Schedule 2 to the Constitution (Suspension and Modification) Decree No. 8 of 1967. This Decree repeals an earlier Decree entitled Constitution (Suspension and Modification) Decree No. 1 of 1966. Both Decrees were issued by the Military Government with identical provisos in this regard. For an examination of the legal complications and possible Judicial interpretations of the Decrees and the events surrounding them, see Chapter 4, post. The 1979 Constitution has a similar provision in S.1. It provides "1(1) This Constitution is supreme and its provisions shall have binding force on all authorities and persons throughout the Federal Republic of Nigeria."

88 See *William Marbury v James Maddison 1 Cranch 137*. The Chief Justice was in that case expounding the duty of the Supreme Court in interpreting the written Constitution of the United States of America. In that case the doctrine of judicial review was first asserted by the American Supreme Court.

89 *Ibid.*

90 The Nigerian Constitution differs with the American Constitution in this respect. For the power of the American Courts to review the constitutionality of laws was not expressly states in the Constitution. Thus Lord Bryce writes: "There is a story told of an intelligent Englishman who, having heard that the Supreme Federal Court was created to protect the Constitution and had authority given it to annul bad laws, spent two days in hunting up and down the Federal Constitution for provisions he had been told to admire. No wonder he did not find them, for there is not a word in the Constitution on the subject." See Bryce: *The American Commonwealth* (1917 ed.) Vol. I, p.252.

> Where any question as to the interpretation of this Constitution or the constitution of a Region arises in any proceedings in any Court of law in any part of Nigeria (other than the Supreme Court, the High Court of a territory or a court-martial) and the court is of the opinion that the question involves a substantial question of law, the court may, and shall if any party to the proceedings so requests, refer the question to the High Court having jurisdiction in that part of Nigeria; and the High Court shall - (a) if it is of opinion that the question involves a substantial question of law, refer the question to the Supreme Court; or (b) if it is of opinion that the question does not involve a substantial question of law, remit the question to the Court that made the reference to the disposed of in accordance with such directions as the High Court may think fit to give.[91]

Where any question as to the intepretation of the Constitution arises in the High Court itself and it is of the opinion that the question involves a substantial question of law, the High Court should if any party to the dispute requests or might on its own volition refer the matter to the Court of Appeal.[92] After the case had been referred to the Court of Appeal, it would give decision and the court in which the question arose should dispose of the case in accordance with the decision of the Court of Appeal or Supreme Court.[93] The provisions as regards interpretation of the Constitution under the 1963 Constitution broadly correspond with the provisions under the 1960 Constitution.[94] Under the 1960 Constitution, the Federal Supreme Court was called upon to interpret S.33(10) of the Western Region of Nigeria Constitution. This arose from the case of *Akintola v Governor of Western Nigeria and Adegbenro*.[95] The plaintiff in that case was the Premier of the Western Region of Nigeria. He was removed from office by the Governor of the Region - exercising the power conferred on him under S.33(10) of the Constitution of the Western Region. The plaintiff sought

(a) a declaration that the Governor had no right to remove him from office under S.33(10) of the Constitution of Western Nigeria without a prior resolution of decision of he Western House of Assembly reached on the floor of the House to the effect that the Premier, i.e. plaintiff, no longer commanded the support of the majority of the members of the House;

(b) an injunction to restrain the Governor from purporting to relieve the plaintiff of his office as Premier in the absence of the aforementioned decision or resolution of the House and to restrain the defendants from usurping or permitting anyone to usurp the

---

91 S.115 of the Constitution of Federation (1963).

92 S.220 of the Constitution of Federation (1979).

93 S.219 *Ibid.*

94 See S.108 of the Nigeria (Constitution) Order in Council, 1960, S.1. 1652, 1960.

95 (1962) 1 All N.L.R. 442; see also (1962) 11 I.C.L.Q. 919.

said office unless and until the plaintiff resigned or is constitutionally relieved of the office;

(c) a declaration that the purported removal of the plaintiff from the office of Premier by the Governor was invalid and of no effect.

There was no doubt that the Governor was constitutionally empowered to remove the Premier. The question was under what circumstances could the Governor remove the Premier. The test is laid down in the constitution itself which reads as follows:

> Subject to the provisions of subsections (8) and (9) of this section, the Ministers of the Government of the Region shall hold office during Governor's pleasure: provided that (a) the Governor shall not remove the Premier from office unless it appears to him that the Premier no longer commands the support of a majority of the members of the House of Assembly;[96] and (b) the Governor shall not remove a Minister from Office except in accordance with the advice of the Premier.[97]

The issues which the Federal Supreme Court under S.108 of the Nigerian Constitution 1960 was called upon to be decided were:

(1) whether the Governor could validly exercise the power to remove the Premier from office under S.33 (10) of the Constitution of Western Nigeria without prior decision or resolution on the floor of the House of Assembly showing that the Premier no longer commanded the support of the majority of the House?

(2) whether the Governor could validly exercise the power to remove the Premier from Office under S.33 (10) of the said Constitution on the basis of any materials or information extraneous to the proceedings of the House of Assembly?

The Federal Supreme Court answered the first question in the negative i.e. that the Governor could not remove the Premier from office unless a resolution was passed in the House of Assembly to the effect that the Premier no longer commanded the support of a majority of the House. Consequently the Supreme Court found it unnecessary to go into the next question.[98]

The circumstances leading to the removal of the Premier emanated from a rift in the Action Group which was the party in power in the Western

---

[96] The point in issue here is how the Governor is to exercise this discretionary power to accord with the letter and possibly the spirit of the Constitution. From the cases we shall examine it will be seen that the exercise of statutory discretionary powers has no objective test as such. It is subjective and in the absence of bad faith and other undesirable influences the courts do not usually interfere with acts which are apparently within the powers conferred on the person in question.

[97] S.33(10) of the Constitution of Western Nigeria, 1960. i.e. the Fourth Schedule to the Nigerian (Constitution) Order in Council, 1960.

[98] This was reversed by the Privy Council; see *Adegbenro v Akintola 1963 A.C. 614.*

Region of Nigeria at this material time. The Action Group had called upon Chief Akintola to relinquish the Premiership of the Western Region. Instead of heeding to this, Chief Akintola asked the Governor to dissolve the House of Assembly. This being within the constitutional discretionary powers of the Governor, he refused to grant the request for dissolution.[99] Chief Akintola having rejected demand of his party, the Action Group, to surrender the Premiership of the Western Region, the party then decided to see to his removal from office. On May 21, 1962, a letter was addressed to the Governor of the Western Region to this effect. The letter reads as follows:

> *Your Excellency,*
> We the undersigned being a majority of the House of Assembly declare that we no longer support Chief Samuel Ladoke Akintola as Premier. We hereby request Your Excellency to remove the said Chief Samuel Ladoke Akintola from his office as the Premier in accordance with powers vested in you in Section 33 (10) of the Constitution of Western Nigeria. We have the honour to be, Sir,
> *Your obedient servants ...*[100]

On the receipt of this letter, the Governor wrote a letter to the Speaker of the House of Assembly to ascertain whether those whose names appeared on the letter were members of the House of Assembly. The Speaker replied and confirmed that all the sixty-six signatories were members of the House of Assembly. Meanwhile at a joint meeting of the federal executive council of the Action Group a resolution was passed and embodied in another letter to the Governor expressing lack of confidence in the Premier, Chief A.L. Akintola and praying the Governor to remove him from office. The meeting also removed Chief Akintola from the office of Deputy Leader of the party, the Action Group. It was on the strength of all these that the Governor acted and removed Chief Akintola from office of Premier of the Western Region. The wording of the instrument removing the Premier was couched in such a way as to exhibit with little or no doubt the discretionary power of the Governor in this respect. It reads as follows:

> Whereas it appears to me that Samuel Ladoke Akintola, Premier of the Western Region no longer commands the support of a majority of the Members of the House of Assembly, now therefore, I, Adesoji T. Aderami ... Oni of Ife, Governor of the Western Region of Nigeria, in exercise of powers vested in me by Section 33, sub-section (10) of the Constitution of Western Nigeria, set out in the First Schedule to the Nigeria Constitution Order-in-Council, 1960, do hereby remove the said Samuel

---

[99] The Governor was empowered under S.31(4) to refuse a request to dissolve the House if he considers that the government of the Region could be carried on without a dissolution or if such a dissolution would not be in the interest of the Region.

[100] For these letters, see Nigeria Hansard cols. 2194-2196, May 29, 1962 (Daily Parts).

> Ladoke Akintola from his Office as Premier of the Western Region with effect from this date.[101]

The Federal Supreme Court in reaching the decision which was subsequently reversed by the Privy Council, basically relied on the argument that viewing the Constitution of the Region as a whole, there was an inference that the Premier could only be removed from office on the basis of a resolution in the House that the Premier no longer commanded the support of the majority of the members of the House. It was contended that the Constitution of the Western Region was a deliberate attempt to write down the conventions of the United Kingdom Constitution. It may be observed that the crux of the whole matter lay in the clause, "if it appears to him" which forms part of S.33 (10) of the Constitution of Western Nigeria. It is submitted that this clause made it apparent that the Governor was empowered to act purely in his discretion in matters relating to the ascertainment of the fact that the Premier had or had no longer the support of the majority of the members of the House. But the exercise of discretion in cases pertaining to duties imposed by law, should not be arbitrary, unduly influenced by undesirable circumstances and should not be tainted by bad faith. Where the power of discretion had been exercised in good faith and reasonably the courts do not usually interfere. Thus in *Fraser v Minister of National Revenue*[102] (a Canadian case), the Minister refused to make depletion allowance to the appellant company in respect of their assessment to income tax for the fiscal year 1940-41; for the exhaustion of timber limits owed by the Crown on which the company had been licensed to cut timber. It was hold *inter alia*, that in exercising his discretion not to make any depletion allowance the Minister could not be said to have transgressed the bounds of his discretion so as to justify any interference by the court with his decision. Their Lordships after a thorough examination of the case laid down the rule guiding the exercise of discretionary statutory powers as follows:

> The creteria by which the exercise of a Statutory discretion must be judged ... is well settled that if the discretion has been exercised *bona fide*, uninfluenced by irrelevant considerations and not arbitrarily or illegally, no court is entitled to interfere even if the court, had the discretion been theirs, might have exercised it otherwise.[103]

---

101 The letter was dated May 21, 1962.

102 (1949) A.C. 24.

103 (1949) A.C. 24 at p.36.

In *Sharp v Wakefield*[104] Lord Halsbury L.C. said "The Minister must act according to the rules of reason and justice not according to private opinion." Discretion was defined in *Rooke's Case*[105] as follows:

> Discretion is a science or understanding to discern between falsity and truth, between wrong and right, between shadows and substance, between equity and colourable glosses and pretences, and not to do according to their wills and private affections.

In its decision the Federal Supreme Court was of the view that 'Section 33(10) was an attempt to write down constitutional, *(sic)* conventions of the English Constitution.' The Court also maintained that although section 33(2) empowered the Governor to use his deliberate judgment in appointing a Premier, it did not state that the Governor could use his own deliberate judgment in removing him from office. It is difficult to agree with that reasoning. Even though the conventions of the British Constitution have been written in the Nigerian Constitution, the written constitution should be interpreted without recourse to the unwritten conventions.[106] The vagueness of some of these conventions and the weaknesses of their incorporation by reference have been the main reason why the Constitutions of the newer independent States of the Commonwealth are usually drafted with marked explicitness.[107]

Brett, F.J. in his dissenting judgment pointed out that when all the parallels relating to the relationship between the unwritten Constitution of the United Kingdom and the written Constitution had been examined, the task of the Court in Nigeria remained that of construing a written Constitution. It is impossible to resist agreeing wholly with the point made. There was no ambiguity in Section 33(10) of the Constitution of Western Nigeria, 1960; the powers vested in the Governor was discretionary and once he had exercised them in good faith, it is submitted that from the authorities referred to above, the Court should not interfere. It was a similar view which led the Privy Council into reversing the decision of the Federal Supreme Court. It was left to the Governor to exercise the statutory or constitutional discretion *bona fide*, uninfluenced by irrelevant considerations and not arbitrarily but with reason and justice and once he had done so, the Courts would not be entitled to interfere.

Under the circumstances, it was not shown that the Governor had not acted with good judgment. The Region then was operating party system of

---

104 (1891) A.C. 173 at p.179; see also Lord Thankerton in *Pioneer Laundry & Dry Cleaners v Minister of National Revenue (1940) A.C. 127 at 136*, Lord Kenyon C.J. in *Wilson v Rastall (1792) 10 E.R. 1283.*

105 77 E.R. 209 at 210.

106 Cf. Their Lordships' view in the judgment of the Privy Council delivered by Viscount Radcliffe in *Adegbenro v Akintola (1963) A.C. 614 at p.628.*

107 See S.A. de Smith: *"The New and Its Constitutions"* (1964), p.78 *et seq.*

government and a Governor could reasonably think that a party which put a person in office was entitled at any time to ask for his removal. *A fortiori*, when a letter was written to the Governor by the party itself as well as sixty-six party members of the House of Assembly. While we agree that British practice should be emulated, justice compels us to interpret a written constitution which basically is an embodiment of British constitutional practice. Where, therefore, the conventions of the British Constitution are written and form part of the written law, the courts are not entitled to import into the written constitution when called upon to interpret it, conventions which had not been written into the Constitution. Consequently we must accept that the decision of the Privy Council was the right one as that was an irresistible emanation from written Constitution.[108] It must be pointed out, however, that in a democratic State, it would be undesirable to allow discretionary powers to be concentrated in the hands of a person without adequate checks. There is no doubt that the better practice should be to remove a Premier from office after a vote of no confidence had been passed in the House of Assembly. But this will not blind us to the fact that if no such provision is made in a written Constitution, the courts will not be entitled to import such practice into the written constitution when called upon to construe it.

After the Privy Council's decision - reversing the decision of the Federal Supreme Court and upholding the removal of Chief Akintola as legal, the Western House of Assembly passed a law amending the Constitution of the Region.[109] This amendment operated to restore the decision of the Federal Supreme Court to the effect that no removal of the Premier would be legal unless a resolution was passed in the House of Assembly that the Premier no longer commanded the support of the majority of the House. The amendment was expressed to operate retrospectively from the 2nd day of October, 1960.

The 1963 Constitution carefully avoided making a provision for the removal of the Premier or Prime Minister as the case may be. As the constitution was apparently silent on that, it is hoped that the traditional British Convention of the Constitution would be followed; that is, when a government is defeated on a vote of no confidence in the House of Commons or the House of Representatives as the case may be, it will resign.

---

108 Their Lordships observed: "According to any ordinary rule of construction weight must be given to the fact that the Governor's power of removal is not limited in such precise terms as would confine his judgment to the actual proceedings of the House ..., *ibid*, at p.629.

109 See the Constitution of Western Nigeria (Amendment) Law, 1963, Legislation of Western Nigeria, 1963. The Federal Prime Minister introducing a motion for ratification of the Constitution of Western Nigeria (Amendment) Law, 1963, showed that Chief Akintola received two successive votes of confidence by 79 and 80 members respectively in a House of 117 members. See House of Representatives Debates, 3rd June, 1963.

As we have seen, the Republican Constitution of 1963 was made the supreme law of the land. Any law whether enacted or otherwise which is in conflict with the constitution is void. It must be pointed out that the position was the same under the 1960 Constitution.[110] It was under this Constitution that the Federal Supreme Court was called upon to determine the validity of an Act of the Federal Parliament. This was an interesting case, for in this case of *Doherty v Balewa*,[111] the Federal Supreme Court dauntlessly declared certain sections of the Act of the Federal Parliament *ultra vires* the Constitution and therefore void. The Commissions and Tribunals of Equity Act, 1961 was passed and made applicable throughout the Federation. The Act provided, inter alia, that the Prime Minister could, whenever he deemed it expedient, institute a Commission of Inquiry "into any matters or thing within or affecting the general welfare of the Federal Territory, or into any matter or thing within Federal competence anywhere within the Federation."[112] The Act then went on to purport to oust the jurisdiction of the courts. It provided as follows:

> The fact that a commission is issued under this section shall be sufficient proof of the proper exercise by the Prime Minister of his authority to do so; and neither the Commission itself nor any action of the Prime Minister in relation thereto shall be enquired into in any court of law.[113]

In pursuance of the powers under the Act, the Prime Minister i.e. the defendant, appointed a Commission of Inquiry into the activities of a bank licensed under the Banking Ordinance (Cap.19) and carrying on business in the Western Region and the Federal Territory of Lagos. In the instant case, the plaintiffs sought a declaration that the Commissions and Tribunals Enquiry Act, 1961, under which the Commission of Inquiry was appointed was unconstitutional generally, or, if not, that certain sections thereof were unconstitutional and therefore void. The High Court of Lagos under S.108 of the Constitution referred the matter to the Federal Supreme Court to determine

(1) whether or not the Commissions and Tribunals of Enquiry Act, 1961 was within the legislative powers of the Federal Parliament insofar as it purported to have effect to matters and things within Federal competence anywhere in the Federation.

---

110 See S.1 of the Nigeria (Constitution) Order in Council, 1960.

111 (1961) 1 All N.L.R. 604.

112 S.3(1) of the Commissions and Tribunals of Enquiry Act, 1961, see Laws of the Federation of Nigeria and Lagos, 1961.

113 S.3(4) *Ibid.*

(2) whether or not S.3(4) of the Act was constitutional and valid or contravened SS.21, 31 and 108 of the Constitution of Nigeria.[114]

(3) Whether or not SS.8(c), 8(a) 15(a) and 18(1)(b) of the Commissions and Tribunals of Enquiry Act, 1961 were valid under the Constitution or contravened SS.20 and 21 of the Constitution.[115]

The Federal Supreme Court held that the Federal Parliament could legislate for the whole of the Federation on those matters only in respect of which it was specifically empowered so to legislate under the Constitution. That Item 44(a) of the Executive legislative List permitted legislation making provision for Tribunals of Enquiry and matter pertaining thereto, but was not intended to be so wide as to provide generally for the attendance of witnesses, disclosure of information and the production of documents as these matters could not be legitimately regarded as incidental to legislation establishing or regulating tribunals or Commissions of Enquiry. The Court went on to declare that the Commissions and Tribunals of Enquiry Act, 1961 in making for such matters, was insofar as it applied to the entire Federation, in excess of the powers of Parliament under the Constitution and was therefore unconstitutional. The Court then judged the constitutionality of the Act in relation to the Federal Territory of Lagos and held that the Act was valid in respect of the legislative power of Parliament. It was obvious that the Court would declare *ultra vires* and void S.3(4) of the Act which as we saw earlier, was couched in such a way as to oust the jurisdiction of the courts in matters affecting the Commission of Inquiry. This it did. It follows therefore that the Federal Supreme Court did not declare the whole Act unconstitutional but certain sections of it which could not stand under the Constitution. From the decision of the Federal Supreme Court appeal was made to the privy Council.[116]

Their Lordships held that the Act of 1961 was valid insofar as it authorised tribunals or commissions of inquiry of any sort without compulsive powers into Federal matters; but that it was not within the legislative power of the Federal Parliament insofar as S.8(a) to (d) - which included the giving of compulsive powers to the Commissioners to take evidence on oath, to compel the attendance of witnesses and the production of documents - purported to have effect in relation to matters and things

[114] S.21 of the 1960 Constitution made elaborate provisions for 'due process' in relation to cases arising from fundamental rights and freedoms. S.31 made provision for recourse to the High Court for redress where any of the provisions of Chapter III had been contravened in relation to that person. S.108 vested in the High Court and subsequently to the Federal Supreme Court the power to interpret the Constitution.

[115] S.20 of the Constitutions provided that no person shall be deprived of his personal liberty save in certain specified cases.

[116] Balewa v Doherty (1963) 1 W.L.R. 949.

"within Federal competence anywhere within the Federation."[117] Like the Federal Supreme Court their Lordships found no difficulty in declaring void and without effect S.3(4) which could have operated to exclude any judicial review of the acts of both the Commissioners and the Prime Minister. This provision was glaringly *ultra vires* and could not stand under our Constitution. Section 15(a) which imposed "a fine of fifty pounds or to imprisonment of three months to be imposed by the Commissioners and recoverable or enforceable in the same manner as a fine or imprisonment imposed by a Magistrate's Court," was declared void. Equally Section 18(b) which dealt with contempt "whether the act was or was not committed in the presence of Commissioners sitting in commission" was declared invalid. This sub-section also imposed a fine of ten pounds.

It follows that the Privy Council broadly upheld the decision of the Federal Supreme Court and after minor changes in the Supreme Court's decision, dismissed the appeal. Both decisions deserve every commendation. We are operating a written Constitution. The Constitution is, as we pointed out earlier, the fundamental law of the land. This fundamental law has endowed the Courts with the power to interpret the Constitution; consequently any enactment which derives its validity from the Constitution should be subject to interpretation by the Courts. Acts emanating from such enactments, whether they are that of the executive or quasi-judicial bodies appointed by the executive, should be subject to judicial review. From this point of view, the provision of S.3(4), which as we saw earlier, was designed to oust the jurisdiction of the Courts for any action of the Prime Minister and the commission was not only *ultra vires* and consequently a nullity but also deplorable. Such a provision could hardly find accommodation in any democratic country's constitution whether written or unwritten.

It may be observed that where commission of inquiry is appointed by the executive in the sphere where this is constitutional, the jurisdiction of the courts should not be excluded. In such a case, the courts would be in a position to issue *certiorari*[118] where there is, *prima facie*, case for that. Any

---

117 The powers given or purported to be given to the Commissioners under the Act were sweeping. The deplorable aspect of the legislation being that the courts were purported to be ousted in respect of any act done by the Commission of Inquiry or the Prime Minister. S.8(d), for instance, provided that the Commissioners should have "the power to issue a warrant to compel the attendance of any person who, after having been summoned to attend, fails to do so, and does not excuse such failure to the satisfaction of the Commissioners, and to order him to pay all costs which may have been occasioned in compelling his attendance or by reason of his refusal to obey the summons, and also to fine such person a sum not exceeding five pounds, such to be recoverable in the same manner as a fine imposed by a Magistrate Court."

118 *Certiorari* will issue to quash on order made by an administrative body if it acted in a judicial or quasi-judicial capacity. If a statutory tribunal makes an order which is in excess of its powers, *certiorari* will issue to quash the order. See *R. v Northumberland Compensation Appeal Tribunal, Ex parte Shaw 1952 1 K.B. 338*. It was laid down in this case that a decision of an inferior court,

aggrieved person would be entitled to bring his case before a court of law. As several sections of this Act, i.e. the Commissions and Tribunals of Inquiry Act, 1961, had been nullified, we may venture to suggest the repeal of the whole enactment and if necessary, pass another legislation which could take root under the Constitution.

Just as the Constitution of the Federation was expressed to be the supreme law of the nation, so were the Regional Constitutions made supreme laws of the respective Regions. Thus S.5(1) provided as follows:

> Subject to the provisions of this Constitution and the Nigeria Independence Act, 1960, the constitution of each Region shall have the force of law throughout that Region and if any other law is inconsistent with that constitution, the provisions of that constitution shall prevail and the other law shall, to the extent of the inconsistency, be void.[119]

It follows that any law in any Region which could be proved to be in conflict with the Constitution of the Region will be void.[120] Thus in *Olawoyin v Commissioner of Police*[121] the constitutional validity of S.59C(1) of the Northern Region High Court (Amendment) Law, 1960 was in question. The appellant was convicted and sentenced in the Provincial Court at Ilorin. From the Conviction and sentence in the Provincial Court he appealed to the native Courts Appellate Division of the High Court. Consequently he found occasion to question the constitutional validity of S.59C(1) of the enactment which provided for the composition of the Appellate Court. It reads as follows:

> A Court of the Native Courts Appellate Division of the High Court shall be constituted of three judges, two of whom shall be judges of the High Court and one of whom shall be the Grand Kadi, or the Deputy Grand Kadi or such other judge of the Sharia Court of Appeal as the Grand Kadi shall appoint.[122]

The issue was therefore referred to the Federal Supreme Court under S.108 of the Constitution of the Federation. The questions which fell to be answered by the Supreme Court were, *inter alia*, as follows: 'Whether the

---

such as statutory tribunal was liable to be quashed on issue of *certiorari*, on the ground that there was an error on the face of the record. *Certiorari* also issues where a tribunal makes a mistake of law or exceeds its jurisdiction - Per Lord Denning at p.346.

119 The Nigeria (Constitution) Order in Council, 1960, S.1. 1652, 1960.

120 The 1963 Constitution has been modified as follows; "Provided that the Constitution of a Region shall not prevail over a Decree, and nothing in this subsection or in the constitution of a Region shall render any provision of a Decree void to any extent whatsoever." See Constitution (Suspension and Modification) Decree 1966. Supp. to Official Gazette Extraordinary No. 20, Vol. 53, 4th March, 1966; the 1966 Decree has been repealed by Decree No. 8 of 1967 which has the same title and contains the same *proviso*.

121 (1961) 1 All N.L.R. 203.

122 See N.R. No. 14 of 1960; this sub-section in question is reproduced in (1961) 1 All N.LR. at p.209.

provisions of S.59C of the Northern Region High Court Law insofar as they make the Grand Kadi or Deputy Grand Kadi or an appointee of the Grand Kadi capable to sit as a member of the Appellate Division of the High Court have not been invalidated by the provisions of Chapter IV of the Constitution of Northern Nigeria;[123] and whether the Appellate Division of the High Court is properly and adequately constituted by two Judges of the High Court.' The Federal Supreme Court held that any law which provided for the sharing of the functions of the High Court and its judges with other person must, unless the Constitution expressly permitted it, be regarded as inconsistent with the Constitution and invalid. The Court further held that the Constitution of the Northern Nigeria (Nigeria Constitution) Order in Council, 1960, 3rd Schedule did not expressly permit of the sharing of such functions of the High Court or its judges with other person. It was strongly contended for the Respondent that S.142A(13) of the Nigeria (Constitution) Order in Council, 1954 expressly provided for legislation for the appointment of person other than High Court Judges to act.

The argument then went on, that in the light of such provision and in view of S.4 of the Order - saving existing Courts, that S.59C was within the legislative competence of the Northern Region legislature. The Federal Supreme Court, while agreeing that S.59C could not be validly attacked under the 1954 Constitution held that S.142A(13) of the 1954 Constitution was merely an enabling section and once the power conferred by it had been exercised, it was spent. As the section was not repeated in the 1960 Constitution, the Constitution had to be interpreted accordingly.

The Court went on to make a very important observation; that the Court in interpreting a Constitutional instrument is not entitled to refer to extraneous evidence, such as, in the instant case, the Report on the Resumed Conference on the Constitution of Nigeria; unless the words used in the Constitution are ambiguous.[124] After the decision the Northern

---

123 Chapter IV of the Constitution of Northern Nigeria made provisions for the establishment of High Court for the Region but there was no provision empowering the sharing of functions of the High Court with other persons as the Grand Kadi.

124 *Cf. Katikiro of Buganda v Attorney-General (1961) 1 W.L.R. 119;* in this case their Lordships upheld the refusal of the Court of Appeal for Eastern Africa to admit in evidence a White Paper for the purpose of construing one of the constitutional instruments in force in the Protectorate of Uganda, on the ground that they "found no ambiguity which would justify the admission of extraneous evidence" - at p.128. One of the most important functions of the judiciary is the intepretation of Statutes, which in our own case and other countries with written constitutions include the Constitutional instruments themselves. The practice of the courts in the common law world is to construe a statute or a written Constitution without recourse to extraneous materials. Thus there is no judicial power to "fill gaps" in a statute or written constitution. Lord Simonds restated this principle in *Magor and St. Mellons R.D.C. v Newport Corporation (1952) A.C. 189,* when he said: "The duty of the court is to interpret the words that the legislature has used, those words may be ambiguous, but, even if they are, the power and duty of the court to travel outside them on a voyage of discovery are strictly limited." - at p.191. See also Lord Wright in *Assam*

Region legislature passed a law which amended the Constitution of the Region and restored the status quo.[125] The fact that the legislation was passed which in effect abrogated the decision does not detract from the principle that any enactment whose validity cannot be established under the Constitution cannot stand.

As we have seen, the superiority of a written Constitution over other laws of the nation is not unique to Nigeria. In countries with written Constitutions which had been expressed to be the supreme laws of the land, any laws which are in conflict or *ultra vires* the constitution are void and the courts are under a duty to declare accordingly. Thus in *Australian Communist Party v The Commonwealth,*[126] the High Court of Australia held that the Communist Party Dissolution Act, 1950 was *ultra vires* the Parliament of the Commonwealth and invalid. The Court was of the view that the Act could not be supported by S.51(XXXIX) read with S.16 of the Constitution or under an implied power to make laws for the preservation of the Commonwealth and its institutions from internal attach and subversion. This case provides one of the classic examples of dauntless decisions emanating vividly from constitutional construction. The Judges may not like communism as a philosophy of life, but once they were in the judicial arena, they had to cast off all personal prejudices and construe a written constitution as men of integrity. In another case, both the High Court of Australia and the Privy Council were confronted with the interpretation of the Constitution of the Commonwealth of Australia. The issue in this case, *Attorney-General for Commonwealth of Australia v Colonial Sugar Refining Co.*[127] was whether the compulsive powers given to commissioner under the Royal Commissions Acts of 1902 and 1912 were valid under the

---

Railways & Trading Co. Ltd. v Inland Revenue Commissioners (1935) A.C. 445 at 458. Denning L.J. in Magor's case advocated filling of gaps but this was strongly criticized by Lord Simonds in the House of Lords in the same case. Lord Simonds said: "It appears to me to be a naked usurpation of the legislative function under the guise of interpretation ... If a gap is disclosed, the remedy lies in an amending Act." - *(1952) A.C.* at p.191. It is submitted that this is the correct view on the subject. Statutory or Constitutional interpretation is one of the primary roles of the judiciary but judicial interpretation should not be replaced by judicial legislation which cannot be accepted. Here we differ with the practice predominant in the Continent where courts freely have recourse to *travaux preparatoires* or legislative materials. Courts in the common law world refuse to have regard to such documents, although the rule is not as strict in the U.S.

125 See Constitution of Northern Nigeria (Amendment) Law 1961.

126 *(1950-51) 83 C.L.R. 1.* It is interesting to note that in the case of *Amalgamated Society of Engineers v Adelaide Steamship Co. (1920) 28 C.L.R. 129* the method of reading into the Constitution certain views which were in fact not written down in the constitutional instrument was exploded. The idea took root since the case of *D'Emdem v Pedder (1904) 1 C.L.R. 91* and was followed ever since until the *Engineers' Case.* The High Court of Australia in the *Engineers' Case* stated that it was 'the chief and special duty' of the Court to interpret the Constitution by 'finding the intention from the words' of the Constitution - *(1920) 28 C.L.R. at p.142.* See also W.A. Wynes: *Legislative, Executive and Judicial Powers in Australia* (3rd ed. 1962) p.15

127 (1914) A.C. 237.

were valid under the Constitution. In holding that the powers purported to be given by the Acts were *ultra vires* under the Constitution, their Lordships observed:

> There Lordships hesitate to differ from the judges with the special knowledge of the Australian Constitution ... but the question they have to decide depends simply on the interpretation of the language of an Act of Parliament ... Without redrafting the Royal Commissions Act and altering them into a measure with a different purpose, it is, in their Lordships' opinion, impossible to use them as a justification for the steps which the Royal Commission on the Sugar Industry contemplates in order to make its inquiry effective. They think that these Acts were *ultra vires* and void so far as they purported to enable a Royal Commission to compel answers generally to questions, or to order the production of documents, or otherwise to enforce compliance by the members of the public with its requisitions.[128]

Before arriving at this conclusion their Lordships had to examine the provision of S.51 where the Parliament of the Commonwealth of Australia was empowered to make laws for peace, order and good government but there was a limited sphere in which the power was to operate. This was vividly brought out by the words "with respect to," following by a list of enumerated specific subjects.[129] As with every written constitution, the Parliament could only act within the ambit of the Constitution. It cannot tread outside the prescribed path without the Courts declaring the move *ultra vires*. It follows that as long as the Parliament or a Legislative Assembly acts within the constitution in respect of a legislation, the courts will not allow such legislation to be successfully attached. Thus in the case of *Olajire v Superintendent-General of Local Government Police*,[130] the High Court of Western Nigeria was called upon to declare *ultra vires* SS.13 to 19 of the Western Region Local Government Police Law.[131] S.13 provided for the

128 *Ibid* at p.257. *Cf.* This case with *Balewa v Doherty (1963 1 W.L.R. 949* and *Doherty v Balewa (1961) 1 All N.L.R. 604* where, as we have seen, both the Federal Supreme Court of Nigeria and the Judicial Committee of the Privy Council held certain sections of the Commissions and tribunals of Enquiry Act, 1961 *ultra vires* and void.

129 In the British North America Act 1867, i.e. the Constitution of Canada, a similar clause appears in S.91 without much restriction as in the Australian Constitution. S.91 provides: "It shall be lawful for the Queen by Advice and Consent of the Senate and House of Commons, to make laws for the peace, order, and good government of Canada, in respect to all matters not coming within the Classes of Subjects assigned exclusively to the Legislatures of the Provinces ..." Under the powers expressed to be conferred on it, the Domiion Parliament passed the Canadian Temperance Act, 1878 which in effect, uniformly prohibited the sale of intoxicating liquors except in wholesale quantities or for certain specified purposes. In the case of *Charles Russel v The Queen 1882 App. Cas. 829*, the validity of the Act under the Constitution was questioned Their Lordships held that the Act of 1878 was within the legislative competence of the Dominion Parliament and therefore valid, thus upholding precisely the decision of the Supreme Court of Canada.

130 (1961) 1 All N.L.R.826.

131 Cap. 70, Laws of the Western Region of Nigeria, 1959, Vol.IV

appointment of the Superintendent-General of the Local Government Police Force by the Governor. The Objector in the instant case was charged with an offence by the Respondent before Ilesha Grade "A" Customary Court. The main issue in this case was whether the said SS.13 to 19 of the legislation were *ultra vires*. Sections 98(4) and 98(7) of the Constitution of the Federation[132] insofar they purported to provide for the appointment of a Superintendent-General of Local Government Police Forces.

Somolu J. held that the Provisions of Sections 13 to 19 inclusive of the Western Region Local Government Police law were not contrary to or *ultra vires* the Constitution of the Federation, 1960. The learned Judge in holding that the appointment of a Superintendent-General of Local Government Police was constitutional said as follows:

> In my view, where there is a power conferred, there is the implied construction that all means of exercising that power to the best advantage will be conceded to the donee of such power. It is not necessary for the details of such provisions to be set out in a Constitution, it is enough if the material outline of that power is clearly set out.[133]

For this statement the Judge relied heavily on the judicial pronouncement of Marshall C.J. in *McCulloch v Maryland.*[134] It reads as follows:

> A constitution, to contain an accurate detail of all the subdivisions of which its powers will admit, and of all the means by which they may be carried into execution would partake of the prolixity of a legal code, and could scarcely be embraced by the human mind ... Its nature therefore requires, that only its great outlines should be marked, its important objects designated, and the *minor ingredients*[135] which compose those objects be deduced from the nature of the objects themselves ... But we think that the sound construction of the constitution must allow to the ... legislature that discretion, with respect to the means by which the powers it confers are to be carried into execution, which will enable that body to perform the high duties assigned to it, in the manner most beneficial to the people ... *Let the end be legitimate, let it be within the scope of the constitution,*[136] and all means which are appropriate, which are plainly adapted to that end, which are not prohibited, but consistent with the letter and spirit of the constitution, are constitutional."

While we would agree with Somolu J. that on true construction of S.98(7) of the Constitution of the Federation, 1960, SS.13 to 19 of the Western

---

[132] S.98(4) of the Constitution of the Federation, 1960 provided as follows: "Subject to the provisions of this section, no police force other than the Nigeria Police Force shall be established for Nigeria or any part thereof." Then S.98(7) made an exception as follows: "Nothing in this section shall prevent the legislature of a Region from making provision for the maintenance by any native authority or local government authority established for a province or any part of a province of a police force for employment within that province."

[133] (1961) 1 All N.L.R. 826 at 832.

[134] (1819) 4 Wheat 316.

[135] Emphasis supplied.

[136] *Ibid.*

Region Local Government Police Law could not be held to be *ultra vires*; the reasons he gave for his decision could lead to dangerous consequences if not accepted with care and reservations. It must be pointed out that the American method of statutory construction differs with the English and our method with regard to filling of gaps and the use of extraneous materials.[137] We would not agree that a constitution should contain only "material outline." This method of drafting has led to many difficulties. As we pointed out earlier, a Constitution as the organic law of the land, must be complete in all respects and should make no room for "filling in" of any gap as the America Constitution.[138] The American Constitution has been described as a "short and terse" document. Authorities in American jurisprudence realise the inadequacies of the Constitution. Thus a well known author in American Constitutional Law writes: "To understand the American governmental system, one must study the leading decisions of the Supreme Court which interpret the Constitution, for much of the 'filling in' is done by that Court."[139] In construing our Constitution, the Judges should proceed with the British or (to be more exact) the English method of Statutory interpretation or construction.[140] The true meaning of the Constitutional provision must be constructed out of the words used in the documents.[141] Our present Constitution could not justifiably be deemed to have mapped out only the "material outline;" on the contrary, it was drafted like a United Kingdom Statute and is therefore a complete verbal embodiment of the intention of the law-makers - and must be construed as such by the Courts and the execution especially when the latter has occasion to implement certain provisions of the Constitution. It follows therefore that before getting started with the interpretation of the Constitution there must be a presumption that the Constitution is complete, supreme, and that it has spelt out all the powers it intended to invest; anything done outside the express powers is *ultra vires* and void.

From this point of view, it might be said that we have been advocating the positivist[142] approach in constitutional or statutory interpretation. But

---

137 See D. Lloyd: *Introduction to Jurisprudence*, 1965, p.387. The author shows that the laxer American method has led to abuse.

138 *Cf Olawoyin v Police (1961) 1 All N.L.R. 203.*

139 Rocco J. Tresolini: *American Constitutional Law*, (Macmillan, New York), 1959, p.45.

140 We have seen how Lord Simonds in the House of Lords in *Magor and St. Mellon R.D.C. v Newport Corporation (1952) A.C. 189 at 191* vigorously repudiated any idea of 'filling in' gaps in statutory interpretation. See also Lindley J. in *Hancock v Lablache (1878) 3 C.P.D. 197 at p.201*, where the learned Judge refused to fill in what appeared to be an omission in the Married Women's Property Act, 1870.

141 Unless there is a glaring case of ambiguity, when other rules of construction should be prayed in aid.

142 Cf. McWhinney: *Judicial Review in the English-Speaking World* (2nd Ed.), p.16,

some on the other hand favour what has been termed liberal approach in constitutional interpretation. The positivists adopt a self-imposed limitation and avoid any straying away, in the name of liberalism, from the actual words used in the Constitutional Instrument or Statute. This, as we have pointed out, is the traditional English method of Statutory interpretation. The idea behind this method is that the intention of the law-maker should predominate; that is to say, that the constitutional document or the Statute should be construed in a manner to carry out the intention of the law-makers. Thus Lord Blackburn in *Edinburgh Street Tramways v Torbain*[143] said:

> I quite agree that in construing an Act of Parliament we are to see what is the intention which the Legislature has expressed by the words, but then the words again are to be understood by looking at the subject-matter they are speaking of and the object of the legislature, and the words used with reference to that may convey an intention quite different from what the self-same set of words used in reference to another set of circumstances and another would or might have produced.

It follows that where the words of the Statute or the Constitution are unambiguous, the courts must restrict themselves to those actual words used.

The Privy Council found it expedient to express opinion on the method to be adopted in interpreting a written constitution. Thus in *Attorney-General for Ontario v Attorney-General for Canada*,[144] their Lordships in holding that the 1875, 1891 and 1906 Acts passed by the Dominion Parliament authorising the Executive Government of the Dominion to obtain by direct request answers from the Supreme Court of Canada on questions both of law and fact were *intra vires* and consequently valid said:

> In the interpretation of a completely self-governing Constitution founded upon a written organic instrument, such as the British North America Act (1867), if the text is explicit the text is conclusive, alike the what it directs and what it forbids. When the text is ambiguous, as for example, when the words establishing two naturally exclusive jurisdictions are whole enough to bring a particular power within either, recourse must be had to the context and scheme of the Act.[145]

It therefore means, as we have seen earlier, that it is only when the words are ambiguous that the courts may resort to extraneous aids (these of course do not include *travaux preparatoires*) and even under such circumstances 'the power and duty of the courts to travel outside the words used on a voyage of discovery are strictly limited.'[146]

---

143 (1877) 3 App. Cas. 58 at 68.

144 (1912) A.C. 571.

145 *Ibid* at p.583.

146 Per Lord Simonds in *Magor's Case* ante.

The advantages of adopting the positivist method of interpretation and the disadvantages of the liberal approach are obvious. There is little doubt that the latter would lead to abuse; for when the door is so thrown open it will be very difficult to check the scramble for judicial legislation. Where would one draw the line? It is not easy to foresee all the dangers that would follow from that, especially in Nigeria where the interpretation of the Constitution is not restricted to the Supreme Court.[147] It is therefore our suggestion that the positivist method of interpretation be used in the interpretation of our Constitution. On the other hand, where it is apparent that the Constitution intends that the Courts should use their judgment in determining certain issues then the courts should adopt a functional interpretation; that is to say, to interpret in such a way as to give due regard to the letter and the spirit of the Constitution. For instance Section 27 of the 1963 Nigerian Constitution provides:

> (1) Every citizen of Nigeria is entitled to move freely throughout Nigeria and to reside in any part thereof; and no citizen of Nigeria shall be expelled from Nigeria or refused entry thereto.
>
> (2) Nothing in this section shall invalidate any law that is reasonably justifiable in a democratic society - (a) restricting the movement or residence of any person within Nigeria in the interest of defence, public safety, public order, public morality or public health.

The Courts are under this section empowered to determine by themselves from the facts of each case what is reasonably justifiable. Thus in *Williams v Majekodunmi*,[148] the Federal Supreme Court held that the restriction of the plaintiff under the Emergency Powers (Restriction Order) Regulations, 1962 in such a way as to deprive him even the right to appear in person to plead his own case before the Court was not reasonably justifiable.

---

[147] See S.115 of the 1963 Constitution of the Federal Republic of Nigeria.

[148] (1962) 1 All N.L.R. 324.

Chapter 4

Judicial Attitude With Regard To The Constitution (Suspension And Modification) Decree[1a] And The Events Surrounding It.[1b]

1. *Events Leading to the Promulgation of the Decree*

On 15th January, 1966, an army revolt took place in Nigeria. It transpired that the revolt was planned by young army officers at the head of which was Major Chukwuma Nzeogwu who was serving with a unit of the Nigerian Army stationed at Kaduna in Northern Nigeria. The revolt which simultaneously took place at Kaduna (the Capital of Northern Region), Lagos and Ibadan (The Capital of Western Region), paralysed the civilian administration in most parts of the country. The Federal Prime Minister, Sir Abubakar Tafawa Balewa and the Federal Minister of Finance, Chief Festus Okotie-Eboh were kidnapped by the soldiers. The Premier of the Northern Region, Sir Ahmadu Bello, the Sardauna of Sokoto and the Premier of the Western Region, Chief S.L. Akintola as well as certain senior army officers were killed in the revolt.

The Federal Parliament was then in session. It met or about fifteen minutes before adjourning after a motion to that effect was moved by Mr. R.B.K. Okafor who was recently promoted to be a Minister of State. By then there was growing fear that the Prime Minister was no longer alive, for no one could say something about what had become of him. It must be pointed out that the situation then had a grave constitutional consequence. For section 87(9) of the Constitution provided that 'the office of a Minister of the Government of the Federation other than the Prime Minister shall become vacant if the office of Prime Minister becomes vacant'. Section 87(8) provided that the office of the Prime Minister should become vacant: '(a) when, after any dissolution of the House of Representatives, the Prime Minister is informed by the President that the President is about to re-

[1a] The Decree No. 8 was promulgated March 17, 1967 and repeals an earlier Decree No. 1 promulgated on 4th March, 1966. Both,were entitled Constitution (Suspension and Modification) Decree. The Decree No. 8 was fully published in the *Daily Times* of 18th March 1967.

[1b] The Original heading of this Chapter had "Likely" before Judicial. This was because this chapter was written shortly after the military take-over of 1966. I felt highly satisfied when the views I expected in this work as my Ph.D. thesis were seemingly applied by the Supreme Court of Nigeria in 1970 in the well known case of *E.O. Lakanmi v. The Attorney General* (West) (1974)4 E.C.S.L.R. 713.

appoint him as Prime Minister or to appoint another person as Prime Minister; or (b) if he ceases to be a member of the House of Representatives otherwise than by reason of a dissolution of Parliament'. It may be said that one of the situations contemplated by (b) is death of a Prime Minister. For it stands to reason that the office of Prime Minister will be vacant if he is dead. It follows that if the Prime Minister was dead (which was most likely) during the time Members of Parliament were meeting, the Office of Prime Minister was then vacant. From this point of view, it may be argued that the Offices of the Ministers of the Government were automatically vacant by the operation of the law[2]

However, in the evening of the same 15th January, 'a cabinet meeting' was held and was attended by two N.P.C. leaders and some N.C.N.C.ministers. Following this meeting Dr. Orizu, the Acting President was said to have been asked to appoint an Acting Prime Minister. Dr. Orizu, was then acting for the President, Dr. Azikiwe who was in London for medical reason. Dr. Orizu was reported to have refused to appoint an Acting Prime Minister in the absence of Prime Minister Sir Balewa; his reason being that he was trying to get in touch with the President Dr. Azikiwe. It might be observed that the Acting President, Dr. Nwafor Orizu was placed in a very difficult position; it was not unreasonable for him to insist on hearing from the President before he could act under such extra-ordinary situation. Events were by then very fluid and he might have thought certain actions might turn out to be rash. But things went quickly beyond the expectation of the ordinary men.

On January 16, 1966, another 'cabinet meeting' took place and was presided over by Alhaji Zanna Bukar Dipcharime. After that meeting 'the rump of the Cabinet' handed over administration of the country as a temporary measure to the army and the police under the control of Major-General John T.U. Aguiyi-Ironsi.[3] On the same day the acting President, Dr. Orizu told the nation in a broadcast that he had been advised by the Council of Ministers that they had unanimously decided to hand over the government of the Federation to the Armed Forces in view of the precarious situation in the country. As soon as the acting President finished his broadcast, the Supreme Commander and the head of the Military Government, Major-General Aguiyi-Ironsi followed and announced decrees for suspensions of the offices of the President and the Prime Minister.He also announced that Parliament was suspended. He equally decreed for the suspension of the Offices of the Regional Governors and Premiers and the suspension of Regional Legislatures. He then went on to decree that there should be a military government in each region of the Federation and that Regional Military Governments headed in each case by

---

2 S. 87(9) of the 1963 Constitution of Nigeria

3 Major-General Aguiyi-Ironsi was the General Officer Commanding the Nigerian Military Forces.

Governor should be responsible to the Federal Military Government.[4] These measures were later embodied into one document entitled Decree No. 1 of 17th January, 1966 [5]

An interesting legal question which might fall to be considered could be whether those who 'handed over' power to the head of the Military Forces were actually in a position to do so in the eye of the law. It was evident from facts which emerged afterwards that the Prime Minister of the Federation was no longer alive during the material time when the 'hand-over' of power was made to the army and the Police. It might be argued that no one, except perhaps those who carried out the revolt, could say precisely when the Prime Minister actually died. But if we assume for the purpose of this legal reasoning that he was dead before the 'hand-over' was made, then the question arises whether any 'hand-over was made in law. It is submitted that if the Prime Minister was dead before the 'hand over', then no such hand-over was made in law.[6] For the moment the office of the Prime Minister was vacant by reason of the death of the holder of that Office, the Offices of Ministers of the Government of the Federation would be vacant accordingly.[7] From this point of view, it might be argued that unless a new Prime Minister was appointed and he adopted the existing men as ministers of his cabinet there was no Council of Ministers as such because those members of Parliament were no longer ministers as provided in the Constitution. If on the other hand the Prime Minister was still living at the time of the 'hand-over', then it might be argued that he still retained his seat as a member of Parliament and consequently his cabinet was still legally constituted and capable of functioning. But the question would remain that even under such circumstances could the cabinet take such a great decision without the authority of the Prime Minister a *fortiori* nobody having been appointed acting Prime Minister. Surely no person can delegate the power which he has not got - *delegatus non potest delegare*. But the matter does not end here.

As we have seen above both the Premiers of the Northern and the Western Regions of Nigeria were killed instantaneously during the army revolt. Section 34 sub-section (8) off the Constitution of Northern Nigeria provided:

> The office of the Premier shall become vacant - (a) when, after any dissolution of the Legislative Houses of the Region,the Premier is informed by the governor that the Governor is about to re-appoint him as Premier or to appoint another person as

---

[4] For more details of the events starting from 15th January, 1966, see *West Africa* No. 2538 of 22 January, 1966 - especially pp. 82, 83, 105 & 106. See also G.N. 147 & 148, Federal Gazette, 1966.

[5] See Nigerian Gazette extraordinary No. 20, Vol. 53 of 4.3.1966

[5] That is to say, in accordance with the Constitution.

[7] S.87(9) of the 1963 Constitution.

Premier; or (b) if he ceases to be a member of one or other of the Legislative Houses otherwise than by reason of a dissolution of the Legislative Houses[8]

Sub-section (9) of the same section then provided that 'the office of a Minister of the Government of the Region other than the Premier shall become vacant if the Office of the Premier becomes vacant'. It may then be said that after the death of these two Premiers, the Offices of the respective ministers of the respective Governments would be vacant. For as we earlier observed, it stands to reason that a deceased person ceases to be a member of the Legislation.

The Doctrine of Civil or State Necessity

If, therefore, the Offices of the members of the governments of the Federation, the Northern Region and the Western Region became vacant as the result of the deaths of the said gentlemen, or if consequent to their deaths the governments were paralysed with the danger of the greater part of the country plunging into anarchy could something not be done to save the nation from slipping into chaos? It is submitted that if our courts are confronted with such a difficult issue for determination in view of the fact that it was not feasible to comply with the letters of the Constitution under the melting circumstances, they may pray in aid the doctrine of State Necessity,[8a] which could legalise an otherwise unconstitutional or illegal act. Thus Sir William Scott said in The Gratitudine:[9] "Necessity creates the law, - it supersedes rules; and whatever is reasonable and just in such cases, is likewise legal." Braction in his famous work declared that that which otherwise is not lawful, necessity makes lawful - *id quod alias non est licitum, necessities licitum facit.* [10] This doctrine of the common law is also known as the doctrine of *Civil necessity*. It may, therefore, be said that under the doctrine of necessity those members of Parliament who were de facto members of the government of the Federation could legitimately hand over the administration of the country *temporarily* to any organ of the State that could hold the country together in peace and tranquility - thus ensuring that law and order prevailed; *salus reipublicae est supreme lex* - safety of the State is the Supreme law. It follows that when the State is in danger of collapsing anything could be done to save it. Thus Darling J., in *In re an Arbitration between Shipton, Anderson & Co. and Harrison Brothers* [11]

---

8 Constitution of Northern Nigeria, N.N. No. 33 of 1963. See also S. 33 (8) of the Constitution of Western Nigeria, W.N. No. 26 of 1963.

8a C.F. *E.O. Lakanmi v. The Att.-General* (West) (1974)4 E.C.S.L.R. 713.

9 (1801) 3 C. Rob. at p. 266.

10 Bracton, *Treatise, folios, 93E and 247A, 'De legibus et Consuetudinibus Angliae*, quoted in Jennings: *Constitutional problems in Pakistan* 1957, p. 299.

11 (1915) 3 KB 676.

described the *maxim salus populi supreme lex* [12] as not only a good maxim but treated it as 'an essential law'.

We may here refer to almost analogous situations in the English legal history as recorded by Chitty J. in his book.[13] The learned author referred to two memorable occasions in which Parliament had assembled in an illegal manner, that is to say, without the authority of the King. These instances, the learned author pointed out, were when the Parliament assembled and restored Charles II and the Parliament of 1688 which handed over the British Crown to William III. The learned author maintained: 'that in both these instances the necessity of the case rendered it necessary for the Parliament to meet as they did, there being no King to call them together and necessity supersedes all law.'

2. *The Decree No. 1 of 1966*

As we have seen, the administration of the country was handed over to the Army and the Police under the supreme command of Major-General Aguiyi-Ironsi. We must point out at this stage that it is not our intention to go into the political question whether the revolt succeeded or whether it was crushed. We are, therefore, dwelling with what might be the judicial determination of the issues arising from the apparent upheaval in our body politics.

After the handing over of the administration of the country, followed by the respective suspensions afore-mentioned, a Federal Military Government was formed. This consisted among others, of the Major-General who became the Head of State and Supreme Commander - as well as the Head of the Federal Military Government; the Military Governors of the Regions - i.e. the Northern, Eastern, Western and Mid-Western Regions of Nigeria;

---

[12] Safety of the people is the supreme law.

[13] Chitty, *Prerogatives of the Crown (1820 ed.) p. 68*, Maitland in his book, *Constitutional History of England (1950 ed.), pp. 283-6* closely examined the legality of what happened when William, Prince of Orange became the King of England and the validity of legislation after James dissolved the Parliament and fled from London on 11th December, 1688. On the Convention Parliament which was summoned subsequently Maitland wrote: "It is difficult for a lawyer to regard the Convention Parliament as a lawfully constituted assembly. By whom was it summoned? Not by a King of England, but by a Prince of Orange. Even if we go back three centuries we find no precedent. The Parliaments of 1327 and 1399 were summoned by writs in the King's name under the Great Seal. Grant that Parliament may depose a King, James was not deposed by Parliament; grant that Parliament may elect a King, William and Mary were not elected by Parliament. If when the convention met it was no Parliament, its own act could not turn it into a Parliament. The act which declares it to be a Parliament depends for its validity on the assent of William and Mary. The validity of that assent depends on their being King and Queen; but how do they come to the King and Queen?" From this attractive legal reasoning, it follows that in strict law the Convention Parliament not being summoned by the King was not a lawful Parliament, with all that would have been the terrible undesirable consequences but as Chitty pointed out, the necessity of the situation legalised otherwise illegal acts.

the head of the Police Force and the head of the Navy. The Federal Military Government then proceeded to suspend certain sections of the Constitution of the Federation and those of the respective Regions and to modify others by the said Decree No. 1 of 1966.

Section 1 of the Decree provided as follows:

"(1) The provisions of the Constitution of the Federation mentioned in Schedule 1 [14] of this Decree are hereby suspended.

"(2) Subject to this and any other Decree, the provisions of the Constitution of the Federation which are not suspended by sub-section (1) above shall have effect subject to the modification specified in relation to that constitution in Schedule 4 of this Decree."

Like Section 69 of the Constitution, Section 3 of the Decree provided that the Federal Military Government should have power to make laws for the peace, order and good government of Nigeria or any part of it with respect to any matter whatsoever. It was equally provided that the Military Governor of a Region should not have power to make laws with respect to any matter included in the Exclusive Legislative List; that, therefore, confined the Governors to the spheres in which the civil administrations

---

[14] In Schedule 1 was listed many very important sections of the Constitution of the Federation which were decreed to be suspended. These include *inter alia* S.4 which provided for the procedure to be followed in the alteration of the Constitution; S.5(2) to (6) which equally made provision for the procedure to be followed in the event of any alteration to the constitution of a Region; S.16, which dealt with powers of Parliament; SS. 34 to 49, which dealt with the Office of the President of the Republic S.50(5) which provided for the Office of a member of the Electoral Commission of the Federation; SS. 51 to 74, which dealt with constituencies, Elections, determination of questions of membership of Parliament and many other matters having to do with Parliament and its legislative powers; SS. 76 to 87, which dealt with income tax and estate duty, trade and commerce, Banks and Banking, Electricity and Gas and others relating to commerce; and the matters relating to the exercise of Executive powers in the Federation; SS. 89 to 96, these cover establishment of Council of Ministers and matters relating therewith and the exercise of President's powers; one of the most striking suspensions was Section 114 which dealt with original jurisdiction of the Supreme Court; it is however remarkable that the provisions protecting fundamental rights and freedoms were not suspended. It seems that the suspension aimed at those sections from which political controversy might arise; for instance, S.116 dealing with Advisory jurisdiction of the Supreme Court was suspended. For more of the suspended sections see Schedule I of the Decree, Supp. to the Official Gazette Extraordinary No. 20, Vol. 53, 4th March 1966. Schedule 2 of the Decree provides for modifications 'of the provisions of the Constitution of the Federation not suspended by S.1(1).' Important among these was a proviso added to S.1 of the Constitution of the Federation. It reads - "Provided that this Constitution shall not prevail over a Decree, and nothing in this Constitution shall render any provision of a Decree void to any extent whatsoever." This was added because S.1. of the Constitution makes void any law which 'is inconsistent' with it and the Constitution was expressed to prevail, and the other law nullified to the extent of such inconsistency. A similar proviso was added to S.5(1) of the Constitution of the Federation so that 'the constitution of a Region shall not prevail over a Decree'. In Schedule 3 were listed all the suspended sections in the Regional Constitutions and Schedule 4 the corresponding modifications.

operated. The Federal Military Government was empowered to make laws by means of Decrees and the Military Governors of the Regions could make laws by means of Edicts. Thus Section 4 of the Decrees provided as follows:

> "(1) The power of the Federal Military Government to make laws shall be exercised by means of Decrees signed by the Head of the Federal Military Government.
> "(2) The power of the Military Governor of a Region to make laws shall be exercised by means of Edicts signed by him.
> "(3) A Decree or Edict may be made known to the public by means of a sound or television broadcast, or by publication in writing or in any other manner."

The powers vested in the respective governments of the Federation were assuredly far-reaching. The Regional Governors were left with the vast legislative powers which lay with the former civilian legislatures, for as is well known, residual powers in Nigeria rest with the Regions. It follows that under the new order, the Military Governors could make any laws provided that they did not encroach with those in the Exclusive List, and in the case of any matter included in the Concurrent List prior consent of the Federal Military Government was obtained. One would not have quarrelled with any temporary measures directed at obviating the dangers which were threatening the security of the State. But no amount of dangers would justify the exclusion of the courts to determine issues arising from the measures taken. But Section 6[15] of the Decree No. 1 provided that "No question as to the validity of this or any other Decree or of any Edict shall be entertained by any court of law in Nigeria". It follows that the jurisdiction of the courts was ousted not only in respect of the alteration of the Constitution itself by the Decree No. 1 of 1966, but also with regard to future Decrees of the Federal Military Government and the Edicts of the Governors of the respective Regions. It is submitted that Section 6 of the Decree went too far.

It might be argued that there was need for that particular provision because in the absence of that there could be many litigations which would embarrass the Military Governments and may even hold up certain quick measures which were urgently required for the restoration of peace and order. But the efficacy of a provision like Section 6 of the Decree No. 1 does not lie in an enactment as such but on the attitude of the Judges themselves. We may here recall the case of *Doherty v. Balewa16* where Section 3(4) of the Commissions and Tribunals of Enquiry Act, 1961, which provided *inter alia*, that 'neither the Commission itself nor any action of the Prime Minister in relation thereto shall be enquired into in any court of law' was nullified by the Federal Supreme Court.

---

[15] This is now Section 5; See Decree No. 8 of 1967, post.

To have excluded the courts was not necessary. The Judges are supposed to be men of integrity who can easily appreciate the need to take certain measures to preserve law and order. They would have in fact upheld any reasonable measures taken in this respect even if those measures apparently contravened the respective Constitutions or any other law of the land. Hence the Judges have always prayed in aid the doctrine of civil necessity [17] to valid otherwise invalid measures. A pronouncement of that nature would enhance the confidence of the people which any government whether civil or military requires for proper and even effective administration. As Kelsen put it, a new order may acquire legitimacy through effectiveness and acquiescence.[18] A total exclusion of any means whereby the legality of a measure having force of law could be determined would not promote the confidence of the people which might generate the acquiescence and register the effectiveness.

The Decree however set up an Advisory Judicial Committee which consisted of the Chief Justice of Nigeria, who was to be the chairman, the Chief Justices of Northern Nigeria, Eastern Nigeria, Western Nigeria and Mid-Western Nigeria, and the Chief Justice of Lagos; the Grand Kadi of the Sharia Court of Appeal and the Attorney-General of the Federation. The Solicitor-General of the Federation was to act as secretary of the Committee. It was not specifically stated in the Decree what was the real function of the Advisory Judicial Committee but by its nature and name,ss the Committee was supposed to advise on the legality of the measures taken by the Federal Military Government. It is submitted that whatever might have been the broader function of the Advisory Judicial Committee, the setting up of a body like that, although consisting of the most eminent men in the judicial hierarchy, should not have been considered a justification for ousting the jurisdiction of the courts to determine the validity of Decrees and Edicts. In any system of government, outside perhaps a dictatorship, there must be some checks of some kind to avoid abuses which are inherent in the frailties of human nature. Surely a Military Governor of a Region will be more careful in dishing out Edicts if it is apparent to him that their validity might be tested in a court of law and that the Judges might rule this way or that way about the legal validity of such Edicts. It is, therefore, submitted that nothing would have been lost, in fact something might have been gained in the nature of more public confidence, if Section 6 of the

[17] In a Cyprus case, *Att.-Gen. of the Republic of Cyprus v. Mustafa Ibrahim of Kyrenia & others (1964) 3 J.C.C. 114* (post) Josephides J. after giving the conditions under which doctrine of civil or State necessity may be applicable said: ."A law thus enacted is subject to the control of this Court to decide whether the aforesaid pre-requisites are satisfied."; for the pre-requisites see post.

[18] This idea was upheld by the Pakistan Supreme Court in *The State v. Bosso (1958) 2 P.S.C.R. 180* post.

Decree ousting the jurisdiction of the courts was omitted from the Decree completely.

As was evident from events which are notorious enough, Nigeria is a complex country. Under such circumstances which have long exhibited themselves and culminated in the eruption of January 15, 1966 and rolled on to the cataclysm of the 29th July, 1966 and some months following, a strong Judiciary is needed. But the Judiciary could not, and in fact cannot, play its part effectively and adequately if its jurisdiction is ousted in certain vital issues which concern the very existence of Nigeria as a Nation. The politicians, divided by tribal allegiance found it difficult to find enduring solution to the country's problems; the army appeared to have equally encountered the same difficulty.

The result was that the Judiciary and the Police stood highest in the estimation of the people. This, therefore, buttresses the contention that the Judiciary should not be excluded as was done in the Decree.

3. *The Decree No. 8 of 1967*

The Decree No. 1 continued to be in force until it was repealed[19] by the Decree No. 8 promulgated on March 17, 1967.We may pause here to give a brief account of the events leading to its promulgation.

On the 29th of July, 1966, another army revolt took place in Nigeria. Some, in fact, regard that as a mutiny. The incident was not widespread, none the less, the Head of State and the Supreme Commander of the Armed Forces was killed, and Lieutenant Colonel Yakubu Gowon (as he then was) assumed power in place of Major-General J.T,U, Aguiyi-Ironsi the said Head of State.

From July, 1966, events seemed to have drifted badly as certain units of the Federation did not appear to have recognised the change in the Federal Military Government as well as the order of things in the Army. However, the Military leaders of the country met at Aburi in Ghana, on January 4 and 5 1967. They agreed on certain vital issues and the country was saved from uncertainty which beclouded its destiny. However, there were some differences in the interpretation of the decisions reached in the Aburi meeting. The Constitution (Suspension and Modification) Decree No. 8 of 1967 was promulgated "to reflect" the decisions reached at the said meeting. We do not propose to go deep into all the provisions of this Decree which went much further than the Decree No. 1 in introducing new changes in the Nigerian body politic. For instance, Section 3 of the Decree No. 8 provides that "The legislative and executive powers of the Federal Military Government shall vest in the Supreme Military Council; and the legislative power shall be exercised by means of Decrees signed by the Head of the

---

[19] See S.15 of the Constitution (Suspension and Modification) Decree No. 8 of 1967

Federal Military Government." Section (2) then provides that "The power of the Military Governor of a Region to make laws shall be exercised by means of Edicts signed by him."

The Supreme Military Council now consists of the Head of the Federal Military Government who is the Chairman of the Supreme Military Council; the Military Governors of Western Nigeria, Eastern Nigeria, Northern Nigeria, and the Mid-Western Nigeria, and the Military Administrator of the Federal territory; the Head of the Nigerian Army; the Head of the Nigerian Navy; the Head of the Nigerian Air Force; the Chief of Staff of the Armed Forces; the Chief of Staff Nigeria Army; and the Inspector-General of the Nigerian Police [20] The Head of the Federal Military Government was also the Commander-in-Chief of the Armed Forces [21]

The Decree No. 8 like the Decree No. 1 in its schedules listed the sections of the Constitution of the Federation and those of the Regions which have been suspended. There are also modifications which broadly correspond with those in Decree No. 1 (which we have seen). Section 5 of the Decree No. 8 reproduced section 6 of the Decree No. 1. This provides that 'No question as to the validity of this or any other Decree or any Edict shall be entertained by any court of law in Nigeria'. Having dealt at length with a similar provision in the Decree No. 1, we may only emphasis that such a provision designed to exclude the Courts is unnecessary, for the Courts are sufficiently responsible to deal with any delicate issues coming before them as we shall see presently from decided cases in other countries when such countries were under trying constitutional crises.

4. *The Validity of the Decree* [22]

Although it is provided that no question as to the validity of any Decree or any Edict shall be entertained.by any court of law in Nigeria, nevertheless, we deem it necessary to examine the legal and constitutional issues raised by the Decree itself which was issued to suspend certain sections of the Constitution and modify some provisions therein. As we pointed out earlier, it is for the courts to rule that their jurisdiction had actually been ousted.[23a] As no test case has in fact been brought before our courts to

---

[20] S.6., *ibid.*

[21] S.14., *ibid.*

[22] As a possible judicial pronouncement on the validity of the Decrees No. 1 and No. 8 would be the same, we therefore discuss the issues involved by referring simply to 'the Decree - although Decree No. 8 is the present law.

[23a] As evidenced under the English legal history, Judges in many occasions resisted any attempt by any person or authority to swerve or silence them in their onerous task of administration of justice. *Holdsworth* in his book, *History of English Law Vol. V. p. 348* pointed out that during the Tudor period judges sometimes refused to obey commands which in their opinion were contrary to law. *Lord Denning* in his book, *The Road to Justice (1955) p.10* records a clash between King James and

determine the validity of the Decree in which the exclusion of the court is laid down;[23b] it is difficult to forecast accurately what might be the attitude of our judges in this respect. They might simply rule that they have no jurisdiction - Thus upholding Section 5 of the Decree. Such a ruling would be unhelpful and dangerous in that it will enshrine in our legal system a dangerous precedent which would remain after the Decree bad been repealed. A provision in an enactment which provides that the people of Nigeria should not question the validity of Decrees and Edicts issued by the respective governments for the administration of the affairs of the country 'in any court of law in Nigeria', should not be allowed to stand by our courts.

Assuming that a section like Section 5 which aimed at ousting the jurisdiction of the courts never existed in the Decree or that the courts are prepared to entertain a case brought before them to test the validity of the Decree (Section 5 notwithstanding), they may view such a case in this light: If there is a revolution in a sovereign State and a new order emerges and completely displaces the old order and abrogates a written constitution which was the supreme law of the land,[24] and replaces that constitution with an entirely new constitution; if there is effective administration of the affairs

---

a great judge called Sir Edward Coke. The King sought to interfere with the judges in their determination of a case by consulted the King. In refusing this Coke said: "Obedience to His Majesty's commend to stay proceedings would have been a delay of justice, contrary to the law, and contrary to oaths of the judges." - *The case of Commendams (1616) Hobart 140*, In a recent test case brought before the High Court of Rhodesia, (which we herein refer to as *Baron and Madzimbanuto's Case 1966*) challenging the legality of the Smith regime and the emergency regulations under which they were detained. The judges of the High Court were bold to entertain the case and declared the regulations of the regime illegal - see *The Evening News (London) Sept. 9, 1966, p.l.* The Court however recognised that the regime was the effective Government in Rhodesia and to avoid chaos the court should give effect to such measures of the Government under the 1961 constitution of Southern Rhodesia. In arriving at this ruling the Court was guided by the doctrine of State necessity which it prayed in aid when aced with such apparently difficult case.

23b In the recent case of The Military Governor, Ondo State & or. V. Victor Adegoke Adewumi, (1988) 3 N.W.L.R. (pt. 82) 280, the Supreme Court of Nigeria held that any edict or State law which was inconsistent with the provisions of S. 6 and S. 236 of the 1979 Constitution was void. It consequently anulled section of the Chieftaincy Edict which ousted Courts' jurisdiction.

24 In Ghana, there was a military coup d'etat on Thursday, February 24th, 1966. Out of this coup emerged a body called the "National Liberation Council issued a Proclamation entitled" "Proclamation for the Constitution of a National Liberation Council for the Administration of Ghana and for other matters connected therewith". In Paragraph 2 the 1960 Ghana Constitution was expressly suspended. The Paragraph provides as follows: "With effect from the 24th day of February, 1966 and subject to any decree that the National Liberation Council may make, the operation of the Constitution of the Republic of Ghana which came into force on the 1st day of July, 1960 (as Subsequently amended) shall be suspended." For this Proclamation See, SPC/A10188/4, 460/2/66, Printing Division) Accra-Teme, Ghana. Where a Constitution is wholly abrogated or even wholly suspended, there will be little or no co-application as long as there is a new set-up of fill the gap thus created. Greater complication arises where the new order proceeds to amend the old constitution contrary to the procedure laid down in the constitution itself.

of the State by the new order and the people acquiesce in that administration, it may be said that there is a complete break in the legal continuity. the revolution above mentioned need not be an army revolution, for as Professor de Smith recorded in his book,[25] the Pakistan Supreme Court [26] recognised that the suspension of the 1956 Constitution of Pakistan was a legal revolution' In such a case, no great difficulty arises, for the new order will be regarded as having acquired legitimacy through effectiveness and acquiescence.[27] It follows that if after the events which followed the incident of the 15th January 1966. the Constitution of the Federation of Nigeria as well as those of the Regions were expressed to be abrogated and replaced with an entirely new Constitution and the people of Nigeria acquiesced to that, the principle stated above would apply.

A greater legal difficulty would arise if the new order resorted to amend the Constitution which was in existence prior to the emergency of the new order. This was what happened in Nigeria. The Federal Military Government issued the Decree No. 1 which was made to operate as from 17th January, 1966 to alter the 1963 Constitution of the Federation[28] as well as the respective Regional Constitutions. The question which the courts might be called upon to answer could be whether such alterations were valid.

Section 1 of the 1963 Constitution provided:

> This Constitution shall have the force of law throughout Nigeria and, subject to the provisions of Section 4 of this constitution, if any other law (including the Constitution of a Region) is inconsistent with this Constitution, this Constitution shall prevail and the other law shall, to the extent of the inconsistency, be void.

Section 4 referred to above made provisions for the alteration of the Constitution. After providing that 'parliament may alter any of the provisions of this Constitution'; it then listed out certain sections of the Constitution and also the Schedule therein which an Act of Parliament altering 'shall not come into operation unless each legislative house of at least three Regions has passed a resolution signifying consent to its having effect'. Subsection (2) of section 4 provided that "A bill for an Act of Parliament under this section, ... shall not be passed in either House of parliament unless it has been supported on second and third readings by the votes of not less than two-thirds of all the members of that House."

---

25 *The New Commonwealth and it constitution (1964) p. 218.*

26 *The State v. Dosso [1958] 2 F.S.C.R. 180.*

27 *he State v. Dosso [1958] 2 P.S.C.R.. 180*

28 The Decree No. 1 has been repealed by Decree No. 8, as has been shown, the Decree No.8 also was designed to suspend certain sections of the 1963 Constitution and modify some others. Thus, in this respect, the legal results are the same; both Decrees are entitled: Constitution (Suspension and Modification) Decree.

Similar provisions were made for the alteration of the constitution of any of the Regions.[29]

It follows that for any alterations in the respective constitutions to be valid, such alterations must be according to the provisions laid down in the Constitutions for amending them. From this point of view it is apparent that there was no compliance with the Constitution in respect of the alterations effected through the Decree. Consequently the courts might rule that the Decree is unconstitutional, that is to say, invalid. But that is not the only answer to the problem; in fact such a ruling, although very correct, might not help the situation for it might once more plunge the country into chaos and law and order might break down.

Under such circumstances, the courts might look outside the Constitution and pray in aid the common law doctrine of State necessity to validate an otherwise invalid constitutional alteration. As we have seen, the army revolt paralysed the civilian administration which finally collapsed. The affairs of the nation had to be administered; law and order had to be preserved to save the nation itself from collapse. If those who were called upon to save the nation (Whether they were soldiers or civilians) reasonably felt that to carry out their task, the alteration of the Constitution was imperative political or State necessity would operate to make such alteration valid. As Bracton,[30] put it *id quod alias non est licitum, necessitas licitum facit* _ That which otherwise is not lawful, necessity makes lawful; and of course, the well known maxim of *salus reipulicae est suprema lex* - safety of the State is the Supreme law. Willies, J. Said in *Philips v. Eyre:* [31] "... there may be occasions in which the necessity of the case demands prompt and speedy action for the maintenance of law and order at whatever risk..." Munir, C.J. in Special Reference by the Governor-General [32] of Pakistan said:

---

29 See S.5 of the 1963 Constitution of the Federation of Nigeria, No. 20 of 1963.

30 Bracton. *op.cit.*, folios 39E and 247A.

31 (1870) 6 Q.B.1. In *Attorney-General v. De Keyser's Roval Hotel 1920 A.C. 508,* Lord Moulton said: ... the Grown, to whom the defence of the realm was entrusted, had wide prerogative powers as taking or using the lands of its subjects for the defence of the realm when the *necessity* arose. But such necessity would be in general an actual and immediate necessity arising in face of the enemy and in circumstances where the rule *Salus populi suprema lex* was clearly applicable." at p. 552. In other words, the circumstances must be instant and overwhelming. In the sphere of international law necessity could be pleaded as a defence for an illegal act. Thus Schwarzenberger said: "A State of necessity would be merely a factual set of circumstances which might amount to a justification of, or excuse for, a breach of international law." Schwarzenberger, Vol. 1, *op.cit.*, p. 643.

32 P.L.D. [1955] F.C. 435; see report of the case in Jennings: *Constitutional Problems in Pakistan* (1957) p. 259 et seq.

> I held on the authority of that[33] case and the observations in *Tilonko v. Attorney-General of Natal*[34] that where civil authority is paralysed by tumult, all acts done by the military which were dictated by necessity and done in good faith will be protected even if there be no bill of indemnity. Of course the duty of army commander arises where there is a revolt, insurrection or disturbance of the public order, but the principle which permits and occasionally demands, the exercise of emergency powers is not limited to those cases and equally Governs a situation where the Head of the State is required the act in a case of necessity when the Legislature is not in being.[35]

A situation which closely resembled that which prevailed in Nigeria at the time the constitution was altered arose in Cyprus (although not on all fours). Cyprus had been operating a difficult and complicated Constitution[36] which finally ran into a deadlock. The deadlock degenerated into armed conflict between the two main communities - the Greek and the Turkish Cypriots. Under such an atmosphere of hostility between the two groups, it was almost impossible for them to sit together in Parliament. the House of Representatives under Article 62 of the Constitution of the Republic of Cyprus, 1960 was to consist of fifty members, thirty-five of whom were to be communally elected. The communalism was also ensured in the composition of the Courts. It was provided under Article 133 of the 1960 Constitution that "A Supreme Constitutional Court will be established composed of one Greek, one Turk, and a neutral judge. The neutral judge will be President of the Court." The membership of the supreme Court of Justice consisted of two Greek members and one Turkish member plus a neutral person who was to serve as the President of the Court.

When there was hostility between the two communities it became obvious that unless something was done very quickly, the administration of the affairs of the State would come to a standstill. The President of the Republic, Archbishop Makarios was a Greek. The Greeks formed the majority of the population. The President faced with mounting problems as the result of the deadlock proceeded to take certain measures to save the situation irrespective of whether or not those measures were valid under the Constitution. One of these measures was the establishment of a new

---

33 *Muhammed Umer Khan v. The Crown* [1953] P.L.R. Lahore 825.

34 (1907) A.C. 93.

35 In the *Reference*, the Court in Pakistan held that while no legislature was in existence on account of the dissolution of the Constituent Assembly and Federal Legislature, inherent legislative powers were vested in the Governor-general by virtue of the common law doctrine of civil necessity. The Constituent Assembly was dissolved by a Proclamation of Governor-General on the ground 'that the Assembly had lost the confidence of the people and could no longer function'. the Court therefore applied the doctrine of civil necessity to validate the measures taken by the Governor-General..

36 For opposite examination of this complex document, see de Smith, *op.cit.*, p. 282 at seq. See also Catherine D. Papastathopoulos: *Constitutionalism and Communalism. The Case of Cyprus* [1965] University of Toronto Law Journal, p. 118.

Supreme Court of Cyprus. The new Supreme Court was established under the Administration of Justice (Miscellaneous Provisions) Law, 1964, In *Attorney-General of the Republic of Cyprus v. Mustafa Ibrahim of Kyrenia & others* [37] the validity of the law under which the new Supreme Court was established was questioned. The interesting thing was that the very Supreme Court was to determine the validity of its very existence. It is equally interesting to note that the Judges exercised in their judgment a very high degree of integrity and approached the issues before them objectively.

In that case three appeals were filed by the Attorney-General against granting of bail, pending trial by Assizes to three persons on criminal charges. The three accused persons were Turkish Cypriots and were charged with offences of preparing war or warlike undertaking and of using armed force against the Government, contrary to section 40 and 41 of the Criminal Code, Cap. 154. Before the hearing on the merits of the appeals, Counsel for Respondents, Mr. Benberoglou, took two preliminary objections. He contended that the Administration of Justice (Miscellaneous Provisions) Law, 1964 under which the Supreme Court was established never came into force due to lack of proper promulgation as required under Articles 47(e) and 52 of the Constitution. Counsel equally contended that the 1964 Law lacked proper publication as required under Article 3(1)(2) of the Constitution. he also maintained that the 1964 Law was void for unconstitutionality in that Section 3(1)(2) thereof contravened Articles 153(1) and 133(1) of the Constitution of Cyprus; Section 9 Contravened Article 146 and 152, Section 12 contravened Articles 159(1)(2) and 155(3); he finally contended that Section 15 of the 1964 Law contravened Article 179(1)(2) of the 1960 Constitution of Cyprus. Vassiliades J. in his judgment summarised the conditions which existed in Cyprus at the very time the Law was enacted as follows:

(a) a state of revolt, i.e. armed rebellion and insurrection against the established government of the Republic;

(b) armed clashes between organised groups resisting the authority of the State, and the forces authorised by the government to assert the authority of its organs:

(c) loss of life, damage to property, interruption of communications, and upsetting of law and order in the affected areas, with all the consequent repercussions on life assertion of authority and actual physical control over areas of State territory, by the insurgents and their political leaders and commanders, to the exclusion of the authority of the established Government of the Republic;

(e) presence of, with the consent of the Government, international troops within the State territory under a Commander acting for, and

---

37 (1964) 3 J.S.C.I (Judgment of the Supreme Court).

upon orders from an Authority outside the State, i.e. Secretary-general of the United Nations and the Security council thereof, for the declared purpose, *inter alia*, of preventing armed clashes between combatants, with a view to the maintenance of peace and the prevention of bloodshed; without, however, exercising authority or assuming in any way government responsibility." His Lordship then touched the crux of the matter:

(f) inability of the State-Government, pending a political settlement in the international circles,[38] to combat the insurgents in order to re-establish its authority and resume its responsibility in the affected areas, owing to the presence and intervention of the said foreign troops, and corresponding uncertainty, as to when the one or the other of the combating forces may eventually prevail, so as to assume the responsibility of government in the maintenance of law and order in the territory to the Republic.[39] His Lordship showed that the stalemate had endured for several months.

Turning to the first contention, i.e. that the 1964 Law never came into force because it lacked proper promulgation as provided in the Constitution, his Lordship said: "This argument would seem to be sufficient to seal the fate of the new Law - i.c. the 1964 Law. He went on" "I believe that there can be no doubt that if the new Law came to be enacted within the first months of the life of the Republic (to satisfy, for instance, the provisions of Article 190) it could not stand the weight of this argument. But from August, 1963, the Constitutional Court, and from June 1964 the High Court ceased to function. The fact remains that both these superior Courts ceased to function; and together with them the whole system of the administration of Justice in the Republic was in danger of collapse." [40] It follows that according to the letters of the Constitution, the 1964 Law should be held invalid.

---

[38] One of the most complicated and rigid aspects of the Cyprus 1960 Constitution was the international character of this unique organic law. To the Constitution was annexed two international agreements - the Treaty of Guarantee concluded between the Republic, Greece, Turkey and Britain, and the Treaty of Alliance between the Republic, Greece and Turkey. These treaties were expressly given constitutional force, see Article 181 of the 1960 Constitution. For the Treaty of guarantee, see Cmnd. 1093 (1960), 86-87; and for the treaty of Alliance, see ibid. 88-90. the international compromise is generally known as the Zurich Agreement. The Treaty of Guarantee provided that in the event of a breach of the treaty the powers should consult together and that if concerted action then consult together and that if concerted action then proves impossible each of the powers may take individual action to re-establish the state of affairs created by the treaty. Under treaty of Alliance Greece and Turkey were to keep armed contingents on the island of Cyprus. The Treaties may be said to be a clog on the independence of Cyprus and added to the predicament in which the country found itself.

[39] *ibid.*, at p.5.

[40] *ibid.*, at p. 13.

The Court Then proceeded to examine the submission of the attorney-General. He submitted that the 1964 Law was enacted 'on sound legal foundation: the generally accepted principle of the *law of necessity* [41] for the preservation of fundamental services in the State.' The learned Attorney-General further defended the 1964 Law from the attack that it was unconstitutional by the same principle of the law of necessity. His Lordship on this said: "So it seems to me that it is really, on the force of the legal concept - or expediency - known to Jurisprudence as the defence of necessity that the case for the appellant rests, in support of the validity of the new Law. And on the sound practical view, that law is made for man, and not man for the law" [42] The learned Judge emphasised: "The fact that the Attorney-General of the Republic defends this new Law, by the defence of necessity, points ... in the direction that its validity cannot otherwise be defended." The Court then arrived at the decision of upholding the submission of the learned Attorney-General of Cyprus to accept the principle of the law of necessity in validating the enactment of the Administration of Justice (Miscellaneous Provisions) Law, 1964 and the measures taken thereunder. The Court concluded as follows:

> This Court now, in its all-important and responsible function of transforming legal theory into living law, applied to the facts of daily life for faced with the question whether the legal doctrine of necessity... should or should not, be read in the provisions of the written Constitution of the Republic of Cyprus. Our unanimous view and unhesitating answer to this question is in the affirmative.[43]

Josephides J., agreeing with the judgment of the Court delivered by Vassiliades J. said that the Constitution should be interpreted to include the doctrine of necessity in exceptional circumstances. The learned Judge was of the view that the doctrine of necessity should be treated as implied exception to particular provisions of the Constitution 'in order to ensure the very existence of the State'. He then gave certain prerequisites which must be satisfied before the doctrine of necessity may become applicable:

(a) an imperative and inevitable necessity or exceptional circumstances;
(b) no other remedy to apply;
(c) the measure taken must be proportionate to the necessity; and
(d) it must be of a temporary character limited to the duration of the exceptional circumstances.

A law enacted during the period should be subject to the control of the Courts to decide whether the aforesaid prerequisites were satisfied, that is to

---

41 Emphasis supplied.

42 *ibid.*, at p. 17.

43 *ibid.*, at p. 25.

say, whether there existed necessity and whether the measures taken were justifiable under the circumstances.

The doctrine of necessity may be prayed in aid to justify or legalise measures only when they are taken to avert extremely melting and dangerous situations which threaten the safety of the State. Like public policy, the the doctrine of State or civil or political necessity, if not checked, could be dangerously abused.[44] So the conditions laid down in the judicial pronouncement of Josephides J. should serve as useful guide in the application of the doctrine of necessity which is now accepted as a principle of law.

As the situation is Cyprus when the Administration of Justice (Miscellaneous Provisions) Law, 1964 was enacted nearly completely resembled that which prevailed in Nigeria when the Decree No. 1 of 1966 was issued to alter the Constitution of Nigeria, this decision by the Cyprus Supreme Court would undoubtedly have great persuasive influence in the Courts of Nigeria should an action be brought for the determination of the validity of the Decree.

In France the doctrine is known as the 'theory of exceptional circumstances'. According to Counseiller d'Etat Raymond Odent: "The jurisprudence emanates from the thought that the whole social organisation is destined to ensure the life of the country or, to use a more juridical expression, public order, and that law is a means the object of which is to organise the public powers to this superior end. Jurisprudence was thus led to appreciate that there was a hierarchy in the juridical rules and that the executive authorities were behaving more in conformity with the spirit of constitutional institutions by a temporary encroachment on legislative prerogatives than by limiting themselves to narrow conventionality or by remaining inactive when such inactivity imperils public order. Administrative jurisprudence has therefore always refused to consider that the executive power was irremediably bound by a system conceived for a period of normality, adapted to the needs of normal period, but inadequate in case of exceptional circumstances."

The learned author then went on to make the point we have been stressing in connection with the exclusion of the Courts in respect of Decrees and Edicts issued in Nigeria [45] He said. "Also, in case of

[44] In *Gregson v. Gilbert (1783) 3 Dougl. 232*, 150 slaves were pushed overboard because water was running short. The perpetrators pleaded doctrine of necessity. The action was on insurance policy in respect of loss of slaves; a new trial was ordered to decide whether the act was in fact necessary; In consequence of the case statutes were passed prohibiting recovery under insurance policies where slaves were thrown overboard. See also Glanville Williams: *"Defence of Necessity" (1953) C.L.P., p. 228*

[45] It will be recalled that the Decree provides that 'no question as to the validity of this or any other Decree or any Edict shall be entertained by any court of law in Nigeria'. We still maintain that this section, Section 5 of the Decree, is unnecessary and should not have been included in the Decree. It

exceptional circumstances all authority emanating from the executive power has the legal and moral obligation to take, for the duration of the circumstances and under the control of the administrative judge, all measures strictly necessary for the accomplishment of the mission entrusted to it even if the measures taken normally belong to the competence of the legislature." He continued" "So that the executive have the legal power to exceed not only their own normal extent of authority, but even the normal extent of authority of the executive power. Three conditions must exist simultaneously. Two of these conditions result from the nature of the circumstances: *first*, it is necessary that the circumstances, in terms of the time and place, have, an undeniable and potently exceptional character; *secondly*, it is necessary that the authority which has normal competence in the matter has not got the physical or juridical possibility to intervene and, consequently, to take proper steps to avert the circumstances. The *third* condition refers to the end to be achieved: this and must be of such importance that if it were not achieved, one of the fundamental tasks of public power could not be accomplished." [46]

The theory of exceptional circumstances as expounded by the learned author broadly agrees with the common law doctrine of necessity. In *R.v. Stratton*,[47] the Governor of Madras acted illegally and unconstitutionally in refusing to count the votes of some of the members of his council. councillors accordingly imprisoned him for eight months and carried on the government themselves. Upon being put to trial on indictment in England, they set up the defence of necessity. Whereupon Lord Mensfield directed the jury that the defence was one of 'civil or State necessity'. In the process of the direction his Lordship said:

> In India you may suppose a possible case, but in that case, it must be imminent, extreme necessity; there must be no other remedy to apply to do, they must appear clearly to do it with a view of preserving the society and themselves ... What immense mischief would have arisen to have waited for the interposition of the council at Bengal?

Following the direction and after the consideration of the case, the jury returned a verdict of guilty. His Lordship made it clear in this important case that to amount to a justification, there must appear imminent danger to government and individuals; that the mischief must be extreme, and such as would not admit a possibility of waiting for a legal remedy. The situation

---

casts great doubt on the integrity and the independence of our judiciary..On the judicial review of the measures taken when impelled by necessity see *Ex parte Milligan 71 U.S. (1866) esp. 122-125* (post).

46 Conseiller d'Etat Raymond Odent: "*Contentieux Administratif*", University of Peris (1961), Vol. I, pp. 137-8-translated in (1964) 3 J.S.C. at pp. 112-3.

47 21 St. St. Tr. 1222; see also Lord Coleridge, C.J. in *Reg. v. Dudley end Stephens* (1884) 14 Q.B.D. at p. 285.

must be such that the safety of the government must well warrant the experiment. 'The necessity will not justify going further then necessity obliges; for though compulsion takes away the criminality of the acts which would otherwise be treason, yet it will not justify a man in acting farther then such necessity obliges him or continuing to act after the compulsion is removed.'[48] It follows that the measures taken will be measured in the light of such overwhelming circumstances. Any act unduly excessive or unreasonable will not be justified.

The United States Supreme Court was in the case of *Ex parte Milligan*[49] faced with a very difficult issue in which necessity was pleaded as a defence for an apparent illegal criminal trial. In that case, one Lambdin P. Milligan applied to the Circuit Court of the United States for the District of Indiana for a writ of habeas corpus to be discharged from an alleged unlawful imprisonment. From that court, the case went to the Supreme Court of the United States upon a certificate of division from the judges of the Circuit Court. Milligan, a citizen of the United State was during Civil war arrested by the military authorities, tried and sentenced by them to be banged.

The charges preferred against him were: (1) conspiracy against the United States; (2) giving aid and comfort to the enemy; (3) inciting to insurrection; (4) disloyal practices; (5) violation of the the laws of war. The government contended that the trial by military tribunal was justified as an act of necessity. Three questions were put to the Supreme court as follows: 'On the facts stated in the petition and exhibits ought a writ of habeas corpus to be issued? Whether M. on the facts stated ought to be discharged from custody as prayed in the petition? and whether the military commission had jurisdiction legally to try and sentence Milligan in manner, and form as stated in the petition?' The Supreme Court answered the first two questions in the affirmative and the third one in the negative.

Before reaching their decision, the Court found as a fact that the State of Indiana was not during the Rebellion, 'a resident of any of the States whose citizens were arrayed against the government'. It was on this point which Milligan insisted and claimed that his right to be tried by jury was guaranteed to him by the Constitution of the United States. Consequently, he maintained, his trial was illegal and amounted to infringement of the constitution. In rejecting the defence of necessity as a justification for the military trial the Court observed: "It is difficult to see how the safety of the country required martial law in Indiana." It went on: "It follows ... that there are occasions when martial rule can be properly applied. If, in foreign invasion or civil war, the courts are actually closed and it is impossible to administer criminal justice according to law, then, on the theatre active military operations, where war really prevails, there is a necessity of furnish

48 *Ibid.*, at p. 1230.

49 71 U.S. 3 (1866).

a substitute for the civil authority, thus overthrown, to preserve the safety of the army and society[50]

The Court did not see any justification for the trial of Milligan by a military tribunal while the ordinary courts were open. Equally the defence of necessity could not be sustained because, although it recognised that 'necessity creates the rule', the situation in Indiana at that time never warranted the measures taken in Milligan's case. The Court observed that the measures 'could have been enforced in Virginia, where the national authority was overturned.'[51] It follows that where necessity[52] is pleaded as a defence for a justification of an action, especially that of the executive or an action approved by the executive, it is for the Courts in an action challenging the validity of such measure to decide whether there was in fact a necessity to justify such step.

The doctrine of necessity or the law of necessity as it is sometimes called[53] is becoming increasingly popular in many countries; although it may be very useful to justify the measures taken, for instance, to preserve the safety of the nation; it must be carefully watched, for as we indicated above, it can be abused. Hence it is necessary that the courts should have jurisdiction to determine the validity of such measures.

---

50 *ibid.*, 1127.

51 *ibid.*

52 For the 'defence of necessity' in other aspects of American legal system, see *(1921) 21 Columbia Law Review. p. 71.* In delivering the opinion of the Federal Court of Pakistan in the *Special Reference (supra footnote 25)* Munir, C.J. in dealing with the doctrine of necessity cited George Chalmers' work, *"Opinions of Eminent Lawyers"*. At pp. 29 and 30 of that work the author quoted where what was apparently illegal was supposed in case of necessity to have been legal. The opinion was that of Lord Chief Justice Holt on the forfeiture of Lord Baltimore's charter of Maryland and the grant of it to another governor. The question in that case was whether, before Lord Baltimore's forfeiture of his charter was adjudged, Maryland could be granted to another Governor. On that the Lord chief Justice said: "I think it had been better, if an inquisition had been taken, and the forfeiture committed, by the Lord Baltimore, had been therein found, before any grant be made to a new governor; yet, since there is none and it beings in a case of necessity, I think the King may by his commission constitute a governor, whose authority will be legal."

53 Jennings: *op.cit.*, p. 298.

Chapter 5.

The Judiciary as a Unifying Force in the Nigerian Legal System.

In Chapter One we tried to show the types of legal systems which were in existence before the inception of the British administration. The British Administration was mainly responsible for the welding of the various units of the country into one administrative entity. By Section 19 of the Supreme Court Ordinance, 1876, the Supreme court was required to observe and enforce the observance of any law or customs existing in the Colony of Lagos or territories subject to its jurisdiction; such law or custom not being repugnant to natural justice, equity and good conscience, nor incompatible either directly or by necessary implication with any enactment of the Colonial Legislature. With the gradual expansion of the British Authority far into the hinterland the jurisdiction of the Supreme Court expended. So that by 1914 (the year of the amalgamation of the southern and Northern Nigeria) the judicial regime established since 1976 fully predominated in the entire areas as one unit. Just as the customary or native laws were allowed to exist and given official recognition, the customary or indigenous courts continued to function. The arrangement precisely remains even to the present day.

However. the administrative of justice by customary courts is always within the supervisory eyes of the High Court. Thus Tew, J. said: *In re Native Court of Onitsha*, "If a person is imprisoned by a native tribunal acting without jurisdiction, then I have no doubt that this court (i.e. the Supreme (Court) can, and will, grant a writ of habeas corpus, at any rate where the cause has arisen, within the local limits of its jurisdiction."[1] Again in *Re Effiong Okon Ate*, [2] Butler Lloyd rejected a claim based on customary law, to the personal property of a deceased person who happened to be slave-born. The Court was of the view that to allow such a claim would be contrary to natural justice as well as the Slavery Abolition Ordinance.

The task of the Courts in administering the laws which predominated in the country before the introduction of federalism was not as onerous and complicated as the period which has witnessed the regionalisation of the judiciary itself. Under the federal set-up, each Regional legislature had

---

1 (1928) 9. N.L.R. 65 at p.

2 (1930) 10 N.L.R. 65, C.F. *Kodieth v. Affram (1930) I.W.A.C.A. 12* - where a similar decision was reached in a case from the Gold Coast (now Ghana).

power to make any law as long as such law was not contrary to the constitution.[3] Armed with such powers (the residuary powers rest with the Regions), the Regions legislated on those matters enumerated in the constitution.[4]

With such a seemingly divergent set-up, it would appear at first sight that there would be resurrection of what would amount to different legal system in the country. fortunately, as we shall see presently, the courts have done a lot to harmonise the different legal set-ups with the result that one will be accurate when he speaks of the Nigerian legal system in law and in fact. We will then examine the main factors which help to make this a reality.

The Application of the Rules of Precedent [5]

We may pause here to examine the position of the Courts of Appeal and the Superior Courts in the judicial hierarchy and see how their decisions are regarded as binding on other courts. Such adherence to the rules of precedent contributes enormously to cohesion, certainty and unity which are essential in a legal system such as our own. The Privy Council, which at one time stood at the apex of judicial hierarchy, was the last Court of appeal. The next in rank was the West African Court of Appeal followed by the former Supreme court. As was shown in Chapter One, the West African Court of Appeal was established in 1928 but its jurisdiction extended to Nigeria in 1933.[6] With the introduction of Federalism and the establishment of the Federal Supreme Court; appeals to the West African Court of Appeal Ceased.[7] With regard to the judicial Committee of the Privy Council, appeals to it ceased with the introduction of Republican Constitution in 1963.

With the abolition of appeals to the West African Court of Appeal and the Privy council, the Supreme Court which was established under the 1963

---

[3] The legislative powers of the respective Regions are now vested in the respective Military Governors since the introduction of military regime in the country. The Governors legislate by Edicts.

[4] The Legislative and Executive power of the Federal Military Government is now vested in the Supreme Military council. See Constitution (Suspension and Modification Decree (no.8) of 1967. Under this Decree, the power to appoint the Judges in the Regions is vested in the respective Military Governors and the power to appoint Judges of the Supreme court vested in the Supreme Military Council.

[5] It may be said that the rule of precedent is connected with the idiosyncrasy of man to follow examples. In this context, precedent means past decisions. Under this rule a lower court is bound by the decision of a higher court.

[6] See, the West African Court of Appeal Ordinance, 1933.

[7] It took some time before the Federal Supreme Court got started with its functions in this respect. The first reported decision was given on the 17th February, 1956 - *(R. v. Udo Akpakpan [1956] F.S.C.R.1.)* It appears that until then appeals continued to go to the West African Court of Appeal.

1963 Constitution was elevated to the pinnacle of authority in the judicial hierarchy; a position hitherto occupied by the Judicial Committee of the Privy Council. It was therefore made the final Court of Appeal. Appeals from the High courts of the Regions lay to the Supreme Court whose decision is, of course, final.

We have now to see how or to what extent these eminent courts are bound by their own decisions or the decisions of others, if any, above them. The privy council's decisions bind all the Courts below. That is to say, from he West African Court of Appeal downwards. An important question then arises: to what extent is the Judicial Committee of the Privy Council bound by its own decisions? The Privy Council does not consider itself absolutely bound by its previous decisions. Where the Board considers it expedient so to do, it could depart from its previous decisions.[8] The attitude of the Board in this regard was explained by Viscount Simon in the case of *Attorney-General for Ontario and Others v. Canada Temperance Federation and Others.*.[9] His Lordship delivering the judgment of the Board stated as follows: 'The appellants' first contention is that Russell's case[10] was wrongly decided and ought to be overruled. Their Lordships do not doubt that in tendering humble advice to His Majesty they are not absolutely bound by previous decisions of the Board, as is the House of Lords[11] by its judgments. In ecclesiastical appeals, for instance, on more than one occasion, the Board has tendered advice contrary to that given in a previous case, which further historical research has shown to have been wrong. But on constitutional questions it must be seldom indeed that the Board would depart from a previous decision which it may be assumed will have been acted on both by governments and subjects.' And dealing with the particular case sought to be overruled, which would of course affect the Act in question, his Lordship pointed out that the Canada Temperance Act, 1878 had 'been put into operation for varying periods in many places in the Dominion, under its businesses must have been closed, fines and imprisonments for breaches of the Act have been imposed and suffered.' With regard to *Russell's case* he pointed out that the decision had stood for sixty years.

---

[8] In *Mercantile Bank of India, Ltd. v. Central Bank of India. Ltd.[1938] A.C. 287* the Privy Council reversed its previous decision on a matter arising from mercantile law. Again *Nkembule (Gideon) v. R. [11950] A.C. 379,* it refused to follow a previous decision of its down in a criminal case

[9] [1946] A.C. 193., at p. 206.

[10] *Russell. v. The Queen (1882) 7 App. 829* - where the Privy Council held that the Canada Temperance Act, 1878 was within the legislative competence of the Dominion Parliament under S.91 of the constitution of Canada, i.e. the British North America Act, 1867, on the ground that it related to the peace, order and good government of Canada, and did not deal with any of the matters exclusively reserved to the provinces by S.92 of the constitution.

[11] The statement with regard to the House of Lords has recently modified its attitude in this respect - see infra.

Now two main points emerge from this judicial pronouncement; the Board will depart from its decisions in matters which are not constitutional, if it transpires that such decisions were wrong. But in constitutional matters, the Board usually feels reluctant to depart from its previous decision where it is too late. That is to say, where the previous decision had been acted upon both by the governments and the subjects. It may be observed that what might be meant by this latter statement was that such a decision of the Board sought to be overruled must not be glaringly wrong. For their Lordships appeared to have thought that *Russell's case* was not fully established to be wrong. It is submitted, therefore, that if a highest Court of Appeal which considers that it is not bound by its decisions is of the view that a previous decision which it gave was wrong, such decision should be overruled whether the matter is constitutional or not; the case for overruling such a decisions is even stronger whether the decision was given on constitutional question. The reason for this is because it is easier to overrule a wrong decision than to amend a written Constitution, the final Court of Appeal should feel bound to put matters right by overruling such decision whether it was of its own or otherwise, even if such a wrong decision had been acted on.

Another question is, which of the decisions of the Privy Council are binding on Nigerian Courts and up to what time? It may be stated that as the Privy Council was the highest Court of Appeal until 1963, when appeals to it ceased, all the decisions of the Privy Council in cases going to the Board from Nigeria, should be binding on all Nigerian Courts which were in existence before appeals to the Board were terminated. The Nigerian Courts in this respect, include the present Courts that possess the same status as those which were in existence when appeals to the Board ceased. The present Supreme Court which has, *de jure*, taken the place of the Privy Council with regard to Nigeria is however in a different position, from this point of view. We shall deal with that later. It remains to state that the decisions of the Judicial Committee of the Privy Council on issues coming before the Board from countries other than Nigeria during the said period, are equally binding on the Nigerian courts aforementioned; provided always that the fact of such cases are similar. It therefore means that all such decisions of the Privy Council are still binding on the Nigerian courts cessation of appeals to the board notwithstanding. However, the decisions of the Board given after the termination of appeals should only be of very high persuasive authority.

From the Judicial Committee of the Privy Council we now come to the West African court of Appeal. The West African Court of Appeal was second in rank to the Privy Council. Appeal from the former Supreme Court lay to the West African Court Appeal until such appeals ceased officially in 1954 when the Nigerian judicial system was re-organised. It may then be stated that all the decisions of the West African Court of Appeal given before appeal to the Court ceased will be binding on the Nigerian Courts from the High courts downwards. The Federal Supreme Court which replaced the West African Court of Appeal would, of course, not be bound by those decisions and could depart from them if it chose to do so. The view that the decisions of the West African Court of Appeal are binding on the High courts in Nigeria finds support in the recent case of *Jelo Tsamiya v. Bauchi Native Authority* [12] where Jibowu, Ag. C.J.F. disapproving the attitude of the High court of Northern Nigeria[13] in not following the decision of the West African Court of Appeal [14] because the High Court felt that the decisions was given *per incuriam*, stated: 'We do not quarrel with the High Court's decision not to follow their own decisions, if they felt that the decisions had been reached *per incuriam*, but there is no precedent for their refusing to follow a previous decision of the West African Court of Appeal on the subject matter of the inquiry because they consider that that decision had been reached *per incuriam*.' He then went to issue what amounted to a warning is respect of the future attitude of the High Courts. He said: 'With respect to the learned Chief Justice and other members of the Court (i.e. the High Court), it must be pointed out that it is not for an inferior court (i.e. a lower Court) to say that a decision of the higher court was reached *per incuriam*; that is a privilege of the higher Court if, after reconsidering its former decision, it is satisfied that the previous decision had been reached *per incuriam*.'

This judicial pronouncement struck a right note because the rules of precedent and in fact the unity in our legal system will be thrown into jeopardy if lower courts can arrogate to themselves the power to depart from the decisions of higher courts. Hence his Lordship further observed:[15] 'When the High Court found itself in such a position that it could not follow a previous decision of a higher Court by which, according to the comity of courts, they are bound, the proper course, it appears, was for the High court to have reserved questions of law under Section 20 of the Federal Supreme Court (Appeals) ordinance for the consideration of the Federal Supreme Court in order to give that court, which has taken the place of the West African Court of Appeal, the opportunity of reconsidering previous decisions in the light of the questions reserved with a view to giving a considered ruling on the question of law raised on the issues involved.'

It may be observed, however, that where a decision of a higher court was given *per incuriam*, i.e. in ignorance of the provisions of a statute or some other law, the lower Court will be placed in a great difficulty if there is

---

[12] [1957] N.R.N.L.R. 73 at pp. 82-3.

[13] See *Fagoji v. Kano Native Authority* [1957] N.R.N.L.R. 57.

[14] See *Gishiwa Ghana v. Bornu Native Authority* (1954) 14 W.A.C.A. 587.

[15] [1957] N.R.N.L.R. at p.83.

is no provision in on enactment for referring such cases to the highest Court in the land other than by appeal. For in such a case a wrong decision will be blindly followed. The only solution therefore lies in an enactment which should make reference of issues to the Supreme Court in all cases for it will be most undesirable to allow lower Courts to depart from the decisions of either the Privy Council, the West African Court of Appeal, the former Federal Supreme Court or the present Supreme Court.

From the West African Court of Appeal we come to the former Supreme Court. This Supreme Court cannot be equated with the present Supreme Court. Rather it may be said that the former Supreme Court was really only a High court of Justice. This is borne out by Section 11 that of the Supreme Court Ordinance of 1876 [16] which provided that the Court should 'possess and exercise, all the Jurisdiction, powers and authorities... which are vested in or capable of being exercised by Her Majesty's High Court of Justice in England as constituted by the Supreme Court of Judicature Acts 1873 and 1875.' If follows, therefore, that the former Supreme Court was in the same status as the present High Courts of the States. The relationship between the former Supreme Court and the present High court could then be determined, with regard to rules of precedent, in the light of the general practice under English law.

Under English law, and of course, the prevailing practice in Nigeria, a Judge of the High Court sitting alone is not bound by the decisions of another High Court judge sitting at first instance. He will, however, treat such decisions as of strong persuasive authority, and will refuse to follow such decisions only after considerable hesitation and with a clear statement of the reason for such a departure. Thus in the case of *In re Hilles-Drake*, [17] Simonds, J., in refusing to follow the decision of another judge in the case of *In re Gunther's will Trusts* [18] because he thought it had 'little cogency' stated: 'Ought I in the circumstances to follow this decision? I think not. Uniformity, consistency, certainty in the law, those are highly important attributes of our legal system, and I would not advance my opinion against the considered judgment of Farewell J. if I thought that by doing so I made a breach in the principle which judges of co-ordinate jurisdiction are bound to observe, but, in my opinion, it is the judgment in *In re Gunther's Will Trusts*, followed by Bennett, J. *In re Oram [1940] Ch. 1001* which is out of line with authority, and is inconsistent with long established principle and practice.'

---

[16] No. of 1876.

[17] [1944] 1 Ch. 236 at p. 241.

[18] (1939) Ch 983.

In *Jiboso v Obadine*,[19] Charles, J., refused to follow the view which he expressed in an earlier case,[20] which view was followed by Medarikan, J. in *Eke v. Odolofin*. [21] this was because, as the learned Judge put it, 'the decision of Duffus, J. in *Akohwero of Okan v. Emeyebor* [22] was right and that my opinion in Ntiashagwo's case and, with respect, the reasons of Mederikan, J. in *Eke v. Odolofin* were wrong.'[23] The above cases illustrate that a Judge of the High Court can depart from the decision of another High Court Judge if he has a strong reason for doing so.[24]

Having seen that the former Supreme Court was in the same status as the present High Court and that a judge of the High Court can depart from the decision of another judge of the High Court (although with strong reasons); it follows, therefore, that the present High Courts can depart from the judgment of a judge of the former Supreme Court. The position is however, different with regard to the decisions of the Full Court of the Supreme Court. The Full Court was usually composed of three judges. The Full court may be compared with the Court of Appeal. From this point of view, a Judge of the High Court today, should not depart from decisions of the Full Court of the former Supreme Court. Where any wrong decision of the Full Court is discovered, it should be the duty of the present Supreme Court to overrule it.[25]

From the consideration of the position of the former Supreme Court and its Full Court, we now come to deal with the Regional High Courts. As was pointed out earlier, with the regionalisation of the Judiciary in 1954, each Region had its own High Court. However, a careful study of the

---

19 [1962] N.N.L.R. 303

20 *Ntiashagwo v. Amodu [1959] W.N.L.R. 273.*

21 [1961] 1 All N.L.R. 404. The point of conflict in those cases was whether a document which did not comply with the Illiterates protection Act was a complete nullity or whether such non-compliance rendered the document voidable only at the instance of the illiterate person whom the Act sought to protect. The view that the non-compliance rendered such document a nullity was held by the learned Judges in the cases referred to above but later dissented from and not followed.

22 [1959] W.R.N.L.R. 83.

23 [1962] W.N.L.R. at p. 307.

24 See equally, Bray, J. in *Forster v. Baker [1910]2 K.B. 636, 638* where he stated 'I have always understood that one judge is not bound by the decision of another Judge on a point of law at nisiprius. And du Percq. J. was of the same view in *Green V. Berliner and Others* [1936] 2 K.B. 477, 494.

25 The present Supreme, Court, like the house of Lords in the united Kingdom has power, and in fact, is under a duty to correct errors in the law brought about by duty to correct errors in the law brought about by the wrong decisions of the lower courts. for instance, in *Fibrose Spolka Akcyine v. Fairbairn Lawson combe Barbour, Ltd.* [1943] a.G. 32, the House of Lords overruled the decision of the Court of appeal in *Chandler v. Webster [1924] 1 k.B. 493*, on the issue of frustration of contract. See also the case of *Hill v. William Hill Ltd.* [1949] 2 K.B. 696 - both were cases dealing with wagering.

attitude of the Judges of the High Courts in these Regions shows that the Judges always look beyond their respective Regions and follow the decisions of their counterparts in other Regions. For example, in *Jiboso v. Obadine,* [26] Charles, J. deciding a case in the High Court of Western Nigeria refused to follow his earlier opinion but rather followed as one of the most important authorities, a decision of smith, J., in *United Africa company Ltd. v. Edem* [27] in the High Court of Northern Nigeria. The learned Judge (Charles, J.) was at pains when he discovered that the view he expressed in an earlier case was at variance with those expressed by his brother Judges, and retracting he said: 'This opinion was given without knowledge of the Judgments of Smith, J. and Duffus, J. in *United Africa Company Ltd. v.Edem and Akohwere of Okan v. Emayebor, supra.*

While it is obvious that the Regional High Courts are bound by the decisions of the former Federal Supreme Court and the present Supreme Court and the Court of Appeal, a question may then be posed whether the decisions of Regional High Courts now State High Courts bind one another? It may be stated that as a general rule, as was pointed out earlier, a decision of one High Court Judge will not be binding on another High Court Judge. But such a decision must be treated as of strong persuasive authority. It is of utmost importance that Judges of the High Court should follow the decisions of other judge of co-ordinate jurisdiction. This enhances uniformity and certainty in the legal system. In *Olawoyin v. Attorney-General of Northern Region,* [28] Brown, C.J. said that 'It would therefore appear to be clear that while a judge sitting at first instance will accord great weight to a previous decision of a judge of co-ordinate jurisdiction and will only depart from it with reluctance and after the most careful consideration, he commits no breach of principle if he does - for he is not bound by it.' It follows therefore that a Judge of the High Court in one state is not bound to follow the decision of another Judge in the High Court of another state, just as he is not bound by such decision of such a Judge in his State. But in practice the Judges of the High Courts have followed the decisions of their brother Judges in other States. And they should continue to do so.

A different situation, however, arises in cases of appeals. It would appear that a decision of the High Court in its appellate capacity will be binding on the High Court both on its original and appellate jurisdiction. Dealing specifically on this point Brown, C.J. in *Olawoyin v. Attorney-*

---

[26] [1962] W.N.L.R. 303.

[27] [1958] N.R.N.L.R. 33.

[28] [1960] N.R.N.L.R. 53 at p. 58. C.F. *In re Hillas-Drake, National Provincial Bank v. Liddell. [1941] 1 Ch. 236, 241* - a judge of the Chancery Division of the High Court departed from the decision of another judge of that Division, see other cases at footnote 24.

General of Northern Region [29] and praying in aid the principle enunciated in the case of *Young v. Bristol Aeroplane Company Ltd.*[30] stated as follows:

The Court of Appeal is bound to follow its own decisions and those of courts of co-ordinate jurisdiction, with three exceptions:-

(1) the court is entitled and bound to decide which of two conflicting decisions of its own it will follow;
(2) the court is bound to refuse to follow a decision of its own which, though not expressly overruled, cannot in its opinion, stand with a decision of the present Supreme Court, House of Lords - and, no doubt, of the Privy Council;
(3) the court is not bound to follow a decision of its own if it is satisfied that the decision was given per incuriam, that is to say, where material cases or statutory provisions which show that the court has decided a case wrongly were not brought to its attention.

It follows, therefore, that the High Court in its appellate capacity is entitled to decide for itself which of two conflicting decisions of its own it will follow. Again the Court must refuse to follow any of its previous decisions which cannot stand with a decision of the Privy Council, the West African Court of Appeal, the Federal Supreme Court or the present Supreme Court; even if such a decision has not been expressly overruled by the aforementioned higher Courts. Equally the High Court in exercising its appellate jurisdiction is not bound to follow a decision of its own if it is satisfied that such a decision was reached per incuriam,[31] that is to say, in

---

29 1960 K.B. N.R.N L.R. at p. 58.

30 [1944] K.B. 718 at p. 729, per Lord green, M.R. The decision in Young's case was followed in the case of Police Authority for *Huddersfield v. Watson [1947] 1 K.B. 842* where the Divisional Court stated that it was bound by its own previous decisions in the same way and subject to the same exceptions as the Court of Appeal; and considering an earlier decision in the case of *Garvin v. Police Authority for City of London 1944 K.B. 358*, Lord Goddard, U.J. said: 'I think we ought to hold that we are bound by this decision and I say so for this reason ...' then he quoted with full approval the principles laid down by the Court of Appeal in Young's case - supra. His Lordship went further to restate the general principles on the subject as follows: 's judge of first instance, unless he is convinced the judgement is wrong, would follow it as a matter of judicial comity. He certainly is not bound to follow the decision of a judge of equal jurisdiction. He is only bound to follow the decisions which are binding on him, which, in the case of a judge of first instance, are the decisions of Court of Appeal, the House of Lords and the Divisional Court.' - at p. 848. See also *Melia Ltd. v. Preston & another [1857] 2 Q.B. 380*.

31 With regard to decisions reached per incuriam Lord Greene, M.R. in *Young v. Bristol Aeroplane Co. Ltd. 1944 1 K.B. at p. 729* stated that 'where the court has construed a statute or a rule having the force of a statute its statute or a rule having the force of a statute its decision stands on the same footing as any other decision on a question of Law, but where the court is satisfied that an earlier decision was given in ignorance of the terms of a statute or a rule having the force of a statute the position is very different. It cannot, in our opinion, be right to say that in such a case the court is entitled to disregard the statutory provision and is bound to follow a decision of its own given when that provision was not present to its mind. cases of this description are examples of decisions

ignorance of a relevant statute or enactment, or a rule having the force of a statute, or the decision of the Privy Council, West African Court of Appeal, the Federal Supreme Court or the present Supreme Court. If the High Court in the exercise of its appellate jurisdiction discovers that a decision of any of the higher Courts had been reached *per incuriam*, it should refer such a matter to the Court of Appeal which should examine the issue very carefully; and if satisfied that such a previous decision was in fact reached per incuriam, should overrule and correct the error in the law.

Special Position of the Supreme Court of Nigeria

As was indicated earlier, the Supreme Court, created under the 1963 Constitution, is now the final court of appeal for the whole country. It replaced the Privy council as the highest Court of appeal for the country, and, of course, with its creation the Federal Supreme Court ceased to exist. Under the Jurisdiction: 1979 Constitution [32] it was provided that 'The Supreme court shall have jurisdiction, to the exclusion of any other court of law in Nigeria, to hear and determine appeals from the Court of Appeal.' It was also provided that 'An appeal shall lie from decisions of the Court of Appeal to the Supreme Court as of right in the following cases -

(a) where the ground of appeal involves questions of law alone, decisions in any civil or criminal proceedings before the Court of Appeal;
(b) decision in any civil or criminal proceedings on questions as to the interpretation or application of the Constitution;
(c) decisions in any civil or criminal proceedings on question whether any of the provisions of Chapter IV of the Constitution has been is being or likely to be, contravened in relation to any person.
(d) decisions in any criminal proceedings in which any person has been sentenced to death by the Court of Appeal or in which the court of Appeal has affirmed a sentence of death imposed by any other Court.
(e) decision on any question whether any person has been validly elected to any office under the constitution or to the membership of any legislative house or whether the term of office of any person

decisions given per incuriam.' Again, in police authority for *Huddersfield v. Watson 1947 1 K.B. 842 at p. 847* Lord Doddard, C.J. said: 'what is meant by giving a decision per incuriam is given a decision when a case or a statute has not been brought to the attention of the Court and it has given its decision in ignorance or forgetfulness of the existence of that case or that statute. Now see *James Orubu v. National Electoral Commission & ors*(1988)5 N.W.L.R. (pt 94) 323; *Maclean v. Inlaks* (1980) 8-11 S.C.1. *Odeola v. Coker* (1981)5 S.C. 197; *Akinsanya v. UBA.* (1986) 4N.W.L.R. (pt.35) 273.

32 Now S. 213(1) of the 1979 Constitution appals lie from the Court of Appeal as an intermediate Court.

has ceased or the seat of a person in a legislative house has become vacant; and

(f) such other cases as may be prescribed by any law in force in any State[33]

Equally, it was provided that an appeal shall lie from decisions of the Court of Appeal to the Supreme Court with the leave of the court of Appeal or the Supreme Court in cases where the ground of appeal involves questions of fact. mixed law and and fact. [34]

The present Court of Appeal was created by the the 1979 Constitution.[35]

The determination of the Supreme Court in any appeal to it is final.[36]

From what we have seen, it becomes evident that the Supreme Court is placed in such a position that enables it to entertain appeal from any issue whether civil, criminal or constitutional from any part of Nigeria. The fact that the Supreme court is placed in such a position makes it very possible for it to reconcile conflicting decisions in the States High courts through the Court of Appeal; overrule those decisions which it thinks to be wrong thus correcting errors in the law and bringing uniformity in the legal system. Example, Taylor, F.J., delivering the Judgment of the Federal Supreme Court in the case of *Adegbenro v The Attorney-general of the Federation and others* [37] on issue relating, inter alia, to the office of the Premier of Western Nigeria recalled a decision of that Court on an issue which came before the Court from the Northern Region. His Lordship put it thus: "It would be contrary to the established practice of this Court, as laid down is *Olawoyin v. Attorney-General, Northern Region,* [38] to pronounce on the validity of a law except at the instance of a person who has shown that his rights have been invaded or threatened." Perhaps no example could be more apposite then the corrective pronouncement of Jibowu, Ag. C.J.F. (as he then was) in the case of *Jelo Tsamiya v. Bauchi Native Authority* [39] where he disapproved of the action of the High Court of Northern Nigeria in not following a decision of the West African Court of Appeal; and then directed that in any case where the High court thought that a decision of a higher

---

[33] S. 213(2), 1979 Constitution

[34] S. 213(3) *ibid.*

[35] S. 217 1979 Constitution.

[36] S. 215 *ibid.*

[37] [1962] 1 All N.L.R. 431 at p. 437.

[38] [1961] All N.L.R. 269. The present Supreme Court as we have seen, replaced the Federal Supreme Court and does what the Federal Supreme Court was doing in this regard.

[39] [1957] N.R.N.L.R. 73, 82, 83.

Court was reached per incuriam, such a matter should be referred to the Supreme Court for appropriate action by it.

The decision of the Supreme Court not only serves as a guide but also in most cases settles conflicting views in the law. Thus in *The Queen v. Chief Ozogula II, Ex parte Chief Ekpenga,* [40] the Federal Supreme Court resolved an important issue when it held that the performance of certain traditional ceremonies required of a chief on the death of a person belonging to a class of chiefs under customary law was a public duty for which an order of mandamus would lie. Again, it may be said that the decision of the Federal Supreme Court in granting the order of Certiorari in the case of *The Queen v. The Governor,Eastern Region and Another, Ex parte Ojiegbo Ikoro of Ngodo* [41] cleared the doubt raised in an earlier decision in the High court of Eastern Nigeria in the case of *The Queen v. The Officer Administering the Government of Eastern Nigeria. Ex parte Onyehalu* [42] Equally, it may be said that the judicial pronouncement of Quashie Idun, Ag. F.J. to the affect that a document which did not comply with the provisions of the illiterates Protection Act, Cap. 88 was not a nullity [43] settled at last the conflicting views held by Judges on the subject. There is no doubt that that statement of the law by his Lordship while delivering the judgment of the Federal Supreme Court on an Appeal from the decision of the High Court of Northern Nigeria led to the corrective decision in the case of *Jiboso v. Obadine* [44] - in the High Court of Western Nigeria.

The Supreme Court and Precedents

Now, it remains for us to examine whether the Supreme Court is bound by its previous decisions. It may be stated that the Supreme Court, like the Judicial Committee of the Privy Council, does not consider itself absolutely bound by its previous decision and will depart from such decision if the interest of justice requires that. In other words, the Supreme Court can depart from its previous decision with strong reasons. Thus in *Maizabo and Others v. Sokoto Native Authority,* [45] the appellants were convicted of intentional homicide under customary law and sentenced to death. The High

---

40 [1962] W.N.L.R. 136.

41 [1962] 1 All N.L.R. 40.

42 [1960] E.N.L.R. 33. for a discussion on the last two cases see Chapter 6, post

43 See S.C.C.A., Zarie v. Okon [1960] N.R.N.L.R. 34 at p. 38 where the learned Judge delivering the Judgment the Illiterates protection Ordinance (now Act) Cap. 88 said that failure to comply with the provisions of the Ordinance renders a document unenforceable."

44 [1962] W.N.L.R. 303, in that case the earlier views and decisions to the contrary were expressly stated to be "wrong" and the view of the Federal Supreme Court was followed with approval.

45 [1957] F.S.C.R. 13; 1957 N.R.N.L.R. 133. Vide also, *Eperokon v. University of Lagos* (1986) 4 NWLR pt. 34 162

Court of Northern Nigeria had dismissed the appeals because on the authority of the Federal Supreme Court decisions[46] they were precluded from considering the question of manslaughter. In overruling the previous decisions of its own the Federal Supreme Court held that where a Native Court had imposed a Punishment in excess of that permitted by the Criminal Code or other enactment, the Appellate court might either substitute the proper penalty or if for any reason it was not in any position to do so, order a new trial of the appellant. In delivering the judgment of the Federal Supreme Court de Lestang, F.J., stated that ' there can be no doubt that this court decided in Jelo Tsamiya's case [47] that where a person had been properly convicted on intentional homicide in a Native court applying Maliki law and sentenced to death, but that offence might have been manslaughter under the Criminal Code, the High court in its appellate jurisdiction ought not to order a retrial so as to make it possible for a verdict of manslaughter to be found. In *Fagoji's case* this Court merely followed its previous decision in *Jelo Tsamiya's Case.*

'Having regard, however, to the great importance of this matter and in particular since it affects the life to the subject, we felt it right to hear fresh arguments with a view to reconsidering, if necessary, the decisions of this Court in the two cases under reference.' Reconsideration of the two cases was in fact effected by the Court and it came to the conclusion that the decision in Jalo *Tsamiya's case* was 'too wide' and ought not to be followed. It may be observed that the decision of the Supreme Court to the effect that it was not absolutely bound by its previous decision is a good and laudable one; for even the House of Lords which had held [48] itself absolutely bound by its previous decisions had recently [49] modified its

---

46 See *Jelo Tsamiya v. Bauchi N.A. [1957] N.R.N.L.R. 73 (F.S.C., and Fagoji v. Kano N.A.* [1957] N.r.N.L.R.

47 Supra.

48 See *London Street Tramway Co. v. London County Council* [1898] a.C. 375.

49 In a statement in the House of Lords on July 26, 1966 on behalf of the Law Lords, Lord Gardiner, L.C. showed how essential it is to allow proper development of the law. He said: "Their Lordships regard the use of precedent as an indispensable foundation upon which to decide what is the law and its application to individual cases. It provides at least some degree of certainty upon which individuals can rely in the conduct of their affairs, as well as rigid adherence to precedent may lead to injustice in a particular case and also unduly restrict the proper development of the law. They propose, therefore, to modify their present practice and, while treating former decisions of this House as normally binding, to depart from a previous decision when it appears right to do so. In this connection they will bear in mind the danger of disturbing returning retrospectively the basis on which contracts, settlements of property and fiscal arrangements have been entered into and also the especially need for certainty as to the criminal law. This announcement is not intended to effect the use of precedent elsewhere then in this House." See *"Practice Statement (Judicial Precedent)" [1966] 1 W.L.R. 1234.* Also the Supreme Court of the United States of America can depart from its previous decisions. See Lewis Mayers: *"The American Legal System"*, Herper & Brothers, New York (1954) p. 351 et seq.

attitude in that regard. However, it may be further observed that while necessary departure from previous decision would obviate the danger of making the law static and enhance the growth which is necessary in the law, the Supreme Court should only make such departure where it is absolutely necessary, for certainty in the law is equally essential.

Chapter 6

Control of Inferior Tribunals by the High Court

'The High Court has an inherent power, unfettered by statute, to control inferior tribunals in a supervisory capacity. Such control is by means of *certiorari* [1] to keep the inferior tribunal within the law, within bounds and within such jurisdiction as the legislature deemed fit to confer upon it.'[2] There is no doubt that "Our Law on certiorari (and other prerogative orders) is based on the English Law."[3]

Historically, the instruments of control at common law have been *certiorari*, prohibition, *mandamus* and *habeas corpus*. *Habeas corpus* is an ancient safeguard for the liberty of the subject. The old writ which was found in Edward I's reign, was merely a command by the Court to someone to bring before itself person or persons whose presence was necessary to some judicial proceedings. However, habeas corpus is of limited practical importance in modern administrative law.

Apart from the above, there are also injunction and declaration. On declaration, Denning L.J. (as he then was) in 1955 said. "Since *Barnard v National Dock Labour Board [1953] Q.B. 18* I take it to be clear law that the Queen's courts can grant declarations by which they pronounce on the validity or invalidity of the proceedings of statutory tribunals.[4] Usurpation and abuse of power by public authorities may be challenged by means of action for injunctions and declarations. Compared with the common law remedies, injunction and the declaratory orders are more flexible and adaptable instruments of judicial control. For instance, the technicalities arising from judicial precedent and the subtle test of what is a 'judicial act' which surround certiorari may be avoided completely in declaratory proceedings. Injunction is an order restraining a person or persons from doing an illegal act. It is an equitable remedy which can lie against a private

---

[1] And other prerogative writs (now Orders). post.

[2] *he Queen v. District Officer & Others, Ex parte Etim Atim* [1961] 1 All N.L.R. 51 at p.58, per Ademola, C.J.F.; see also *The State v Wogu & Others, Ex p. Nwabisi* [1965] N.M.L.R. 219 at pp.222-3.

[3] Per Duff, J. in *The Queen v The Governor in council, Western Nigeria, Ex p. Oyebola [1962] W.N.L.R. 360,364*

[4] *Haeley v Minister of Health* [1955] 1 Q.B. 221 at p. 227

individual or a public body.[5] But we are more concerned here with injunctions against public bodies.

Inferior [6] tribunals in this respect include customary courts, administrative tribunals - and even a person, for example, a minister, when he is required to act judicially. Thus a tribunal can be a court of justice or a judicial authority. Dealing with this point Scrutton, L.J. said "... certiorari is intended to bring into the High Court the decision of the inferior tribunal. in order that the High Court may be certified whether the decision is within the jurisdiction of the inferior court." He went on: "There has been a great deal of discussion and large number of cases extending the meaning of 'court'. it is not necessary that it be a court in the sense in which this court is a court; it is enough if it is exercising after hearing evidence, judicial functions in the sense that it has to decide rights after hearing evidence between a proposal and an opposition."[7] It follows that it is not necessary that the tribunal which is subject to control should be strictly a court; it is enough if the body in question has to determine rights and interest after hearing evidence. It is not necessary that there should be a *lis inter partes, stricto sensu.*

Another means of control of the inferior tribunals is by appeal where there is a statutory provision to that effect. In Nigeria, a decision of a magistrate in a criminal case may be appealed against on the ground of want of or excess jurisdiction. Appeal also lies on the ground that the magistrate was personally interested in a case before him or that he was biased to the detriment of justice. In England certiorari will undoubtedly lie in such cases. It must, however, be pointed out that there is in practice no conflict between prerogative orders and appeals as remedies. For generally, a prerogative order, for example, certiorari will issue after all other remedies have been exhausted. However, the Federal Supreme Court has held that *certiorari* will lie notwithstanding the existence of an alternative remedy, i.e. by way of appeal, "when that alternative remedy means going to some other tribunal where the appellant is not likely to get help to remedy the injustice

---

[5] See *Pride of Derby and Derbyshire angling Association Ltd. and Another v British celanese Ltd. and Others* [1953] 11 Ch. 149 - Injuction was granted against the Derby corporation and the British electricity Authority restraining them from continuing nuisance by polluting a river, post.

[6] The word 'inferior' is not used in a derogatory sense. it is generally used to denote those tribunals which are required to act within prescribed jurisdiction. They are therefore generally regarded as tribunals of limited jurisdiction. thus Willes, J. in *Mayor of London v Cox (1967) L.R. 2 K.L. 239, 259, 263* said that ' the rule for jurisdiction is that nothing shall be intended to be outside to the jurisdiction of a Superior Court but that which specifically appears to be so; and,. on the contrary, nothing shall be intended to be within the jurisdiction of an inferior court but that which is so expressly alleged.' see also *Peacook v Bell 30 L.J. (Q.B.)*

[7] *R.v. London County Council, Ex p. Entertainments Protection Association. Ltd.* [1931] **2 K.B. 2.5.** at p. 233; see equally *R.v. Electricity Commissioners* [1924] 1 K.B. 171, post and *Reg. v The Governor in Council, Western Nigeria* [1962] W.N.L.R. 93 post.

done to him."[8] It will appear that in certain cases, the only remedy open to an aggrieved person in the Northern Region will be an appeal to a higher tribunal; as section 27 of the High court Law[9] provides that 'No order of mandamus, of prohibition or of certiorari and no injunction under the provisions of section 25 shall be made or granted by the High court in respect of any proceedings in a native court or in the Sharia Court of Appeal save such as may be necessary in the exercise of its powers under section 32 of the constitution of the Federation or any other Law under that section.' It follows that the prerogative orders will lie in the native Court or the Sharia Court of Appeal where there is a breach of any of the fundamental rights and freedoms entrenched in the Constitution of the Federation. It may be observed that in view of the complex native Court set-up in the Northern Region, as we have seen in Chapter One, and in view of the obvious weakness of appeal system as a means of control,[10] it is suggested that section 25 of the said Law be amended so as to allow the prerogative Orders to lie in all respects.

We shall now deal in greater details with the main instruments of control beginning with the common law prerogative orders:

1. Certiorari

Denning L.J., dealing with the grant of the order of certiorari to quash the decision of a statutory tribunal said that 'the Court of King's Bench has an inherent jurisdiction to control all inferior tribunals, not in an appellate capacity, but in a supervisory capacity. This control extends not only to seeing that the inferior tribunals keep within their jurisdiction, but also to seeing that they observe the law. The control is exercised by means of a power to quash any determination by the tribunal which, on the face of it offends against the law'[11] The order of certiorari is a means of bringing up to the High Court a decision of an inferior tribunal or 'judicial'[12] authority in order that its legality may be investigated. The decision will be quashed if there is want or excess of jurisdiction or error on the face of the record or denial of Natural Justice.

The old writ [13] of certiorari was couched in commanding fashion demanding certain record or records to be sent "forthwith" to the King's

---

[8] *Regina v District Officer & Others, Ex parte Eti Atem* [1961] 1 all N.L.. 51 at p.57 per Ademola, C.J.F.

[9] Cap. 49. Laws of Northern Nigeria, (1963) Vol. II p.911.

[10] See the dictum of Ademola C.J.F. footnote No. 8 supra.

[11] *R. v Northumberland Compensation Tribunal, Experte Shaw* [1952] 1 All E.R. 122 at p.127.

[12] The term 'Quasi- Judication vested in a person or body outside the system of ordinary Courts.

[13] As we indicated earlier the prerogative writs are now orders, see Administration of Justice (Miscellaneous Provisions) Act, 1938, S.7 1 & 2 Geo. 6, C. 63 Habeas Corpus was unaffected.

court to be examined.[14] The purpose of controlling inferior tribunals through this medium was to ensure that they did not exceed their jurisdictions. With the abolition of the Star Chamber in 1640, the central control exerted by the Star Chamber over justices of the peace could have vanished but fortunately, the vacuum task being properly undertaken by the Court of the task being properly undertaken by the Court of the King's Bench which became almost the only co-ordinating authority until the modern times which have seen a better development of the order which is now used as a key instrument of control exercised strictly in legal and not in political sense.[15]

As we pointed out above, certiorari will lie[16] against an inferior tribunal where there is:

(i) want or excess jurisdiction;
(ii) error on the face of the record of the tribunal; and
(iii) denial of natural justice in the proceedings.

Thus Atkin L.J. pertinently stated that 'Wherever any body of persons having legal authority to determine question affecting rights of subjects, and having a duty to act judicially, act in excess of their legal authority they are subject to the controlling jurisdiction'[17] of the High Court exercised through the prerogative orders, in this case, through certiorari or prohibition. An important requirement, as we have seen, for certiorari to issue is that the person or persons against whom it is to issue must be under a duty to act judicially, Thus certiorari has been held to issue against a customary court,[18] an administrative officer reviewing the decision of a Native or Customary court,[19] kingmakers making appointment to fill a chieftaincy

---

[14] The actual wording of the writ was reproduced by Denning L.J. in R.v. Northumberland Compensation Appeal Tribunal Ex. p. Shaw '1952] 1 All E.R. at p.128.

[15] See Wade H.W.R., Administrative Law, 1961 pp.97-8. For more details see de Smith S.A. Judicial Review of Administrative Action, 1959 p.271 et seq.

[16] However, certiorari will not lie for purely ministerial act, that is to say, such executive act which involves policy making and where the person vested with the power to do the act was not required to act judicially: See *The Queen v The Governor in Council. W.R. of Nigeria, In re Adeniji [1961] W.R.N.L.R. 81* - it was held that an enquiry before deciding to dissolve a local government council. It must be pointed out, however, that there is no general definition as such for what is a "ministerial" act. It depends on the statute conferring the power and the interpretation of such statute by the Court. See further, de Smith op.cit p.30. See also *Arike v Governor, N.R. [1961] 1 All N.L.R. 379.*

[17] *Rex v Electricity commissioners, Ex p. London Electricity Joint Committee company [1920] Ltd. 7 Ors.* [1924] 1 K.B. 171 at p.205.

[18] *The State v. Wogu & Ors.* [1965] N.M.L.R. 219; In re Umuolu village Group Court, Ex p. Maceulay and ben [1953 2 N.L.R. III

[19] *Reg. v.District Officer & Ors. Ex p. Eti Atem* (1961] 1 All N.L.r. 51; *Reg. v The Governor, Eastern Region &^Another, Ex.p. Ojiegbo Ikoro of Ngodo* [1961] 1 All N.L.R. 40.

vacancy, as well as a suusequent approval by the Governor in council.[20] Equally certiorari has been held to lie against the Patents Appeal Tribunal[21] a legal aid committee[22] a valuation court,[23] a minister conducting a police enquiry,[24] and a rent tribunal.[25] In the recent case of *Regina v Patents Appeal Tribunal ex.parte Baldwin & Francis Ltd.*,[26] the Court of Appeal, approving an earlier decision,[27] held that Patent Appeal Tribunal was an inferior tribunal to which an order of certiorari would issue.As we have seen above, there are three main grounds under which certiorari may issue:-

(i) Want or excess jurisdiction

Certiorari will issue against an inferior tribunal if it acts in want or excess of its jurisdiction. Thus in the *State v Wogu and Others*,[28] the High Court of Eastern Nigeria held that certiorari would issue to quash convictions by a Customary Court because the convictions were made under a section of the Criminal Code which did not exist.[29] The Court also held that although the Customary Courts were empowered to exercise jurisdiction in cases of people conducting themselves in manner likely to cause breaches of the peace,[30] the penalties imposed were in excess of the jurisdiction of the District Court. In another case of In re Umulou Village Group Court.[31] *certiorari* was issued to quash the convictions of the applicants because sentence imposed by the Native Court were in excess of the jurisdiction of the Court. In *The Queen v District Officer & others Ex. parte Etim Atem*, Ademola, C. J. F. said:[32] "It has been stated that certiorari is discretionary, it will nevertheless be granted *ex debito justitia* to quash proceedings which the Court has power to quash, where it is shown that the Court below has acted without jurisdiction or in excess of jurisdiction". In that case it was

---

20 *Reg. v The Administration, Western Nigeria, Ex p. Bamgbedu* [1962] W.N.L.R. 344.

21 *R.v Patents Appeal Tribunal (1957) 1 W. L. R. 248*

22 *R.v Manchester Legal Auid Cinnuttee* [1952] 2 Q.B. 413

23 *R.v. East Norfolk Local Valuation Court* [1951] 1 All E.r. 743.

24 *Errington & Others v Minister of Health 919530 1 K.B. 249, see also r. v Minister of Health, ex p. Yaffe (1930) 2 K.B 98.*

25 *R.v Paddington Rent Tribunal, ex po. Bell Properties [1949] 1 K.B. 66.*

26 (1959) 1 Q.B. 105

27 *Reg. v Patents Appeal Tribunal Ex. p. Champion Paper & Fibre Co* (1957) 1 W.L.R. 248; (1957) 1 All E. R. 227.

28 (1963) N. M. L. R. 219

29 The Applicants were said to have been convicted under S.249(5) of the Criminal Code.

30 Under S.246*d° of the Criminal Code

31 (1953) 2 N.L.R. III,See also *R v Governor Eastern Region 1962 1 All N. L.R.40 and Regina v Bullock 1963 3 W L. R. 911.*

32 (1961) 1 All N.L.R 51 at p. 57

held that certiorari would issue to quash the decision of a District Officer for acting in excess of his powers in a land dispute. It follows that the discretion which the High Court exercises in this respect is a discretion which justice requires. For if an application for the Order is made by the party aggrieved and not merely by one of the members of the public unaffected personally, the order should be granted ex debito justitiae.[33]

Equally certiorari will lie against a customary Court for denying a person right to appeal against his conviction by the court; as that would be exceeding its jurisdiction. Thus in *The Queen v The President and Members of Akugbene Grade 'C' Customary Court*,[34] the High Court of Western Nigeria held that citing of sections of the Customary Court Law by a party to a suit who was not a legal practitioner could not amount to contempt of Court; and the denial of a right of appeal to the applicant by the customary court amounted to the court exceeding its jurisdiction. Consequently certiorari was issued to quash the proceeding and conviction.

A suitable question which has engaged the Courts in a number of cases is whether certiorari would lie to quash a decision where an inferior judicial authority has acted without jurisdiction at all. In *The Queen v The Officer Administering the Government of Eastern Nigeria, Ex, parte Ouvehelu & others* [35] it was held that certiorari would not lie to quash proceedings because the Governor who decided the case had no jurisdiction under the Customary Courts Law,[36] to entertain the appeal. In reaching this decision the court was of the view that the proceedings before the Governor were void *ab initio* and that being so certiorari would not lie. The presiding judge quoted the submission of the Crown Counsel (on which he relied) thus: 'Mr. Okadigbo, Crown Counsel, on behalf of the first respondent submitted that the Governor having no jurisdiction to entertain the appeal the proceedings were void ab initio and so certiorari proceeding would not lie'. He relied on statements of the law cited in II Halsburys 3rd Edition at page 136 paragraph 255 and page 141 paragraph 266.[37] The two authorities referred to appear to be very distinguishable from the instant case. The first one, *Weston v Sneyd;* [38] in that case, a justice of the peace was sued for assault in the High Court and damages of £100 claimed.Before that action, the plaintiff had already sued the same justice in county court claiming £50.

---

33 *R v Postmaster General, ex.parte Carmichael* (1928) 1 K. B. 291. 299 per Avory, J., See also *R. v.Manchester Legal Aid Committee Ex. p. R.A. Brand & Co-Ltd.* (1952) Q. B. 413.

34 (1960 W. R. N. L. R. 146; see also *R v The President, Ogoja Province Experte 1h p-ah Onah of Igogobe* (1957) 2 F.S.C.R. 30

35 (1960) E. N. L. R. 33

36 No 21 of 1956, Laws of Eastern Region of Nigeria, 1956 P. A. 135. This repealed the Native Court Ordinance but saved appeals pending before the Governor.

37 (1960) E. N. L. R. at p. 34.

38 (1857), I H. & N. Hurilston & Norman 703; 156 E. R. 1095.

But the Justice Protection Act, 1848[39] provided that 'no action shall be brought in any county court against a justice of the peace for anything done by him in the execution of his office if such justice shall object thereto.[40] The assault was alleged to have been committed by the defendant in the alleged execution of his office. Exercising his right under the said statute, the defendant registered his objection. However, on the same day after receiving the written notice about the objection, the plaintiff gave a written notice to the effect that he had abandoned his intention to proceed with the court proceedings were commended for the £100 damages.

Thereupon, the defendant applied to the High Court for and 'obtained' a writ of certiorari to remove the cause of the action from the County Court to the High Court (i.e. the Queen's Bench Division). The Court was of the view that as soon as the notice under the statute was given., the proceeding in the County court thereafter were null and void. Hence, under the circumstances, as the statute had rendered the proceedings null and void, certiorari was not granted. The difference between this case and that of the *Queen v The Officer Administering the Government of Eastern Nigeria, supra*, could be seen from the facts of the two cases. In the former, the proceedings were expressly made null and void by statute as soon as a notice by justice objecting to the proceedings in the County Court against him was given. The latter was a question of the Governor acting without jurisdiction, in this particular case, the jurisdiction which he had always had had ceased.[41] It is submitted with respect, that the Governor's action was more of a person acting without or in excess of his jurisdiction. It was not doubted that the Governor had been acting and indeed could act in judicial capacity in matters relating to appeals.

Neither could it be cogently argued that the facts of the case of *The Queen v The Officer Administering the Government of Eastern Nigeria, supra,* were similar to that of Re Daws (1838).[42] This was the second authority relied upon. In that case an unauthorised coroner's clerk, described as 'really a stranger', conducted what purported to be an inquest in the coroner's absence. In the eyes of the law, it was no inquest at all, it was a complete nullity, for the clerk was no coroner at all but signed the

---

[39] II & 12 Vict C. 44, s. 10.

[40] The section went on to render null and void any proceedings taken in the County Court after the notice had been served.

[41] S.70(2) (c) of the Customary Courts Law, 1956 provided that 'wherever on the coming into operation of this Law a cause or matter is, in accordance with the provisions of the Native Court Ordinance pending on appeal before the governor, then the Governor shall, in accordance with the provisions of the Native Courts Ordinance, deal with the causes or matter.' The appeal in question was not 'pending' before the Governor as was provided. In that regard the Governor by hearing it acted in excess of his jurisdiction.

[42] Re Daws (1838) 8 Ad. & E. (Adulphus & Ellis) 936; 112 E.r. 1095.

inquisition, "C.A., Coroner." Eight months later the father of the deceased applied for certiorari to bring it up and have it quashed on the ground that a *melius inquirendum* was necessary. In refusing the rule Lord Donman , C.J. stated: If you wish to take any further proceeding and have a right to do so, how can you be prevented by the act of a person calling himself the coroner but really a stranger? I think that to grant this rule would be doing a *very unnecessary act*,[43] to set on foot a very undesirable proceeding.

The case of In re Daws was distinguished in *The Queen v The Governor, Eastern Region and Another, Ex parte Ojiegbo Ikoro of Ngodo*;[44] in that case, a Senior District officer entertained an appeal from a decision of a native Court presided over by a district Officer who had given judgment against a certain Respondent. The Senior District Officer had no power under the law to hear an appeal from a Native Court when it was presided over by a District Officer; although the Senior District Officer had jurisdiction to entertain an appeal from a Native Court. It then followed that the Senior District Officer acted without jurisdiction when he entertained an appeal from the Native Court presided over by a District Officer. An application was made to the High Court of Eastern Nigeria for an order of certiorari to quash the decision of the Senior District Officer who had reversed the decision of the Native Court presided over by the district Officer. The High Court in refusing the order for certiorari was of the view that as the Senior District Officer acted without jurisdiction, the proceedings before him were complete nullity and that certiorari would not lie. The High Court followed the decision in *Re Daws*. An appeal was made to the Federal Supreme Court. The Federal supreme Court held that certiorari lay to quash the decision of the Senior District Officer. In delivering the judgment of the Court, Bairamain, F.J. stated: The learned Judge was of opinion that the decision in *Re Daws*, 1838, 8 Ad. & El. 936, was not distinguishable in principle from the present case, and went on to hold that: Mr. Floyer having no legal authority to embark upon the appeal the proceedings are an absolute nullity and certiorari proceedings do not lie. I think that the learned Judge had no report of the case before him.' His Lordship then gave the facts in *Re Daws* and the Lucid Judicial statement of Lord Danman, C.J. and then proceeded to say:

> Mr. Floyer, as a Senior District Officer could sit as a court under the Native Courts Ordinance and hear appeals from Native Court decisions; but he could not hear appeals from a Native Court which had sat with a District Officer as its president. That he did: his decision was invalid. The decision from it to the governor was dismissed, but that, of course, did not make it valid.' [45]

---

43 *ibid*, at p. 938, 112 E.R. at p. 1096. Emphasis supplied.

44 [1962] 1 All N.L.R. 40.

45 *ibid.*, at pp. 42-42.

His Lordship, in this regard, then concluded by saying 'The present case is by no means similar to that of In re *The queen v The Officer Administering the Government of Eastern Nigeria*,[46] for as we have seen in that case, the Governor had legal authority to hear appeal from the Native Courts as was provided in the Native Courts Ordinance. Under the Customary Courts Law, 1956, the Governor had jurisdiction to hear appeals that were "pending" before the Law came into operation. So in that case, the Governor heard an appeal which was not "pending" before the Customary Courts Law came into operation. It is submitted that the mere fact that the governor could not hear certain appeals that time did not make him 'a stranger' as was the case in *Re Daws*, supra. The governor's act was more of a person exceeding his jurisdiction under an enactment; and it may be observed, was similar to that which gave rise to *The Queen v The Governor, Eastern Region and Another, Ex parte Ojiegbo Ikoro of Ngodo ante*. It may be further observed that it is doubtful if the case of *The Queen v The Officer Administering the Governor of Eastern Nigeria. Ex parte Onyebula* [47] can still stand in view of the Federal Supreme Court decision in *The Queen v The Governor, Eastern Region and another, Ex parte Ojiegbo Ikoro of /Ngodo*.[48]

ii. Error on the face of the Record of the Tribunal

In the case of *Rex v Northumberland Compensation Appeal Tribunal, Ex. parte Shaw* [49] Singleton L.J. said:

> Error on the face of the proceedings has always been recognised as one of the grounds for the issue of an order of certiorari. I can find no authority for saying that in this respect there is any distinction to be drawn between proceedings of a criminal nature and civil proceedings.

It follows that certiorari will issue to quash the decision or Order of an inferior tribunal if there is any error in point of law or any defect in point of form appearing on the face of the record of the tribunal. The principle applies as his Lordship pointed out, in civil as well as criminal cases. Thus in the aforementioned case, the Divisional Court was upheld by the Court of Appeal in holding that certiorari would be granted to quash a decision of an

---

[46] [1960] E.N.L.R. 33 (ante).

[47] *ibid*

[48] [1962] 1 All N.L.R. 40. In *R v Administrator. Western Nigeria, Ex Ex p. Bamgbedu [1962] W.N.L.R. 344*, the kingmakers appointed the person they wanted to be a chief to fill a vacancy in a ruling house. subsequently, and before their first appointment was set aside, they appointed another person to the same chieftaincy. It was held that the second appointment was without effect. Certiorari was without effect. Certiorari was granted to quash it.

[49] [1952] 1 K.B. 338 at p. 341.

inferior tribunal because there was an error on the record arising from erroneous computation of the compensation due to the application.

In *The Queen v The Governor of Eastern Region, Ex parte Nnodi and Another* [50] Many-Plange, J. in refusing leave to apply for an order of certiorari to quash the proceedings of a Native Court as well as that of the District Officer, demarcating certain boundary, held *inter alia* that there was no error on the face of the record to warrant the order.

An important question in this respect is, *what is a record?* Record is said to consist of 'all those documents which are kept by the tribunal for a permanent memorial and testimony of their proceedings.'[51] Although whenever any controversy arises as to what should or should not be included in the record of a tribunal, the High court should determine such a question. However, it seems that the court of the King's Bench always requires that the record of such tribunal should contain, or recite, the document or information which initiated the proceedings and thus give the tribunal its jurisdiction and also the document which contained their adjudication.[52] In cases of records coming from the Customary Courts, the records should contain, in cases of Land disputes, not only the whole evidence of witnesses, elders or chiefs, the decision of the Court, but also a clear map or plan of the land in question. In criminal cases, the offence committed by the convicted person and a reference to the appropriate written law contravened.[53]

iii. Denial of Natural Justice:

The cardinal rules of natural justice are, no man shall be a judge in his own cause - *nemo judex in causa sua,* and requirements: each party must be given reasonable notice of the case he has to meet, and he must be given an opportunity of stating his case and answering to allegations against his - *audi alteram partem.* In criminal cases the latter rule is expressed thus - no one ought to be condemned unheard.

These rules of natural justice are so fundamental and necessary in the administration of judicial and quasi-judicial functions that a breach of any of them may lead to setting aside or quashing the decision reached in such proceedings. A decision or determination reached in breach of any of the rules of natural justice renders it voidable and not void, 'nevertheless it is to

---

50 [1959] E.N.L.R. but see *R. v Medical Appeal Tribunal Ex p. Gilmore* 1057] 1 Q.B. 575.

51 See Blackstone's Commentaries Vol. III. p.24.

52 *R.v Northumberland Comp. App. Tribunal* [1952] All E.R. 122, 131.

53 The requirement is essential because, as we have seen in *The State v Wogu & Others Ex parte Nwabisi & Others* [1965] N.M.L.R. 219,the applicants were convicted under an alleged section of the Criminal Code which in fact did not exist. The High Court quashed the convictions as there was error in law on the face of the record, as well as the tribunal exceeding its jurisdiction in inflicting penalties.

be avoided when brought under review, and upon objection taken'.[54] We now examine the rules more closely:

(a) No man should be a judge in his own case - *nemo judex in causa sua.*

Certiorari will lie to quash a decision of an inferior tribunal when it acts in breach of the rule of natural justice. Thus in the case of *The Queen v The Acting Provincial Secretary, Uyo, Ex parte Imeh,*[55] it was held that the order of certiorari would be granted to quash the conviction of the applicant because the Native Court which tried him in the case of *"Native Court v J.D Imeh"*[56] was a party to the case. It was equally held that the applicant was not given opportunity to plead to the second charge nor give opportunity to be heard on it. In his judgment, Kaine, Ag. J., said: I have not bothered myself about the fact that there is no consolidation in criminal cases because much latitude is often given to Native Courts because of their inexperience in legal matters, but where the Native Court uses such a latitude against the principles of natural justice, as to give judgment on a case when no plea was taken, a halt must be put to it." And in touching another point the learned Judge continued: "If the Native Court is the prosecutor, is it not against the principles of natural justice for the Native Court to be the judge in its own matter?"[57] There is no doubt that under the circumstances the Native court in that case acted in breach of the rules of natural justice by not giving the applicant an opportunity to plead in a criminal charge against him - no one should be condemned unheard. Again, the Native Court acted wrongly by being a prosecutor and judge in the criminal suit against the accused; that was clearly against a fundamental rule of natural justice.

The main reason why a man should not be a judge in his own cause is to obviate any possibility of bias or partiality which militates against administration of justice. It is not necessary to establish that the interested party who happened to be a judge or one of the judges was influenced or did influence one of the judges. The important thing is not what actually happened but what might appear to happen. Thus Lord Hewart, C.J., said in a case[58] where a conviction by the justices was quashed because the clerk

---

[54] *Dimes v Grand Junction Canal Proprietors* (1852) 3 H.L.C. 759, 792, 110 E.R. 301 at p. 325 per Lord Brougham; see also *The Queen v The Administrator, Western Nigeria, Ex parte Ojetola & Others* [1962] W.N.L.R. 313, 315

[55] [1959] E.R.N.L.R. 59

[56] *Iman Clan Court Criminal Suit Nos.* 371/57 and 373/57

[57] [1959] E.R.N.L.R. at p. 60

[58] *The King v Sussex Justices, ex. D. McCarthy [1924] 1 K.B.* 256, at pp. 258-9.

to the justices who happened to have some interest in a civil proceeding connected with the criminal case retired with the justices: 'It is said, and, no doubt, truly, that when the gentleman retired in the usual way with the justices, taking with him the notices or the evidence in case the justices might desire to consult him, and that he scrupulously abstained from referring to the case in any way. But while that is so, a long line of cases shows that it is not merely of some importance but is of fundamental importance that justice should not only be done, but shall manifestly and undoubtedly be seen to be done.' His Lordship then went on: 'the question is whether he was so related to the case in its civil aspect as to be unfit to act as clerk to the justices in the criminal matter. The answer to that depends not upon what actually was done but upon what might appear to be done'. He concluded with the dictum which should ever remain green in the minds of everyone called upon to act judicially; Nothing is to be done which creates even a suspicion that there has been an improper interference with the course of justice.

Where therefore it is established before the High court that an inferior tribunal has exposed itself to a likelihood of improper interference with its administration of justice by being a judge in its cause, the High Court will intervene to remedy the situation.[59] For it is absolutely essential that the public should be reassured that justice has been done. Thus in a case[60] where the House of Lords set aside a decree of Lord Chancellor Cottenham, granting an injunction to and confirming the title of a company in which he had some interest; Lord Campbell said: "No one can suppose that Lord Cottenham could be, in the remotest degrees, influenced by the interest that he had in this concern; but my Lords, it is of the last importance that no man is to be judge in his own cause should be sacred. And that it is not confined to a cause in which he is a part, but applies to a cause in which he has an interest. Since I have had the honour to be Chief Justice of the court of Queen's Bench, we have again and again set aside proceedings of inferior tribunals because an individual, who had an interest in a cause, took a part in the decision."

(b) *Audi alteram partem* - ' Hear the Other side".

As we have seen, this rule of natural justice requires that opportunity be given to a person to prepare and state his case and answer charges or

---

[59] *Modibbo v Adamawa N.A.* [1956] N.R.N.L.R. 101 - conviction set aside because some members of the Lamido's court were interested parties in the criminal charge against the accused. See eqally *Bauchi v Bauchi N.A. 1957 N.R.N.L.R. 156* - conviction was also set aside because the proceedings were conducted before the Chief Alkali when the charge against the accused in that case was one of abusing the Alkalis.

[60] *Dimes v Grand Junction Canal Proprietors* (1852) 3 H.L.C. 759, 793; 10 E.R. 301, 315. See also *R.v Sunderland Justices* [1901] 2 x.B. 357, Order made by Justices v[illegible]s deliberated on the matter.

allegations against him. A breach of this rule will, as we have seen, render a decision of an inferior tribunal voidable, and such a decision will be avoided if and when the matter is taken up to the High Court. Thus in *The Queen v The Governor in Council, Western Nigeria, Ex parte Adebo,* [61] the High Court of Western Nigeria held that certiorari would lie to quash an order of the Governor in Council deposing that he applicant as Olofin of Ilishan because the chief was not given an adequate opportunity to prepare his defence against the charges made against him nor was he heard in the determination of a matter which affected his rights and interest, the Governor in Council being required, in the determination of such issues, to act judicially.

In his judgment, Charles J. stated [62] that 'it is important to recognise that there is a presumption that when the Legislature confers a power[63] on an authority to make a determination affecting an individual in his property or person, it intends that the power shall be exercised judicially in accordance with the rule of natural justice that the individual concerned must be given an adequate opportunity to be heard.' It follows that certiorari will be granted to quash a decision or determination of inferior tribunal, whether it is judicial or quasi-judicial, if such tribunal conduct its proceedings in such a way as to deprive a party affected an opportunity to be heard.[64] The principle applies in civil as well as criminal proceedings. For as we have seen in *The Queen v The Acting Provincial Secretary, Uyo, Ex parte Imeh,* [65] the High Court granted an order of certiorari to quash the conviction of the applicant who was convicted by a Native court on a charge in which he was not given an adequate opportunity to plead or answer to the charge preferred against him.

The rule of natural justice which requires each party to be heard and given adequate opportunity in that regard is embedded in any enactment requiring an inquiry to be made by a member of the executive or any other person before doing an act. Where the rule is infringed, the High Court will intervene, Thus in *The Queen v The Resident, Ijebu Province, Ex parte Oshunlaja* [66] where the Governor in Council approved the appointment of a

---

61 [1962] W.N.L.R. 93.

62 *ibid*, at p. 98. However, the absence of an oral hearing or an opportunity to be heard orally before an inferior down in writing and submitted to such tribunal does not necessarily amount to a denial of the rule of natural Justice: *The Queen v The Director of Audit, Western Region, Ex p* '• *Oputa & Others* [1961] 1 All N.L.R. 659.

63 *See Meradane Nosque (Board of Trustees) v Badi-ud-dian Mahmud & Another [19660 1 All E.R. 545 P.C.* - Order of Minister quashed because being required by statute to act judicially, he acted contrary to natural justice by not giving the party affected opportunity to be head. (An appeal from the decision of the Supreme Court of Ceylon).

64 *See Smith v The Queen (1978) 3 App. Cas. 614, 624, 625 P.C.*.

65 [1959] F.R.N.L.R. 59; see also *Auzinawa v Kano N.A. [1956] F.S.C.R. 27.*

chief, which appointment was made without "due enquiry", Ademola, C.J. (as he then was) said that 'the Court is precluded by law from interfering in the matter of selection of a chief; it will therefore not interfere but it will be standing between the executive and the members of the public, so far as the legislature on the point permits; and if something is being done which is contrary to natural justice, or certain things required by law are not done, it will interfere.'

The above judicial statement brings us to an important question, viz., Can certiorari lie despite an express provision in an enactment excluding the Order? It may be said that normally, when an enactment, for instance, an Act of Parliament, expressly excludes the order of certiorari, the High Court will be bound by the statute. However, such an enactment could not provide a shield against irregularities, nor will the High court feel precluded if an inferior tribunal is challenged before it for acting in excess or without jurisdiction, or in breach of the rules of natural justice; or contrary to certain sections of the law and thus revealing an error of law on the face of its records[67]

In *Rex v Moreley*[68] it was stated that 'the jurisdiction of this court is not taken away (in respect of grant of writ of certiorari) unless there be express words to take it away'. In *Ex parte Bradlauch*[69] an important question which faced the Court was whether certiorari could lie notwithstanding its express exclusion in a statute. The statute in question was described as, an Act for Regulating the Police Courts in the Metropolis. It provided that 'no information, conviction, or other proceeding before or by any of the said magistrates, shall be quashed or set aside, or adjudged void or insufficient for want of form, or be removed by certiorari into Her Majesty's Court of Queen's Bench.'[70] The order issued by the inferior court in this case did

[67] In *R.v. Mahony [1910] 2 I.R. 695 at 742-3*, Gibson, J. was of the view that Certiorari would issue for breach of rule of natural justice and error of law on the face of the record privative provisions notwithstanding. In *Re Gilmore Application [1957] 1 All F.R. 796* it was held that certiorari would issue to remove into the High Court and quash a decision of a medical appeal tribunal because of an apparent error of law on the record despite the privative provision in the National Insurance (Industrial Injures Act, 9 & 10 Geo. 6 c. 62 s. 36(2). This made the decision of the medical tribunal "final". However, in *New Zealand . Waterside Workers' Federation Industrial Association of Workers v Frazer & Others [1924] N.Z.L.R.* might be effectively taken away by a privative provision in a statute in case of error on the face of the record of an inferior tribunal but such a provision will be ineffective in case of such tribunal acting in excess of its jurisdiction. In Nigeria, the case of *The Queen v The Governor in Council, Western Nigeria, Ex p. Adebo [1962] W.N.L.R. 93* shows that the High Court will grant order of certiorari in cases of breach of the natural justice - *audi alteram partem and Ex p. Odubote [1961] W.M.L.R. 95* for error of law in implementing the provisions of a statutes privative provisions notwithstanding. It seems therefore that the view expressed in *R.v. Mahony*

[68] (1760) 2 Burr. (Burrow) 1041,1042; 97 E.R. 966, 967.

[69] (1878) 3 Q.B.D. 509.

[70] 2 & 3 Vict. C. 71, Section 49.

not state the existence of matter essential to its jurisdiction. It was held that certiorari would issue to quash the order of the metropolitan magistrate for the destruction of the applicant's books which were said to be obscene publication. Referring to the section which excluded certiorari, Cockburn, C.J. said that 'the section does not apply when the application for the certiorari is on the ground that the inferior tribunal has exceeded the limits of its jurisdiction.'[71] Mellor, J., was however, more direct when he said: "It is well established that the provision taking away the certiorari does not apply where there was absence of jurisdiction. The consequence of holding otherwise would be that a metropolitan magistrate could make any order he pleased without question."[72]

In a recent case of *Regina v His Honour Judge Sir Donald Hurst, Ex parte Smith*,[73] the Court of Queen's Bench firmly established that certiorari could lie despite an enactment precluding its issue if an inferior tribunal acts without jurisdiction. In that case the Court was confronted by two sanctions of the County Court Act, 1959;[74] section 107 provides that "Subject to the provisions of any other Act relating to county courts, no judgment or order of any judge of county, nor any proceedings brought before him or pending in his court, shall be removed by appeal, motion, certiorari or otherwise into any other court whatever, except in the manner and according to the provisions in this Act mentioned." The provisions contemplated in section 107 could be found in Section 115 (1) of the Act which provides that, 'The High Court or a judge thereof may order the removal into the High court, by order of certiorari or otherwise, any proceedings commenced in a county court, if the High Court or judge thereof thinks it desirable that the proceedings should be heard and determined in the High Court.

The question before the High court was whether certiorari could be granted to quash the directions of a county court judge in respect of removal of certain names, including that of the applicants from the register of electors. It was held that the county court judge had no jurisdiction to give the directions in question, consequently certiorari would issue to quash the directions.

Lord Parker, C.J. referring to the two sections of County Courts Act said: 'Looking at those two sections it is to be observed that the only remedy by way of certiorari dealt with is in regard to the removal of the proceedings.from one court into another and not for the purpose of quashing. Notwithstanding that, I am quite satisfied that certiorari will lie in this case.' His Lordship went further to say, 'I am quite satisfied that

---

71 *ibid*, at p.513.

72 *ibid*,

73 [1960] 2 All E.R. 386.

74 7 & 8 Eliz. 2 C. 22.

certiorari will lie against a county court judge if he has acted without jurisdiction, notwithstanding the sections of the County courts Act, 1959.'[75] It follows that the order of certiorari will be granted to quash decision of a judge or magistrate of an inferior court or any other person required to act judicially if such a court or person acts without jurisdiction, notwithstanding any enactment excluding the order of *certiorari*.

As we have seen, there were certain provisions excluding prerogative orders in Section 27 of High court law, Northern Region, in respect of proceedings in a Native Court or Sharia Court of Appeal. It does not appear that there has been any direct challenge to this exclusion yet. However, in the case of *The Queen v Governor in Council, Western Nigeria, Ex parte Odubote* [76] the High Court of Western Nigeria had to deal with the provisions of an enactment which expressly excluded the prerogative orders. This was section 3(1) of the Administration of Justice (Crown Proceedings) Law, 1959.[77] It provided as follows:

"The High Court shall not have jurisdiction to issue an order of mandamus, order of prohibition or any order of certiorari to the governor or to the Governor in Council in respect of -

(a) the approval or setting aside of the appointment of any chief;
(b) the suspension or deposition of any chief;
(c) any decision of the Governor or any Governor in Council in a dispute with regard to the appointment to a chieftaincy;
(d) any other thing required to be done by the Governor or the Governor in Council under any enactment relating to chiefs."

In the case referred to above an application was made for an order of certiorari to quash the order of approval and recognition of the appointment of one Adebayo Soile as the Otunba (Obomu) of Omu, because the recognition and approval order was made without jurisdiction owing to the absence of the essential conditions precedent to the exercise by the Governor in Council of his powers under section 37(3) of the Appointment and Recognition of Chiefs Law, 1954. It was also contended *inter alia* on behalf of the applicant that the order and the proceedings relating to it were *ultra vires* having violated the provisions of sections 7(3) and 8 of the said Law. The only defence relied upon by the respondent was that notwithstanding the irregularities alleged, any act done or omission made under the said Law could not be questioned by way of certiorari in any court because of section 3 of the Administration of Justice (crown

---

75 *ibid*, at p.389.

76 [1961] W.N.L.R. 95.

77 Legislation of the Western Region of Nigeria, 1960 p. A 11.

Proceedings) Law, 1959.[78] It was held that *certiorari* would issue to quash the approval and recognition order of the Governor in council notwithstanding section 3 of the Administration Justice (Crown Proceedings) Law, 1959.

The High court was of the view that the Governor in council acted without jurisdiction because 'the power of the Governor in council is to give approval to appointments to which the Law applies. In this case, the Governor in Council has given approval and recognition under the Law to an appointment to a chieftaincy to which the Law had not been applied at the time the holder was appointed chief. It is quite clear, therefore, that the condition necessary for the exercise of his power does not exist.'[79] It follows therefore, that provision ousting the jurisdiction of the High Court in respect of prerogative orders will not apply where an inferior tribunal.acts without jurisdiction. As Fatayi Williams, J. in his judgment appositely said:

> 'It is, in my view, settled law that where a statute seeks to take away the jurisdiction of a superior court, that privative provision will not be effective where the inferior court or body exercising judicial or quasi-judicial function has acted in violation of the statute or has acted without jurisdiction.[80]

In *Colonial Bank of Australia v William* [81] it was stated by the Privy Council that 'notwithstanding the privative clause in a statute, the Court of Queen's Bench will grant a certiorari to quasi a decision of an inferior tribunal when it acts without jurisdiction. The Federal Supreme Court in the case of *R.v. The Governor in Council. Western Region. Nigeria, Ex parte Ojo* [82] was of the view that 'it is settled law' that despite words taking away certiorari, the Court will issue certiorari for manifest defect of jurisdiction in the tribunal which made the order, and the objection may be founded on the character and constitution of the inquiry, or the absence of some preliminary proceedings which was necessary to give jurisdiction to the inferior court. It may therefore be observed that the no-certiorari or privative provisions in the statutes are not generally effective as the courts will feel more obliged to interfere where there is a clear case of an inferior tribunal acting without jurisdiction or in excess of its jurisdiction,[83] or where there is a breach of the rule of natural justice by not giving a party affected an adequate

---

78 No. 3 of 1960

79 [1961] W.N.L.R. 95, 98.

80 *Ibid*, at p.

81 (1874) 30 L.T. 238.

82 [1962] W.N.L.R. 62.

83 *The Queen v Governor in Council, Western Nigeria, Ex parte Odubote ante; R.v. Hurst, Ex p. Smith ante; New Zealand Waterside Workers' Federation Industrial Association of Workers v Frazer 1924] N.Z.L.R. 689, Ex parte Bradlaugh (1878) 3 Q.B.D. 509*

opportunity to be heard,[84] or where there is an error of law on the face of the record of such tribunal.[85] Equally certiorari will lie to quash a decision of an inferior tribunal where there is a manifest fraud, private provision in a statute not withstanding.[86] As was established in *Re Gilmore Application supra* a privative provision may spell out no particular prerogative order to be excluded but couched in such a way to imply a blanket exclusion of any control by the High Court through prerogative orders. Such words as "shall be final" are used. It may be said that as these privative provision do not effectively operate to exclude the courts, their inclusion in statutes, therefore, appears to be unnecessary. From this point of view, it will not be surprising if the High Court of the Northern Region rules that the Court has jurisdiction to grant prerogative orders in appropriate cases in respect of decision or findings of Native Courts and Sharia Court of Appeal, the preclusion of such jurisdiction by the High Court Law[87] notwithstanding.[88]

Military Tribunal

A military tribunal is an inferior tribunal and therefore subject to control by the High Court through the order of certiorari.[89] If military tribunal exceeds its jurisdiction or acts without jurisdiction, the High Court may on application grant an order of certiorari to quash the proceedings. Thus in a case[90] where man was tried by a court martial after his release from military duty, it was held, on his application to the High Court for a writ of *habeas corpus* on the ground that the court martial had no jurisdiction to try him, that writ of habeas corpus should issue for the prisoner's immediate release. The order of certiorari equally went to bring up the proceedings of the court martial and get them quashed.

---

84 *The Queen v The Governor in council. Western Nigeria. Ex p. Adebo* [1962] W.N.L.R. 93; *R. v Hahony [1910] 2 I.R. 695, at pp. 742-3.*

85 *Re Gilmore Application 1957 1 All E.R. 796; R.v. Mahony supra; The Queen v The Governor in council Ex p. Odubote [1961] W.N.L.R. 95.*

86 *Colonial bank of Australia v willan* (1874) 30 L.T. 237, 238, P.C.

87 Cap.49, S.32, Laws of Northern Nigeria, 1963.

88 Similar provisions in the (U.K) County Courts Act, 1959 s.107 (7 & 8 Eliz. 2 C.22) did not effectively exclude the High Court's jurisdiction to grant order of certiorari: *R. v Hurst, Ex p. Smith* [1960] 2 All E.R. 386; nor was, as shown above, S.3(1) of the Administration of Justice (Crown proceedings) Law, 1959, No. 3 of 1960, Legislation of the Western Region of Nigeria, 1960.

89 And other prerogative orders as well as the prerogative writ of *habeas corpus*. See Lord Loughborough in *Grant v Gould 1972) 2 H.Bl. (Blackstone, II) 69, 100; 126 E.R. 434, 450* where he said: 'Naval Courts Martial, Military Courts Martial, Courts of Admiralty, Courts of Prize, are all liable to the controlling authority, which the Courts, of westminister Hall have from time to time exercised.

90 *Rex v Governor of Wormwood Scrubs Prison, Ex Parte Boydeil* (1948) 2 K.B. 193.

It appears, however, that the courts are usually reluctant [91] to interfere with the determinations of military tribunals where they act within jurisdiction but fail to observe certain rules, such as *audi alteram partem*. That is to say, where a decision was reached by a military tribunal as 'a disciplinary authority of a disciplined service.' The idea behind this judicial self-restraint, so to speak, is to avoid, as they say, any interference which might operate to weaken discipline in the armed forces. Also, they maintain that as the grant of the prerogative orders is discretionary, it is left to the courts to use their judgments in carrying out the task. Thus in the case of *The Queen v The Officer Commanding,Second Battalion, The Queen's Own Nigeria Regiment, Ex.parte Uangbaoje*,[92] the applicant had been dismissed from the Regiment and also sentenced to detention for 28 days by the respondent for military offences contrary to the Royal Nigeria Military Forces Act, 1960.[93] He applied for an order of certiorari on the ground that he was not given an opportunity to be heard nor allowed to call witnesses in his defence. Counsel for the respondent contended inter alia, that even if the court had jurisdiction to issue an order of certiorari, it should nonetheless refuse to make the order as that would be prejudicial to military discipline.It was held that the High Court has jurisdiction to issue an order of certiorari to quash a decision of a military tribunal where such a decision was reached without jurisdiction. The court,however, dismissed the application,being discretionary the court had to dismiss the application 'unless special circumstances are shown calling for the discretion being exercised the other way.'

From the report of the case, it was not shown that the allegations made by the applicant were not established. It therefore follows that it is only in cases where military tribunals acted without jurisdiction that *certiorari* would issue. This idea appears to spring from the case of *In re Mansergh94* where an officer serving in the British Army in India was court-martialled convicted and dismissed from the service, applied for a writ of certiorari to quash the conviction and sentence on the ground that the court martial had no jurisdiction over him. This contention did not appear to hold from the facts of the case. The application was dismissed. In his judgment, Lord Cockburn, C. J. stated that 'when the civil rights of a person in military service are affected by a judgment of a military tribunal where the tribunal has exceeded its jurisdiction or acted without jurisdiction,this court ought to interfere to protect these civil rights.

---

[91] *R.v The Army Council, Ex.p. Ravensroft* (1917) 2 K.B. 504, 513;Roberts' Case, 1879, Manual of Military Law (1929) 142; *R. v Secretary of State for Awr Ex. p. Martin* (1949) 1 All E. R. 242 *R. v O/C Deport Battalion, R.A.S.C. Colchester, Ex.p.Elliot* (1949)1 All E.R. 373.

[92] (1962) W. N. L. R. 368.

[93] No. 26 of 1960

It may be observed that literal interpretation of the judicial pronouncement in the above mentioned case by restricting the power of the courts to interfere only to cases where a military tribunal acted without jurisdiction or in excess of its jurisdiction could give rise to many hardships on the part of persons subjected to court martial. If the idea is not checked, it might result, in the final analysis, in judicial self-exclusion which might apparently be regarded as judicial self-restraint. Lord Cockburn, C.J. in his classic statement referred to the "civil rights of a person in military service. Obviously the rights to fair trial and fair trial presupposes right to be heard and adequate opportunity for one in trial to defend himself in person and through the witnesses he could call to buttress his defence. Again, the case of *In re Mansregh* specifically dealt with jurisdiction and was decided on that point.The allegations made in *The Queen v The Officer Commanding, Second Battalion, The Queen's Own Nigerian Regiment, Ex.parte Uangbaoje* were denial of right to be heard and to call witness. It is submitted, with great respect, that if allegations of denial of right to be heard is established, certiorari should issue to quash the decision of a military tribunal. That a man should not be condemned unheard is a sacred rule of natural justice. The laws of God and man both give the party an opportunity to make his defence, if he has any. I remember to have heard it observed by a very learned man upon such an occasion,that even God himself did not pass sentence upon Adam, before he was called upon to make his defence.[95] Again, although the grant of certiorari is discretionary, 'if the application for a certiorari is made by a party aggrieved, then it ought to be granted *ex debito justitiae*, and the Court has not the general discretion which it would have when the application is made by one of the public who is not personally concerned.[96]

There is no doubt that a military tribunal would be more cautious in deciding cases coming before it if it is conscious that its decision might be quashed by the High Court by means of *certiorari* if it fails to observe the elementary principles of justice. Cases are indeed rare where such tribunals act without or in excess of their jurisdiction, as most of the cases handled by them obviously come within their jurisdiction as the people usually affected are men on active service. So, the High Court should issue certiorari in cases where the Order ought to lie, other than for absence or excess jurisdiction on the part of a military tribunal.[97] While it is necessary

---

95 *The King v University of Cambridge* (1723) 1 Str. (Strange) 557 at p.567; 93 E.R. 698, 704. per Fortescue, J. - University's decision to deprive B. of his degrees was declared a nullity because he had not been first heard in his own defence.

96 Per Avory J. in *R. v Postmaster-General Ex p. Carmichael* (1928) 1 K.B. 294 at p.299

97 For cogent and classic argument for civil control over courts martial, see D.C. Holland, "*The law of Courts Martial,*" 1950 3 C.L.P. *(Current Legal Problems)* p. 173. esp. 174 et. seq. Here Professor

that discipline should not be jeopardised it is equally necessary that not only must justice be done but seen to be done.

2. Prohibition

A prohibition is a prerogative order which issues out of the High Court primarily to restrain an inferior tribunal from exceeding its jurisdiction, or acting in breach of the rules of natural justice. Blackstone defined prohibition as follows: 'A prohibition is a writ issuing properly out of the King's Bench being the King's prerogative writ; ... directed to the judge and parties of a suit in any inferior court, commanding them to cease from prosecution thereof, upon the suggestion that either the cause originally, or some collateral matter arising therein, does not belong to the jurisdiction, but to the cognizance of some other court.'[98] Prohibition was a powerful weapon of the Court of the King's Bench in earlier times, when that Court was competing for jurisdictions with other Courts such as the ecclesiastical and the Admiralty Courts. From this point of view, prohibition is a more powerful instrument of control than certiorari, for it can issue to prevent unauthorised proceedings in an ecclesiastical court, whereas *certiorari* will not lie to review the decision of an ecclesiastical court.[99] The penalty for disobedience against an order of prohibition is attachment and committal for contempt. The order of prohibition which has replaced the old writ is just as powerful as the old writ.

The rules governing the issue of the order are similar to those regarding the issue of *certiorari;* the only difference being that the order of prohibition does not lie when once a final decision has been given. In practice it is usually wiser for an applicant to ask for the two orders of prohibition and certiorari together. As Wrottesley, L.J. observed, while the one prevented the other cured, none the less it is the fact that the effect of an order of prohibition is not merely to prevent the making of an order should it arrive in time, but is also to prevent the enforcement of it should it arrive after it has been made,[100] It follows that where an application is made 'for prohibition or certiorari,' the High Court may grant prohibition if it is not too late, that is, if the inferior tribunal has not made a decision, but if it has made a decision on the matter, certiorari might issue to quash such decision. Thus in *Rex v Electricity Commissioners, Ex parte London Electricity Joint Committee Company (1920) Ltd. and Others,*[101] an application involved the

---

Holland firmly established a clear case: that the civil courts should "keep a vigilant eye on courts martial and exercise a strict control over them."

[98] Blackstone Comm. Vol. 3 p.105. *L.P.D.C. v Fawehinmi (1985) 2 N.W.L.R. (pt.7) 300 S.C.*

[99] *Rex v Chancellor of St. Edmundsbury and Ipswich Diocese Ex parte White 1948 1 K.B. 195.*

[100] *ibid* at p.215.

[101] (1924) 1 K. B. 171.

two orders. In coming to the conclusion to grant a writ of prohibition instead of *certiorari*, Atkin, L.J. said: 'I think therefore that the appeal should be allowed, so far as the writ of prohibition is concerned, and that the rule for the issue of the writ should be made absolute. So far as the writ of certiorari is concerned, the matter becomes unimportant.'[102]

In that case, the Court held that a writ of prohibition should issue to restrain Electricity Commissioners from proceeding with a scheme which was *ultra vires*. On the close relationship between certiorari and prohibition Atkin, L.J. observed that he could see 'no difference in principle between certiorari and prohibition, except that the latter may be invoked at an earlier stage. If the proceedings establish that the body complained of is exceeding its jurisdiction by entertaining matters which would result in its final decision being subject to being brought up and quashed on certiorari, I think that prohibition will lie to restrain it from exceeding its jurisdiction.' This statement clearly shows the value of the two orders, but it would be, it may be said, a contradiction in terms if it is said that there is no difference between the two writs or orders. Such idea will lead to one of the remedies flourishing at the expense of the other. They provide different remedies, and it may be observed that in many cases prohibition would serve better purpose. For instance, if a statutory authority embarks on a project which would amount to its exceeding its jurisdiction or acting *ultra vires*, it would be more expedient and possibly less wasteful to stop the statutory authority right in time with an order of prohibition instead of waiting till the last moment and then pray for an order of certiorari. It is better to nip the illegality in the bud, and the job is better done with an order of prohibition. The above illustration could compare favourably with what happened in the case of *Rex v Electricity Commissioners, supra*.

Also, where an inferior tribunal commences its function in a manner not authorised by statute, it is better to apply for an order of prohibition to restrain such tribunal from proceeding as constituted than to wait for the whole proceedings to be completed and then to challenge the legality. Thus in the *Queen v Thomas (Chairman of Thomas Commission of Inquiry) and Others, Ex parte Edukugho*,[103] an application was made for an order of prohibition to restrain the first and second defendants from proceeding with the Itsekiri Communal Land Trust Commission of Inquiry in excess of the jurisdiction conferred on them by statute; in that they appointed or allowed the third and fourth defendants to act as Counsel and Accountant respectively to the said Commission of Inquiry. Having found the allegation proved, Oyemade, J., held that prohibition should issue to restrain the Commission from proceeding with the said Counsel and the Accountant. The Commission was none the less allowed to go on with its proceedings

---

103 *ibid* at p.210.

104 (1962) W.N.L.R. 330.

without the two representations to present the case for the Commission as that was not authorised by statute. It would have entailed more waste if the Commission of Inquiry had been allowed to go on and afterwards to proceed with certiorari to quash its findings.

In *R. v Minister of Health, ex parte Davis* [104] prohibition was considered as an appropriate remedy to prevent the Minister of Health from proceeding with the confirmation of an *ultra vires* housing scheme. Where, however, an *ultra vires* scheme had been carried out or where an inferior tribunal had given a wrong interpretation of the powers conferred on it by statute, resulting in it exceeding its jurisdiction and there is a probability that the excess of jurisdiction would continue, the High Court could quash the decision of the inferior tribunal to embark on the illegal course with an order of certiorari and a prohibition to prevent the tribunal from continuing to exceed its jurisdiction. Thus in *Rex v Paddington Rent Tribunal, Ex parte Bell Properties Ltd,*[105] it was held that certiorari would issue to quash a decision which had already been made by a rent tribunal, and prohibition would equally issue to prohibit the tribunal from continuing to act in excess of its jurisdiction.

Prohibition will also be granted to restrain a person who has an interest in a matter from acting in any way as a judge. Parke, B., made this clear in *Dimes v Proprietors of Grand Junction Canal* [106] when he observed that 'if this had been a proceeding of inferior court, one to which a prohibition might go from a court in Westminster Hall, such a prohibition would be granted the proceedings, upon an allegation that the presiding Judge of the court was interested in the suit.' The extent of interest which disqualifies a person in this respect does not seem to be relevant nor is it necessary to show that the judgement of the person in question is actually influenced by the interest he had in the matter. For the law does not measure the amount of interest which a judge possesses. If he has any legal interest in the decision of the question one way he is disqualified, no matter how small the interest may be. The law in laying down this strict rule, has regard not so much perhaps to the motives which might be supposed to bias the judge as to the susceptibilities of the litigant parties. One important object, at all events, is to clear away everything which might engender suspicion and distrust of the tribunal, and so to promote the feeling of confidence in the administration of justice which is essential to social order and security.[107]

---

[105] (1929) 1 K.B. 619.

[106] (194) 1 K.B. 666.

[107] (1852) 3 H.L.C. 759, 785; 10 E.R. 301, 312, a decree of Lord Chancellor Cottenham set aside because he had financial interest in the company involved in the matter

[108] Per Lush, J in *Sergeant & Others v Dale* (1877) 2 Q.B.D. 558, 567 - held, prohibition should be granted where a bishop who was disqualified from acting in a certain matter because of his interest

Lord Campbell, C.J. in Ex Parte Medwin & Hurst [108] also pointed out that the law is wisely jealous on this head: and the slightest real interest in the issue of a suit incapacitates anyone from sitting as Judge in it, although it may be certain that in fact that interest, from its real or proportionate insignificance, cannot create any bias in his mind. It follows therefore, that a breach of the rule of natural justice that a man shall not be a judge in his own cause grounds an order of prohibition.

Equally prohibition will issue to restrain a person from deciding a case where it is established that he is biased one way or the other. Thus in an Irish case of *Rex (Ree and Others) v Davison,* [109] it was held that prohibition should be granted to prohibit a magistrate who had earlier in a case openly demonstrated animosity against the accused persons from proceeding with the case. Boyd J. unreservedly stated: "As to the question of bias, I am very decidedly of opinion that Mr. Davison was disqualified from hearing or adjudicating in this case,"

It may also be said that the order of prohibition will lie to restrain an inferior tribunal from proceeding with the implementation of a decision which was reached in breach of the rule of natural justice of audi alteram partem - hear the other party. As in *Rex v North, Ex parte Oakey,* [110] a vicar was alleged to have been responsible for the damage of a screen in a church and was in his absence ordered by a Consistory Court to pay for the repair; was held to have not been given an opportunity of being heard in his defence. Consequently a writ of prohibition was issued to stop the order of the Consistory Court from being implemented against the vicar. Dealing with this particular point of giving a person an opportunity to be heard in his own defence, Atkin L.J. stated that 'it appears to me that the vicar is entitled to a prohibition, the order being a breach of the fundamental principle of law, that a person is entitled to have notice of a claim against him and to be heard before he can be deprived of his property.' In conclusion his Lordship further observed that 'the order, being made without jurisdiction, was wholly without effect, and nothing could be validly done under it.'[111]

In the above pronouncement his Lordship used the term 'fundamental principle of law.' The term, however, was not specific but it appears that he chose to use the term instead of the well-known term natural justice and any other generic term appears to be the same. For a breach of the rules of natural justice had been in some cases equated with acting without

---

was in fact doing so. See also *Roberts v Humby 3 M. & W. 120, 126; Buggin v Bunnett 4 Bur. 2035, 2037; Gorham v Bishop of Exeter 15 Q.B. 52, 64, 65*

109 (1853) 1 E. & B. (Elias & Blackburn) 609, 614; 118 E.R. 566, 567.

110 (1913) 2 I.R. 342, 354. See also *Rex (Courtney) v Emerson* (1913) 2 I.R. 377.

111 (1927 1 K.B. 491.

112 *ibid,* at p. 505.

jurisdiction.[112] Although the main difference still remains that a breach of a rule of natural justice renders a decision voidable[113] to be avoided by the High Court if an when the decision is challenged, but a decision reached without jurisdiction is ipse jure void.[114]

An important point in which there appears to have been varied views is whether prohibition issues at the discretion of the Court or whether the Court is obliged to issue one once sufficient legal grounds have been established. Earlier decisions on the subject appeared to point to the view that the grant of the writ of prohibition at the instance of an applicant was a matter purely within the discretion of the Court.[115] The view was dissented from by Willes J [116] who made a distinction between case where a want of jurisdiction in the proceedings of the inferior court or tribunal concerned was apparent in its proceedings and where it was not. Where the want of jurisdiction is apparent, the writ of prohibition at the suit of a party is not in the discretion of the Court. And quoting an earlier case [117] his Lordship declared that 'if called upon we are bound to issue out writ of prohibition as soon as we are dully informed that any Court of inferior jurisdiction has committed such a fault as to found our authority to prohibit The question then remains, what are the defects that authorise and require us to issue the writ of prohibition? The answer is, that they are in every case of such a nature as to show a want of jurisdiction to decide the case before them.' On the other hand where the defect is not apparent, and depends upon some fact in the knowledge of the applicant which he had an opportunity of bringing forward in the Court below, and he has thought proper, without excuse, to allow that Court to proceed to jurisdiction without setting up the objection, and without moving for a prohibition in the first instance, although it should seem that the jurisdiction to grant a prohibition in respect of the right of the Crown is not taken away, for mere acquiescence does not give jurisdiction, yet, considering the conduct of the applicant, the importance of making an end of litigation, and the order though of right, is

---

113 *Reg. v Paddington North and St. Marylebone Rent Tribunal, Ex. p. Perry* (1956) 1 Q.B. 229 at p.237 per Lord Goddard, C.J.

114 *Dimes v Proprietors of Grand Junction Canal* (1852) 3 H.L.C. 759, 792.

115 See *Sergeant v Dale (1877) 2 Q.B.D. 558, 568; Reg. v The Administrator, Western Nigeria, Ex p. Bamgbedu (1962) W.N.L.R. 344, 353; Reg. v The Governor, Eastern Region* (1962) 1 All N.L.R. 40, 42; a fortiori, Re Daws (1838) 8 Ad. & E. 936. See also Lord Mansfield in *Buggin v Bennett 4 Burr. 2035.*

116 *Clay v Snelgrove 1 Ld. Raym. 578, per Holt, C.J.; Wharton v Pits 2 Salk. 548, overruled in Velthasen v Ormsby 3 T.R. 315.*

117 *Mayor of London v Cox* (1867) L.R. 2 H.L. 239.

118 *Burder v Veley* 12 Ad. & E. 263.

not of course, the Court would decline to interpose, except perhaps upon an irresistible case.[118]

It follows, therefore, that where the applicant is the party affected in proceedings before an inferior tribunal which patently has no jurisdiction over the matter prohibition should issue, and the High Court has no discretion in such a case. But, if the want of jurisdiction is not apparent and the applicant knew of such want of jurisdiction and allowed the proceedings to go on to the end, and having no excuse for that, such as disability, malpractice or lack of opportunity to initiate proceedings for an order of prohibition, the High Court will not in such case be precluded from exercising the discretion by refusing the remedy sought.[119] The view that the grant of the order of prohibition to an affected person where the want of jurisdiction is apparent on the face of the proceedings of an inferior tribunal is obligatory on the High Court, was recently emphatically buttressed by the judicial pronouncement of Lord Goddard C.J., He stated:[120] "If the defect of jurisdiction is apparent on the face of the proceedings, the order of prohibition must[121] go as of right and is not a matter of discretion."[122]

Also, the High Court will issue prohibition on the ground of absence of jurisdiction even if there is an alternative remedy, such as, an appeal. There is no technical obstacle to the co-existence of a right to appeal and to a prohibition.[123] As the power of prohibition is in no case taken away by the privilege of appeal; for, as Lord Denman, C.J. put it: 'If called upon, we are bound to issue our writ of prohibition, as soon as we are duly informed that any Court of inferior jurisdiction has committed such a fault as to found our authority to prohibit, although there may be a possibility of correcting it by appeal. For there is no reason for driving the subject to that expensive process.[124] As was pointed out earlier, it is better to apply for an order of prohibition as soon as it becomes obvious that an inferior tribunal is

---

[119] *Mayor of London v Cox* (1867) L.R. 2 H.L. 278, 283.

[120] See *Channel Coaling Company v Ross & Another* (1907) 1 K.B. 145; In *Buggin v Bennett 4 Burr.* 2037, Lord Mansfield held that the Court was not bound to issue a prohibition at the instance of a party who acquiesced in the proceedings of the inferior court except where the absence of jurisdiction was apparent on the face of proceedings of the inferior court. And Lopes, L.J. said that 'where the want of jurisdiction is patent, the grant of the writ prohibition is of course': *Farquharson v Morgan* (1894) 1 Q.B.D. 552, 557.

[121] (1953) 1 All E.R. 863 at p.866.

[122] Emphasis supplied.

[123] It may be observed that where an application for prohibition is made by a person who is not a party in the proceedings, a stranger, so to speak, prohibition may issue at the discretion of the court.

[124] *R. v Comptroller-General of Patents, Ex parte Parke Davis & Co.* (1953) 1 All E.R. 562, 865, see also *Turner v Kingsbury Collieries Ltd.* (1921) 3 K.B. 169; Sweetland v Turkis Cigarette Co. (1899) 80 L.T. 472.

[125] *Burder v Valey* (1840) 12 Ad. & El. (Adolphus & Ellis) 233, 263; 113 E.R. 801, 812; see also Rex v Nort, Ex parte Oakey (1921) 1 K.B. 491, 506 per Atkin, L.J.

exceeding its jurisdiction even if there exists a right of appeal. In such a case prohibition will be more expedient, appropriate and less expensive.

3. Mandamus

An order of mandamus is a judicial remedy which issues from the High Court to compel the performance of a duty of a public nature - such a duty may be statutory. The Order issues at the discretion of the Court, and usually where no other remedy is available. The writ of mandamus was described by Blackstone as 'a command issuing in the King's name from the King's Bench and directed to any person, corporation or inferior Court of jurisdiction, requiring them to do some particular thing, therein specified, which appertains to their duty or office.[125] In *Doctor Bentley's Case* [126] a broader description of the writ was given thus: "Mandamus or mandatory writs are very ancient, as old as Edward the First, if not older; and the two main ends of them are to expedite justice and to prevent oppression in great bodies of men, such as corporation. Returns of mandamus's are answers to the King's commands; they therefore ought to be true and clear; and indeed they require the utmost certainty, even much greater than an indictment; for that may be traversed; but here the King can't traverse, but if the return be not clear, a peremptory mandamus goes; for if the party quibbles or prevaricates, he is supposed not to be able to give a better answer." The penalty for disobedience was attachment and committal for contempt.

Again, Bowen, L.J. in *Regina v The Commissioner of Inland Revenue, In re Nathan,*[127] stated that a writ of mandamus is a high prerogative writ, invented for the purpose of applying defects of justice. By Magna Charter the Crown is bound neither to deny justice to anybody, nor to delay anybody in obtaining justice. If, therefore, there is no other means of obtaining justice, writ of mandamus is granted to enable justice to be done. As we have seen above, for an order of mandamus to issue there must exist a public duty which the person or persons against whom the order is directed have not carried out or feel reluctant to perform. Thus in In the Matter of the Application of Araoye of Ile Esa, [128] the respondent who

---

126 Blackstone Commentaries Vol. 3, 110.

127 (1723) 92 E.R. 818, 819; Fortescue 202, 204. Now vide: *Fawehinmi v Akilu (1987) 1 N.W.L.R.* (pt.51) 554; (1987) 4 N.W.L.R. (pt.67) 797, S.C.; *Garba v University of Maiduguri* (1986) 1 N.W.L.R. (pt. 18) 550.

128 (1884) 12 Q.B.D. 461, 478.

129 (1958) W.R.N.L.R. 36. An appeal from the decision of that case was, however, allowed on the ground that the appellant was not given opportunity to be heard and that the person against whom the mandamus issued had earlier indicated that he was prepared to perform the duty; see *Layanju v Araoye (1959) F.S.C.R. 154*. But the principle established in the High Court in respect of performance of a duty imposed by customary law in that regard being a public duty and grounding the order of

was required by the native law and custom to give approval to the appointment of the applicant to a chieftaincy known as The Esa of Ire refused to do so. It was held that mandamus should issue to compel him to perform the public duty of recognising *the applicant in accordance with native law and custom. In a similar case of Regina v Chief Ozogula II. Ex. parte Chief Ekpenga,*[129] the Federal Supreme Court of Western Nigeria ordered the appellant by mandamus to perform certain traditional ceremonies which by the customary law he was under a duty to perform on the death of a class of chiefs.

This decision has cleared the doubt raised in the case of *Layanju v Araoye* [130] as to the question whether a person who is required by customary law to perform certain chieftaincy ceremony has a public duty to perform. It may be observed that where native law and custom require a person to perform a certain function which the people regard as *sine qua non* in a particular chieftaincy or other matter, and such function is not repugnant to natural justice, equity and good conscience, there is a duty of public nature which should ground mandamus. However, mandamus will not issue unless it is shown that the person who is under such a duty has refused, on demand, to perform it.[131] Nor does mandamus lie to compel exercise of a discretionary power.[132] But the discretion in this respect is a judicial discretion; so that if the person or persons or an inferior tribunal, although having power to exercise a discretion, passes a resolution not to entertain applications having to do with the exercise of a discretion, mandamus, on application to the High Court, will issue to compel the inferior tribunal to accept the applications for consideration by the body in question.[133]

It follows, therefore, that the order of mandamus will issue to compel an inferior tribunal to exercise its jurisdiction where it refuses or feels reluctant to do so, just as prohibition will restrain such a tribunal from exceeding its jurisdiction. An inferior tribunal will be held to have refused to exercise its jurisdiction only when it has been guilty of such a wilful

---

order of mandamus still stands. This had been finally settled by the Federal Supreme Court in the *Queen v Chief Ozogula II Ex parte Chief Ekpenga* (1962) W.N.L.R. 136, post.

130 (1962) W.N.L.R. 136.

131 (1959) F.S.C.R. 154.

132 *ibid.*

133 *The Queen v Western Urhobo Rating Authority, Ex parte Odje* (1961) 1 All N.L.R. 796

134 *Rex v London County Council, Ex parte Corrie* (1918) 1 K.B. 68- held mandamus should issue to compel justices who were to grant licences, to receive application for consideration. They had earlier passed a resolution that no new permits were to be granted.

delay as to amount to a refusal.[134] Equally it has been held that mandamus would lie against magistrates who refused to issue summonses because they 'acted upon a consideration of something extraneous and extra-judicial which ought not to have affected their decision, and which, it seems, was the same as declining jurisdiction.'[135] Again where the justices had asked for money before granting licences, it was held that the illegal collection of money vitiated their determination, resulting in there being no real hearing; consequently mandamus was to go against them.[136]

It must be pointed out that for mandamus to issue, it is necessary to establish a specific legal right in the applicant who may not have a corresponding specific legal remedy. Thus in *Azuike v The Senior Education Officer, Umuahia Province* [137] the applicant who was a candidate at the First School leaving examination of the Eastern Nigeria Ministry of Education claimed that he was successful in the said examination. He supported his claim with a publication in a newspaper called the Eastern Express published at Aba on the 21st February 1962. He claimed that he was one of the eight candidates who were interviewed by the Senior Education Officer, Umuahia. Certificates were issued to successful candidates but none was issued to the applicant; equally the other seven aforementioned candidates received nothing. None of the eight candidates received any communication from the Ministry intimating to them that they were successful in the said examination. The applicant in support of his application for an order of mandamus to compel the respondent to issue him with the said certificate, submitted a document which showed that his and the certificates of some others were "withheld". The High Court of Eastern Nigeria held that the application should be refused. The Court was of the view that the applicant did not establish a clear legal right to warrant a mandamus.

It may be observed that the main pivot in the case should be the establishment of the fact that the applicant did pass his examination. If the Court was satisfied that in absence of fraud, the applicant was successful in the examination and his certificate was in fact "withheld" and the respondent did not satisfy the Court in matters having to do with the alleged interview,

---

35 *R.v. Central professional Committee fcr Opticians, Ex p. Brown* [1949] 2 All F.R. 519. See also *Rex v Port of London Authority, Ex p. Kynoch Ltd.* [1919] 1K.B. 176.

136 *Reg.v. Adamson 7 Others, Justices of North Shields* (1875) 1 Q.B. 201, 2005 per Cockburn, C.J.

137 *Reg.v Adamson & Others Justices* [1898] 1 O.B. 663; see also *Reg. v Cotham & Another, Justices et al* [1898] 1 Q.B. 802 - Justices in exercising their licensing power acted upon considerations outside the statute, he'd determination not according to law, and that mandamus ought to go commanding them so to hear and determine: *Reg. v De Rutzen & Others, justices of Glamorganshire* (1875) 1 Q.B. 55: *Rex v Board of Education* [1910]2 K.B. 165.

138 *Azuike v The Senior Education Officer Umuahia Province*, (unreported yet decided in the High Court of Aba Judicial Division. Eastern Nigeria by Idigbe, J. on 21st Nov. 1963 Suit No. A/M.29/1963.

it would be hard to see why the applicant would be regarded as having failed to establish a legal right to ground a mandamus. He paid 15/6d as entrance fee for the said examination; and if he in fact passed the examination and his result or, a fortiori his certificate was withheld, the Court, on proper proof of the material facts would issue mandamus in that respect.[138] Even though the Court has discretion to issue an order of mandamus and can exercise it one way or the other; nevertheless where the right which the applicant seeks to enforce is the performance of a duty of a public character, which cannot be secured at all if mandamus is refused, the Court should, on proper grounds being established, issue a mandamus.[139] As we have seen earlier, mandamus will issue to compel a public authority to perform a duty which it is required by law to carry out and which it has refused on demand to perform. Where, therefore, say, an education officer, in a proper case, refuses to issue a certificate, mandamus will issue to compel him to carry out his duty which is apparently of a public character.

Thus Chagla, C.J. in *Nayak v Benjan Barucha* said:

> When a writ of mandamus is asked for, the first question that the Court has to determine is whether there is any statutory obligation upon the officer concerned and the next question is whether the officer had failed to discharge that obligation.[140]

It may be said that on tne whole, the application of the high prerogative order of mandamus is wider than the order of certiorari or prohibition for the order of mandamus may lie in cases where neither certiorari nor prohibition may lie. For instance, where the proceedings of an inferior tribunal are regular on their face and the tribunal acted within its jurisdiction neither certiorari nor prohibition may lie; yet if such tribunal, as we have seen has been influenced by extraneous or extra-judicial consideration mandamus will issue to compel the inferior tribunal to act according to law.[141]

4. *Habeas Corpus*

Habeas corpus is a high prerogative writ which is directed to a person who, prima facie, is illegally[142] holding another in custody; and commanding that person to bring the body of the prisoner so that the Court may make some

---

139 See *Dr. Bentley's Case* (1723) 29 E.R. 92 E.R. 818, Mandamus was granted to restore Richard Bentley to his degree of doctor of divinity. He was degraded by a vice-chancellor's court.

141 (1951) 53 Bom. L.R. 654 66i (an Indian case).

142 *R.v Cotham [1898] 1 Q.B. 802; R.v. De Rutzen & Others. Justices of Glamorganshire* (11875) I C.B. 55; *R.v. Adamson & Others, Justices of North Shields* (11875) 1 Q.B. 201.

143 As Coleridge, J. in *Rex v Greenhill* (1830) 111 E.R. 922. 928 put it: A Dabees corpua procede on the fact of an illegal restraint.

order as to what should be done with the person detained.[143] This great bulwark of liberty of the individual is according to Blackstone "directed to the person detaining another, and commanding him to produce the body of the prisoner with the day and cause of its caption and detention, *Ad faciendum subjiciendum et recipiendum*, to do, submit and receive whatsoever the Judge or Court awarding such writ shall consider in that behalf."[144] As all instrument of judicial control, *habeas corpus*, as we shall see presently, is not only very useful but also very effective. Any disobedience to the writ amounts to contempt of court and attracts a heavy penalty.[145]

Habeas corpus is a generic name for a group of writs of very ancient origin.[146] The Common feature of the writs was a command by the Court

---

144 .See *R.v Earl Ferrerb* (1758) 1 Burr. 631; Cox v Hakes (1890) 15 App. Cap. 506; daring do v Rord [1892] A.C. 326: Secretart if *State for Home Affairs v O'Brueb* [1923] A.C. 803, 669; *Zabrovsky v Officer Commanding Palestine* [1947] A.C. 246; In matter of Allen [1860] 30 L.J. Q.B. 38, post.

145 Blackstone Commentaries 3 p. 131

146 In *Search's Case (1588) 1 Leon. 70 74 E.R. 65*, the applicant had been arrested by the Steward of Marshalsey, for himself causing the arrest of one Mabbe (probably according to law). Mabbe had obtained Letters of Protection from the Queen. On application for writ of habeas corpus, the Court of Common Pleas discharged Search from custody, and, on his subsequent re-arrest, the Court issued an attachment against Mabbe and his friends. In a more recent case of *Egan v General Macready and Others* [1921] 1 I.R. (Irish Reports) 265 O'Connor, M.R. held that writ of *habeas corpus* should issue for the release of E From prison because the military tribunal, which was not a court-martial, was 'constituted in some way unknown to the law; - of some military'. When a notice of appeal was given and it was intimated to the Court that the Crown did not propose to release prisoner, what amounted to a dialogue ensued: O'connor M.R. I will not listen to any such to the writ. The writ must be answered in the ordinary way. Has the writ been obeyed? Lynch, K.O.: No.: my Lord. O'Connor, M.R: Then I will order a writ of attachment to issue against the three parties for whom Serjeant Hanna appears. It is a deliberate contempt of court a thing unprecedented in this Court and the whole history of British law. On the following day sergeant Hanna, K.C. stated that the Government had decided to release the prisoner pending the hearing of appeal - *ibid*, at p. 280. The pronouncement of his Lordship was not an over-statement for even in *Darnel's Case (1627) 3 St. Tr.1*, the writ was obeyed; see *infra*. Again in *Homi Rustamjee Pordiwalla v Sub-Inspector Biag & Others A.I.R. (All India Report) (1944) Lab. 196*, a Barrister was arrested in lahore, India, and his *habeas corpus* application was suppressed. The Labore High Court fined the two officers responsible for that for contempt of Court Rs. 100 and 50 each. A strong waming was disused by the Court against any attempt to disobey the writ.

147 These include *habeas corpus ad respondendum, habeas corpus ad satisfiendum, and habeas corpus ad faciendum et recipiendum*, usually known as *habeas corpus cum causa*. Equally there were: (i) writ *de Homine Replegiando* which lay against the sheriff, e.g. royal agent and the private person; (ii) *Writ de Manucaptione* - was only available for persons indicted of larceny before sheriffs by inquest of office and (iii) writ *de Odie et Atia* this lay in favour of a man in prison on an appeal of homicide, i.e. at the suit of a private person. The writ was directed to the Sheriff to hold an inquest whether the accused was accused on good grounds or of 'hatred and malice'. for more details, see *E. Jenks: "The Story of Habeas Corpus"* (190) 18 L. Ć.R.64, see also Maxwell Cohen: *"Some consideration on the Origins of Habeas Corpus" (1938) 16 Can. Bar Rev. 92 and A.T.Markose: Judicial Control of Administrative Action in India (1956)* Madres. P. 113.

for the production of named person before it so that appropriate order might be made by the Court. The term *habeas corpus* which is Latin may be translated: "You must have the body", and the rest of the order goes on: produced before the Court.

Habeas corpus in its long history continues to grow from strength to strength - as a strong weapon by which the Court protects the liberty of the individual. In the year 1588 in *Search's Case,*[147] the Court of Common Pleas discharged, search from unlawful custody, and, when he was re-arrested, the Court issued an attachment against those responsible. In another case, *Howel's Case,*[148] *habeas corpus* was directed to the steward and marshal of Marshalsey, for one Howel who was committed to his Custody. In the return to the writ it was stated that the prisoner was committed *per mandatum Francisci Walsingham Militis Principalis Secreterij et unius de privato concilio deminae reginae.* The Court held the return to a be insufficient, for not stating the cause. Whereupon the steward amended his return and stated that the committal was 'by the opinion and order of the whole privy council'. The Court reluctantly admitted the return as good but emphasised that the prisoner must always be produced and if it shall seem good to the Court, that the prisoner shall have his privilege, and shall be dismissed, he shall be discharged, but if not, then he shall be remanded.' The Court was of the view that if a person was committed by the whole of the Privy Council, no cause for such committal ought to be alleged. Such a situation was obviously not a healthy one for the shield of liberty.

Things appeared to have drifted down to the *Darnel's Case* [149] also known as the *Five Knights' Case.* Darnel and four others were cast into prison because they would not subscribe money to the King, Charles I. The warrant, signed by two members of the Privy council alleged for cause only *per speciale mandatum regis* - by special order of the King. Darnel applied to the king's Bench for a *Habeas Corpus,* which was at once issued. The Court of the King's Bench, after entertaining lengthy arguments in favour of the prisoners remanded them to prison - having, perhaps, at the back of their minds what happened to Sir Edward Coke,[150] the great Judge, when he wanted to defy the King and assert the independence of the judiciary, the Judges of the King's Bench could not do otherwise.

---

148 1 Leo, 70; 14 E.R. 65.

149 1 leanard 74 E.R. 66.

150 (1627) 3 St Tr. 1.

151 See *The case Commendams (1616) Hobart 140 ante*

The case triggered off a wave of reaction culminating in the Petition of Right, 1628[151] This was a victory for the Parliament, for it abolished the power of the Crown to imprison without cause shown; and established that no freeman should be imprisoned or detained without causes being shown. The Petition of Right no doubt helped to improve the position of *Habeas Corpus*, nevertheless the *Habeas Corpus* Acts, 1640,[152] 55 1679[153] and 1816 [154] buttressed and modified the common law prerogative writs. It must, however, be pointed out that by this time *habeas corpus ad subjicicendum* had established itself as the dominant writ. The old common law rules regarding this writ were therefore modified and made more effective by Statute: when therefore we use the term *habeas corpus simpliciter*, we mean *Habeas corpus ad subjiciendum*.

As we pointed our earlier in the chapter, the prerogative writs as part of the common law of England have been 'received' or to be more apposite, inherited in Nigeria as part of our legal system. The rules governing the writ as modified in 1679 continued to operate in many parts of Nigeria. Recently, however, the Western Region enacted a Law known as the Habeas Corpus Law.[155] Section 3 of the law broadly corresponds with section 1 of the 1679 Act. It provides as follows:

> 3. Upon the issue of any writ of habeas corpus directed to any person to produce the body of any prisoner in his custody for any criminal or supposed criminal matter (other than for treason or felony plainly and specially expressed in the warrant of commitment) and the said writ being served in accordance with the provisions of this Law, the person to whom the writ is directed shall, within three days after the service of the writ, make return thereto or bring or cause to be brought the body of the prisoner before the court (i.e. the High Court) by which the writ was issued or before any judge before whom the writ is made returnable and shall then certify the true cause of the prisoner's commitment and detainer.

The enactment[156] then dealt with application for the writ to a judge in vacation. It provides that if any prisoner is committed or in custody during a vacation, he or any person on his behalf may apply to any judge, who shall upon production of a copy of the warrant of commitment or of an affidavit that a copy of such warrant was refused to be given to the applicant by the person by whom the prisoner is detained, and upon a request in writing by the applicant attested and subscribed by two witnesses present at the making

---

152 3 Car. I.C. 1.

153 16 Car. I.C. 10.

154 31 Car. 2 C.2.

155 56 Geo. 3. C. 100

156 Cap. 42 Laws of the Western Region of Nigeria, 1959 vol. II.The Law in its marginal notes refers to sections of the Habeas Corpus Act, 1679, 31 Car. II C. 2., see Statues at Large Vol. 8 p. 432 for the Act of 1679.

157 S.5. *ibid*, this broadly corresponds with section 10 of the 1676 act, *ibid*.

making thereof, issue a writ of *habeas corpus* under the seal of the court, directed to the Officer or person in whose custody the prisoner is detained. The section then prescribes penalty for any such judge refusing to issue the writ by providing that "if any judge refuses any writ of *habeas corpus* required by this section to be issued upon being moved for as aforesaid, he shall forfeit to the prisoner or person aggrieved the sum of five hundred pounds to be recovered by action as for debt in any court of competent jurisdiction."

As we have seen the Courts do not hesitate to inflict heavy penalty for disobedience to the writ. The Law, like the Habeas Corpus Act, 1679 makes that abundantly clear by providing as follows:

> "6(1) If any person to whom a writ of habeas corpus is directed or his servant or agent neglects or refuses to make due return to the writ habeas corpus or to bring the body of the prisoner according to the demand thereof within the time prescribed by this Law, or upon demand made by the prisoner or any person on his behalf refuses to deliver or within six hours after such demand does not deliver to the person so demanding a true copy of the warrant of commitment of such prisoner, every such person in whose custody the prisoner is detained shall for the first offence forfeit to the prisoner or person aggrieved the sum of one hundred pounds and for the second offence the sum of two hundred pounds and shall be and is hereby made incapable of holding or executing this office."[157]

No prisoner delivered or set free upon any writ of habeas corpus shall at any time be again committed or imprisoned for the same offence by any person whatsoever other than by the legal order and process of the High Court. If any person acts in contravention of the Law by knowingly recommitting or imprisoning the person or causing him to be recommitted or imprisoned he shall forfeit to the prisoner or person aggrieved, the sum of five hundred pounds to be recovered by an action as for debt in any court of competent jurisdiction.[158]

As we have seen, the common law rules regarding habeas corpus were made more effective by statute. The Habeas Corpus Act, 1816[159] in section two provides that any disobedience of the writ amounts to contempt of court and punishable as such. Equally section 13 of the *Habeas Corpus* Law, Western Region, provides that if any person to whom a writ of habeas is directed, upon service of such writ, wilfully neglects or refuses to make a return to or obey such writ he shall be deemed guilty of a contempt of the Court.

The grant of the writ of habeas corpus appears to be in some cases at the discretion of the court and in some other obligatory. Thus for the writ

---

158 *ibid.* See also S.4 of the 1679 Act.

159 S.7, *ibid.* Cf. of the 1679 Act.

160 56 Geo. 3 C.100, Statutes at Large (1816) 56 p.505

to issue, the applicant must establish a *prima facie case* regarding the illegality of the restraint or imprisonment. Up to that stage, therefore, it may be said to be discretionary, for it is for the Court to decide whether or not such a case has been made out. After a *prima facie* has been established, the court is bound to issue the writ. This view buttressed by section 10 of the 1679 Act and section 5 of the Western Region Law which impose a penalty of five hundred pounds on a judge refusing to grant the writ during vacation. Such amount shall be payable to the prisoner or person aggrieved. The gravity of such refusal is borne out by the fact that in 1969 the penalty was five hundred pounds, although not very frequently employed like the prerogative orders, is still an effective instrument with which the High Court controls inferior tribunals; and in some cases even private individuals when they subject others to illegal imprisonment.[160] It is however hard to see cases in our society to-day where an individual can arrogate to himself the power to imprison, say his debtor without the authorities intervening. Where therefore, an inferior tribunal acts without jurisdiction and a person is sent to prison thereby, habeas corpus will issue to deliver him from the illegal imprisonment. Thus in *In Re Native Court of Onitsha.*[161] N who was a witness for the defence in a charge against two men in a Native court, was himself brought before the same court on a charge of inciting two men to perform second burial in a way 'contrary to native law and custom.' Instead of convicting him for the charge the Native Court convicted him on what they thought to be an offence but for what the accused was never charged. The court members recorded a conviction in the following terms: "Accused one (1) year. I.H.L. (that is, imprisonment with hard) for refusing to ask peace from Obi Kosi (the chief) and complainant." He was accordingly sent to prison to serve term.

He applied to the Station Magistrate who was vested with the power to review the decisions of the Native Court but the Magistrate refused to exercise his statutory power. No appeal lay to the then supreme Court (i.e.

---

161 The writ was used to set free slaves during the period when slavery was still lawful in some parts of the world; See *Sommersett's Case (1772) 20 St. Tr.1; Forbes v Coobrane (11815) 2 B. & C. 448* and in *The Slave Grave (1827) 2 Hag. Adm.*: It was held slavery was illegal in England, thus while in England *habeas corpus* would issue to free a slave.

162 (1928) 9 N.L.R. 65; see also *Mark Porrtt's case (1844) Oriental Cases by F. Perry p. 414*, where an inferior tribunal, i.e. a court martial convicted an army officer of embezzlement and frau and sentenced to be 'transported as a felon for seven years.' Under the statute, i.e. Indian Mutiny Act, 3 & Vict. C.37, the sentence must be confirmed by the commander-in-chief in the area, i.e.Bombay Presidency. Instead of conforming with the statute in this regard, the Governor, C.J. Hapier "approved and confirmed" the sentence. While the prisoner was about to be deported, he applied for a writ of habeas corpus, questioning the legality of the proceedings. Perry, J. held that as the Governor acted without jurisdiction, and as confirmation of the sentence of the court martial was vital for its legality, the prisoner was being held without legal justification. Habeas corpus was granted and he was discharged - the commander-in-chief having intimated that he did not intend to subject the prisoner to what would amount to a new trial.

the High court.) Whereupon the prisoner applied to the Supreme Court for *habeas corpus*, on the ground that the court acted without jurisdiction. Few, J. held that as the Native Court acted without jurisdiction the Supreme Court had power to interfere to right the wrong in the interest of justice. Consequently *habeas corpus* issued for the release of the applicant from the illegal detention. The Learned Judge after observing that the station Magistrate was wrong in refusing to exercise his power of review of the decision of the Native Court as provided in section 17 of the Native Court Ordinance in favour of the applicant in view of the extremely harsh sentences stated that the Magistrate would not have allowed such a sentence to stand, 'if he had not been influenced by extra-judicial considerations'. He then went on to say: 'The offence of which the applicant was convicted was quite different from the offence with which he was charged. If the Court had imposed a punishment which it was not empowered to impose by the terms of its warrant, it seems to me quite clear that this Court could issue a writ of *habeas corpus* on the ground that the Native Court had acted without jurisdiction, just as much as if the person sentenced had been a person not subject to the jurisdiction of the Court and not consenting thereto, If then a Court sentences a person to imprisonment for an offence other than that with which he has been charged and for which he has been tried, is it going too far to say that that court had acted without jurisdiction and that this Court, though it cannot entertain an appeal, will intervene to prevent an illegal sentence from being carried into effect."[162]

As we have shown, a decision reached by an inferior tribunal when acting without jurisdiction is a nullity. It follows then that as the Native court acted without jurisdiction in that respect, the inevitable consequence was that the sentence and imprisonment were without legal validity and habeas corpus rightly issued to deliver the applicant from illegal detention. Another point which was not taken up in the case was, by convicting a person of an offence quite different from the one with which he was charged under the circumstances amounted to not giving him opportunity to be heard in his defence. This is obviously contrary to natural justice and had been equated with acting without jurisdiction.[163] Such a decision in breach of natural justice, although only voidable is liable to be avoided by the High court. And in the case under consideration, as the Station Magistrate refused to review the case and set aside the apparent illegal decision of the inferior tribunal, the High court (the then supreme Court) rightly intervened to right the wrong with a writ of *habeas corpus*.

---

163 *ibid*, at p. 69

164 *Regina v Paddington North and St. Marylebone Rent Tribunal, Ex p. Perry [1956] 1 Q.B. 229, 237 ante.*

The above case may be favourably compared with the case of *In Re Allen*[164] on the specific point of the issue of habeas corpus in case of illegal detention in prison. In that case, A, a military officer on service in the East Indies was rightly tried and convicted of manslaughter by a general court martial. The court-martial derived its jurisdiction from section 40 of the Mutiny Act, 1857.[165] A was sentenced to 4 years imprisonment. The proceedings took place in the East Indies and the prisoner was to serve his sentence there. But after some months at Agra he was directed to be removed to England in military custody to complete the term of his sentence. The manner of his transfer to a prison in England was not in conformity with the provisions of the Act. Allen applied for a writ of habeas on the ground that his detention in a prison in England was illegal. Cockburn, C.J., after examining the relevant provisions held that 'there is no order in writing under either of these sections (i.e. Sections 40 and 41 of the 1847 Act), by virtue of which the keeper of the Queen's Prison can keep Lieutenant Allen in custody'.[166] The writ of habeas corpus was consequently granted for the release of the prisoner.

There was no doubt as to the legality of the conviction of the prisoner. But the matter did not rest there; the legality of his being kept in the prison in England was not established to the satisfaction of the Court with the result that the detention was held illegal. Being illegal, the prisoner was entitled to be discharged on a writ of *habeas corpus*. It must be pointed out, however, that the High Court does not and cannot grant writ of habeas corpus to a person serving a term of imprisonment prescribed by a tribunal of competent jurisdiction.[167] But if a person is kept in prison after expiration of his term of imprisonment the writ will issue to deliver him.[168] Equally *habeas corpus* will issue to deliver a person from unjustifiable restriction imposed by the order of the executive. Thus in *Eshugbayi Eleko v Officer Administering the Government of Nigeria,*[169] the Governor of Nigeria, purporting to act under the Deposed Chiefs Removal Ordinance, ordered the appellant to 'leave the Colony (of Lagos) and the province of Abeokuta, Ijebu and Ondo' within a specified time. when the order was not obeyed, the Governor then ordered that the said Eleko be deported 'forthwith to Oyo in the Province of Oyo.' The Eleko was ordered into custody, and while he was there he applied for writ of *habeas corpus*; contending

165 (1860) 30 L.J. Q.B. 38.

166 20 Vict. C. 13.

167 (1860) 30 L.J. Q.B. at p.44.

168 Where there is error of law in the conviction and right of appeal exists, the remedy lies only in appeal, *Gwaram v Superintendent of Prisons, Kano [1960] N.R. N.L.R. 5.*

169 *Re Featherstone (1953) 37 Cr. App. R. 146*

170 [1931] A.C. 662; see also *Reg. v Governor of Brixton Prison, Ex parte Armah [1966] 3 W.L.R. 828*

(i) that he was not a native chief,
(ii) that he had not been deposed
(iii) that there was no native law and custom which required him to leave the area, and that consequently the conditions did not exist entitling the Governor (under the Ordinance) to make the said orders.

Having failed in the Supreme Court of Nigeria, the appellant appealed to the Privy Council which allowed the appeal, thus reversing the judgment of the Full Court of the Supreme Court. Their Lordships directed that a rule nisi should be made to order 'the officer administering the Government of Nigeria and the District Officer of Oyo to show cause why a writ of habeas corpus should not issue directed to them to have the body of Eshughayi, Eleko, immediately before the Court at Lagos to undergo and receive all and singular such matters and things as the Court shall then and there consider of concerning him in this behalf.'[170] The grounds to be investigated according to their Lordships order corresponded with those listed as objections by the Eleko.

It follows therefore that those grounds established *prima facie* case for the grant of habeas corpus; consequently as the High Court failed to issue the writ, an appeal from the decision of the Supreme Court which affirmed the decision of the High Court was allowed by the Judicial Committee of the Privy Council. In an earlier case. *Eshugbayi Eleko v Officer Administering the Government of Nigeria, (No. 1)* [171] the Privy Council allowed the appeal of Eleko from the decision of the Full Court of the Supreme Court which decided that where an application for a writ of habeas corpus was refused by a Judge of the Supreme Court (i.e. the High Court) no other Judge of the Court, on the same facts, had jurisdiction to entertain another application. Delivering the judgment of the Board, Lord Hailsham, L.C. stated:[172] 'If it be conceded that any judge has jurisdiction to order the writ to issue, then in the view of their Lords each judge is a tribunal to which application can be made within the meaning of the rule, and every judge must hear the application on the merits. It follows that, although by the Judicature Act the Courts have been combined into one High Court of Justice each of that Court still has jurisdiction to entertain an application for a writ of habeas corpus in term or in vacation, and that he is bound to hear and determine such an application on its merits notwithstanding that some other judge has already refused a similar application. The same principle must apply in case of the judges of the Supreme Court of Nigeria.'

---

171 *ibid*, at p. 675.

172 [1929] A.C. 459.

173 *ibid.*, at p. 468.

This rule of successive applications may be said to be the law on the subject in Nigeria although some doubt has been cast on it by a recent English decision of *In re Hastings (No. 2)* [173] where it was held that an applicant for a writ of *habeas corpus* in a criminal cause or matter, who had once been heard by a Divisional Court of the Queen's Bench Division could not be heard again, on a renewal application made on the same evidence and on the same grounds.

Compared with other prerogative orders it may be said that the writ of *habeas corpus* is a powerful wind which knows no restraint when it blows to carry away to freedom a person in an illegal detention. It is a writ of right and granted *ex debito justitae*.[174] To decide on the validity of a detention habeas corpus may review any act judicial, quasi-judicial or administrative or even private while if the order for the detention is purely private mandamus will have no place and if it is ministerial the other two prerogative orders will not be helpful. From this point of view, it may be said that the writ of habeas corpus takes pride of place amongst the prerogative Orders as an instrument of control in the hands of the High Court. It may be suggested that other states in Nigeria should follow the example of the then Western Region in embodying in a new enactment the provision of the Habeas Corpus Acts 1679 and 1816. This will not only enhance uniformity in the law but also help to make more accessible documents embodying the law on the subject.

Declaratory Judgment

From the realm of common law instruments of judicial control we now come to a comparatively new and growing remedy popularly known as action for declaration. We have, however, adopted the term declaratory judgment in that it appears to be more apposite; for as will be seen presently in this part of our study, force behind this instrument of judicial control lies in the generally recognised sanctity of judicial decision. Declaration therefore, differs from other remedies in that it does not carry the sanction of attachment and committal for contempt of court. But this in practice does

---

[174] [1959] 1 Q.B. 358. This decision has been statutorily approved. See S.14 (2) of the Administration of Justice Act, 1960, S & 9 Eliz. 2 C. 65 which provides that 'Notwithstanding anything in any enactment or rule of law, where a criminal or civil application for habeas corpus has been made by or in respect of any person, no such application shall again be made by or in respect of that person on the same grounds, whether to the court or judge or to any other court or judge, unless fresh evidence is adduced in support of the application; and no such application shall in any case be made to the Lord Chancellor.'

[175] *R. v Cowle (1759) 2 Burr. 834. 855* per Lord Manfield, C.J., *Re Newton (1849) 13 Q.B.D. 716*. Release on *habeas corpus* is not, however, an acquittal: *R.v Officer Commanding Depot Battalion, R.A.S.C., Colchester, Ex parte Millot, [1949] 1 All F.R. 373, 379* per Lord Goddard C.J. Nor may habeas corpus be used as a means of appeal: *Gwaram v Superintendent of Prisons, Kano [1960] N.R.N.L.R. 5; Ex parte Corke [1954] 2 All E.R. 440.*

not appear to reduce the value of this flexible remedy. The issue determined by a declaratory judgment becomes *res judicata*. The judgment forms a binding precedent.

In an action for declaration the plaintiff does not pray for any order requiring the defendant to act as in mandamus or refrain from acting as in prohibition or injunction. He merely asks the Court to declare his legal position *vis-a-vis* the defendant. For example, that the plaintiff is under no duty to do something; or that he has a right, power or privilege; and in the sphere of private law mostly, that the defendant is under a duty to do something or is liable to the plaintiff in the matter.

The origin of action for declaration has been linked with what is known to Scottish law since the middle of 16th century and called "action of declaration."[175] Borchard points out that England came to adopt this judicial measure through the long agitation of Lord Brougham who in steering his bills through the House of Commons eloquently showed the amount of benefits enjoyed by Scotland in enabling persons who apprehend future litigation to proceed by way of a declaratory action to have their rights determined. The efforts to enshrine vividly this valuable instrument of judicial control and remedy into the English legal system came to full fruition in 1850. By the Chancery Act of 1850[176] (described as 'An Act to diminish the Delay and Expense or Proceedings in the High Court of chancery in England'), it was provided that the High Court of Chancery after hearing a case shall have the power "to determine the Questions raised therein or any of them, and by Decree to declare its Opinion thereon, and so far as the Case shall admit of the same, upon the Right involved therein, without proceeding to administer any Relief consequent upon such Declaration; and that every such Declaration of the said Court contained in

---

176 See E. Borchard: *Declaratory Judgments (1941 2nd ed.) p. 125*. Delivering his opinion in the House of Lords in the case of *Earl of Mansfield v Stewart (1846) 5 Bell 139. 160* Lord Brougham stressed how advantageous declaratory action could be as evidenced in Scotland. He said: 'I cannot close my observation in this case without once more expressing my great envy, as an English lawyer, of the scotch Jurisprudence, and of those who enjoy, under it, the security and the various facilities and conveniences which they have from that most beneficial and most admirably contrived form of proceeding called a declaratory action. Here, you must wait till a party chooses to bring you into court, here, you must wait till possibly your evidence is gone; here, you have no means whatever, in ninety cases out of a hundred, of obtaining the great benefit of this proceeding.' See also *"Developments in the Law: Declaratory Judgments - 1941-1949" (1949) 62 Harvard Law Rev. 787, esp. 790-91. It may be observed however, that Hodge v Att-Gen. (1839) 3Y. & C. (Yound & Collyer) Ex.343, 160 Eng. R. 734* suggest very strongly that declaratory judgment was not unknown to the Exchequer Division for in that case it was held that the Court could 'declare the plaintiffs as equitable mortgagees, entitled to hold possession of the property until the Crown should think fit to redeem.' The Court however, declined to decree the sale of the legal estate (because of lack of jurisdiction) as it vested in the crown. Vide equally: *Olaniyan v. University Lagos (1985) 2 NWLR (Pt.9) 599 SC*. Now under S. 6 (6) (b) of the 1979 Constitution a person can sue any Government in Nigeria.

177 13 & 14 Vict. C. 35

any such Decree shall have the same Force and Effect as such Declaration would have had, and shall be binding to the same Extent as such Declaration would have been, if contained in a Decree made in a suit between the same parties instituted by Bill."[177] The Court was also empowered, 'if it shall see fit so to do' to send any case or cases for the opinion of any of the Common Law Courts before proceeding to make the declaration. Equally the Court was given the power to refuse to decide a case, i.e. to make a declaration 'if it shall be of opinion that the questions raised thereby cannot be properly decided upon.'

There is no doubt that this enactment contemplated vesting in the Court wide powers to make declarations at its discretion. Again, in 1852 an Act [178] provided that "No Suit in the said Court (i.e. the High Court of Chancery) shall be open to objection on the Ground that a merely declaratory Decree or Order is sought thereby, and it shall be lawful for the Court to make binding Declarations of Right without granting consequential Relief. Despite the seemingly extensive powers granted under these enactments, the judges resorted to giving them very restrictive constructions[179] which nearly defeated the objects of the Act.

However, the reforms introduced by the Judicature Act of 1873 paved the way for remedying the situation. In 1883 the Supreme Court of Judicature under its rule-making power promulgated the celebrated Order XXV, Rule 5. This Order which more particularly aimed at removing the obstacle placed in the law by the decision in *Rooke v Lord Kensington* [180] provides that "No action or proceeding shall be open to objection, on the ground that a merely declaratory judgment is sought thereby, and the Court may make binding declarations of right whether any consequential relief is or could be claimed or not."[181] By the Order it was made abundantly clear that a plaintiff could not only ask for affirmative declaration, that is to say, that he had right but also could pray for a negative declaration, i.e. that defendant had no right, thus absolving the plaintiff of any liability likely to be claimed by the defendant. Thus in *Guaranty trust Company of New York v Hannay & Company*,[182] the Court of appeal held that the Court had power under the said Order XXV rule 5 to make a declaration at the instance of a plaintiff to the effect that the plaintiff was not liable to the defendant in an existing or possible action. The action referred to in that case was

---

178 S.14, *ibid.*

179 *Chancery Procedure Act, 1952, 15 & 16 vict. c. 86.*

180 See *Garlick v Lawson (1853) 10 Hare, App.I xii; 68 Eng. 391; 44 E.R. 441: Bright v Tyndall (1876) 4 Ch.D. 1189, 196; Rooke v Lord Kensington (1856) 2 K. & J. 753; 69 E Rep.,986* - no jurisdiction to render declaration in absence of right to coercive relief.

181 *ibid.*

182 See 7 Statutory Rules and Orders 54 (1883).

183 [1915] 2 K.B. 536.

case was pending in a court in the United States where a new trial had been ordered. In his judgment Bankes, L.J. stated that 'the framers of the rule must have had the previously existing practice in mind, and have provided both for the case of declarations of right and those which are not.'[183] The judgment demonstrates vividly that a plaintiff need no longer have a cause of action to entitle him to the relief. However, the relief claimed must be something which it would not be unlawful or unconstitutional or inequitable for the Court to grant. Also, the relief does not extend to enable a stranger to the transaction to go and ask the court to express its opinion in order to help him in other transactions.

It may be expedient at this stage to consider whether action for declaration is a legal or equitable remedy or relief. It seems to be the general view that the remedy is neither legal (i.e. common-law) or equitable. It is therefore *sui generis;* [184] for it seems to be as much legal as equitable. The relief is, for instance, not subject to the restrictions of equity that irreparable injury or inadequacy of legal remedy be alleged or established. In *Chapman v Michaelson* [185] Cozens-Hardy, M.r. stated: 'The simple answer is that this is not an equitable relief. It is mere accident that the judgment has been given in the Chancery Division and not in the King's Bench Division, since this action might perfectly well have been brought in the Common Law Courts." Agreeing with the view Farewell, L.J. added that 'you cannot now have recourse to the old equitable practice to explain, and still less to limit, a novel practice created by the Judicature Act and a power given to the High Court and not to one division of the High court to the exclusion of the other.'

Although Order XXV Rule 5 greatly enhanced the efficacy of declaratory action, the decision in 1911 in the case of *Dyson v Attorney-General* [186] resuscitated the jurisdiction of the High court to award declaratory judgment against the Crown represented by the Attorney-General.[187] In that case the Court of Appeal held that the Court had jurisdiction to declare that certain forms signed by the secretary to the

---

[184] *ibid.*, at p.571. Pickford L.J. expressed similar views when he said: 'I think therefore that the effect of the rule is to give a general power to make a declaration whether there be a cause of action of not, and at the instance of any party who is interested in the subject-matter of the declaration". - ibid, at p. 562.

[185] See *Crollard v Northern Life Ins. Co. 200 S.W. 2nd (1947) 375; Cobb v Harrington (1945) 144 Tex. 36; 190 s.W. 2d 709* (American cases).

[186] [1909] 1 Ch. 238 at 242. See also *Gray v Spyer [1921] 2 Ch. 549 at 557* where Younger L.J. expressed the view that the re-lief is 'neither law nor equity' And in *Ansford v New Plymouth Finance C. Ltd. [1933] N.S.L.R. 209 at 214*, reed J. stated that action for declaration 'was not a proceeding seeking equitable relief' - (securities declared illegal and void). However equitable principles are prayed in aid by the Courts where useful.

[187] [1911] 1 K.B. 410; [1912] 1 Ch. 158.

[188] See *Hodge and Others v Attorney-General (1839) 3 Y. & co. Ex 343, 160 E.R. 734. Supra.*

Commissioners of Inland Revenue requiring the plaintiff to deliver certain returns under a penalty not exceeding #50 were invalid and that the plaintiff was entitled to disregard them. That is to say, that he was under no obligation to comply with the requisitions in any of the forms. It is difficult to resist quoting the lucid judicial pronouncement of Cozens-Hardy, M.R. in this famous case. He said:

> "It is urged that in the present action no relief is sought except by declaration, and that no such relief ought to be granted against the Crown, there being no precedent for any such action. The absence of any precedent does not trouble me. The power to make declaratory decrees was first granted to the Court of Chancery in 1852 by section 50 of 15 and 16 Victoria, Chapter 86, under which it was held that a declaratory decree could only be granted in cases in which there was some equitable relief which might be granted if the plaintiff chose to ask for it: See *Rooke v Lord Kensington (1856) 2 K. & J. 753*. The jurisdiction is, however, now enlarged by Order XXV, rule 5... I can see no reason why this section should not apply to an action in which the Attorney-General, as representing the Crown, is a party."[188]

From what we have seen in Chapter two, dealing with the reception of English law and earlier in this chapter, it will now be evident that a large part of the Nigeria Law originated from English law. There is no doubt that the enactments dealing with declaratory judgment were received in Nigeria as 'statutes of general application'. It may, therefore, be said that this historical account on the subject is a historical account of part of English as well as Nigeria legal system. In some cases, however, certain enactments in Nigeria have expressly incorporated by reference the powers and jurisdiction of the High court of Justice in England, to be exercised by the High Court in Nigeria. For example, Section II of the then High court Law of Northern Nigeria provides that the Court shall possess and exercise all the jurisdiction powers and authorities which are vested in or capable of being exercised by Her Majesty's High Court of Justice in England.

In *Olawoyin v Attorney-General, Northern Region* [189] Usworth, F.J. dealing with the section of the High Court law[190] observed that 'the High Court of Justice in England) the same power to make a declaratory judgment under Order XXV Rule 5 of the Rules of Supreme Court.' "It may be observed that the Order referred to is applicable throughout Nigeria. *Olawoyin's case* is very important in that it decided that the High court has jurisdiction to make a declaratory judgment at the instance of a party interested in the subject-matter having to do with fundamental rights entrenched in the Constitution. It was pointed out in the case that as there

---

189 [1911] 1 K.B. at p.417.

190 [1961] 1 All N.L.R. 269.

191 Section 11 of the 1955 High Court Law, N.R., now see s.13 of the high Court law, Northern Region Cap. 49, Laws of Northern Nigeria, 1963 vol. II.

was no express exclusion of High Court's jurisdiction in this regard, such jurisdiction was unaffected by the Constitutional provisions.

It follows therefore that the High court has jurisdiction in an action for declaration to inquire into the constitutionality of an enactment. Also where a person is empowered by the Constitution to do something, the High Court will entertain a declaratory action challenging the conduct of such person in carrying out his function.[191] Equally where a person feels that his constitutional or legal right has been infringed by the executive, an action for declaration may be the best method of getting redress.[192] And where statute does not expressly and effectively exclude the jurisdiction of the High court, a person can pray for and obtain a declaration that installation of a person to a certain chieftaincy by kingmakers is contrary to the local Native Law and custom.[193] Again where a public officer was empowered to declare a customary law pertaining to the appointment to a certain chieftaincy, an action for declaration was held to lie to the effect that the Minister, (who was here held to be a public officer') made an invalid declaration.[194]

Declaratory judgment is increasingly becoming the most popular means of controlling inferior tribunals. In *Barnard and Others v National Dock Labour and Others*,[195] the London Dock labour Board, purporting to exercise their statutory powers delegated their disciplinary functions to a port manager. This was contrary to the Dock Workers (Regulation Employment) Order, 1947 which required the Board to delegate such powers to 'local board'. The plaintiffs were suspended by the manager. Appeals by the plaintiffs to the appeal tribunal were dismissed. In an action for declaration the plaintiffs prayed the Court to declare that they were wrongly suspended and that the original notices of suspension served on them were *ultra vires* and invalid. The Court of Appeal had no difficulty in declaring that the local board had no power express or implied to delegate its quasi-judicial disciplinary functions to the port manager. Such action being *ultra vires*, the suspensions and decisions of the appeal tribunal were complete nullity. In an earlier case of *Cooper v wilson*,[196] the watch

---

192 *Akintola v Aderemi (Governor of Western Nigeria) [1962] 1 All H.L.R. 442. ante.*

193 *Adegbenro v The Attorney-General of the Federation and Others [1962] 1 All N.L.R. 431; Dr Chike Obi v Waziri [1961] 1 All N.L.R. 37; Ndiwe v Waziri [1963] 1 Nigeria Bar Journal 39 ante.*

194 *Ademola II & Others v Akinwande Thomas & Others (1946) 12 W.A.C.A 81.*

195 *Odubote v The Minister of Local Government and Minister of Chieftaincy Affairs for Western Nigeria [1962] W.N.L.R. 112.*

196 [1953] 2 Q.B. 18.

197 [1937] 2 K.B.309; see also *Davis v Carew-pole & Others [1956] 1 WL.R. 833*, which shows that the High Court has power to exercise control over Domestic tribunal. It was held that the plaintiff was entitled to a declaration that the action of the National Hunt Committee in declaring him 'a disqualified person' was *ultra vires* and void.

committee of the Liverpool City Council dismissed a police serjeant who had already terminated his service by due notice of resignation. There was also an infringement of the rule of natural justice in the proceeding before the committee owing to the presence of the chief constable during the committee's deliberations. The Court of Appeal held that on both grounds the serjeant was entitled to a declaration that the order of the watch committee was invalid. Again in *Vine v National Dock Labour Board,*[197] the House of Lords upheld the decision of Ormerod J. in granting damages and a declaration to a dock worker that his dismissal was illegal, *ultra vires* and void because the local labour board had no power to delegate to a disciplinary committee their disciplinary powers.

The value of declaratory judgment cannot be over-emphasized, the flexibility of it makes it applicable in a great number of cases[198] and it is not saddled by restrictions and conditions precedent which predominate in the common-law remedies or instruments of judicial control, nor is it riddled so much by the niceties of equity. All that is required of a plaintiff is to establish a *locus standi*' that is to say, that he has sufficient or material interest in the matter. The Court in exercise of its discretion will refuse to entertain a case where the plaintiff fails to establish a *locus standi*, for before granting a declaration the Court will be satisfied that the plaintiff had suffered a damage or is in the immediate danger of suffering a damage. In *Olawoyin v Attorney-General, Northern Region* [199] it was held that only a person who was in imminent danger of coming into conflict with a legislation or whose normal business or other activities had been interfered with by or under the enactment could obtain a declaration that the Law was unconstitutional. As the plaintiff could not establish such standing, the High Court could not make a declaration *in vacuo*. In an American case of *Commonwealth of Massachusetts v Mellon.*[200] Mr. Justice Sutherland delivering the opinion of the Supreme Court stated: 'The party who invokes

---

198 [1957] A.C. 488.

199 For example, in purely private law, declaratory judgment is very valuable. Thus in *Onyekonwu v Okeke [1961] E.N.L.R. 48*, the High Court of Eastern Nigeria granted a declaration to the effect that an "Okpala" i.e. the first son in the family had no legal power to effect an 'out-right' sale of an 'ancestral' land. That is to say, that the Okpala held only a life interest in the family land and could not sell it without the consent of the members of the family. See also *Alade v Bucknor [1962] W.N.L.R. 67* where a sale of such land was declared void by the High Court of Western Nigeria. Declaratory action is widely employed in the field of land law, where because of concept of ownership of land in African customary law, there is always the tendency to go to the Court to declare that one piece of land or the other belongs to the plaintiff or his family; see for example, *Madukolu v Nkemdilim [1962] 1 All N.L.R. 67; Solaru v seriki [1962] 2 All N.L.R. 180; Alade v Aborisade (1962) W.N.L.R. 74*. It was also used to challenge appointment of additional traditional member of a local council: *Conde v The Minister of Local Govt., Western region of Nigeria [1962] 2 All N.L.R. 186*; and appointment of a special Member of a House of Assembly: *Fashanu v Governor, Western Region [1955-6] W.R.N.L.R.138*.

201 262 U.S. 447, 488 (1923).

the power must be able to show not only that the statute is invalid but that he has sustained or is immediately in danger of sustaining some direct injury as the result of its enforcement and not merely that he suffers in some indefinite way in common with people generally.' A similar decision was arrived at in the case of *Onyia v Governor in Council, Western Region and Others.* [201] The Court made it clear that an individual cannot institute a proceeding in his private capacity to enforce a public right unless he can show that he has a particular or special interest in the matter or that he has sustained special damage over and above that suffered by members of the public generally.

It may be observed that because of the flexibility of declaratory action, coupled with less antagonism between the parties - as opposed to proceedings for coercive remedies, the remedy is growing somehow to the disadvantage of the common-law remedies or instruments of judicial control. However, a person praying the High Court for a declaration will be better advised to couple that with a supplication for injunction where necessary, to enhance the efficacy of the declaratory judgment. Thus in *Law v Chartered Institute of Patent Agents*,[202] the plaintiff sought for a declaration that the proceedings of an inferior or domestic tribunal were invalid and an injunction to restrain the members from erasing his name from the Register of Patent Agents. Eve, J. held that because the tribunal was acting judicially, but while doing so, wrongly acted as both accusers and judges, the rule of natural justice was infringed; consequently the plaintiff was entitled to the declaration and injunction sought.

Injunction

Having seen how useful declaratory judgement is, we now come to what is purely in the domain of equity. An injunction, which is an equitable remedy, is a judicial order restraining the commission or continuation of a wrongful act. Compared with other methods of judicial control which we have seen, injunction operates mostly as a private law remedy. Nevertheless, whenever injunction is employed as an instrument of control of an inferior tribunal by the High Court, the efficacy cannot be doubted. Being a coercive measure, a disregard of an order of the Court issued as an injunction will amount to contempt of court and punishable as such.

If an injunction forbids commission or continuation of an act, it is said to be prohibitory; where it orders a positive act to be done as a reparation, it

---

202 (1962) 2 All N.L.R. 174. See also *Ekundare v Governor in Council, Western Region et al. (1961) 1 All N.L.R. 149; Clark v Epsom Rural District Council (1929) 1 Ch. 287; London Passenger Transport Board v Moscrop (1942) A.C. 332* (no interference with any private right of respondent, he was not entitled to a declaration that the condition was unlawful without joining the Attorney-General as a party).

203 (1919) 2 Ch. 276.

is *mandatory*. The latter is however sparingly granted. The remedy is further divided into what are known as *perpetual* and *interlocutory* injunctions. A perpetual[203] injunction issues after a judicial determination of an issue; while an interlocutory one is granted soon after a writ has been issued, directing immediate cessation of the act complained of whilst the matter is being determined by the Court.[204] In certain cases, however, the Court will require a plaintiff to give an undertaking to indemnify the defendant for any financial loss resulting from such interlocutory injunction if the plaintiff fails in his action.

Historically this remedy was developed by the Court of Chancery as far back as the 14th century - especially in the field of private law. By the sixteenth century, however, the Court of Exchequer extended its jurisdiction into the sphere of equity. This assumption of general equitable jurisdiction which was described by Pollock C.B. as usurpation [205] was resisted for sometime but later acquiesced in. The relief granted by the Court of Exchequer in this field included injunction. With regard to the Court of Chancery, injunction was a strong weapon with which it used to restrain persons from enforcing Common Law rights in violation of equitable principles. This particular injunction was known as common injunction. The Common Law Courts vigorously resisted this exercise of equitable jurisdiction. The matter came to a climax during the reign of James I in the *Earl of Oxford's Case*.[206] Ellesmere, the Lord Chancellor and Sir Edward Coke, the Chief Justice clashed. The former asserted the right to exercise the equitable jurisdiction by common injunction, but the latter disputed that. The Chancellor sternly maintained that the Court of Chancery had the right to set aside judgments obtained by oppression or fraud, "not for any error or defect in judgment, but for the hard conscience, of the

---

204 See *Niger Chemists Ltd. v Nigeria Chemists (1961) 1 All N.L.R. 171, post; J. Lyons & Sons v Wilkins (1899) 1 Ch. 255* - perpetual injunction granted to restrain defendants from watching or besetting either the plaintiffs' workers or the works of a sub-manufacturer for the purpose of persuading or otherwise preventing persons from working for them; see also *The Taff Vale Railway Company v The Amalgamated Society of Railway Servants (1901) A.C. 426, 432; Hendricks v Montagu (1881) 17 Ch.D. 638; North Cheshire and Manchester Brewery Co. v Manchester Brewery Co. 1899) A.C. 83. Young v Ladies Imperial Club (1920) 2 K.B. 523, post; Law v Chartered Institute of Patent Agents (1919) 2 Ch. 276.*

205 See for instance, *Thompson-Schwab and Another v Costaki and Another (1956) 1 W.L.R. 335*, where the Court of Appeal upheld the decision of Parry, J., granting an interlocutory injunction in an action seeking to prohibit the defendants from continuing private nuisance. The Court has a discretion to issue interlocutory or interim injunction where the applicant establishes that "there is a serious question to be tried." *Paul Okwueze v Afam Ekwuaju (1975) 5 E.C.S.L.R. 331; American Cyanamid Co. v Ethicon Ltd. (1975) A.C. 396. S. Kufeji v A Kogbe (1961) 1 All N.L.R. 113.*

206 See *Attorney-General v Halling (1846) 15 M. &W 687, 694, 153 E.R. 1027, 1030.* In that case, a full account of how the Court of Exchequer came to exercise equitable jurisdiction was given. See also Holdsworth, W.S: *A History of English Law Vol. I pp. 240;41.*

207 (1615) 1 Ch. Rep. 1.

party." The matter was referred to James I for settlement. James I decided the issue in favour of the Lord Chancellor and ordered him to continue to give such equitable relief, notwithstanding any determination at the Common Law, "as shall stand with the merit and justice of their cause, and with the former, ancient and continued practice and presidency of our Chancery."[207] Thus common injunction endured until it was abolished by the Judicature Act of 1873.[208]

In the field of public law, the value of injunction was enhanced by section 9 of the Administration of Justice (Miscellaneous Provisions) Act 1938 which abolished Informations in the nature of *quo warranto.* And provides that "In any case where any person acts in an office in which he is not entitled to act and an information in the nature of *quo warranto* would, but for the provisions of the last foregoing sub-section, have lain against him, the High Court may grant an injunction restraining him from so acting and may (if the case so requires) declare the office to be vacant."[209] In *Akintola v Aderemi and Adegbenro* [210] the High Court of Western Nigeria granted an injunction against the second defendant restraining him from acting as the Premier of Western Nigeria. The Court was of the view that the removal of the then Premier was contrary to the Constitution of the Region; consequently the appointment of the second defendant as the Premier of Western Region by the Governor of the Region was invalid. The legal battle which followed this decision was a long one.[211] But the case still demonstrates that the High Court has jurisdiction to restrain by injunction, a public officer or authority[212] from acting in contravention of the law.

---

208 (1615) 1 Ch. Rep. App. 11-26.

209 See S.24(5), 36 & 37 Vict. C.66. For more details, see Keeton G.W: *An Introduction to Equity (1960 5th ed.) p.327 et seq.; de Smith, op.cit Chap. 10 generally and Hanbury H.G.: Modern Equity (1962 8th ed.) p.562 et seq.*

210 S.9(2) 1 & 2 Geo. 6 C.63. This enactment, a U.K. Act, has been adopted in Nigeria, see for example, S.25 of the High Court Law (Northern Nigeria) Cap.46, Laws of N.N. 1963 Vol. II.

211 (1962) W.N.L.R. 197.

212 The case went on reference to the Federal Supreme Court; see *Akintola v Aderemi and Adegbenro (1962) 1 All N.L.R. 442*. The decision of the High Court of Western Nigeria was upheld. On appeal to the Privy Council, it was held by the Board, that the former Premier was validly removed from office by the Governor; see *Adegbenro v Akintola (1963) 3 All E.R. 544;* (1962) 1 All N.L.R. 465. For what happened in that case see Chap. 9, *post*.

213 See *Attorney-General v Ashbourne Recreation Ground Co. (1903) 1 Ch. 101* - held-Court could enforce by-laws by injunction in an action brought by the Att.-Gen. at the instance of the local authority; *Metropolitan Asylum District v Hill (1881) 6 App. Cas. 193* - injunction was granted to restrain a local authority from causing unlawful damage; see also *Broadbent v Rotherham Corporation (1971) 2 Ch. 31; Pride of Derby and Derbyshire Angling Association Ltd. and Another v British Celanese Ltd. (1953) 1 Ch. 149* - injunction granted to restrain local authority from polluting river; and *Odubote v The Minister of Local Government and The Minister of Chieftaincy Affairs for*

The High Court will issue injunction to restrain an inferior tribunal from acting on its decision or determination where such tribunal its proceedings in a way contrary to the rule of natural justice. Thus in *Law v Chartered Institute of Patent Agents* [213] it was held that the members of the council of the defendant institute acted in contravention of the rule of natural justice for being accusers as well as judges against the plaintiff. Consequently injunction was granted to prohibit them from erasing the plaintiff's name from the Register of Patent Agents. The rule which was contravened is the well-known rule that no one shall be a judge in his own cause. For in such a case the possibility of bias is obvious and it is no defence that the person or persons concerned were not in fact biased in the determination of the issue. Eve, J. struck a right note when he stated in the course of his judgement: "Each member of the council in adjudicating on a complaint thereunder is performing a judicial duty, and he must bring to the discharge of that duty an unbiased and impartial mind. If he has a bias which renders him otherwise an impartial judge he is disqualified from performing his duty. Nay, more (so jealous is the policy of our Law of the purity of the administration of justice), if there are circumstances so affecting a person in a judicial capacity, as to be calculated to create in the mind of a reasonable man a suspicion of that person's impartiality those circumstances are themselves sufficient to disqualify although in fact no bias exists. One such circumstance which has always been held to bring about disqualification is the fact that the person whose impartiality is impugned has taken part in the proceedings, either by himself or his agent as prosecutor or accuser."[214]

Western Nigeria (1962) W.N.L.R. 112 - injunction and declaration were sought because a Minister declared a customary law the validity of which the plaintiff contested. Held the plaintiff was entitled to succeed. Equally a public authority can obtain injunction to restrain an individual from doing a wrongful act where no other punishment seems adequate: *Attorney-General v Sharp (1931) 1 Ch. 121* - injunction was granted to restrain the defendant from acting in breach of local statutory regulation as he appeared to be unaffected by fines imposed against him.

214 (1919) 2 Ch. 276.

215 *ibid* at p.289. Also in *Andrews and Others v Mitchell (1905) A.C. 78*, the House of Lords upheld the decision of the Court of Appeal granting injunction against the expulsion of the respondent by a Friendly Society because he was not heard by the Committee which arrived at the decision. See equally *Young v Ladies' Imperial Club Ltd. (1920) 2 K.B. 523.*

Chapter 7

The Courts and the Fundamental Rights and Freedoms

1. *Events leading to the incorporation of these Rights and freedoms into the Nigerian Constitution.*

The incorporation of the provision safeguarding the fundamental rights and freedoms of the individual into the Nigerian Constitution emanated from the compromise reached in the 1957 Constitutional Conference . The issues which confronted the Conference were so delicate in so much that not only was the Conference threatened with a total breakdown but also the very existence of Nigeria as a nation.

As we have seen earlier in this study, the growth of federalism in Nigeria witnessed the growth and entrenchment of political parties in the respective Regions. The unfortunate result was that there never emerged a really national political party capable of at least forming the government of more than one Region. The more glaring feature of these political parties was that they drew the majority of their support primarily on linguistic or tribal basis . Under this atmosphere of political sectionalism , the three main political parties in Nigeria flourished. The Northern People's Congress (N.P.C.) predominantly Hausa , controlled the Northern Region and formed the Regional Government with little or no opposition. The National Convention of the Nigerian Citizens (N.C.N.C.) which *ex facie*, was national, gradually hardened by political vicissitudes to what amounted to a Regional political party and thus controlled the Eastern Regional Government . The party largely drew its support from Igbo population . The Action Group party was found by Yoruba Elements and formed the Government of the Western Region .

What therefore emerged from the political spectacle was a situation in which there were three main political parties, three main languages and three formidable Regional Governments. In these Regions, there were minority areas who feared political eclipse after the withdrawal of the British Administration as the result of the grant of independence to Nigeria . Matters were therefore brought to a head at the 1957 Constitutional Conference. As was pointed out earlier, the country was disproportionately divided into three; the Northern Region was greater in size than the rest of the units of the Federation put together.

At the 1957 Constitutional Conference, Chief Awolowo , who led the delegation of the Action Group [1] submitted two proposals which would have operated to weaken the dominant position of the N.P.C. The two proposals were:

1.the creation of number of new states out of the existing Regions;
2.the entrenchment in the Constitution of a set of fundamental rights.

The first proposal would have diminished the crushing size of the Northern Region - this has always been the hunting fear of the southern politicians . The second proposal would have made it easier (as was anticipated) for the opponents of the N.P.C. to operate freely in the Northern Region. The N.C.N.C. which formed the Government of the Eastern Region favoured the idea of creation of new States but rejected any question of creation of a new state from the Eastern Region as long as the Northern region was left intact. The party was of the view that it was from the Region that the Southern Cameroon was carved out and that it was therefore realistic that it should suffer no further diminution unless the North agreed to creation of a large number of new States. The N.P.C. which formed the Government of the Northern Region bluntly rejected any idea of creation of new states in the North.

The British Government would have agreed to the creation of more states if that was agreed to by all the Nigerian delegation . But unfortunately no such agreement emerged and to save the Conference from complete breakdown thus hampering the question of grant of independence , a compromise was reached to incorporate in the Constitution provisions to safeguard fundamental rights .[2] The Secretary of State's legal advisers were therefore asked to prepare, "in the light of the memorandum submitted to the Conference and the discussions on them, draft clauses for insertion in the constitutional instruments ."[3]

It follows therefore that the question of creation of new States foundered.

On thein in minority and the fears they entertained, the Conference agreed that "a Commission of Enquiry should be appointed to ascertain the facts about the fears of minorities in any part of Nigeria and to propose means of allaying these fears whether well or ill founded."[4] Noting that the desire for creation of new states partially arose from the fear of minorities, the Conference agreed that "the commission would be empowered as a last resort to make detailed recommendation for the creation of one or more new States, specifying the areas to be included and the governmental and administrative structure most appropriate." It must be pointed out that while

---

[1] That is to say, the Government of the Western region.
[2] Cmnd. 207 (1957) p.32.
[4] *Ibid.* p.13.

favouring in principle the idea of creation of new States to ensure a balance of power amongst the units of the Federation, the British Government made it clear that a fragmentation of the country into small uneconomically viable states would not be desirable.[5]

Following the agreement reached at the 1957 Constitutional Conference a four-man Commission of Enquiry under the chairmanship or Sir Henry Willinck , a former British Cabinet Minister , was set up. The Commission arrived in Nigeria on November 23, 1957 to carry out its onerous task.[6]

Contrary to the hopes raised in minority areas , the Commission did not recommend the creation of any State. It was of the view that the creation of such States would create more problems than serve as panacea.[7] However, the Commission in its Report [8] recommended inter alia that feasible and appropriate means of allaying the fears of the minorities should be the incorporation into the constitutional instrument of the provisions safe-guarding fundamental rights and freedom. This, it was proposed, should be based mainly on the European Convention for the Protection of Human Rights and Fundamental Freedoms concluded on November 4, 1950 under the framework of the Council of Europe .[9]

The 1957 Constitutional Conference was followed by yet another one in the following year - the fourth in eight years. This Conference was held in London from September 29 till October 27, 1958. Once more the Action Group was adamant on the need for creation of new States . The N.C.N.C. and the N.P.C. were in accord in requiring the shelving of creation of more States till after independence. They were of the view that creation of more states was not then expedient. The colonial Secretary, Mr. Allan Lennox-Boyd , who was the chairman of the Conference emphasised that independence would have to be postponed if the delegates could not agree on the question of new States. At this point the Action Group had to back down and the conference agreed instead to accept the Minorities commission Report[10] and entrench the fundamental rights provisions in the Constitution.

Consequently the Nigerian (Constitution) (Amendment No. 3) Order in Council 1959 was made to give effect to the agreement reached at the Conference. The Order in council came into force on the 24th day of October 1969. Section 69 of the Order provided for the amendment of the

---

5 *Ibid*, p.14.

6 See Ezera, K., p.252; See also Odumosu, op.cit. pp.241-244.

7 See Report of the constituency delimitation Commission, 1958; Federal Government printer, Lagos, 1958.

8 Cmnd. 505, 1958, pp. 97-103.

9 Cmnd. 8969; European treaty Series, No.5.

10 See Report by the Resume Nigerian Conference, Cmnd. 469 1958, pp. 3-9, 22-23

Principal Order as set out in Section 29 of the Nigerian (constitution (Amendment No. 2) Order in council, 1959 by insertion of sections 244, 245, 246 and 247. These sections which dealt inter alia, with enforcement of the fundamental rights reference to tribunal and review of certain provisions, were made subject to the Sixth schedule of the Order. The Sixth Schedule was entitled - "provisions to be inserted as Sixth Schedule to Nigeria (constitution) Order in council 1954',[11] and thus the fundamental rights and freedoms provisions were incorporated into the Nigerian Constitution of 1954. These provisions were equally included in the Nigeria (Constitution) Order in Council, 1960 as Chapter III of the Constitution.[12] As the fundamental rights and freedoms provisions appeared to be valuable in Nigeria as evidenced in certain judicial decisions , they were transplanted root and branch to the Republican Constitution of 1963 and retained their place as chapter III of the constitution.[13]

The question one has to consider is to what extent the entrenchment of fundamental rights and freedoms provisions in the Nigeria Constitution are an apposite substitute to the creation of new states and to what extent that entrenchment operated in fact to allay the fears of the minorities . Before getting started, it may be observed that the said provisions in actual fact protect the individual irrespective of the community in which he belongs. The individual who belongs to the community which constitutes the majority linguistic or ethnic group in Nigeria is protected by the provisions just as an individual in the minority area . The minorities seek protection[14] from the excesses bordering on oppression by the majority. It is submitted that the minorities appeared to be satisfied with the inclusion of fundamental rights and freedoms provisions in the Constitution as a solution to their problem because just like a drowning person, they grappled at the least momentary object -- being under a precarious situation . The fundamental rights provisions are valuable in any democratic society, they serve as bulwark against oppression by any organ of the State[15] But the fact remains that they in the last analysis and in practice do not protect

---

[11] S.9. 1772, 1959

[12] S.9 1652, 1960; this is generally called the Independence Constitution.

[13] Constitution of the Federal Republic of Nigeria, Government Printer, Lagos, 1963

[14] See, D.C. Holland, "Human rights in Nigeria" (1962) 15 C.L.p. 145 at p.146. See also de Smith, S.a. Fundamental rights in the New commonwealth (1961) 10 I.C.L.Q. 83, 215

[15] See *Taylor v. Thomas 22 Wall. (Supreme Court, U.S.A.) 479*; see also *Bate J. in Cheranci v. Alkali Cheranci [1960] N.R.N.L.R. 24 at p.28* - and Justice Willer in *Citizens Savings & Loan Association v. Topeka (1874) 20 Wall. 655., 662*, See equally Jackson J. in *Board of Education v. Barnette (1943) 319 US at p. 624*

such.[16] There is no doubt that the provisions help to allay the fears of the minorities.

As we have seen earlier, for a federal state to thrive no one unit or component of it should be so large as to dominate the rest. The position which the people of Nigeria found themselves during and after the 1957 and 1958 Constitutional Conferences was that the Northern Region was larger than the rest of the Regions of the Federation put together. It is submitted that the root cause of the Nigerian administrative difficulties could be found in the fear of the Southern Regions of the domination by the North. There should have been an agreement to create new states at the Conference, to ensure some balance of power . This however should not have been to create some small states that could not find their feet economically, socially and administratively. The Northern Region should have at least been divided into two Regions. It might be argued that creation of more states should not have been preferred to independence under any circumstances. But of what use then is independence (If we may put it that way) when the country is plunged into crisis after crisis, thus depicting that there is something fundamentally wrong in the body politic of the nation. While we concede that independence was very essential issue at the conference and any other thing should be settled after it (as the delegates agreed), why then was the problem of creation of more states not tackled, after independence?[17] From this point of view we may say that recent events in Nigeria have shown that the inclusion in the Constitution of the Fundamental rights and freedoms provisions did not remove the fear of certain sections of the country against domination or oppression by another. Minority area, is a relative term. A section of the country which in one respect is regarded as a majority area may on the other hand constitute a minority area in the amalgam of the units of the country. Thus the southern states feel that they are placed in perpetual minority as long as the Northern Region remains a solid block. Where no other compromise could be reached, the ultimate solution should be to divide the Northern Region but there could be some atom of balance of power and removal of fear and distrust which have bedeviled the country.

2. *Position in Other Constitutions*

Under the British Constitution (which is unwritten) there are no formal guarantees of liberty apart from the declarations of rights which could be

---

[16] Sir Ivor, Jennings was of the view that the experience of India, Pakistan and Ceylon reveal that one should not attempt to deal with the problems of minorities by constitutional guarantees of Bills of Rights. See Jennings, *Some characteristics of the Indian constitution* (1953) 48, 54. See also the *Approach to Self-Government (1956) pp. 100, 110* by the same learned author

[17] Both the N.C.N.C. and the N.P.C. were of the view that independence should be granted and after that the question of creation of more states should be settled. see Ezera, op.cit. p. 253

found in the ancient characters and limitations on the arbitrary power of the Crown imposed by the Revolution settlement of 1688 and other earlier celebrated constitutional landmarks. Examples of these are the Magna Carta of 1215 which begins "The GREAT CHARTER of LIBERTIES OF ENGLAND" and it gave "to all the freemen of our Realm these liberties underwritten, to have and to hold to them and their heirs of Us and Our Heirs for ever", for practical purposes worth a hundred constitutional articles guaranteeing individual liberty;"[18] the Petition of Right of 1628[19] and the Bill of Rights of 1689. The traditional British attitude is to distrust declarations of fundamental rights and freedoms and prefer instead the negative approach of the common law.[20]Jeremy Bentham who attached little or no importance to the declarations of rights spared no words in his condemnation of them as evidenced in his comments on the French revolutionary Declarations of rights of Man:

> Look to the letter, you find nonsense - look beyond the letter, you find nothing....... Natural rights is simple nonsense: natural imprescriptible rights, rhetorical nonsense —nonsense upon stilts. But this rhetorical nonsense ends on the old strain of mischievous nonsense: for immediately a list of the pretended natural rights is given, and those are so expressed as to present to view legal rights ."[21]

Sir Ivor Jennings was more direct:

> 'In Britain we have no Bill of Rights; we merely have liberty according to law and we think - truly I believe, that we do the job better than any country which has a Bill of Rights or a Declaration of Rights of Man."[22]

Wheare in his writing on what a Constitution should contain said:

> The ideal Constitution, then, would contain few or no declarations of rights, though the ideal system of law would define and guarantee many rights. Rights cannot be declared in a Constitution except in absolute and unqualified terms, unless indeed they are so qualified as to be meaningless - and we have seen may examples of this. It is in the ordinary law itself that the careful definition of rights can be best undertaken, with the added guarantee that the law, since it has been passed by a legislature, may in most cases be in line with dominant public opinion . To confine a

---

[18] Dicey, A.V., *Law of the Constitution, 10th ed. p.199*

[19] This document enrolled on the Statute book as 3 Car. 1 C 1 contained protests against taxation without Consent of Parliament, arbitrary imprisonment the use of commissions of martial law in times of peace and billeting of soldiers upon private persons. To these protest the King had to yield

[20] See D.C. Holland, (1962) C.L.P. p.15

[21] *Anarchical Fallacies" in Works (ed. Bowring) Vol. 2, pp. 497, 501*

[22] The Approach to *Self-government* (1956) p.20

> Constitution to the bare statement of the rules which establish the principal institutions of the State may seem unduly austere[23]

A close look at these apparent rejectiuns and criticism shows that they follow broadly from two ideas, viz. the total dislike of natural law by some positivists like Bentham and his followers who associate declaration of rights with natural law. Secondly, the difference between the British constitution , which is unwritten, and many other Constitutions which are written. A written constitution , such as the Nigerian Constitution or the American Constitution is the supreme law of the land, no Act of Parliament or say of Congress can stand if it is contrary to the Constitution (chapter 3 ante). In Britain, the Parliament is supreme. It can enact any law whatsoever and the Courts have no power to review Parliamentary legislation and to declare it *ultra vires* or unconstitutional.[24] There is therefore no distinction between laws which are "constitutional" or "fundamental" and those which are not.[25] The mere fact that the individual's rights are not "guaranteed" or described as fundamental and entrenched in the Constitution does not mean that he is wholly unprotected under the British constitution . The individual in Britain is as free and protected as his counterpart in any democratic country with a written constitution which is subject to judicial "review ". Individual liberty , for example, is secured by judicial decisions determining the rights of the individual in particular cases brought before the Courts. Thus Lord Atkin delivering the Judgment of the Board in *Eshugbayi Eleko v. Government of Nigeria* [26] said: "The Governor acting under the Ordinance acts solely under executive powers , and in no sense as a Court. As the executive he can only act in pursuance of powers given to him by law. In accordance with British Jurisprudence no member of the executive can interfere with the liberty or property of a British subject except on the condition that he can support the legality of his action before a court of justice ." A similar assertion was made by Lord Wright in *Liversidge v Anderson* [27] after delving into history to show how

---

23 Wheare K.C., *Modern Constitutions* (Oxford University Press) 1951 pp. 71-72. For more critical analysis on the subject, see Dicey, *op.cit.* - generally and de Smith op.cit. p.162 et seq

24 Thus in Glover v. Officer Administering Government of Nigeria ((1949) 19 N.L.R. 45 at p.48 Ames J. Said: ".....it is no more possible for a plaintiff to sue the Officer Administering the Government for a declaration that the Ordinance is "void and in operative than it would be to bring a similar action against the highest, or any servant of the Crown in a Court in England for a similar declaration about an English sic Act of Parliament which has gone through all stages of enactment including receiving the Royal Assent." In that case the plaintiff attacked the validity of an Ordinance. It was held that an Ordinance (such as the Epetedo Lands Ordinance, 1947) passed by the legislature and Assented to on behalf of the Crown could not be questioned. This decision was of course given long before Nigerian Independence.

25 See *O. Hood Phillips, Constitutional Law (2nd ed. 1957) p.22.*

26 (1931) A.C. 662 at p.670

27 (1942) A.C. 206 at pp.260-261

the struggle for the liberty of the individual had gone on in the centuries past, his Lordship went on:

> All the courts today, and not least this House, are as jealous as they have ever been in upholding the liberty of the subject . But that liberty is liberty confined and controlled by law, whether common law or statute. It is, in Burke's words, a regulated freedom. It is not an abstract or absolute freedom . Parliament is supreme. It can enact extraordinary powers of interfering with personal liberty .....in the constitution of this country there are no guaranteed or absolute rights . The safeguard of British liberty is in the good sense of the people and in the system of representative and responsible government which has been evolved."

It follows that although the United kingdom Parliament has unlimited power to make any law invading the rights and liberty of the individual , in practice it has lived up to the expectation of not taking undue advantage of this unlimited legislative power.

The United States of America Constitution contains Bill of rights. These are more particularly listed in the first eight amendments of the Constitution and of course the famous fourteenth Amendments. Being part of the constitution which is the Supreme law of the land any law which is contrary to any of the rights shall be declared unconstitutional and consequently void[28] The rights listed in the Constitution of the United States like those of Nigeria are 'fundamental' in that while ordinary rights may be altered by the Legislature in its ordinary mode of legislation, the fundamental right guaranteed in the constitution can only be changed through the rigorous way of Constitutional amendment.

The French have had a written Constitution since the overthrow of the *ancien regime,* but *stricto sensu,* the constitutional situation in that country is more similar to that which predominates in Britain than the United States . In France like Britain, the Parliament is omnipotent. There is no judicial "review " of legislation in that no court in France can declare any law passed by the French Parliament to be unconstitutional and consequently void. The Preamble[29] to the Constitution of 1958 like that of 1946 "solemnly affirms" the Declaration of the Rights of Man of 1789, but this Preamble is not enforceable in a Court of law . It can be compared with a Coronation Oath which likewise could not be enforced. This is not to say that the individual in France is wholly unprotected from any excesses of the executive or other organs of the State . In place of the judicial review of enacted laws, the French constitution provides for a scrutiny of measures to be enacted into law. This important function is performed by an extra-judicial body known as the constitution Council composed of the

---

[28] See *Thomas v. Collins (1944) 323 US 516*, Here a state statute was invalidated for violating the first Amendment of freedom of speech, or of the press and the right to assemble peaceably; see also *Lovell v city of griffin (1937) 303 US 444*

[29] For more details see Maurice Craston, *Human Rights today pp. 74-76.*

Presidents of the Republic who should be ex-officio members . The council's declaration as to the constitutionality or otherwise of a Bill is final. Article 61 of the Constitution provides that every "organic law " must be submitted to the council. It follows that the rights and freedom of the individual are subject to the unlimited power of the legislature . Although Article 66 of the constitution makes provision for the protection of the individual liberty there is no provision to the effect that any enactment contrary to this provision should be void and the courts in France unlike those in the United States have not established the dominant right to declare a legislation unconstitutional when it corrodes the rights and freedom of the individual. As the rights mentioned in the French constitution are not judicially enforceable they cannot be said to be "guaranteed" in the sense that any act by any organ of the State which is repugnant to them should be void[30]

The British North America Act , 1867,[31] i.e. the Constitution of Canada does not contain Bill of rights as such. However, it provides for safeguards in certain denominational schools. Thus section 93 reads: "In and for each Provision the Legislature may exclusively make laws in relation to Education, subject and according to the following Provisions: "(1) Nothing in any such Law shall prejudicially affect any Right or Privilege with respect to Denominational School which any class of Persons have by Law in the Province at the Union."[32] To ensure equality between the two rival languages, section 133 provides that "Either the English or the French Language may be used by any person in Debates of the Houses of the Parliament of Canada and of the Houses of the Legislature of Quebec , and both these Languages shall be used either in the respective Records and Journals of those Houses and either of those Languages may be used by any Person in any Pleading or Process in or issuing from any Court of Canada established under this Act, and in or from all or any of the Courts of Quebec . The section then went on to provide that "the acts of the Parliament of Canada and of the Legislature of Quebec shall be printed and published"in Both English and French languages. But despite the absence of the apparent embodiment in the constitution of the Bill of rights or fundamental rights and freedoms, the Supreme Court of Canada has shown remarkable boldness in its decisions by reading into the Constitution implied prohibitions against derogation from civil liberties . In *Reference re Alberta Statutes* [33] Duff C.J. referring to the Constitution of Canada said: "The preamble of the statute, moreover, shows plainly enough that the

30 C.F. Basu D.D., *Commentary on the Indian Constitution Vol. I (1965) p.127*

31 30 & 31 Vict., C.3

32 See also Sub-sections (2) and (3), ibid.

33 [1938 S.C.R. 100 at 133

constitution of the Dominion is to be similar in principle to that of the United Kingdom . The statute contemplates a parliament working under the influence of public opinion and public discussion . There is no controversy that such institutions derive their efficacy from the free public discussion of affairs, from criticism and answer and counter-criticism, from attack upon policy and administration and defence and counter attack from the first and fullest analysis and examination from every point of view of political propaganda ." Continuing with the aspect of the case dealing with measures which could operate to restrict freedom of speech and the press , his Lordship sternly said: "Any attempt to abrogate this right of public debate or suppress the traditional forms of the exercise of the right (in public meeting and through the press) would, in our opinion, be incompetent to the Legislatures of any one of the provinces as repugnant to the provisions of the British North American Act. .."[34] Consequently the Acts were invalidated by the Supreme Court.

In its eagerness to protect civil rights implied in the written constitution of Canada, the Supreme Court found no difficulty in declaring *ultra vire*s [35] "An Act to protect the Province of Quebec against communistic Propaganda."[36] The Court has affirmed the principle that no one may be condemned or deprived of his rights without being heard[37] In *Saumnur v. The City Quebec*,[38] the Supreme Court upheld the right of Jehovah's Witnesses to distribute pamphlets in the streets. It has granted damages against police officers for the break-up of an admittedly orderly religious meeting conducted by a minister of the sect [39] These judgments of the Supreme Court desire every commendation in view of the fact that there were no Bill of Rights in Canada either forming part of the Constitution or standing as a separate enactment. There was however an enactment in 1960.

The Canadian Bill of Rights , "An Act for the Recognition and Protection of Human Rights and Fundamental Freedoms"[40] was passed by the Parliament of Canada in 1960. Part I of the Act called the Canadian Bill of Rights, recognises and at the same time declares existence and continuance in Canada of the following rights and freedoms, without

---

[34] ibid, at p. 134.

[35] *Switzman v. Elbling 1957 s.C.R. 285*

[36] R.S.Q. 1941, C. 52

[37] *L'alliance des Professeurs Catholiques do Montreal v Labour Relations Board of Quebec 1953 2 S.C.R. 140* The Certificate of the appellant was revoked by the Board without the appellant being heard or given opportunity to be head

[38] .1953 2 S.C.R. 299

[39] Chaput v Roman 1955 S.C.R. 834

[40] '8 & 9 Eliz. 2 C.44 (1960)

discrimination arising from race, national origin, colour, religion or sex the right of the individual to life, liberty, security of the person and enjoyment of property and the right not to be deprived thereof except by due process of law the right of the individual to equality before the law and the protection of the law , freedom of religion , freedom of speech , freedom of assembly and association and freedom of the Press . Section 2 provides that "Every law of Canada shall, unless it is expressly declared by an Act of the parliament of Canada that is to say, Act of the Federal Parliament that it shall operate notwithstanding the Canada Bill of Rights, be construed and applied as not to abrogate, abridge or authorise the abrogation... of any of the rights or freedoms..." the section then enumerated more of the rights and freedoms which include *inter alia,* freedom from arbitrary detention , imprisonment or exile, imposition of cruel and unusual treatment or punishment. The right of an arrested or detained person to be informed promptly of the reason for his arrest or detention the right to retain and instruct counsel without delay, or of the remedy by way of *habeas corpus* there are provisions for right to fair hearing, right to the assistance of an interpreter and presumption of innocence until proved guilty. Part II of Act safeguards those rights and freedoms not mentioned in the enactment by providing that "Nothing in Part I shall be construed to abrogate or abridge any human right or fundamental freedom not enumerated therein that may have existed in Canada at the Commencement to this Act." Like the Nigerian Constitution on the subject and the European Convention on Human Rights , the Canadian Bill of Rights permits derogation from the rights and freedoms during times of war, 'invasion or insurrection, real or apprehended; however the Canadian enactment does not provide for derogation from the Bill of rights in other classes of emergencies.

It may be observed that the Canadian Bill of Rights is not a part of the Constitution of Canada. As we have seen from section 2 of the Act, the enactment can be amended or even repealed by an ordinary legislation of the Federal Parliament. The United States , it might be said, followed a better course by incorporating the American Bill of Rights into the Constitution of the United States of America as "Amendment". Such incorporation would make the rights and freedoms secure. On the other hand, it might be argued that being an ordinary legislation , the Act provides for more flexibility and might have been intended to "fortify the courts in their common law convictions , and equally buttress the received convention of legislative restraint where civil liberties are concerned."[41] On the whole, the Canadian Bill of Rights is valuable and covers almost the same grounds as the Chapter III of the Nigerian Constitution. The task of Courts in

---

41 See Bora Laskin: "*An Inquiry into the Diefenbaker Bill of Rights (1959) 37 Can. Bar. Rev. 77*

Canada will now be easier as these rights and freedoms are now spelt out more particularly.

The Indian constitution in its Part II contains elaborate provisions for the protection of Fundamental Rights of the individual. To enhance the sanctity of these provisions, Article 13 of the Constitution of India provides:

1. All laws in force in the territory of India immediately before the commencement of the Constitution, in so far as they are inconsistent with the provisions of this part, shall, to the extent of such inconsistency, be void.
2. The State shall not make any law which takes away or abridges the rights conferred by this Part and any law made in contravention of this clause shall to the extent of the contravention, be void.

This Fundamental Rights[42] provisions run from Articles 12 to 35 of the Indian constitution and broadly cover the same grounds as the Chapter III of the Nigerian constitution.

Most other countries in the new commonwealth have also enshrined in their Constitutions provisions for safeguarding fundamental rights and freedoms of the individual. A close study of these constitutions shows that they follow very closely the Nigerian pattern - being an adaptation of the European Convention on Human Rights .

3. *Position Under International Law*

As we have seen earlier in this chapter, the vogue of inclusion in the Constitutions of the new Commonwealth countries of provisions for the protection of fundamental rights and freedoms gathered momentum after the promulgation of the European Convention on Human Rights and Fundamental Freedoms in 1950.

Long before 1950 international law has recognised the need for the protection of the fundamental rights of man . Grotius in his renowned work[43] published in 1650 recognised as a rule of international law , the doctrine of humanitarian intervention for the protection of human rights. It may be said that the most important of these rights is right to life. Thus even today, it is legitimate under international customary law for a State to intervene to protect her national in the domain of another State when there is apparent danger to their safety. It may be said that this permissible rule of international customary law amounts to an exception to the well-known rule that no State should interfere in the internal affairs of another State.

In 1919 unsuccessful attempt was made to make universal declaration for the protection of human rights. The shocking events of the Second World War , the glaring dangers of racial prejudice and the increasing

---

42 For a more detailed analysis of these provisions, see Basu, op.cit. - generally.

43 *De Jure Bell ac Pacis, Translated Rev. A.C. compbell (1814)*

awareness that unless checked, tyranny would dominate the world and the dignity of man rendered meaningless - these factors combined and pressed on the member States or the United Nations to adopt on the 10th December 1948, the Universal declaration of Human Rights .[44] Prior to this Declaration, the United Nations Organisation had enshrined in its Charter a provision "To achieve international co-operation in solving international problems... and in promoting and encouraging respect for human rights and for fundamental freedoms for all without distinction as to race , sex, language or religion ..."[45]

The long preamble of the Declaration of 1948 makes evident what it wanted to achieve: "Whereas recognition of the inherent dignity and of the equal inalienable rights of all members of the human family is the foundation of freedom, justice and peace in the world whereas disregard and contempt for human rights have resulted in barbarous acts which have outraged the conscience of mankind, and the advent of a world in which human beings shall enjoy freedom of speech and belief and freedom from fear and want has been proclaimed as the highest aspiration of the common people whereas it is essential, if man is not to be compelled to have recourse, as a last resort, to rebellion against tyranny and oppression, that human rights should be protected by the rule of law ... whereas Member States have pledged themselves to achieve, in co-operation with the United Nations, the promotion of universal respect for and observance of human rights and fundamental freedoms... Now therefore the General Assembly proclaims this Universal Declaration of Human Rights as a common standard of achievement for all peoples and all nations..."

Most of the rights and freedoms enumerated in the Articles of the Declaration accord with such fundamental rights and freedoms listed in Chapter three of the Nigerian Constitution. But there are certain provisions in the Declaration which by their nature could not appear in a justiciable document like a written constitution - Chapter III of the Nigerian Constitution. Examples of these are: Article 23 which provides that "Everyone has the right to work, to free choice of employment to just and favourable conditions of work and to protection against unemployment ; Article 24, "Everyone has the right to rest and leisure, including reasonable limitation of working hours and periodic holidays with pay" and Article 25 sections:

1. Everyone has the right to a standard of living adequate for the health and well-being of himself and his family, including food, clothing, housing and medical care and necessary social services , and the right to security in the event of

---

[44] See *General Assembly Resolution* 217 (iii) See also cmnd. 7662 (1949)

[45] Article 1 (3) of the Charter of the United Nations, Reprinted in U.N. OPI/84 - 07227, 1963 - 150 M.

unemployment, sickness, disability, widowhood, old age or other lack of livelihood in circumstances beyond his control.

2. Motherhood and childhood are entitled to special care and assistance. All children, whether born in or out of wedlock shall enjoy the same social protection.

Obviously some of the rights and freedoms enumerated in the Declaration could not possibly be enforced against the state. None the less, the Declaration is a very valuable and attractive international document . It provides standards which every nation should aspire to achieve. It provides a guide for the formulation of municipal legal documents . It is an elaborate document containing very important provisions calculated to serve as grand protectors of human dignity at a time when it was at its lowest ebb in many parts of the world. Mrs. Roosevelt, the Chairman of the Commission on Human Rights and the principal representative of the United States on the third Committee, said of the Declaration: "It might well become the international Magna Carta of all mankind... Its proclamation by the General Assembly would be of importance comparable to the 1969 proclamation of the Declaration of the Rights of Man, the proclamation of the rights of man in the Declaration of Independence of the United States of America and similar declaration of Independence of the United States of America and similar declarations made in other countries."[46] Our observation about the usefulness of this renowned Declaration (doubts about its binding nature notwithstanding) may be buttressed by what the President of the General Assembly of the United Nations at that time said: "It was the first occasion on which the organised community of nations has made a declaration of human rights and fundamental freedoms. That document was backed by the authority of the body of opinion of the United Nations as a whole, and millions of people, men, women and children all over the world, many miles from Paris and New York, would turn to it for help guidance and inspiration."[47] The Secretary-General of the United Nations in his Report to the General Assembly delightfully said "This declaration, the first attempt in history to write a 'Bill of Rights' for the whole world, is an important first step in the direction of implementing the general pledges of the Charter of the United Nations concerning human rights."[48]

The question therefore is to what extent, if at all, is the Declaration of this international 'Bill of Rights' legally binding on Member States of the United Nations. The Declaration was passed by the General Assembly as a Resolution. Nine States only abstained. During the preparatory discussion many statesmen of the world made it abundantly clear that the document

46 *Official Records of the Third Session of the General Assembly, Part I p.662.*

47 *ibid*, p. 934.

48 *Report to the General Assembly, 1948.*

was completely without binding force . Thus, the Australian delegate remarked that "on many occasions during the debate.... it was stated that Declaration....is not legally binding."[49] The British delegate was more emphatic: "The Declaration was ... devoid of any obligatory Character."[50] Mr. Attlee stated in the House of commons that the British Government did not intend giving legislative effect to the Declaration, for "it is not expected .... that any State, will be able at once to realise all these ideals."[51]

The binding nature of the Declaration could not be determined in isolation with other Resolutions of the General Assembly of the United Nations. The majority view is that the Resolutions of the General Assembly are generally devoid of legal obligation on the part of Member States. This is of course in contrast with the resolutions of the Security Council , which are legally binding. But the assertion that the Resolution of the General Assembly is completely devoid of any legal obligation at least creates an estoppel in international law and "any member of the United Nations will be estoppel from contesting the validity"[52] or legality of those ideals which it had recognised by voting for the adoption of the Declaration of Human Rights and Fundamental Freedoms at the General Assembly of the United Nations. But the question remains whether the individual could enforce any of those rights and freedoms enumerated in the Declaration for his protection.In the first place, there is no supra-national court created to this effect. The individual, *a fortiori*, has no *locus standi* i in the International court of Justice , which is an organ of the United Nations, to enforce any of the provisions of the Declaration . Moreover, it cannot be maintained that the Member States of the United Nations intended the Declaration to be a convention *per se*. But assuming for sake of argument that it technically constituted a convention or treaty, could it be said that such a convention confers a right on the individual Law? The traditional view (ardently still maintained by positivists) is that international law being law of nations is the law between States. Consequently sovereign states are the sole subjects of international law . It follows therefore that the individual, being only an object[53] of international law could only maintain an action through a State ; unless it is expressly stated in a treaty that an individual could enforce a

---

49 See U.N. Doc. Ap/P.V. 181, p.11, Dec. 10, 1948.

50 See U.M. Dec. A/C 3/S.R. 164, p.8, Nov.24, 1948, see. equally Lautherpacht, *'The Universal Declaration of Human Rights, 25 B.Y.I.L. (1948) p.154) at p.356 et seq.*

51 See *Hansard* 'Parliamentary Debates', House of Commons Jan. 18, 1949, 5th Series, Vol. 460,' Col. 17

52 See G. Schwarzenberger (1950) 3.C.L.P. 263 at p.291.

53 See Schwarzenberger G. International law as applied by International Courts and Tribunals Vol. 1 (1957) p.354 et seq.

right conferred on him, directly, i.e. by himself before an international tribunal.[54]

In the 20th century, especially during the second half of the century, the rapid technical and cultural developments have brought the individual closer to the realm of international law, with the result that some are advocating making the individual a subject of international law. While we do not intend to delve too far in this study with regard to the merits of that contention it may be observed that as the cardinal principle in international law is that no obligation can be imposed on a sovereign State without its consent; [55] it follows therefore that if the subjects of international law, i.e. sovereign States , agree, they can confer any enforceable right on the individual[56] or even 'agree that a seemingly object of international law should be deemed to be a subject of international law. Thus in the *Reparation for Injuries suffered in the Service of the United Nations case,*[57] the International court of Justice in its Advisory Opinion held that the United Nations Organisation was intended to exercise and enjoy, and is in fact exercising and enjoying functions and rights which can only be explained on the basis of the possession of a large measure of international personality and the capacity to operate upon an international plane . It is at present the supreme type of international organisation , and it could not carry out the intentions of its founders if it was devoid of international personality. It must be acknowledged that its Members by entrusting certain functions to it, with attendant duties and responsibilities, have clothed it with the competence required to enable these functions to be effectively discharged. Accordingly the Court has come to the conclusion that the Organisation is an international person .[58]

In arriving at its opinion the Court relied heavily on Article 104 of the Charter of the United Nations which provides that the Organisation shall enjoy in the territory of each of its members such legal capacity as may be necessary for the exercise of its functions and the fulfilment of its purposes. It follows that the intention to make the Organisation an international personality emerged from the Charter - a treaty entered into by the States. Equally, by the Lateran Treaty of 1949 the international personality of the Holy see was acknowledged by Italy . It may therefore be said that

---

[54] An example of this is the European convention on Human Rights, *ante*.

[55] See Schwarzenberger G. A manual of International law Vol. 1 (1960) P.26, see especially p.138 et seq.

[56] See European Convention on Human Rights *(supra)*

[57] I.C.J. Reports (1949) p. 173 - Advisory Opinion. The case arose from the Injury suffered by a servant of the United Nations during the Course of his employment. The Court held that by necessary implication and intendment, the U.N. had the implied power to maintain its rights by bringing international claims, and in this case, for the injury suffered through the servant.

[58] *ibid.* at p.179.

whatever may be the merits[58a] of the argument that the individual should be recognised as a subject of international law generally, for practical purposes and the need to avoid confusion between the obligation of the State and that of the individual within the State, as well as the reciprocal rights arising therefrom, this is not feasible and not desirable. For as Oppenheim put it: "Since the Law of Nations is based on the common consent of the individual States, States are the principal subjects of International Law. This means that the Law of Nations is primarily a law for the international conduct of States , and not of their citizens. As a rule, the Subjects of the rights and duties arising from the Law of Nations are States solely and exclusively. An individual being, such as an alien or an ambassador, for example, is not directly a subject of International Law. Therefore, all rights which might necessarily have to be granted to an individual being according to the Law of Nations are not, as a rule, international rights, but rights granted by Municipal Law in accordance with duty imposed upon the State concerned by International Law."[59] It follows therefore that under general International Law, the individual still remains not a subject but an object of the international law. If a treaty is entered into by States to protect his rights and freedoms, it will then be incumbent on the States parties to the treaty to make the provisions of such treaty part of the municipal or national law of the States concerned so that the individual could enforce these rights and enjoy the freedoms on municipal law plane .

On the other hand, as we pointed out earlier, the States can agree to enter into a treaty or convention having supra-national effect. They may agree to set up a Court for the adjudication of issues arising from breaches of the fundamental rights and freedoms of the individual . In such a case, the States could therefore consent to the surrender of some part of their sovereignty[60] by allowing the individuals of the member States to bring action directly to an international court against the defaulting state. This in fact is the case in the European Convention for the Protection of Human Rights and Freedoms concluded within the framework of the Council of Europe.[61] It is submitted that this is the better way of effectively protecting the fundamental rights and freedoms of the individual.

The Preamble to the Convention after referring to the United Nations Declaration of 1948, known as the Universal Declaration of Human Rights went on: "Considering that this declaration aims at securing the universal

---

58a Cmnd. 8969, European Treaty Series No. 5. The Convention was concluded in 1950 and came into force in 1953; Cmnd. 8130 (1951)

59 Oppenheim, L., International Law vol. 1 8th ed. (1955) p.19.

60 The right and ability to surrender part of a sovereign State's sovereignty are attributes of sovereignty ipse jure.

61 Cmnd. 8968, European Treaty Series No. 5 The Convention was concluded in 1950 and came into force in 1953; Cmnd. 8130 (1951)

and effective recognition and observance of the Rights therein declared; Considering that the aim of the council of Europe is the achievement of greater unity between its members and that one of the methods by which that aim is to be pursued is the maintenance and further realisation of Human Rights and Fundamental Freedoms . Reaffirming their profound belief in those Fundamental Freedoms which are the foundation of justice and peace in the world and are best maintained on the one hand by an effective political democracy and on the other by a common understanding and observance of the Human Rights upon which they depend. The Preamble then ended as it started by having great regard to the Universal Declaration: "Being resolved, as the Governments of European countries which are likeminded and have a common heritage of political traditions , ideals, freedom and the rule of law , to take the first steps for the collective enforcement of certain of the Rights stated in the Universal Declaration."

Article 19 of the Convention provides for the setting up of "A European Commission of Human Rights" and "A European Court of Human Rights". Article 25 made history by giving the individual a unique chance. It provides: "(1) The commission may receive petitions addressed to the Secretary-General of the Council of Europe from any person, non-governmental organisation or group of individuals claiming to be victims of a violation by one of the High Contracting parties of the rights set forth in this convention, provided that the High Contracting Party against which the complaint has been lodged has declared that it requires[62] the competence of the Commission to receive such petitions . Those of the High Contracting Parties who have made such a declaration undertake not to hinder in any way the effective exercise of this right."

The human rights and fundamental freedoms enumerated and protected under the Convention are precisely the same as those in Chapter IV of the Nigerian Constitution as the latter is an adaptation of the former. We shall therefore henceforth dwell primarily on the provisions in the Nigerian Constitution, making reference to the Convention where necessary.

4. *Position under the Law of Nigeria*

Nigeria has preferred to leave the guardianship of the constitution and the rights and freedoms guaranteed therein to the regular Superior Courts of the Land. In this respect the High Court of a State of the country is vested with the original jurisdiction to hear and determine any issue arising from the

---

62 The United Kingdom now allows individuals to petition against it; see (1966) Ap & May Crim. L.R. pp. 205 & 266 resp. U.K. has also accepted the compulsory jurisdiction of the European Court of Human Rights. Documents carrying these declarations were deposited with the Council of Europe on Jan. 14, 1966 with immediate effect. Council of Europe press Release C(66)2. See also the Prime Minister's Statement in House of Commons on Dec. 7 1965 H.C. Deb. vol. 722 Co.235.

breach of the guaranteed rights and freedoms. Thus Section 32 of the Constitution provides:

"(1) Any person who alleges that any of the provisions of this Chapter has been contravened in any territory in relation to him[63] may apply to the High Court of that territory for redress.

"(2) Subject to the provisions of Section 115 of this constitution, the High court of a territory shall have original jurisdiction to hear and determine any application made to it in pursuance of this section and may make such orders, issue such writs and give such directions as it may consider appropriate for the purpose of enforcing, or securing the enforcement within that territory of any rights to which the person who makes the application may be entitled under this chapter."

In adopting this method Nigeria followed the example of Canada, India and the United States. In some countries the guardianship of the Constitution and the rights emanating therefrom is entrusted to a special tribunal. In Australia, under the Constitution of 1920, this function was entrusted to a tribunal known as (Verfassungsgerichtschaf). Under thc 1960 Constitution of Cyprus , the function was entrusted to a Supreme Constitutional Court . It may be observed that the better method is to vest in the regular Superior Courts of the land the power to determine issues arising from the breach of the fundamental rights and freedoms guaranteed and protected under the constitution.

As we have indicated earlier, the fundamental rights and freedoms guaranteed under the Nigerian Constitution are enumerated in Chapter IV of the Constitution in the following order:

(A) *Right to Life and Inviolability of the Dignity of Men*

(1) Section 30(1) of the Constitution provides:
Every person has a right to life, and no one shall be deprived intentionally of his life, save in execution of sentence of a Court in respect of a criminal offence of which he has been found guilty in Nigeria.

(2) A person shall not be regarded as having been deprived of his life, in contravention of this section if he dies as a result of the use, to such

---

63 In *Olawoyin v. Att.-Gen. of the Northern Region* 1961 1 All N.L.R.269 it was held that the plaintiff had no *locus standi* o maintain an action challenging the legality of Children's and young persons' Law, 1958 (N.R. N.).28 of 1958) because he could not show that any of his rights had been infringed. The High Court in dismissing the action observed that it would be contrary to principle to make a Declaration in vacuo. In *Maluleke v. Minister of Law and Order 1963* (4) S.A. 206 the High Court of Southern Rhodesia held that the Court had no jurisdiction to entertain acclaim under Section 71 (1) of the Constitution until there had been an actual illegal infringement of the complainant's rights.

extent and in such circumstances as are permitted by law, of such force as is reasonably justified -

(a) for the defence of any person from violence or for the defence of property;

(b) in order to effect an arrest or to prevent the escape of a person detained;

(c) for the purpose of suppressing a riot, insurrection or mutiny.

Most of the rights and freedoms enumerated in this part of the Constitution are not unknown to the general law of Nigeria . Thus with regard to right to life section 306 of the Criminal Code provides that 'it is unlawful to kill any person unless such killing is authorised or justified or excused by law.'[64] It follows that an executioner who carries out the killing of a condemned man has performed a duty and commits no crime in the eye of the law .

Equally the arm of the law will not fall on a person if under reasonable circumstance he kills a man in the following ways:

(i) *In Defence of Oneself or any other Person from Violence:*[65]

A person is entitled to defend himself from an assailant with such reasonable force to prevent the assailant from destroying him. If therefore the assailant is killed during the process, that would not amount to unlawful killing . Such a homicide is justified because it is effected in order to prevent a capital felony.[66] It must be pointed out that if he is being attacked there is a duty to retreat before any fatal blow is struck *se efendendo*.

Homicide is equally excusable where the act was done to preserve the life of another. Thus in *R. v. Rose* [67] the accused was charged with the murder of his father. Evidence was adduced to show that he was living with his mother and father. A violent quarrel ensued as a result of a misunderstanding between the parents. The father, a man of great physical strength forced the mother to the top of the stairs and threatened to kill her with a knife. The accused, a boy of 21 would have been worsted in a fight with his father, being under such strain of circumstances and eager to save the life of his helpless mother, he shot and killed his father. It was held that the homicide was excusable. Lopes J. in the course of his summing up, said:

---

[64] Cap. 42, Laws of the Federation of Nigeria, Vol. II(1958) p. 712

[65] S.286 of the Criminal Code, ibid, See *R. v. Igwe(1938) 4 W.A.C.A. 117*

[66] *Harvel's Case (1221) Maitland's Select Pleas 94 (T.A.C.) in McCluskey v. H.M. Advocate (1959) S.L.T. 26*, the High Court of Judiciary in Scotland declared that to justify a plea of homicide in self-defence it is essential that the fatal resistance should have been made to save the accused's life. See also *Archbold, Criminal Pleading Evidence & Practice 35th ed. (1962) para. 2496. See R. v. Nwibo (1950) 19 N.L.R. 124*

[67] (1884) 15 Cox. CC.540.

> Homicide is excusable if a persc.ı takes away the life of another in defending himself, if the fatal blow which takes away life is necessary for his preservation. The law says not only in self-defence such as I have described may homicide be excusable, but also it may be excusable if the fatal blow inflicted was necessary for the preservation of life. In the case of parent and child, if the parent has reason to believe that the life of a child is in imminent danger by reason of an assault by another person, and that the only possible, fair, and reasonable means of saving the child's life is by doing something which will cause the death of that person, the law excuses that act. It is the same of a child with regard to a parent it is the same in the case of husband and wife.

His Lordship then went on to lay down what amounts to the golden rule on the subject:

> If you think, having regard to the evidence, and drawing fair and proper inferences from it, that the prisoner at bar acted without *vindictive feeling owards his father*[68] when he fired the shot, if you think that at the time he fired that shot *he honestly believed and had reasonable grounds for the belief*, that his mother's life was in imminent peril and that the fatal shot which he fired *was absolutely necessary for the preservation of her life*, then he ought to be excused, and the law will excuse him. from the consequences of the homicide.[69]

The fatal blow must be absolutely necessary for the preservation of lifet; the law will therefore not excuse any reckless destruction of life guise of self-defence or the defence of another. A reckless vendetta will not escape the punishing rod of the law. In *R. v Onyeanaizu*,[70] the accused was convicted of manslaughter instead of murder. With regard to a plea of self-defence, Brown C.J. in his judgment said: "The defence of self-defence is not open to an abnormally nervous or excitable person who, on being assailed by a comparatively minor assault or an assault of any nature which falls short of that which is described in the section, S.286 of the Criminal Code (supra), unreasonably believes that he is in danger of death or grievous harm. Such a person may hope for clemency from other quarters, he cannot expect it from the law.[71]

---

68 Emphasis supplied.

69 *ibid* at p. 541."Self-defence, it is established is not restricted to the person attacked Hale's *"Pleas of the Crown"* Vol. I p. 484 gives as instances master and servant, parent and child, and husband and wife who, if they even kill an assailant in the necessary defence of each other, are excused, the act of the relative assisting being considered the same act of the party himself"; - per Edmund Davies J. in *R. v Duffy 1966 2 W.L.R. 229 at pp. 231-232.*

70 1958 N. R. N. L. R. 93.

71 *ibid*, at pp. 94-95

(ii) *Deprivation of Life in the Defence of Property*

Under Section 282 of the Criminal Code any person who is in peaceable possession of a dwelling house, and any person lawfully assisting him or acting by his authority may use such force as he believes, on reasonable grounds, to be necessary in order to prevent the forcible breaking and entering of the house with intent to commit a felony or misdemeanour therein.[71a] In *R.v Ebi*, [72] the accused was the owner of a magnificent building which was nearing completion when fighting broke out between two rival sections of the community. The rioters badly damaged a large part of this building on the first day. On the following day, the accused who had left the building during the night, returned probably to save what remained of it. While he was there, the riot was resumed and stones were again thrown at his house; whereupon in great exasperation he picked up his brother's gun, dashed out and fired at the crowd - with fatal consequence. It was held that the homicide was justifiable as being in defence of his property. The difference between defence of property and self-defence in this respect is that while one is under a duty to retreat from an assailant in case of self-defence , he is not under such a duty while he is defending his property, 'but may even pursue the assailant until he finds himself or his property out of danger.'[73]

(iii) *Killing in order to Effect an Arrest or to Prevent the Escape of Person Detained*

The constitutional provision is a recognition of the existing law which provides that when a peace officer or police officeen is proceeding lawfully to arrest, with or without warrant, a person for an offence which is a felony, and is such that the offender may be arrested with or without, a warrant and that person takes to flight in order to avoid arrest, it is lawful for the officer concerned or for any person lawfully assisting him, to use such force as may be reasonably necessary to prevent the escape of the person sought to be arrested and if the offence is such that the offender may be punished with death or with imprisonment for seven years or more, then the said person may be killed if he cannot by any other means be arrested.[74]

[71a] See sa. 60, 65 and 66 of the Penal Code, (Northern Region) 1959.

[72] (1936) 3 W.A.C.A. 36.

[73] Archbold, op.cit. para 2512

[74] S. 271 of the Criminal Code, Cap. 42. In *R. v Aniogo (1943) 9 W.A.C.A. 62*, the accused, saw a suspected person at night being chased by a crowd; he then fired and killed the man. It transpired that the deceased was an innocent man lawfully abroad; he only started to run when he felt terrified by a man, and consequently the villagers started pursuing him, suspecting he was a thief. The accused was at first charged with and convicted of murder, but on appeal the conviction was reduced to manslaughter. In *Udo Abot v.The Queen (1953) 14 W.A.C.A. 352*, the accused was charged with murder. Evidence showed that he killed the deceased with matchet when the latter,

It may be observed that this permissive section of our law requires a strict and if necessary a very narrow interpretation n order to obviate any wanton killing of the individual by an officer who may under certain circumstances lose his sense of proportion when confronted withchallenging circumstance. It follows that the section is not a charter for homicide. The officer in question or any person assisting him must be guided by the letters of the law in this respect. The person sought must have committed a felony or he must have been sought in connection with an offence which is a felony. All reasonable means must be exhausted in attempt to apprehend him alive, it is only when no other choice is left should fatal blow be struck.

A person who is unlawfully sought to be arrested is within his right to protect his liberty which he inherently is entitled and which has been guaranteed to him under the Constitution. However, the force he may use to ward off the person arresting him must not be out of proportion and must be reasonable. If he therefore uses force which is considered to be in excess and in so doing causes death, it has been held that such killing would nevertheless be manslaughter only.[75]

(iv) *Deprivation of life for the Purpose of Suppressing a Riot, Insurrection, Meeting or in order to Prevent Commission of a Criminal Offence*

It is lawful for any person to use such force as is necessary to suppress a riot. The force however must be reasonably proportional to the danger.[76] It is lawful for any person equally to use such force as is reasonably necessary in order to prevent the commission of an offence which is such that the offender may be arrested without warrant or in order to prevent any act from being done as to which he believes, on .reasonable ground that it would, if done, amount to any such offence or in order to prevent a person whom he believes, on reasonable grounds, to be of unsound mind, from doing violence to any person or property.[77]

---

unarmed broke into his house at night and stole some meat (pieces of which were found in the deceased's pocket). It was held that the applicant was entitled to apprehend the deceased as a felon but was not justified by the circumstances in killing him, while in fact unarmed. In *R. v Forster (1825) 1 Lew C.C. 187; 168 E.R. 1007* it was held that the killing of a person who was endeavouring to escape from lawful arrest was only justifiable if the arrest was for a felony. If therefore it was for a misdemeanour, the killing would be murder reducible to manslaughter if there was provocation.

75 *R. v Adu* (1954) 14 W.A.C.A. 462; *R v. Dangar* (1944) 10 W.A.C.A. 225: *R. v Nshi* (1944) 17 N.L.R. 103

76 SS.73, 276-7 of the Criminal Code. See also.102 & 103 Criminal Procedure (N.R.)

77 S. 281 *ibid*; See *R. v Rose* (1884) 15 Cox. C.C. 540

It follows then from what we have seen above that although the law of Nigeria prohibits the .deprivation of the life of the individual, in certain cases such deprivation is not only excused but justifiable. It is therefore the duty of the courts to examine each case on its merits and to hold the scale of justice between the State and the deceased's cause on the one hand and the accused on the other. Where it appears to the court that despite the general rule that one has to defend his property,[78] the killing of a thief could not be tolerated under certain circumstances then the killer will have to pay the price for a reckless or unjustifiable homicide.

(v) *Inhuman Treatment, Slavery and Forced Labour*

The law of Nigeria, of which the Constitution is the Supreme Part ensures that the dignity of the human person is not only protected but also respected and free from violation by the State and other individuals. Thus it is provided that 'No person shall be subjected to torture or to inhuman or degrading punishment or other treatment'.[79] The Constitution however does not 'invalidate any law by reason only that it authorises the infliction in any part of Nigeria of any punishment that was lawful and customary in that part on the first day of November 1957.'[80] The Constitution equally provides that no person shall be held in slavery or servitude nor be required to perform forced labour .[81] "Forced labour" does not however include any labour required in consequence of the sentence or order of a court or any labour required of members of the armed forces of the Federation in pursuance of their duties as such or, in the case of persons who have conscientious objections to service in the armed forces or any labour required instead of such service, or any labour required in the event of any emergency or calamity threatening the life or well-being of the community or any labour that forms part of normal communal or other civil obligations.

One of the most degrading things a man can suffer is subjection to slavery . This gross indignity to human person was abolished by the British Parliament throughout the British Empire in 1833. Before this date the

---

[78] *Udo Obot v.R. (1953) 14 W.A.C.A. 352*

[79] S.31 of the Nigerian Constitution. In *Runyowa v R.* 1966 Crim.L.R. 161, the Privy Council in an appeal from Southern Rhodesia held that an enactment which provided for mandatory death sentence might be harsh but the punishment could not be declared inhuman and contrary to. S 60 of the 1961 Constitution. Now see *R. v Brown (1964) 7 W.I.R. 47* at p. 47 sentence of mandatory flogging and hard labour was quashed and described as 'degrading' form of punishment which could have 'detrimental effects'.

[80] S.19 (2) ibid. An example of this type of punishment could be the"symbolic" lashing or punishment of Haddi- a sort of ritual lashing practised in Northern Nigeria, now administered in accordance with The Criminal Procedure (Haddi Lashing) Order in Council 1960 (N.R.)For a description of this lashing see *Nwabueze, Machinery of Justice in Nigeria (1963) pp. 236-237.*

[81] S. 20.

courts in England had held in *Forbes v Cochrane* (1815)[82] and .The Slave Grace (1827)[83] that slavery was illegal in England or in a British ship, even if it was not illegal in the country from which the slave was brought or to which he was to be taken. If such a slave was therefore taken to England he could be set free by habeas corpus.

On the international plane, by the General Act of the Berlin Conference 1881 traffic in slaves was declared to be contrary to the law of Nations.[84]

Under the law of Nigeria apart from the Constitution, slavery is illegal. The Slavery Abolition Ordinance of 1916, while abolishing the legal status of slavery provided that "All persons heretofore or hereafter born in or brought within the Protectorate of Nigeria are hereby declared to be free persons."85 Then the Ordinance went to nullify any contract arising from slave dealing as follows: "Every contract in which it is stipulated or agreed that any person shall be bought or sold, or placed in servitude, or be transferred either as a pledge or security for debt or in any other way, shall be absolutely illegal."[85] While the Ordinance aimed more particularly at abolition of slavery per se, the Criminal Code not only makes slave dealing an offence, but also stipulates the punishment which would fall on perpetrators. Thus section 369 of the Code provides that "Any person who deals, or trades in, purchases, sells, transfers or takes any slave ... or places or receives any person in servitude as a pledge or security for debt whether then due and owing ... or enters into any contract or agreement with or without consideration for doing any of the acts or accomplishing any of the purposes herein above enumerated is guilty of slave dealing and is liable to imprisonment for fourteen years'.[86]

The Courts in Nigeria have always refused to recognise any claim which in any way got tainted with slavery. Thus in *R. v Effiong Okon Ata*

---

[82] (1815) 2 B & C.448; Best J. said "The moment persons put their feet on board a British man-of-war... those persons who before had been slaves were free", *ibid* at p. 467.

[83] 2 Hag. Adm.

[84] Earlier The Congress of Vienna of 1815 declared the slave trade to be "repugnant to the principles of humanity and to the universal laws of morality". By the Treaty of St. Germain in 1919, the African Colonial Powers agreed to endeavour to secure the abolition of slave trade by land and sea. Since then several Conventions have enjoined parties to them "to prevent and suppress the slave trade". The latest on the subject is the Geneva Convention on High Seas 1958; of which almost all the UN Members are parties. Article 13 of the Convention provides that "every State shall adopt effective measures to prevent and punish the transport of slaves in ships authorised to fly its flag, and to prevent the unlawful use of its flag for that purpose. Any slave taking refuge on board any ship whatever its flag, shall *ipso facto* be free". The European Convention on Human Rights in its Articles 3 and 4 provides that "No one shall be subjected to torture or to inhuman or degrading treatment or punishment. No one shall beheld in slavery or servitude. No one shall be required to perform forced or compulsory labour. The exceptions to "forced or compulsory" are broadly the same with those under the Nigerian provisions on the subject.

[85] SS. 3 & 4 Slavery Abolition Ordinance, 1916, Cap. 207; Laws of Nigeria 1948 p. 112.

[86] Criminal Code, Cap. 42.

,[87] a claim by the head of the House (in which an emancipated slave belonged) to the personality of the latter after his death was rejected by the court. Butler Lloyd J. in his judgment said:"The effect of the abolition of slavery was to make all persons equal before the law". His Lordship was of the view that to allow such claim to succeed "would be very largely to render nugatory the provisions of the Slavery Abolition Ordinance.'[88]

The Constitutional provision guaranteeing freedom from forced labour is an entrenchment of an existing law which protected the individual from any such degrading labour. The Nigerian Labour Code incorporating the Forced Labour Convention , 1930 provides that 'any person who exacts forced labour or causes forced labour to be exacted, or who permits forced labour to be exacted for his benefit, shall be guilty of an offence and shall be liable to a fine of five hundred pounds or to imprisonment for two years or to both such fine and imprisonment .'[89] The Code went on to provide that any person who being a public officer or chief, puts any constraint upon the population under his charge or upon any individual memberthereof to work for any private individualcompany or association, shall be guilty of an offence , and shall be liable to a fine of N100 or to imprisonment for a period of six months or to both such fine and imprisonment.[90] The Labour Code then makes exceptions by providing that 'it shall be lawful for any native authority or such other authority as may be prescribed to require the inhabitants of any town or village subject to its jurisdiction to provide labour' for certain amenities: These include construction and maintenance of buildings and for communal purposes; sanitary measures; the construction and maintenance of local roads and paths, construction and maintenance of town or village fences, communal wells and other communal services of a similar kind in the direct interests of the inhabitants of the town or village.

The above provision is very necessary in view of the fact that while there is absolute need to protect the individual or the community from any degrading or forced labour at the present stage of Nigerian development, most of the rural development is done by communal labour of the inhabitants. It would then not be in the interest of the community if individuals are allowed to opt out in any labour directed at improving the communications, providing water supply, preventing erosions and many other pressing needs of the community. But where an individual feels that he could not afford to lose his own day's work by working for the

---

87 (1930) 10 N.L.R. 65.

88 *ibid*, at pp. 65-66. A similar view was held by the West African Court of Appeal in *Kodich v Affram* (1930) 1 W.A.C.A. 12; See also *R. v Abia* (1936) 3 W.A.C.A. 40

89 S.115 of the Labour Code - incorporating Forced Labour Convention, 1930; Cap. 91 of 1946, Laws of the Fed. of Nigeria (1958) Vol. III,

90 S.116, *ibid*.

community on the appointed day, he 'may be excused therefrom on payment of such sum per day, while such labour is being done, as represents the current daily wages for labour;' [91] otherwise the members of the community would demand that such recalcitrant member or members be disciplined. Thus in a recent case, [92a] ten farmers who refused to participate in communal labour organised by Kujama farmers of Northern Nigeria were brought before the Alkali Court. Evidence showed that the Kujama farmers arranged to cut some trees at a river bank in order to prevent wild animals from entering and destroying their farms. The Alkali Court was satisfied that the refusal of the ten to participate in the work which was for the benefit of all was unjustified. The ten farmers were then ordered to pay £2 each or face one month's imprisonment.

(B) *Right to Non-Deprivation of Personal Liberty*

Unless permitted by law, no person should be deprived of his personal liberty . [92b] This is one of the cardinal principles predominating in a free society - and is now enshrined in Section 32 of the Nigerian Constitution which provides as follows:

(1) Every person shall be entitled to his personal liberty and no person shall be deprived of his personal liberty save in the following cases and in accordance with a procedure permitted by law -

(a) in execution of the sentence or order of a court in respect of a criminal offence of which he has been found guilty.

(b) by reason of his failure to comply with the order of a court or in order to secure the fulfilment of any obligation imposed upon him by law;

(c) for the purpose of bringing him before a court in execution of the order of a court or upon reasonable suspicion of his having committed a criminal offence or to such extent as may be reasonably necessary to prevent his committing a criminal offence;

(d) in the case of a person who has not attained the age of twenty-one years, for the purpose of his education or welfare;

(e) in the case of person suffering from infectious or contagious disease, persons of unsound mind, persons addicted to drugs or alcohol or vagrants, for the purpose of their care or treatment or the protection of the community; or

(f) for the purpose of preventing the unlawful entry of any person into Nigeria or for the purpose of effecting the expulsion,extradition or other lawful removal from Nigeria of any person or the taking of proceedings relating thereto.

---

[91] S.119, *ibid.*

[92a] *Kujama Farmers v. Amadu Kujuma & others, The New Nigeria, 21st June, 1966 p. 5.*

[92b] 1979 Constitution.

The section then went on to provide that any person who is arrested or detained shall be promptly informed in the language that he understands, of the reasons for his arrest and detention. Such a person shall be brought before a court without undue delay and if he is not tried within a reasonable time he shall be released either unconditionally or upon such conditions as are reasonably necessary to ensure that he appears before a court of law for his trial when required to do so.

The deprivation of the liberty of the individual unlawfully is a criminal offence under the law of Nigeria. For it is provided under the Criminal Code that any person who unlawfully confines or detains another in any place against his will, or otherwise unlawfully deprives such person of his personal liberty, is guilty of a misdemeanour, and is liable to imprisonment for two years.[93] It follows that the provision in the Code relates to the unlawful act of the individual against the individual while the Constitutional provision shields the individual largely from the excesses of the executive and other organs of the State . Prior to the order established by the Constitution, the Courts have always jealously guarded the liberty of the individual by the writ of *habeas corpus*. Thus in *Eshugbayi Eleko v. Officer Administering the Government of Nigeria,* the Judicial Committee of the Privy Council was faced with one of the most important cases in the fight for individual liberty. The appellant, who was the Head of the House of Dosuma was equally the Paramount Chief of Lagos and known as the Eleko . On August 5, 1925, some of the members of the House of Dosumu met together and purported to depose the appellant from his position as head of the House of Dosumu. Consequently, the Governor, acting in pursuance of the Deposed Chiefs Removal Ordinance , 1916 under which the Governor is given power to deport a chief who had been deposed by him or with his sanction if such deportation was required by customary law or if the Governor was satisfied that it was expedient in interest of peace, order and good government, ordered the appellant to leave Lagos and not to stay in the Provinces of Abeokuta, Ijebu and Ondo.[94] When this order was not complied with by the appellant, the Governor ordered him to be deported to Oyo - relying on the customary law. The appellant applied for a writ of habeas corpus for his release. His contention being,

(1) that he was not a native chief and did not hold an office as such;
(2) that he was therefore not deposed or removed from that office, and the Governor's sanction was consequently irrelevant ;
(3) that there was no native law and custom which required him or any chief or native, whether deposed in the manner alleged against him or

---

93 S. 365 of the Criminal Code. In *R. v Lambo Sokoto (1961) W.N.L.R. 27* the accused was convicted for the unlawful deprivation of the liberty of a girl.

94 1931 a.C. 662

in any other way, to leave the area in question. After a careful examination of the case, the Privy Council made an order directed to the Officer administering Government of Nigeria and the District Officer of Oyo 'to show why a writ of habeas corpus should not issue directed to them to have the body of Eshugbayi, Eleko, immediately before the Court at Lagos '[95] for the determination of his case a anew.[96]

(i) *Circumstances under which Personal liberty may be Lawfully Deprived*

The principle of individual liberty demands that a person who is held on suspicion or charge of a criminal offence must be brought before a court of law for the determination of his guilt or innocence as expeditiously as possible. If therefore the person is brought before the court and it happens that on the arraignment he stands mute, the court will find it difficult to determine any charges against him. When faced with such difficulty, the court will before proceeding with the case determine whether the accused is mute of malice or by the visitation of God If the latter is the case, then the accused will be in the same category as a person who is insane and in such a case he will be detained in any establishment provided for such people.[97] If on the other hand the jury or a judge without jury finds that the accused is in fact in a position to plead but is only trying to deceive the court, or if he pleads loss of memory which is incredible, there is nothing to stop the court from proceeding with the case, and enter a plea of not guilty for him.

The most important issue in a case of unfitness to plead is the burden of proof . In *Reg. v Sharp* [98] Salmon J. held that the onus was on the prosecution to show that the accused was mute of malice . It was established as a rule in M'Naghten's case [99] that everyone is presumed to be sane until the contrary is proved to the satisfaction of the jury. It follows that if the defence raises the plea that the accused is insane, the *onus probabandi* will rest on the defence to show that the accused is insane and therefore unfit to plead .[100] But the burden on the accused to prove his

---

[95] *ibid*, at p.675.

[96] The appellant was later allowed to return to the Iga, the official residence of the Oba of Lagos, although not reinstated to his former position. Earlier the same man had fought for his personal liberty and the Privy Council in *Eshugbayo, Eleko v. Government of Nigeria 1928 A. C. 459* held that the appellant was entitled to make a fresh application to another judge for a writ of habeas corpus notwithstanding that some other judge had already refused a similar application.

[97] In Britain such people are detained in a Broadmoor Institution, see Criminal Justice Act, 1948, S.62.

[98] 1958 1 All E.R. 62; see 1960 1 O.B. 357.

[99] (1843) 110 CL & F. 200

[100] See Viscount Sankey L.O. in *Woolmington v. D.P.P. 1935 A.C. 462*

insanity is on the balance of probabilities not beyond reasonable doubt[101] In *Reg. v. Podela,*[102] the accused was indicted for capital murder. Before the arraignment the accused raised the plea that because of total loss of memory, the accused was unfit to plead to the indictment. After evidence on both sides, the Judge directed the jury and they returned the answer that the accused was not suffering from genuine loss of memory. On the second stage the jury was directed to say that the accused was fit to stand his trial, they brought a verdict accordingly. The trial then proceeded after the accused had pleaded not guilty. He was found guilty and sentenced to death. In delivering the judgment of the Court of Criminal Appeal Lord Parker C.J . restated the common law on the subject as follows:

> "1. In all cases in which a preliminary issue as to the accused person's sanity is raised, whether the issue is contested or not, the jury should be directed to consider the whole of the evidence[103] and to answer the question "Are you satisfied upon that evidence that the accused person is insane so that he cannot be tried upon the indictment?"
>
> 2. If the contention that the accused is insane is put forward by the defence and contested by the prosecution, there is, in our judgment, a burden upon the defence of satisfying, the jury of the accused's insanity. In such a case, so in other criminal case in which the onus of proof rests upon the defence, the onus is discharged if the jury are satisfied on the balance of probabilities that the accused's insanity has been made out.
>
> 3. Conversely, if the prosecution alleges, and the defence disputes, insanity, there is a burden upon the prosecution of establishing it."[104]

It is submitted that if the prosecution alleges that an accused person is insane, the prosecution must prove that beyond reasonable doubt . It follows therefore that a person's liberty may be deprived if it established to the satisfaction of the court that such an accused person is unfit to plead in such a case he may be detained in a lunatic asylum- or the like institution. Where therefore the court deems it expedient to go on with the proceeding[105] or if no question of unfitness to plead arises and in the end the accused is found guilty, then his liberty may be deprived in execution of the sentence or order of the court in respect of such criminal offence of which he has been found guilty.

---

101 *Soderman v.R.* 1936 2 All E.R. 1138.

102 1960 1 O.B. 325

103 In Nigeria where the Judge usually sits alone, this important duty falls on him

104 *ibid*, at p.350.

105 *R.v. Podola 1960 1 Q.B. 325; R. v Ogor 1961 1 All N.L.R. 70*

(ii) *Contempt of Court*

Under the law of Nigeria, contempt of court is a criminal offence. Thus the Criminal code provides that any person who within the premises in which any judicial proceedings is being held or taken, or within the precincts of the same, shows disrespect, in speech or manner, to or with reference to such proceeding, or any person before whom such proceeding is being and or taken, or if a person is called upon to give evidence in a judicial proceeding, he fails to attend or having attended, refuses to be sworn or to make an affirmation or after being sworn or having affirmed, such a person, without lawful excuse refuses to answer questions or produce a document, or remains in the room in which proceedings are being conducted after he had been asked to leave such a room or if a person causes an obstruction or disturbance in the course of a judicial proceeding or if while a judicial proceeding is pending, a person makes use of any speech or writing, misrepresenting such proceeding or capable of prejudicing any person in favour of or against any party to such proceeding, or calculated to lower the authority of the bench; or while a proceeding is pending, a person publishes a report of the evidence taken in such judicial proceeding which has been directed to be held in private if a person wrongfully attempts to interfere with or influence a witness in a judicial proceeding either prior or after he has given evidence such person. found guilty of any of these offences, shall be liable to imprisonment for three months.[106]

The power to punish for contempt of court serves as important set of teeth granted to the judiciary to enhance its prestige, independence and impartiality. Where a person manifests utter disrespect for the court he may in certain cases be summarily committed for contempt of court and his liberty in such a case will be lawfully deprived. Thus in *Mu'Azu of Nunku v. Inspector-General of Police,*[107] where the accused disturbed and interrupted a judicial proceeding in spite of frequent warnings; it was held that the magistrate had the power to commit him summarily for contempt as the magistrate in fact did. It was held in *Onitiri v. Ojomo*[108] that no action for false imprisonment will lie when a magistrate by "acting judicially orders that a person be held in custody pending trial by another magistrate where such a person has committed a contempt of court . In *R.v Jackson,*[109] the accused was committed to prison for two months and

---

[106] S.133 of the Criminal Code.

[107] 1954 21 N.L.R. 34

[108] 1954 21 N.L.R. 19

[109] (1925) 6 N.L.R. 49, see also *R.v. Gray 1900 2 Q.B. 35; R.v. Davis 1906 1 K.B. 32; R.v. Ojukoko & others (1926) 7 N.L.R. Service Press Ltd (1952) 20 N.L.R. 96* a Service Press

ordered to pay costs of the proceedings for publishing articles in his newspaper which made grave aspersions against the integrity and impartiality of the Judges of the Court. In *R.v. Parke,*[110] Wills, J. vividly stated why the courts punish for contempt as follows:

> The reason why the publication of articles like those with which we have to deal is treated as contempt of court is because their tendency of the power of doing that to deprive the court of the power of doing that which is the end for which it exists - namely, to administer justice duly, impartially, and with reference solely to the facts judicially brought before it. Their tendency is to reduce the Court which has to try the case to impotence, so far as the effectual elimination of prejudice and prepossession is concerned. It is difficult to conceive an apter description of such conduct than is conveyed by the expression contempt of Court.

It may be observed that while it is very necessary that those who administer justice should be armed with the weapon of the powers to punish for contempt of court, justice itself and the principle of individual liberty demand that this weapon must be used sparingly especially with regard to comments made after a case has been disposed of by the Court. On this Lord Morris in *Mcleod v. St. Aubyn* said: "The power summarily to commit for contempt of court is considered necessary for the proper administration of justice . It is not to be used for vindication of a judge as a person. He must resort to action for libel. or criminal information . Committal for contempt of court is a weapon to be used sparingly, and always with reference to the interest of the administration of justice. Hence, when a trial has taken place and the case is over, the judge or the jury are given criticism..."[111]

(iii) *Arrest with or without Warrant - for the Purpose of Bringing a Person before a Court of Justice*

With regard to arrest with warrant, a police officer may lawfully effect an arrest of a person on a written warrant for the arrest of such a person granted by a justice of the peace or other .judicial authority who is vested with the power to issue warrants after a sworn information of the commission of criminal offence . The warrant must state clearly the name of the person to be arrested and the offence alleged to have been committed indicated equally. Thus Scott L.J . in *Leachinsky v. Christie* [112] said: "The

---

Limited was found guilty of contempt of court and fined £150 and ordered to pay 25 guineas costs to the Attorney-General.

110 (1903) 2 K.B. at pp. 436-7.

111 (1899) A.C. 549 at 561. The criticism, however, must be constructive and not vindictive or derogatory to the bench. For further details on Contempt of Court see *O.N Rewane: "Contempt of Court in Nigeria Criminal Law"* 1957 3 J.A.L. p. 172 et seq.

112 1946 1 K.B. 1 4 at p.130. See *Christie v Leachinsky* 1947 A.C. 573 (post). See S. 32 of the Criminal Justice Act, 1925.

very essence of the law of arrest of a person suspected of an offence is that arrest is the first step in an intended criminal proceeding against that person ... Summons and warrants of arrest are issued by a justice on an information being laid before him. A warrant of arrest may issue on a summons being disobeyed, or may issue in the first instance. Summonses, warrants, and arrests are mere machinery for securing the attendance of an accused person." His Lordship then quoting from a Statutory provision concluded: "Every information, complaint, summons, warrant or other document laid, issued or made ... shall be sufficient if it contains a statement of the specific offence ." There is no power to issue a general warrant to arrest unnamed person or even to conduct a search in that respect.[113] Dicey in his work appositely states: "The right to personal liberty as understood in England , means in substance a person's right not to be subjected to imprisonment, arrest or other physical coercion in any manner that does not admit of legal justification."[114]

With regard to arrest without warrant, the common law imposes a duty on everyone, whether police officer or private citizen, to arrest any person who in his presence commits a treason or felony or even dangerous wounding . The powers of a police officer , however, are wider in this respect. It must be pointed out that neither the Executive nor any other organ of the State has a right as such, to interfere, through the police or any other way, with the liberty of the individual by means of arbitrary arrest. As was established in *Leach v Money* (1765) and *Entic v Carrington* (1765)[115] a plea of an act of State is no defence to action brought by the individual to vindicate his right. It follows that while the law allows the deprivation of the liberty of the individual in certain circumstances it still jealously guards this inherent, (and under the Constitution) guaranteed right. However, in cases of treason or violent felony , a private person may use whatever force that is necessary for capturing the offender. He may, for instance, shoot him (preferably on the leg) if he cannot otherwise be prevented from escaping if the felon dies under the circumstances, that

---

113 *Leach v Money (1765), 19 St. Tr. 1002; Wilkes v Wood (1763) 19 St. Tr. 11. In Leach v Money, ibid* Lord Mansfield C.J. said: "There is no case for these uncertain warrants ... The magistrate ought to judge and give definite directions to the officer as to the person to be arrested."

114 As well as in Nigeria Dicey, *Law of the Constitution (9th ed.) pp. 207-208. If a person is illegally detained* he may institute a civil proceeding for false imprisonment.Thus in *Ezeani v Ekwealu 1961 All N.L.R.428,* the plaintiff who was arrested and held in custody by the order of the Onitsha County Court was not brought from the prison to the court for the trial of his case on the appointed day. This situation arose due to the default of the Court Messengers who should have gone to collect the accused from the prison; consequently he was held in custody until the following day. In an action for false imprisonment, Palmer J. held that the officer in charge of the prison was liable as the warrant for detention of a prisoner on remand requires him to convey the accused to the court on the appointed day; failing that the detention was wrongful imprisonment.

115 (1765) 19 St. Tr. 1030.

will be a justifiable homicide .[116] There is also power to arrest without warrant where any person is reasonably suspected of having committed treason or felony or dangerous wounding . In cases of this nature, a private person would have no defence to an action for false imprisonment if it transpires that no crime was in fact committed.[117] Where a person is arrested without warrant, he is entitled to be told immediately on what grounds he has been detained unless the reason for the arrest is obvious to the arrested person, for example, if he is caught in the actual commission of the crime ." In *Christie v Leachinsky*[118a] Lord Simon restated the law on the subject as follows:

"(1) If a policeman arrests without warrant upon reasonable suspicion of felony,[118b] or of other crime of a sort which does not require a warrant, he must in ordinary circumstances inform the person arrested of the true ground of arrest . He is not entitled to keep the reason to himself or to give a reason which is not the true reason. In other words a citizen is entitled to know on what charge or on suspicion of what crime he is seized.

"(2) If the citizen is not so informed but is nevertheless seized, the policeman, apart from certain exceptions, is liable for false imprisonment.

"(3) The requirement that the person arrested should be informed of the reason why he is seized naturally does not exist if the circumstances are such that he must know the general nature of the alleged offence for which he is detained.

"(4) The requirement that he should be so informed does not mean that technical or precise language need be used. The matter is a matter of substance, and turns on the elementary proposition that ... a person is, *prima facie entitled to his freedom and is only required to submit to restrains on his freedom if he knows in substance the reason why it is claimed that this restraint should be imposed.*[119]

"(5) The person arrested cannot complain that he has not been supplied with the above information as and when he should be, if he himself produces the situation which makes it particularly impossible to inform him, e.g. by immediate, counter-attack or by running away

---

[116] S.271 of the Criminal Code.

[117] *Walters v Smith & Son Ltd.* 1914 1 K.B. 595.

[118a] 1947 A.C. 573 at pp. 587-588.

[118b] In *Rice v Connolly 1966 2 All E.R. 649*, the right of a police officer to arrest without warrant on reasonable suspicion of felony was recognised but it was held that a citizen is entitled to decline to answer the questions put to him and (prior to his arrest) to accompany the police to a police box to establish his identity.

[119] Emphasis supplied.

> ... these principles equally apply to a private person who arrests on suspicion."

These common law principles are now embodied in the Nigerian Criminal Procedure Act .[120a]

Other circumstances in which the liberty of the individual could be deprived are in fact designed to benefit the individual concerned or to protect the society from any danger which might arise from his being let lose. Thus a person who has not attained the age of 21 years may be restricted for the purpose of his education and welfare persons suffering from infectious or contagious diseases may be isolated from the rest of the community. Equally lunatics and persons addicted to drugs or alcohol may be removed from the community for their treatment and in the interest of community preservation from possible acts of violence from such people. The State has also the right to hold in custody[120b] any person who unlawfully enters Nigeria or where an alien has been told to leave the country, he may be held in custody pending the expulsion of such person from the country. It must be pointed out however, that where such persons are held in custody, there must be no undue delay in taking them out of the country otherwise where the detention is not reasonable a writ of *habeas corpus* may issue on application for their release.

(C) *Determination of the Fundamental Rights or 'Due Process' Provisions*

The Constitution provides that in the determination of a person's civil rights and obligations, he shall be entitled to a fair hearing within a reasonable time by a court or other tribunals established by law and constituted in such manner as to secure its independence and impartiality. Whenever any person is charged with criminal offence , he shall be entitled to a fair hearing within a reasonable time by a court, and the proceedings shall be held in public. The court or such a tribunal may however exclude from its proceedings persons other than the parties thereto in the interest of defence, public safety , public order , public morality , the welfare of persons who have not attained the age of twenty-one years, the protection of the private lives of the parties or to such extent as it may consider expedient, by reason of special circumstances in which publicity would be contrary to the interests of justice or if a Minister of State certifies that publicity of the proceedings of the court or a tribunal would be contrary to public interest Every person who is charged with a criminal offence shall be presumed to

---

120a S.10 Cap. 43. On arrest by private persons, see S.12 *ibid*. See also S.28 of the Criminal Procedure Act 1960 (N.R) see equally SS.26-30 Criminal Procedure Code (W.R).

120b See S.5 of the Aliens (Deportation) Act Cap. 9. See also *Burma v Sarki (Fed. Minister of Internal Affairs)* 1962 2 All N.L.R. 62

be innocent until he is proved guilty. This provision does not however invalidate any law which imposes upon the accused the burden of proving certain facts.[121] Every person who is charged with a criminal offence shall be entitled to be informed promptly, in the language that he understands and in detail of the nature of the offence, and to be given adequate time and facilities for the preparation of his defence; to defend himself in person or by persons of his own choice who are legal practitioners and to examine in person or by his legal representatives witnesses called by the prosecution before any court and to obtain the attendance and carry out the examination of witnesses to testify on his behalf before the court on the same conditions as those applying to the witnesses called by the prosecution. The accused person shall equally be entitled to have without payment the assistance of an interpreter if he cannot understand the language used at the trial of the offence .

The section however recognises the lawful exclusion of legal representation in Customary or Native Courts in different parts of Nigeria.[122] The Constitution went on to provide that no person shall be held to be guilty of a criminal offence on account of any act or omission that did not, at the time it took place, constitute such an offence and no penalty shall be imposed for any criminal offence heavier than the penalty in force at the time the offence was committed. No person who shows that he has been tried by a competent court for a criminal offence and either convicted or acquitted shall again be tried for that offence, or for a criminal offence having the same ingredients as that offence save upon the order of a superior court. Equally no person who shows that he has been pardoned for a criminal offence shall again be tried for that offence.A person shall not in a criminal trial be compelled to give evidence. To protect the individual against dubious criminal offences the Constitution provides that 'No person shall be convicted of a criminal offence unless that offence is defined and the penalty therefore is prescribed in a written law.[123]

These Constitutional provisions serve as codification of the substantive rules of law under the Nigeria legal system. We shall therefore examine them in fuller detail for they essentially make for better administration of justice:

---

121 Prominent among these are of course a plea of insanity by the accused and certain statutory offences.

122 These are Native Courts Law, No. 6 of 1956, the Sharia Court of Appeal Law, the Court of Resolution Law Nos. 16 and 17 of 1960, - (N.R); Customary Courts Law No. 21 of 1956 (E.R), and Customary Courts Law 1959 Cap. 31 (W.R).

123 S.33(12) of the Constitution; on protection from conviction under unwritten law.

(i) *Right to Fair Hearing and Representation by Counsel*

Fair hearing may be defined as just and honest trial, a trial in which an accused person is given every opportunity to defend himself in a criminal proceeding. This implies a defence by himself or through a legal practitioner. It follows that the Courts will not allow any conviction to stand if it is shown that the accused has not been given a fair hearing. Thus in *Gokpa v Inspector-General of Police*[124] the High Court of Eastern Nigeria was called upon to quash a conviction because the accused was denied a fair hearing in a criminal proceeding against him. The appellant in that case was charged on various counts of stealing and forgery. The appellant first appeared before the Magistrate at Ogoni on 27th September, 1960 although the case had been in the Court list since 12th April, 1960. On the first appearance, no plea was taken and the case was adjourned to 25th October, 1960 - at the prosecution's request. On the 25th October, the case was not called. On November 28th,1960 the case again appeared on the list but neither the appellant nor his Counsel was present. Whereupon the Magistrate ordered a bench warrant to issue against the appellant and then adjourned the case to the next day.

On the next day, the appellant, was brought before the Court without his Counsel. The appellant informed the Court that he had Counsel and asked for adjournment to enable his Counsel to appear for his defence. What the Magistrate did was only to adjourn the case to later in the day, although appellant's counsel, and in fact any available, resided in Port Harcourt, not less than 23 miles away. There was no counsel available in the Court there and then. Later in the day, the hearing was resumed. Witnesses were called by the prosecution but the accused did not cross-examine them, in fact he did not take any active part in the proceedings. He refused to give evidence in his defence. The Magistrate found him guilty and sentenced him to two years hard labour on each count to run concurrently. He appealed - contending that the trial contravened the provisions of Section 21(2) (now Section 33(1) of the Constitution, in that he was not given a fair trial. Mbanefo, C.J. held that by depriving the appellant of the right to be represented by Counsel, the action of the Magistrate in that case amounted to denying the appellant the opportunity of a fair trial, contrary to the guaranteed of S.21(2) of the then Constitution. The appeal was allowed.

In course of his judgment his Lordship made a very important observation thus: "It is necessary in dealing with matters of this kind to bear in mind the justifiable anxiety of Magistrates to see that cases are disposed with minimum delay. It is in the accused's interest that it should be so. After six months and several adjournments one can understand the

---

124 (1961) 1 All N.L.R. 423.

Magistrate's desire to dispose of the case. But this should not be done at the expense of giving an accused person adequate opportunity of defending himself."[125]

It may be observed that in this case, it was not shown that the delay in disposing of the case was caused by the accused or his counsel. As his Lordship rightly pointed out,the expeditious disposing of cases of this kind is very necessary in the interest of justice. To have delayed the case for so long was unfair and to have started to be hasty at the eleventh hour and under the circumstances was unjustifiable. To have gone on with the case despite the fact that the accused intimated that he had counsel and no ample opportunity given to him to bring his counsel or any other, and the accused ultimately being convicted, was most unfair; especially as the accused ostensibly refused to take part in the proceeding under the circumstances.

It would have made some difference if the appellant, seeing that his counsel was not present, decided to conduct his case alone. Thus in Shemfe v Commissioner of Police,[126] the appellant contended that he was denied a fair trial because the court refused to adjourn in order to allow his counsel appear. It was shown that his counsel sent a telegram asking for the adjournment of the case to a certain day. But he did not consider it necessary to send another counsel to hold the brief for him. The court refused the request for adjournment and proceeded with the trial. The accused was convicted and sentenced on all the counts after he had conducted his own defence and cross-examined witnesses for the prosecution. Hurley, C.J. held that the trial was not unfair. His Lordship pointed out that the appellate court will not set aside a conviction only on the ground that the accused was deprived of the assistance of counsel where such deprivation was due to his counsel's own default. It may be observed that where a person retains the services of counsel, he should be given opportunity to defend himself through his counsel. A counsel who is briefed must see that he appears[127] or asks another counsel to hold the brief for him. Even where a person is granted assistance of counsel by the State, any attempt to proceed with the case in absence of the counsel would amount to unfair trial.[128] Thus their Lordships in *Galos Hired & Another v*

---

[125] *ibid*, at p.425. Now see *R. Ariori V.M.B.O. Elemo (1983) 1 S.C.13*. The inordinate delay while hearing the case and the Court's delay for several months after close of the case and addresses by counsel was held a violation of the constitutional right of fair hearing. The appeal was allowed by the Supreme Court. Vide equally: *Sunday Okoduwa & Ors. v The State (1988) 2 N.W.L.R. (pt. 76) 333*.

[126] (1962) 2 All N.L.R. 98.

[127] In *R. v Mary Kingston* 32 Cri. App. R. 183 at p. 188 it was pointed out that person who briefed counsel is at common law entitled to his services.

[128] In *Galos Hired & another v the King 1944 A.C. 149*. The Privy Council set aside a conviction by the Protectorate Court of Appeal of Somaliland because the advocate assigned to the accused was not present to defend them when the case came up for hearing and the court of Appeal made

The King[129] observed: "Just as a conviction following a trial cannot stand if there has been a refusal to hear counsel for the accused, so it seems to their Lordships, an appeal cannot stand where there has been a refusal to adjourn an appeal in which the appellant was entitled as of right to be heard by a Counsel assigned to him by the government who was unable, without any default on his part, to reach the court in time to conduct the appeal." Fair trial is a wide concept, it covers almost every aspect of judicial proceeding - pre-supposing an atmosphere of judicial trial untainted with any apparent prejudice nor subjected to any threat within or without the court. Thus the Supreme Court of the United States of America interfered with a State criminal conviction[130] on the ground that the accused persons were denied fair trial. The Court held that five Negroes who had been convicted in an Arkansas court and sentenced to death for the murder of a man were denied due process of law under the Fourteenth Amendment of the United States Constitution because their trial had been dominated by an angry and hostile mob.

To ensure fair trial, a criminal proceeding must be conducted in public unless State security makes it unsafe in a particular circumstance. In *Re Oliver*,[131] Mr. Justice Black, delivering the judgment of the Supreme Court of the United States said: "Whatever other benefits the guarantee to an accused that his trial be conducted in public may confer upon our society, the guarantee has always been recognised as a safeguard against any attempt to employ our courts as instruments of persecution. The knowledge that every criminal trial is subject to contemporaneous review in the forum of public opinion is an effective restrain on possible abuse of judicial power." In that case the accused was a witness before a judge who decided that his testimony was false. The judge there and then sentenced him to sixty-day jail term for contempt. The judge based his decision on confidential evidence which was not revealed the public was excluded from the proceedings. Oliver had no counsel; "no chance to prepare his defence and no opportunity either to cross-examine the other grand jury witnesses or to summon witnesses to refute charges against him. In quashing the conviction the Supreme Court said: "It is the law of the land that no man's

inquiry with regard to the advocate's absence nor found out when he might be expected to be available.

129 (1944) A.C. 149 at p. In *Samson v R. 1958 E.A. 681* the Court of Appeal of Eastern Africa allowed an appeal when Counsel for the accused obtained a leave to withdraw on the ground that he had not had time to see his client; the court then proceeded with the trial instead of adjourning to enable the accused to be represented. See also *Uusufu Gitta v R. (1959) E.A. 211*

130 *Moore Dempsey* 261 U.S. 86; See also *Real v Delanare* 103 U.S. 370, *Frank v Mangum* 237 U.S. 309.

131 333 U.S. 257 (1948) at p.269, 270.

life, liberty or property be forfeited as a punishment until there has been a charge fairly made and fairly tried in a public tribunal." [132]

The right of persons charged with crime to be represented by counsel at their trial is in substance denied where on being arraigned they were not asked whether they had or were able to employ counsel, or wished to have counsel appointed or whether they had friends or relatives who might assist in that regard if communicated with.[133]

Equally the right of one charged with crime to be represented by counsel includes a fair opportunity to secure counsel of his own choice. In *Awolowo v Sarki and Another*,[134] the plaintiff who was facing a charge of treasonable felony[135] instructed one Mr. E.F.N. Gratiaen, Q.C., a practising member of the United Kingdom Bar who had also been admitted to practice in Nigeria, to defend him. On his arrival at the Lagos Airport on November 8th, 1962, Mr. Gratiaen was refused entry into Nigeria by the direction of the first defendant who was then the Federal Minister of Internal Affairs. In his action the plaintiff sought declaration, (a) that he was entitled under the Constitution to be defended in the criminal charge by Mr. Gratiaen Q.C. or any other counsel of his own choice whether British or Nigerian (b) that the order of the first defendant and the Attorney-General of the Federation prohibiting the entry of the gentleman in question into Nigeria for the purpose for defending him in the said criminal charge was *ultra vires* the Nigerian Constitution Section S.21(5c) (now Section 22(5c), and consequently void. The plaintiff equally prayed the court for an injunction restraining the defendant from preventing the said Mr. Gratiaen or any other counsel of his choice from entering Nigeria for the purpose of defending him.

In refusing Mr. Gratiaen to enter Nigeria, the Minister asserted that he was legitimately exercising his powers under Section 13 of the Immigration Act, Cap. 84,which permitted him in his absolute discretion to prohibit any non-native of Nigeria from entering therein. The defendants contended that the plaintiff was not entitled to choose a legal practitioner who could not enter Nigeria as of right for his defence at the said criminal trial. The High Court of Lagos held that the first defendant's refusal to allow Mr. Gratiaen to enter Nigeria was lawful as such power was conferred on him by section 13 of the Immigration Act. It was further held that in exercising his powers under the Act in this respect, the first defendant had not acted contrary to Section 21(5c) of the Constitution as the "legal representatives"

---

[132] *ibid* at p.278. See also Chambers v Florida 309 U.S. 227, 236, 237.

[133] *Powell v Alabama 287 U.S. 45* (1932) Due process of law - right to counsel in this respect, extends to right to counsel even for the preparation for proper defence for the trial that would proceed: - *Cook v U.S.* 267 267 U.S. 517; *Pennoyer v Neff*, 95 U.S. 714.

[134] 1962 L.L.R. 177.

[135] *R. v Omisade & Others* (1964) N.M.L.R. 67 (ante).

mentioned thereunder meant those not under a disability of any sort. That is to say those who could enter the country as of right. The Court was also of the view that first defendant had not acted maliciously.[136]

In the course of his judgement,Udo-Udoma, J. said: "I must state at once that I do not accept as a sound proposition that submission that the provision contained in Section 21(5c) of the Constitution liberally interpreted, can be construed to entitle anyone to bring a counsel from the United Kingdom for the purpose of defending him in a criminal charge. To accept that interpretation would be to strain the language. The Constitution is a Nigerian Constitution, meant for Nigerians in Nigeria. It only runs in Nigeria. The natural consequence of this is that the legal representative contemplated in Section 21(5c) ought to be someone in Nigeria and not outside it."[137] It is submitted with great respect that this dictum went too far that it almost emptied itself of substantial accuracies. Surely the Constitution is not only meant for Nigerians in Nigeria. The Constitution being the Supreme law of the land, like most of the written and even some unwritten law of Nigeria binds Nigerians wherever they may be. It follows equally that the benefits or rights conferred on Nigerians by the Constitution run with them wherever they may be. International law allows States to make laws having extra-territorial effect, a fortiori, to the extent of binding foreign citizens, on condition that such laws are not enforced in any place outside the territorial jurisdiction of the State enacting such laws.[138] So the Nigerian Constitution is not only meant for Nigerians in Nigeria but also Nigerians outside Nigeria. It therefore in some respect runs outside Nigeria. For if one who derives a right under the Constitution is denied such a right when he is outside Nigeria and such right could be exercised from outside the country, the denial would amount to contravention of the Constitution. It is equally submitted that the right guaranteed under S.21(5) now Section 33(6)(c) was not restricted to Nigerian citizens. It applies to "Every person who is charged with a criminal offence." So aliens[139] equally are entitled to shelter under the protective umbrella of the sub-section.

---

[136] The Court however observed that "it is even doubtful whether motive and intention are relevant in a case like the present one in which absolute discretionary power has been given to the first defendant by Parliament" 1962 L.L.R. at p.18. For this the Court relied on the well known case of *Mayor of Bradford v Pickles 1895 A.C. 587 at p.594*. It is submitted with every respect that Pickles' case is not on all fours with the case under consideration. The Minister is here required to exercise a statutory discretion and this must be done in good faith. See *Minister of National Revenue v Wrights Canadian Ropes 1947 A.C. 109; Lord Keyon C.J. in Wilson v Rastall (1792) 100 E.R. 1283 at p. 1288*. It is however not being suggested that the Minister acted with malice.

[137] (1962) L.L.R. 177 at pp.184-5.

[138] See *The Lotus Case (1927) Series A No. 10 (decided by The P.C.I.J.)*.

[139] Aliens for this purpose are persons who are not Nigerian nationals.

It was not disclosed that Mr. Gratiaen did any thing wrong that would have warranted his exclusion from Nigeria especially as he was a member of the Nigerian Bar. From this point of view his exclusion, to my mind, is unsupportable. The incident would have earned Nigeria a very bad name but for the fact that Mr. Victor Durand, Q.C. of the British Bar was subsequently allowed to enter Nigeria and he argued Chief Awolowo's appeal against his conviction.[140]

With regard to right to be represented by Counsel, the Legal Practitioners Act, 1962 has narrowed it down in such a way that the choice of counsel will invariably be within the Nigerian Bar.[141] Whatever may be the case, obstacles should not be put in the way of any person when it falls that one has to choose counsel to defend him in a criminal proceeding. Defence by counsel is very essential to an accused person and to ensure that not only that justice must be done but seen to be done when an accused person requires the services of counsel he must be allowed to avail himself of them. However, refusal of a trial court to appoint counsel for one prosecuted for robbery who requests such appointment on the ground that he is without funds to employ counsel is not a denial of due process of law or right to be defended by counsel.[142]

(ii) *Presumption of Innocence*

The Constitutional provision[143] enshrines the well known rule of the Nigerian criminal law that every person is presumed to be innocent until he is proved guilty. This common law rule was appositely stated by Lord Sankey L.C. in the famous case of *Woolmington v D.P.P.* [144] as follows:

---

140 The appeal was however dismissed; see *R. v Omisade* (1964) N.M.L.R. 67.

141 S.3 of the Legal Practitioners Act, 1962, makes Nigerian citizenship a condition for enrolment in the Nigerian Bar.

142 *Smith Betts v Brady 316 U.S. 454*. The right is bestowed to 'every person who is charged with criminal offence'; it may not be extended to an enquiry set up by the Executive - *Chia Khinsze v Mentri Bensar, State of Selangor (1958) 2 M.L.R. (Malayan Law Journal) 105*. Fair hearing and right to the services of counsel came to be considered in the case of *R. v Eguabor (1962) 1 All N.L.R. 287*. In that case the Federal Supreme Court quashed a conviction because the proceeding was not interpreted to the accused in the language he understood, when it transpired that his counsel turned against him and was no longer in effect conducting the defence for which he had been employed . "It is a miscarriage of justice ... that the counsel should have continued to represent the appellant without the appellant's being aware that the counsel to whom he looked to present his case had gone over to the enemy" - per Brett F.J. at p. 293. There was misunderstanding between counsel and the accused, for Counsel felt that what the accused was telling the court was different from what he told him. Whereupon Counsel disclosed the instructions given to him by the accused. This was strongly disapproved of by the Federal Supreme Court. No such disclosures should be made.

143 S.33(5).

144 (1935) A.C. 462 at p. 481. In *Rex v Buddle Udo Edem Eka* (1945) 11 W.A.C.A. 39 at p.40; Kingdon, C.J. said: "It is fundamental that in a criminal trial the onus is upon the prosecution to

> "Throughout the web of the English Criminal Law one golden thread is always to be seen, that it is the duty of the prosecution to prove the prisoner's guilt ... If,at the end of and on the whole case, there is a reasonable doubt, created by the evidence given by either the prosecution or the prisoner, as to whether the prisoner killed the deceased with a malicious intention, the prosecution has not made out the case and the prisoner is entitled to an acquittal. No matter what the charge or where the trial, the principle that the prosecution must prove the guilt of the prisoner is part of the common law of England and no attempt to whittle it down can be entertained."

The presumption of innocence of an accused person is absolutely essential in the administration of justice. It shields an accused person against any prejudice which might operate against his defence. It leaves a case open and uncontaminated by outside influence and casts the burden of proving on the prosecution. Where therefore a judge fails to direct the jury that the onus of proving the guilt of the accused rests on the prosecution to discharge beyond reasonable doubt, that would amount to disregard of essential form of justice and a conviction arising from such direction may not stand. Thus in *Lawrence v The King.*[145] The Privy Council had to deal with an appeal from a judgment of the Full Court of the Supreme Court of Nigeria. The grounds of the appeal were (1) the absence of any adequate direction to the jury as to the issues they had to try. especially as to burden of proof; (2) the invalidity of the recorded sentence. The accused in that case was an Administrative Officer who was charged on an information containing sixteen counts involving charges of stealing and false accounting. The trial was by jury. In his direction, to the jury, Berkeley J., 'inadvertently' omitted to tell the jury that the onus of proving the guilt of the accused person lay with the prosecution, and that the prosecution must prove that guilt beyond any reasonable doubt - thus demolishing the presumption of the innocence of the accused.

The Privy Council held that the lack of such direction was fatal to the conviction consequently the conviction and sentence were set aside. In delivering the judgment of the Board, Lord Atkin said: "A more important objection is that throughout the Judge's charge he did not give the jury any direction at all as to the onus of proof, or that the accused was entitled to the benefit of a reasonable doubt... The true direction would be that the onus always was on the Crown i.e. the prosecution but if the jury believed that the accused had the money, and were not satisfied that his reason for not

---

prove all the elements which go to make up the offence charged. If it fails to prove any of them the accused is entitled to an acquittal, and if in spite of that he is convicted, he is entitled to have the conviction quashed on appeal.

[145] 1933 A.C. 699; (1933) 11 N.L.R. 6.

accounting for it was true, there was evidence upon which they might if they chose find him guilty of stealing."[146]

The presumption of innocence is a presumption of law. Thus in Williams v East India Company[147] it was held that where the plaintiff declared that the defendants, who had chartered his ship, put on board dangerous substances without due notice to the captain or any other person concerned in the navigation, it lay upon him to prove even such negative averment,'as the law presumed innocence of such a criminal neglect of duty." The constitutional provision in respect of presumption of innocence was closely examined in the case of *Ibeziako v Commissioner of Police.*[148] In that case, a magistrate, acting in accordance with Chapter XVI of the Criminal Procedure Code[149] (dealing with summary trials) took the evidence of some of the prosecution witnesses and then framed a charge against the accused who was brought before him for trial. Section 160(1) of the Code required a magistrate to frame a charge if after taking evidence of the prosecution witnesses or at any previous stage of the case the court i.e. the magistrate was of opinion that there was a ground for presuming that the accused had committed an offence. The accused then pleaded not guilty to the charge and after further evidence he was convicted. He appealed contending that the procedure adopted for his trial contravened the provisions of section 21(4) (now section 33(5) of the Constitution which provided that every person who is charged with a criminal offence should be presumed innocent until he is proved guilty. It was strongly contended that the magistrate who framed the charge must have presumed that the accused was guilty. The Federal Supreme Court held that the Submission that the magistrate must have presumed the accused guilty was ill founded, and that the provisions of Section 21(4) of the Constitution were not infringed. The appeal was dismissed.

It is submitted that although the case was rightly decided, the provisions of the Criminal Procedure Code requiring a magistrate to hold trial of an accused person brought before him, and then to frame charges against the accused, if he 'is of the opinion that there is a ground for presuming that the accused has committed' an offence, requires further examination. It is further submitted that a magistrate who frames a charge against an accused and that accused is tried on those charges, is hardly to be presumed impartial. It is worse when the accused is to be tried by the same

---

[146] *ibid,* at pp. 706-7; pp.6-7.The rule as to burden of proof beyond reasonable doubt is now embodied in S.137 (1) & (2) of the Evidence Act, Cap. 62, Laws of Nigeria, 1958.

[147] (1802) 3 East 192; 102 E.R. 571.

[148] (1963) N.R.N.L.R. 88. Where in a civil case a party bases his pleadings on a crime alleged to have been committed by the other party, such allegation must be proved beyond reasonable doubt - *Ezekwe v Otomewo (1957) W.R.N.L.R. 130.*

[149] Criminal Procedure Code (N.R) Cap. 30, Laws of Northern Nigeria, 1963, Vol. I.

magistrate. For it is not unlikely that such a magistrate might crave to see his charges vindicated by the conviction of the accused. We are not for one moment imputing that a magistrate under such circumstances would be partial. All we are putting forward is that by requiring a magistrate to frame a charge at a stage in his trial of a case appears to expose him to a charge from the defence's side that 'he had gone over to the enemy.'[150] It is difficult to see how presumption of innocence should not be put in jeopardy if a magistrate should after hearing evidence or even 'at any stage of the case' turn to draft a charge against the same accused. Surely it is the duty of the prosecution to investigate a case, draft the charges and get witnesses to support these. If the prosecution fails in this respect and consequently fail to establish a *prima facie* case against the accused, justice demands that such a case should be allowed to fail instead of endangering the independence and impartiality of the Judiciary. We suggest that this part of the Criminal Procedure Code be amended and this delicate duty imposed on the magistrates removed.

(iii) *No Double Jeopardy - i.e. no person shall be punished twice for the same Offence*

The Constitution makes it perfectly clear that a person shall not be put in double jeopardy in respect of the same offence. Thus Section 33(9) (10) of the Constitution provides:-

> No person who shows that he had been tried by an competent court for a criminal offence and either convicted or acquitted shall again be tried for that offence or for a criminal offence having the same ingredients as that offence save upon the order of a superior court; and no person who shows that he has been pardoned for a criminal offence shall again be tried for that offence.

The general principle of the common law is *nemo debet bis vexari*: a man must not be put twice in peril for the same offence. In *R. v Otio Enwa,*[151a] an accused was convicted and sentenced on a charge of rape. During the trial it was discovered that he had already been tried in a Native Court on a charge of adultery on the same facts, found guilty, and sentenced. Kingdon, C.J. delivering the judgment of the court held that there was no jurisdiction to entertain the case as the accused had already been tried and punished before the Native Court. If a person had been indicted for an

---

[150] A term used by Brett F.J. in *R. v Eguabor (1962), 1 All N.L.R. 287 at p. 293* in respect of counsel who apparently turned hostile to his client, the accused, and disclosed his instructions from the accused to the advantage of the prosecution in the open court. As we pointed out earlier, the Supreme Court sternly disapproved of such unfairness to the accused.

[151] (1943) 9 W.A.C.A. 194. The Court relied on S.16 of the Criminal Code which is now repealed by No. 43 of 1945

offence he can plead as a complete defence his former acquittal [151b] or conviction.[152] *autrefois acquit or autrefois convict.* It was held in *Sambasivam v Public Prosecutor, Federation of Malaya* [153] that the plea was available even though the acquittal or conviction took place in a foreign country. It is submitted that this should be the case where such issues are raised in Nigerian Courts, provided the ingredients are the same.

(iv) *Freedom from Conviction Under Undefined Offence*

As was indicated above, because a great part of the law of Nigeria remains unwritten it was felt that the individual must be protected against any dubious criminal charge. Thus Section 33(12) of the Constitution provides that 'no person shall be convicted of a criminal offence unless that offence is defined and the penalty therefore is prescribed in a written law.' This provision is necessary because of the complex nature of the customary or unwritten law. Under civil law, any person can institute any action based on customary law provided he can prove that that custom in which he relies has been accepted as binding as law by the people. That is to say, that the particular custom had crystallised into customary law. But the position is different under criminal law; the liberty of the individual requires a stringent control of the unwritten law and the court will not hesitate to quash any conviction in the customary courts which contravenes the Constitutional provision. Thus in *Aoko v Fagbemi* [154] the High Court of Western Nigeria was called on to quash a conviction by a Customary Court on the ground that it contravened Section 21 (10), now Section 33(12) of the Constitution. In that case, the applicant, a woman, had been convicted and sentenced to a fine of £2.10 or to go to jail for one month by a Grade 'D' Customary

---

[151b] In *Nwali v Inspector-General of Police 1956 1 E.R.L.R. 1* the appellant was charged before a Magistrate with four offences contrary to Section 116 (1) of the Criminal Code. When the prosecution failed to prove certain facts necessary for the conviction of the appellant, he was discharged. The Magistrate, however, stated that he discharged him "not on the merits of the case." After three days he was again charged with precisely the same offences and before the same Court. Whereupon he pleaded autrefois acquit. The Magistrate refused to accept this plea and proceeded with the trial. On this occasion the prosecution proved the facts which they were previously unable to prove, and the appellant was convicted. He appealed. It was held that the appellant's plea of autrefois acquit should be sustained. Consequently the appeal was allowed and the conviction quashed. In his judgment Ainley, Ag. J. (as he then was) said: "If the prosecution fail to prove their case so that the Magistrate, if he does his duty, must decide on the evidence that the accused is not guilty of the offence, charged, he should indicate that that is his decision, and should discharge the accused," ibid, at p.4. This should be the case, for once an accused is discharged and acquitted on a charge, he must not be subjected to double jeopardy. See *Inspector-General of Police v Marke 1957 N.R.N.L.R. 89; Halsted v Clark V. 1944 1 All E.R. 270.*

[152] *R. v Burnham Justices, Exp. Ansorge 1959 3 All E.R. 505*, See especially p.507.

[153] (1950)66 T.L.R. 254.

[154] (1961) 1 All N.L.R. 400.

Court for an alleged offence (this wás a charge of adultery of which she had pleaded guilty). She was also ordered to pay £5 compensation and £1.7.0 costs. Evidence was adduced to show that she was living with another man 'without judicial separation.' It was submitted on her behalf that as there was no written law which she had violated her conviction was contrary to the provisions of Section 21 (now S.22 sub-section (10) of the Constitution. Fatayi Williams, J. (as he then was) upheld the submission and quashed the conviction and ordered all the money paid by the woman to be refunded to her.

(D) *Right to Respect of Privacy and Family Life*

Section 34 of the Constitution provides that "Every person shall be entitled to respect for his private and family life, his home and his correspondence." Sub-section 2 of Section 23, however, provides for exception which protects any law that is reasonably justifiable in a democratic society in the interest of defence, of public safety, public order, public morality, public health or the economic well-being of the community; or for the purpose of protecting the rights and freedom of other persons, fro;m being invalidated.

The Constitutional provisions may be said to have codified the common law on the subject although the exceptions are wider under the Constitution. Under the common law, no one has a right to enter the house of another against his will.[155] In *Great Central Railway Co. v Bates, Lord Hewart*, C.J. said: It appears to be very important that it should be established that nobody has a right to enter premises except strictly in accordance with authority."[156a]

The Nigerian Criminal Procedure Act [156b] authorises entry to premises to effect an arrest under a warrant. Thus section 7 of the Act provides: "If any person or Police Officer acting under a warrant of arrest or otherwise having authority to arrest has reason to believe that the person to be arrested has entered into or is within any place, the person residing in or being in charge of such place shall, on demand of such person acting as aforesaid or such Police Officer, allow him free ingress thereto and afford all reasonable facilities to search therein for the person sought to be arrested." Sub-section (2) of the same section goes on to add to the power conferred. It provides that, "If ingress to such place cannot be obtained under sub-section (1), any such person or Police Officer may enter such place and search therein for

---

[155] Per Beadle, C.J. in R. v Nkomo and Others 1963 (4) S.A. 166 at p.177.

[156a] (1921) 3 K.B. 578 at p.582.

[156b] Cap. 43, vol, II Laws of Nigeria, 1958. In *Elias v Pasmore (*1934) 2 K.B. 164, it was held that inter alia, that the Police may enter premises in order to execute a warrant for arrest, and search a person whom they have lawfully arrested

the person to be arrested, and in order to effect an entrance into such place, may break open any outer or inner door or window of any house or place, whether that of the person to be arrested or any other person or otherwise effect entry into such house or place, if after notification his authority and purpose, and demand of admittance duely made, he cannot otherwise obtain admittance." Under section 8 of the Act any Police Office or other person authorised to make an arrest may break out of any house or place in order to liberate himself or any other person who, having lawfully entered for the purpose of making an arrest, is detained therein.

It follows that even under the Act, before a Police Officer or any person as provided in the Act could enter any premises, he must give notice to the occupier. This might be in a form of a demand to enter but unless that is done, the entry would be illegal. Thus in a Southern Rhodesian case, *R. v Nkomo and Others*,[157] the court was to construe an enactment[158] which was similar to the Nigerian Criminal Procedure Act, Section 7. In that case, Beadle, C.J. posed and answered the most important question in the case as follows: 'Was the action of the Police in forcibly entering room 27 without the permission of and against the will of the owners, lawful, and was the laying of hands on Nkomo lawful?"[159] The learned Chief Justice after dealing with two instances under the Act in which the Police may enter a man's house against his wish, one of which being when the Police are armed with a lawful search warrant, went on and made a very important observation. He said: "It seems implicit from the Act that unless a Police Officer is acting under the provisions of one of these sections he has no right to enter private premises against the wish of the owner." He continued: "Even when the Police are lawfully authorised to arrest a person inside the premises, they may not enter the premises, until they have audibly demanded admission and notified the purpose for which they seek entry."[160] He therefore held that the Police had no right under the Act to enter the said room 27 for the purpose of arresting Mr. Nkomo without permission of, and against the will of the owners.

The Police, however, in execution of their duty, may enter a premises and may remain there if a meeting in which a crime might be committed or which might lead to a breach of the peace is going on.[161a] It must be pointed out that unless a Police Officer is acting under a warrant he cannot claim a right to enter and remain in a private premises. Thus in *Davis v Lisle*, [161b]

---

157 1963 (4) S.A. 166.

158 Criminal Procedure and Evidence act, Cap. 28 (S.R).

159 *ibid*, at p.171.

160 *ibid*, at p.172.

161a *Thomas v Sawkins* (1935) 2 K.B. 249.

161b (1936) 2 K.B. 434.

the respondent, a Police Officer, believing that an offence had been committed by the appellant in causing an obstruction in the highway with a motor lorry, followed the lorry into the appellant's garage for the purpose of making enquiries with regard to the obstruction. The respondent did not obtain the appellant's permission to enter the garage. He had no warrant to that effect. The appellant directed the respondent to leave the premises, but the respondent in refusing to do that claimed that he was entitled to remain there. He was then assaulted by the appellant. It was held that even if the respondent, i.e. the Police Officer, had a right to enter the garage to make inquiries, he became a trespasser after the appellant had told him to leave the premises, and that having been asked to leave the premises he was not therefore acting thenceforward in the execution of his duty; consequently the appellant could not be convicted of assaulting or obstructing the Police Officer in the execution of this duty.

(E) *Freedom of Conscience and Religion*

Section 35 of the Constitution provides that 'Every person shall be entitled to freedom of thought, conscience and religion, including freedom to change his religion, or belief and freedom either alone or in community with others and in public or in private, to manifest and propagate his religion or belief in worship, teaching practice and observance no person attending any place of education shall be required to receive religious instruction or to take part in or attend any religious ceremony or observances if such instructions, ceremony or observances relate to a religion other than his own[162] no religious community or denomination shall be prevented from providing religious instruction for pupils of that community or denomination in any place of education maintained wholly by that community or denomination.'

The freedom guaranteed was not to invalidate 'any law that is reasonably justifiable in a democratic society in the interest of defence, public safety, public morality or public health; or for the purpose of protecting the rights and freedom of other persons, including their rights and freedom to observe and practise their religions without the unsolicited intervention of members of other religions.'

While the Constitution guarantees freedom of thought, conscience and religion, the Criminal Code [163] makes it an offence to disturb religious worship. Section 206 of the Code provides that any person who wilfully

---

162 This particular provision is very essential in view of the fact that in Nigeria like some countries, there are certain public schools where children of different religions are educated. It was held in an American case, School District of Abington Township v Schemp, 364 U.S. 299 (1960) that daily Bible reading in the public school as required by a Pennsylvanian statute as well as the practice of saying the Lord's Prayer in unison was unconstitutional.

163 Cap. 42.

and without lawful justification or excuse, disquiets, or disturbs any meeting of persons lawfully assembled for religious worship, or assaults any person lawfully officiating at any such meeting, or any of the persons there assembled, is guilty of an offence and liable to imprisonment for two months, or to a fine of five pounds. It is equally an offence to insult a religion with an intention that any class of persons should consider it as such. The offence, which is a misdemeanour, is punishable by two years imprisonment.[164]

Religious discrimination is not rife in Nigeria with the result that our courts have not on many occasions been called upon to deal with cases having to do with breaches of the law or the constitution in this respect. However, in *Ojiegbe v Ubani* [165] what apparently was an election petition, turned out to be a case to be fought on religious points. In that case, the applicants filed an election petition disputing the result of an election held on the 12th December, 1959, to the House of Representatives in respect of the Aba Central Constituency. The main objection to the election result was that in the Constituency in question there were between six to seven thousand Seventh Day Adventists whose rights, it was contended, were violated by holding the said election on a Saturday in that they were subjected to disability or restriction by so holding the election on that day. They maintained that it was contrary to the ethics of their religion to do anything or any manner of work on a Saturday being their Sabbath Day. Consequently many of them, for fear of being excommunicated from their Church, refrained from going to the Polls. The interesting aspect of the facts of this case was that when the polling date was fixed by the Governor-General, protests were made by the sect that it was contrary to their religious belief to exercise the right to vote on a Saturday. These people in their protest requested that the polling day should be changed to Friday 11th December, 1959. The request was refused. It was shown in evidence that the defeated candidate lost the election by over twenty thousand votes. The Federal Supreme Court of Nigeria held that even if all the six to seven thousand Seventh Day Adventists in the constituency had voted for the defeated candidate the result would have been the same for he was defeated by over twenty thousand votes. Thus the Court upheld the decision of the High Court of Eastern Region in dismissing the election petition.

It is difficult to see the wisdom behind the procedure adopted in that case, by including in an election petition, a case involving violation of the provisions of the Constitution protecting fundamental rights and freedoms of the voters who happened to belong to a particular religious sect. If an action was brought before the High Court immediately the Electoral

---

164 S. 204, *ibid.*

165 (1961) 1 All N.L.R. 277.

Commission refused a postponement of the date of the election at the request of the seven thousand Seventh Day Adventist voters, the High Court would have been in a better position to make such orders under Section 32 of the Constitution as it might deem expedient to protect the voting rights of such large number of electors in the constituency in question. The High Court should not be expected to do something to protect the voting rights of these people or the religious freedom which was involved as the action was brought *ex post facto*. The election could not be nullified as the Court found out that the abstention of the voters on religious grounds did not affect the result of the election. It follows therefore that those members of the Seventh Day Adventist Church should have brought an action in the High Court to the effect that their religious right guaranteed to them under the Constitution had been infringed. Such action should have been brought as soon as the Chairman of the Electoral Commission refused the request to change the polling date. It would then be left to the High Court to examine all the issues involved and make appropriate decision, which might, if necessary, entail alteration of the date of the election in that particular constituency.

(F) *Freedom of Expression and Freedom to Hold Opinions*

The right of the individual to express his opinion freely is one of the essential characteristics of a free society. This basic right is now guaranteed under Section 36 of the Constitution which provides that every person shall be entitled to freedom of expression, including freedom to hold opinions and receive and impart ideas and information without interference. This freedom both under the Constitution and the substantive law of Nigeria is a freedom hedged around with necessary restrictions. Thus the section under the Constitution goes on to provide that 'nothing in this section shall invalidate any law that is reasonably justifiable in a democratic society, in the interest of defence, public safety, public order, public morality or public health for the purpose of protecting the rights, reputations and freedom of other persons, preventing the disclosure of information received in confidence, maintaining the authority and independence of the courts or regulating telephony, wireless broadcasting, television or the exhibition of cinematography films or imposing restrictions upon persons holding office under the state, members of the armed forces of the Federation or members of a Police Force.

Despite these restrictions, the courts in Nigeria recognise that they have a duty to protect the right of the individual to express his opinion with regard to different aspects of State administration; to criticise fairly and objectively the government of the day, by words spoken or written or through the press. Fortunately, the press in Nigeria, like many other countries in the Commonwealth is virtually free.[166] Brett, F.J. said in *Ogidi v Commissioner of Police*[167] "We fully agree that the law of sedition must not be stretched beyond its function of protecting public order and that it is the duty of the courts to safeguard the right of freedom of expression, which is now embodied in the constitution of Nigeria." A similar judicial pronouncement was made by Shastri J. in *Romesh Thappar v State of Madras* [168] as follows: "... freedom of speech and of the press lay at the foundation of all democratic organisations, for without free political discussion no public education, so essential for the proper functioning of the processes of popular Government, is possible." Freedom of speech and expression is not limited to any particular field of human interest,[169] but assures the broadest tolerable exercise of the right for religious, political, economic and scientific purposes.[170]

Recently in Oliver v Buttigieg,[171] the Privy Council was called upon to validate an order which prohibited circulation of a particular newspaper in certain hospitals. In that case the appellants contended that a circular issued in April, 1962 which prohibited the entry of the respondents newspaper the "Voice of Malta" was not in breach of sections 13 and 14 of the Malta (Constitution) Order in Council, 1961. The appellants who were the Minister of Health and the Chief Government Medical Officer in Malta, in issuing the circular, acted in response to ecclesiastical authorities' condemnation of 'certain newspapers' in Malta, one of which was the newspaper in question, a labour party newspaper. The employees of the hospitals and the branches affected by the ban numbered 2,660 persons. The respondent claimed that the circular in question, insofar as it affected the "Voice of Malta" was an infringement of his constitutional rights of

---

166 See D.C. Holland, *"Freedom of the Press in the Commonwealth" (1956) 9 Current Legal Problem* (C.L.P) 184.

167 (1960) W.R.N.L.R. 201 at p.203.

168 (1950) S.C.R. 594, 602 (Supreme Court Report, India).In *Thornhill v Alabama 310 U.S. 88 (1939)*, the Supreme Court of the United States observed 'that the safeguarding of freedom of speech and press to the ends that men speak as they think on matters vital to them, and that falsehoods may be exposed through the process of education and discussion, is essential to free government.' Consequently it declared that a State statute which made it an offence to go near a business premises for the purpose of influencing or inducing other persons not to have business dealings with or be employed by such person violated the constitutional guarantees of freedom of speech and the press. An enactment which prohibits circulation of certain materials through which information is disseminated is an interference with the right of free speech and press. Thus in *Loveli v City of Griffin 303 U.S. 444 (1937)* the U.S. Supreme Court held that a municipal ordinance prohibiting the distribution without a permit of circulars, handbooks, advertising, or literature of any kind, whether delivered free or sold was invalid on its face as infringing the constitutional freedom of the press. See also *Martin v. Struthers 319 U.S. 141 (1942)*.

169 *Thomas v Collins 323 U.S. 516, 531 (1945)*

170 *Douglas v Jeanette 319 U.S. 157, 179 (1942)*.

171 (1966)2 All E.R. 459.

freedom of expression. The Privy Council held that the prohibition went beyond reasonable orders regulating the conduct of employees during working hours and constituted a hinderance of the respondent in the enjoyment of his freedom of expression, viz. to impart information and ideas without interference. The Board therefore held that the circular which carried the prohibition contravened section 14 (2) of the Constitution of Malta. This case is particularly interesting because the cause of action emanated not from a legislation but merely from executive order which was issued in guise of instruction to ensure discipline during working hours; the Courts were not impressed by this idea nor the view that the prohibition was minimal. It was fully established that the prohibition was an 'interference' in the respondent's freedom of expression which included a freedom to impart ideas and information. The Board took note of the observation of the Court of Appeal of Malta in respect of effect of such prohibition in the circulation of the said newspaper; that "if it were to be held that the present appellants had the right to issue the circular in question naturally the same right would appertain to each and every other Minister and Head of Department in respect of the department under his charge, in such a way that the interference with circulation and reading of his newspaper would be vastly widened and extended with impunity."[172]

This case is particularly important in view of the fact that it is now a common practice for certain Regions and even certain local authorities to ban some newspapers from circulating in their areas. On the authority of the above case and many of the American decisions[173] on the subject, such bans could be successfully challenged in our Courts. A Legislature may however include in an enactment provisions which prohibit publication in a newspaper of intentional falsehood. Thus section 14 of the Eastern Region of Nigeria Newspaper Law, 1955[174] provides that any person who publishes or reproduces in a newspaper any statement, rumour or report knowing or having reason to believe that such statement, rumour or report is false shall be guilty of an offence and liable upon conviction to a fine of £200 or to imprisonment for one year.

In *Attorney-General, Eastern Region of Nigeria v Amalgamated Press of Nigeria Ltd.*,[175] Aimley, C.J. in upholding legality of the 1955 Newspaper Law said: "The Eastern Legislature has not, as I see it, made any attempt to limit or control the sale of the commodity known as a newspaper. Simply they have said that it is an offence to publish in this Region in a newspaper that which is known, or should be known to be

172 *ibid*, at p.467, per Lord Morris of Borth - Y - Gest.

173 *Carlson v California 310 U.S. 106; Schneider v Irvington 308 U.S. 147; Hague v Committee for Industrial Organisation 307 U.S. 496; Thornhill v Alabama 310 U.S. 88 (Supra.)*

174 No. 24 of 1955, Laws of Eastern Region of Nigeria, 1955 p.A. 141 .

175 (1956) 1 E.R. L.R. 12

false. In effect they say "Sell all the newspapers you wish in this Region, but do not publish lies in this Region or we will punish you."[176]

Control over Freedom of Expression

The liberty of expression presupposes liberty according to law. Every person has got the freedom to express his opinion provided that that which he says or writes or prints does not contravene the law, whether civil or criminal. To accommodate this inevitable restriction, the Constitution provides that any such law which might operate as a check on the said freedom shall not be invalidated if it is 'reasonably justifiable in a democratic society'[177] The Control is principally effected through the law relating to defamation, sedition, obscenity, blasphemy and certain statutory restrictions in respect of wireless telegraphy and cinematograph and the law having to do with Official Secrets.

(i) *Defamation*

Defamation may be defined simply as an injury to a person's reputation. A matter is defamatory if it exposes the individual about whom it is published to hatred, ridicule or contempt, or which causes him to be shunned or avoided by other people.[178] It is essential in the law of defamation that the matter complained of must have been published to a third person. If the matter is in writing, printing or in some other permanent form, then it is

---

[176] *ibid*, at p.13. See also *D.P.P. v Associated Newspaper of Nigeria Ltd.* (1959) W.R.N.L.R. 247.

[177] The phrase *'reasonably justifiable in a democratic society'* was adopted from the European Convention on Human Rights which provides for restrictions which "are necessary in a democratic society" - Article 10. But this phrase was not defined. In *Cheranci v Alkali Cheranci 1960 N.R.N.L.R. 24 at p. 29*, Bates J. dealing with the constitutionally and the reasonable justifiability of the Children and Young Persons Law, 1958 (N.R) said: "... the restriction must be reasonably necessary in the interests of public ... Morals, safety or welfare. It must have a real and substantial relation to the object sought to be attained by the restriction ... The restriction must not be in excess of the requirement. In other words the freedom must not be abridged or curtailed unduly or arbitrarily." In *D.P.P. v Obi (1961) 1 All N.L.R. 186 at p.196* Ademola, C.F.J. said that the Federal Supreme Court "must be the arbiter of whether or not any particular law is reasonably justifiable." This duty of course extends to all our courts. Thus in *Pawa v Akangbe (1961) W.N.L.R. 268* Somolu, J. held inter alia that the custom of paying "lada" to the Head of a certain community in Oyo on the sale of each cow by cattle dealers was "reasonably justifiable in the democratice society in Oyo." The learned judge was of the view that the custom was beneficial rather than detrimental to the cattle dealers. Whether or not an act or measure or enactment is reasonable depends on the circumstances of a particular case. The question may be that of fact or law or mixed fact and law. Reasonableness is therefore a relative term depending on the circumstances of the case. In *Glassbrook Brothers v Leyson (1933) 2 K.B. 91*, Lord Hanworth, M.R. expressed the view that "the question whether or not there was an unreasonable refusal or unreasonable demand is a question for the decision of the court as a question of law;" ibid at p.109

[178] Per Lord Blackburn in *Capital and Countries Bank v Henty (1882) 7 App. Cas. 741 at p.771*. See also *Sim v Stretch (1936) 53 T.L.R. 669.*

libel but if it is in the form of spoken words or gestures then it is slander. It is now recognised that defamation through the radio and television is libel.[179]

A defamation may be criminal or civil. Under the Criminal Code, "any person who publishes any defamatory matter is guilty of a misdemeanour, and is liable to imprisonment for one year and any person who publishes any defamatcry matter knowing it to be false is liable to imprisonment for two years.'[180] Defamatory matter in this respect is any matter likely to injure the reputation of any person by exposing him to hatred, contempt, or ridicule, or likely to damage any person in his profession or trade. Such matter may be expressed in spoken words or in any audible sounds, or in words legibly marked, on any substance whatever, or by any sign or object signifying such matter otherwise than by words, and may be expressed either directly or by insinuation or irony.[181] However, the publication of defamatory matter is not an offence if the publication is, at the time it is made, for the public benefit, and if the defamatory matter is true.[182] Absolute privilege attaches to publications made in respect of proceedings in a court of law, legislature[183] or in respect of the instances listed in the Criminal Code.[184] With regard to judicial privilege Lopes, L.J. in *Royal Aquarium and Summer and Winter Garden Society Ltd. v Parkinson*[185] said: "The authorities establish beyond all question this: that neither party, witness, counsel, jury, nor judge can be put to answer civilly or criminally for words spoken in office that no action of libel or slander lies, whether against judges, counsel, witnesses or parties forewords written or spoken in the course of any proceeding before any court recognised by law, and this though the words written or spoken were written or spoken maliciously, without any justification or excuse, and from personal ill-will and anger against the person defamed. This absolute privilege has been conceded on the ground of public policy to insure freedom of speech where

---

179 *See section 3 of the Defamation Act 1961, Laws of Nigeria 1961.* This is so under English law: Defamation Act, 1952 S.1. In *Youssonpoff v Metro-Goldwyn-Mayer Pictures Ltd. (1934) 50 T.L.R. 581*, it was held that a defamatory talking film was libel.

180 S. 375 of the Criminal Code, Cap.42.

181 S.373, *ibid.* For a definition of publication, See S.374 *ibid.*

182 S.377 *ibid*, see also S.393(2) of the Penal Code (N.R) Cap.89.

183 S.26 of the Legislative (Powers and Privileges) Act, Cap. 102.

184 S.378 of the Criminal Code, Cap.42; for qualified privilege see S.379, ibid; see equally S.91 (2) of the Penal Code, Cap. 89 (N.R)

185 (1892) 1 Q.B. 431 at p.451. In that case it was held that a meeting of the London County Council for granting music and dancing licences was not a court within the meaning of the rule by which defamatory statements made in the course of judicial proceeding could enjoy absolute privilege. Consequently a county councillor making a defamatory statement at such a meeting with regard to a person applying for a licence was not entitled to absolute immunity from an action with regard to such statement.

it is essential that freedom should exist, and with the knowledge that Courts of justice are presided over by those who from their high character are not likely to abuse the privilege, and who have the power and ought to have the will to check any abuse of it by those who appear before them.

With regard to civil defamation, a person defamed can sue for damages and vindication of his good name and reputation. It is not proposed to go into fuller details in this aspect of the law of defamation we therefore confine our attention to the aspect that controls freedom of expression. The individual enjoys wider privilege under civil defamation, for the privilege covers those under criminal law and then proceeds to cover more of those occasions known to the common law.[186]

(ii) *Sedition*

Sedition is a common law misdemeanour. It comprises of the publication of a seditious libel, the uttering of seditious words, and conspiracy to do an act in furtherance of a seditious intention. A seditious intention is an intention to bring into contempt or hatred, or to excite disaffection against, the person of the Head of State or Sovereign or the government and Constitution of the State or the Parliament or the administration of Justice.[187] Under the Criminal Code,[188] it is sedition for any person to utter any seditious words or to print, publish, sell, offer for sale, distribute or reproduce any seditious publication or to import any seditious publication with the intention to bring into hatred or contempt or to excite disaffection against the person of the President or Regional Governor or the Government or Constitution of Nigeria or any of the Regions, or the administration of justice in Nigeria or to excite the inhabitants of Nigeria to attempt to procure the alteration, otherwise than by lawful means any other matter in Nigeria as by law established or to raise discontent or disaffection amongst the inhabitants of Nigeria or to promote feelings of ill-will and hostility between different classes of population of Nigeria. But an act, speech or publication is not seditious by reason only that it intends to show that the President or Governor has been misled or mistaken in any of his measures or to point out errors or defects, in the Government or Constitution of Nigeria, or of any Region thereof, as by law established or in legislation or in the administration of Justice with a view to the

---

[186] For more details see *Winfield on Tort, (1963) seventh ed. p. 621 et seq.* A schedule to the Defamation Act, 1961 contains elaborate list of privileged occasions; see the Schedule in Laws of the Fed. of Nigeria, 1961 pp. A429-A431. For Defamation Law in the Western and Mid-Western Regions: see Cap. 32 W. R. Laws 1959.

[187] See Cave, J. in *R. v Burns (1886) 16 Cox 355 at p. 360*; See also *R. v Wallace — Johnson, (1938) 5 W. A. C. 56.*

[188] Sections 50 and 51. Sedition is punishable under the Code by two years imprisonment or N100 fine or to both and for subsequent offence by three years imprisonment.

remedying of such error or defects, or to persuade the inhabitants of Nigeria to attempt to procure by lawful means the alteration of any matter in Nigeria as by law established or to point out, with a view to their removal, any matters which are producing or have a tendency to produce feelings of ill-will and enmity between different classes of the population of Nigeria.

It follows that the law of sedition does not preclude a person from criticising the Government of the day. A statement is not seditious by reason only that it tends to point out the errors or defects in the Government with a view to remedying of such errors or defects. "What is not permitted is to criticise the Government in a malignant manner for such attacks, by their nature tend to affect the public peace.[189]

(iii) *Obscenity*

The earliest law governing obscenity in Nigeria is the United Kingdom Obscene Publication Act, 1857[190] which applies in Nigeria as a statute of general application. Under the Criminal Code, any person who for the purposes of or by way of trade or for the purposes of distribution or public exhibition, makes, produces or has in his possession any obscene writings, drawings, prints, paintings, printed matter, pictures, posters, emblems, photographs, cinematograph films or any other obscene objects, or by other object tending to corrupt morals, is guilty of a misdemeanour and is liable to imprisonment for two years or to a fine of one hundred pounds or to both such imprisonment and fine.[191] It follows that freedom of expression does not mean a licence to write or print obscene things which operate to deprave and corrupt public morals. The common law definition of obscenity in writing was given by Cockburn, C. J. in *R. v Hicklin* [192] as any writing which "tend to deprave and to corrupt those minds that are open to such immoral influences, and into whose hands a publication of this sort may fall and dealing more with the danger of such publications the learned Chief Justice went on to say that they "would suggest to the minds of the young of either sex, or even to persons of more advanced years, thoughts of a most impure and libidinous character."

---

[189] Per Ademola, C. F. J. in *D. P. P. v Obi 1961 1 All N. L. R. 186 at p. 194 (ante)* see also *Queen v Amalgamated Press Ltd.* 1961 1 All N. L. R. 199

[190] 20 & 21. C. 66. This Act, however is no longer applicable in Western and Mid-Western Regions of Nigeria, see Western Region (Laws of England Application) Law, 1959.

[191] S. 232 of the Criminal Code, Cap. 42. See also Obscene Publications Act, 1961 which applies to the Federal Territory, Laws of the Fed. of Nigeria, 1961, p. A. 341.

[192] (1868), L. R. 3 Q. B. 360 at p. 371. In that case a number of copies of a pamphlet entitled "The Confessional Unmasked: showing the depravity of the Romish priesthood, the iniquity of the Confessional, and the questions put to females in confession" were held to be obscene. They were seized and destroyed on the order of the justice of the borough.

The principle laid down in the above case came in for examination *Reg. v Martin*,[193] Stable, J. was of the view that the standard which applied in 1868 for the determination whether a book was obscene could not necessarily be adopted in 1954 or today as different standards might apply. It was then laid down as a principle that in considering whether a book which has to do with relationship of sexes, constitutes an obscene libel, the jury must have regard to the proper functions of a contemporary novel, viz. to hold up a mirror to the society of its own day and place, to present a picture and a record of that society, its manners, customs, attitudes and thought for the information both of its own generation and of posterity. The publication should therefore be judged accordingly to the time and the society in question. Thus in directing the jury Stable, J. appositely said: "Your task is to decide whether you think that the tendency of the book is to deprave those whose minds today are open to such immoral influences and into whose hands the book may fall in this year, or last year when it was published in this country." There is need to protect works which have great literary merit, for it would be of no benefit to the reading public if the creative ideas of people are muzzled unduly. This however, does not mean that the courts should allow any apparently obscene publication to escape the arms of the lay . Society must be protected against those dirty publications which end to deprave and corrupt it.[194]

(iv) *Blasphemy*

Stephen states that a publication is blasphemous if it "contains any contemptuous, reviling, scurrilous or ludicrous matter relating to God, Jesus Christ or the Bible, or the formularies of the Church of England as by law established. It is not blasphemous to speak or publish opinions hostile to the Christian religion, or to deny the existence of God, if that publication is couched in decent and temperate language. The test to be applied is as to the manner in which the doctrines are advocated and not as to the substance of the doctrines themselves."[195] In *Rex v. Taylor* [196] Lord

---

193 1954 1 W. L. R. 11 38 at p. 1139. The book in question was entitled "The Philanderer" by S. Kauffman and published by Martin S. Wardurg Ltd. Following the direction the jury returned a verdict of not guilty.

194 *Shaw v. D. P. P. (1962) A. C. 220.* In that case the applicant published a booklet, the "Ladies Directory", of 28 pages containing names and addresses of prostitutes together with their telephone numbers and advertisement of perverse nature. In dismissing the appeal of the appellant it was held that the test of obscenity under section 1(1) of the Obscene Publications Act, 1959 was whether the effect of the article was such as to tend to deprave and corrupt persons who were likely to read it. The obscenity depends on the articles in question and not on the intention or honesty of the publisher which is irrelevant.

195 Stephen. *Digest of Criminal Law (9th ed.)* p. 163

196 (1675) 1 Vent. 293.

Hale held that blasphemy was Indictable at common law several convictions followed that case.[197] With society becoming more advanced and freer, the prosecution for blasphemy is now rare. Although the law governing blasphemy serves as a check on freedom of speech, the courts do not usually rush to convict a person simply because he propagates a doctrine that is anti-Christian, apart from scurrility or profanity.[198] That freedom of speech is more freely exercised in the field of religion and even views having to do with the existence of God, does not however mean that blasphemy as a crime has become obsolete. The Courts in Nigeria should not hesitate to convict, should any clear case of blasphemy be brought before them.

(v) *Restrictions on Wireless Telegraphy and Cinematograph*

Under the Wireless Telegraphy Act, 1961[199] restrictions are imposed on persons operating private wireless telegraphy stations. Thus section 4 of the Act provides that 'no person shall establish or use any station for wireless telegraphy or install or use any apparatus for wireless telegraphy except under and in accordance with the licence in that behalf.' Any person who contravenes the provisions of this section of the Act shall be guilty of an offence. The licence referred to in the Act is to be granted by the Minister at his discretion.[200] The Act also makes it an offence for any person by means of wireless telegraphy to send or attempt to send any message which, to his knowledge, is false or misleading and is equally to his knowledge likely to prejudice the efficiency of any safety of life service or endanger the safety of any person or any vessel, aircraft or vehicle, and in particular, any message which to his knowledge, falsely suggests that a vessel or aircraft is in distress or in need of assistance or is not in distress or not in need of assistance.[201]

It may be observed that this section of the Act lays down a subjective test in the determination of the guilt of the accused in this regard. But the occasions covered by the section are such grave occasions, such as when aircraft or ships are in danger, and therefore require a more stringent control. It is therefore suggested that despite the wording of the section, the Courts in certain cases should apply the objective test. For instance, a

---

197 *R. v Woolston (1729) Fitzg 64 2 Str. 834 R. V. Williams (1797) 26 St. Tr 653; R v Mary Varile (1819) 3 B & Al. 167; R v Waddington (1822) 1 B & C. 26 R. v Hetherington (1841) 5 Jur. 529; 4 St Tr. (N.S.) 563.*

198 *Bowman v Secular Society Ltd. 1917 A. C. 406.* In that case it was held that it was not criminal to propagate anti-Christian doctrines in that such did not constitute the offence of blasphemy

199 Wireless Telegraphy Act, 1961, No 31 of 1961; laws of the Fed. of Nigeria, 1961. p. A. 273.

200 S. 6. *ibid*

201 S. 10. *ibid*

person sending a distress message in case of an aircraft or ship or giving a counter false message should not be heard to say that he had no knowledge of any likely danger flowing from his reckless act. A reasonable man should have foreseen such danger.

The Cinematograph Act, 1963 [202] places some restrictions on the exhibition of films in Nigeria. Thus section 1 provides that no person shall exhibit or cause or allow to be exhibited any film without the approval for exhibition in Nigeria given by the federal board of film censors under the Act.[203] Under the Cinematograph Ordinance,[204] no film is to be exhibited in the Region without the approval of a censorship committee of the Regional Board of censors.[205]

(vi) *Official Secrets*

The safety of the State makes it imperative that steps should be taken to ensure that certain classified official matters are not exposed to the detriment of the nation. Thus section 1 of the Official Secrets Act, 1962 provides that any person who transmits any classified matter to a person to whom he is not authorised on behalf of the government to transmit it; or who obtains, reproduces or retains any classified matter which he is not authorised on behalf of the government to obtain, reproduce or retain shall be guilty of an offence punishable on conviction or indictment to imprisonment for a term not exceeding two years or a fine of an amount not exceeding one hundred pounds or both in case of summary conviction.[206] It is also provided that any person who for any purpose prejudicial to the security of Nigeria, enters or is in the vicinity of or inspects a protected place or photographs, sketches or in any other manner whatsoever makes a record of the description of, or of anything situated in a protected place; or obstructs, misleads or otherwise interferes with a person engaged in guarding a protected place or obtains, reproduces or retains any photograph, sketches, plan model or document relating to, or anything situated in a protected place shall be guilty of an offence and punishable on conviction as aforesaid [207] It follows that despite the fact that an individual enjoys freedom of expression

---

202 Cinematograph Act, 1963, No. 7 of 1963, laws of the Fed. of Nigeria 1963, p. A.35

203 S. 1 *ibid.* A person who commits any of the offences under the section shall be liable on conviction to a fine of £200. See also Cinematograph (Film Censorship) Regulations, 1964. Parts 1 and III of the regulations were expressed to apply throughout the Federation, and Part II to the Federal Territory of Lagos only.

204 Cinematograph Ordinance Cap. 32; Laws of Nigeria 1948 Vo. VII p. 293. This Ordinance is still in force in the Eastern, Western and Mid-Western Regions of Nigeria.

205 SS. 6 to 8 *ibid*

206 SS. 1, 7, of the Official Secrets Act, 1962, Laws of Nigeria, 1962, p. All 7.

207 S. 2 (1) *ibid.* The Official Secrets (Amendment) Act, 1962 recognises the right of the Legislature of a Region to make laws with respect to public safety of that Region provided such laws are not

both in words spoken, written or printed, he is not allowed to do an act which might endanger or affect the security of the State.

(G) *Freedom of Association & Assembly*

The right of people to form and belong to lawful association is very essential in any democratic society. It is therefore important that people should be free to band themselves into political parties, trade unions and other important organisations which facilitate the smooth running of the State. Thus it is provided under the Constitution that every person shall be entitled to assemble freely and associate with other persons, and in particular he may form or belong to trade unions and other associations for the protection of his interest.[208] The right thus guaranteed is, however subject to the usual restrictions provided always that any law providing the restriction is reasonably justifiable in a democratic society. Mr. Justice Rutledge delivering the judgment of the Supreme Court of the United States in *Thomas v Collins* [209] said "The right of either of workmen or of unions to assemble and discuss their own affairs is as fully protected by the Constitution as the right of businessmen, farmers, educators, political party members or others to assemble and discuss their affairs and to enlist the support of others." And dealing more specifically with State law which tended to restrict the right of the individual to form trade unions and assemble freely, the learned Judge said: "If one who solicits support for the cause of labour may be required to register as a condition to make a public speech, so may he who seeks to rally support for any social, business, religious or political cause. We think a requirement that one must register before he undertakes to make a public speech to enlist support for a lawful movement is quite incompatible with the requirements of the First Amendment."[210]

In another case [211] the same Court in upholding the legitimate right of people peaceably to assemble said: "Those who assist in the conduct of such meeting cannot be branded as criminals ... The question, if the rights of free speech and peaceable assembly are to be preserved, is not as to the auspices under which the meeting is held but as to its purpose not as to the relations of the speakers, but whether their utterances transcend the bounds of freedom of speech which the Constitution protects. If the persons

---

inconsistent with the provisions of the 1962 Act. The Northern Region has re-enacted the 1962 Act, see Official Secrets Law 1963, Cap. 85, Laws of Northern Nigeria Vol. II p. 1417.

208 S. 37 of the Constitution, 1979

209 323 US 516, 539, 540 (1944). The Supreme Court of the United States in that case nullified a state legislation which unduly restricted the right to solicit for labour union membership.

210 The First Amendment of the Constitution of the U.S. A. guarantees inter alia, 'the right of people peaceably to assemble' for any lawful purpose. Cf. S. 26 of the Nigerian Constitution.

211 *De Jonge v Oregon 299 U. S. 353, 365 (1937)*

assembling have committed crimes, if they formed or are engaged in a conspiracy against the public peace and order, they may be prosecuted for their conspiracy or other violation of valid laws." It follows that in absence of *conspiracy* to commit a crime, people have a right to congregate for any purpose whatsoever. Willes J. in *Mulcahy v R.* [212] defined conspiracy as "the agreement of two or more persons to do any unlawful act or to do a lawful act by unlawful means." The same view was expressed by Viscount Simon, L. C. in *Crofter Harris Tweed Co, v Weitch.* [213] He said: 'Conspiracy, when regarded as a crime, is the agreement of two or more persons to effect any unlawful purpose, whether as their ultimate aim, or only as a means to it, and the crime is completed if there is such agreement, even though nothing is done in pursuance of it. The crime consists in the agreement, though in most cases covert acts done in pursuance of the combination are available to prove the fact of agreement.' The *tort of conspiracy* is constituted only if the agreed combination is carried into effect in a greater or less degree and damage to the plaintiff is thereby produced. It must be so, for, regarded as a civil wrong, conspiracy is one of those wrongs (like fraud or negligence) which sound in damage, and a mere agreement to injure, if it was never acted upon at all and never led to any result affecting the party complaining, could not produce damage to him.' It follows therefore that conspiracy to ground an action in tort must have gone beyond mere agreement between two or more persons to do the act in question. There must be a concrete act to the damage of another person or persons. In other words, the person who brings the action must show what damage [214] he has suffered as a result of the conspiracy. But in criminal law the mere agreement to commit a crime is sufficient to constitute the offence. Conspiracy is an indictable offence at common law.

Under the Criminal Code any person who conspires with another to commit any felony, or to do any act in any part of the world which if done in Nigeria would be a felony, and which is an offence under the laws in force in the place where it is proposed to be done, is guilty of felony, and is liable to imprisonment for seven years. Where the conspiracy is to commit an offence which is not a felony the offender will be guilty of a misdemeanour and is liable to imprisonment for two years. The offender

---

212 (1868) L. R. 3 H. L. 306 at p. 317.

213 (1942) A. C. 435 at pp. 439-40.

214 In *Huntley v thornton (1957) 1 W. L. R. 3212*, it was held that the plaintiff who was expelled from his union the Amalgamated Engineering Union (U.K.) and made to resign his employment and obstacles placed on his way to regain the said employment by the members of the Union, was entitled to succeed in an action in tort for damages. This was in fact assessed at £500 and he was asked to apply for injunction if further obstacles were put in his way to secure employment. In *Bonsor v Musicians Union 1956 A. C. 104* it was held that a member of a trade union was entitled to maintain an action for damages against the Union for wrongfully expelling him from the Union. See also *Rookes v Benard 1964 A. C. 1129.*

cannot be arrested without a warrant. It is equally an offence punishable by imprisonment for two years for any person to conspire with another to prevent or defeat the execution or enforcement of any statute or order in council; to cause any injury to the person or reputation of any person, or to depreciate the value of any property of any person to prevent or obstruct the free and lawful disposition of any property by the owner for its fair value; or to injure any person in his trade or profession, or to effect any unlawful purpose or even to effect any lawful purpose by any unlawful means.[215a]

It may therefore be said that people are free to assemble and where necessary enter into association provided they act according to law.

(H) *Freedom of Movement*

Life will be extremely difficult if people cannot move freely from place to place within the State. This freedom is vital not only in respect of social intercourse but also in the interest of many business activities.[215b] (a) Under the Constitution every citizen of Nigeria is entitled to move freely throughout the country and to reside in any part thereof, and no citizen of Nigeria shall be expelled from the country or refused entry thereto. This constitutional guarantee does not, however, invalidate any law that is reasonably justifiable in a democratic society, restricting the movement or residence of any person within Nigeria in the interest of defence, public safety, public order, public morality or public health; or for the removal of persons from Nigeria to be tried outside the country for criminal offences or to undergo imprisonment outside the country in execution of the sentences of courts in respect of criminal offences of which they have been found guilty or imposing restrictions upon the movement or residence within the State of members of the public service, the armed forces or the police force. Equally the guarantee shall not invalidate any law by reason only that the law provides for the removal or exclusion of a person who is or was a chief by reference to a territory or part of a territory from a particular area within that territory.[216]

In Williams v Majekodunmi,[217] the applicant was served with a Restriction Order during the crisis in the Western Region of Nigeria. The

---

215a Section 516-518 of the Criminal Code, Cap. 42.

215b Lord Denning in his book, "The Road to Justice" 1955 p.98 said. "If men are ever to be able to break the bonds of oppression or Servitude, they must be free to meet and discuss their grievances and to work out in unison a plan of action to set things right. Men and women must be free to form themselves into political parties with liberty to criticize the party in power. This is one of the great bulwarks of democracy. So also men must be able to form themselves into trade unions to protect their working conditions."

216 S.38 of the Constitution, 1979.

217 (1962) 1 All N.L.R. 324 (No.1), see also *Williams v Majekodunmi (No. 3) 1962 1 All N.L.R. 413.*

Order stipulated that the applicant "shall be and remain within a distance of three miles from 193 Abeokuta Road, in the township of Abeokuta." The applicant, an eminent member of the Nigerian Bar, filed a Motion on Notice with the Federal Supreme Court for an Interlocutory Injunction to restrain the Defendant from enforcing the Order pending the hearing of an action [218] which the applicant was to institute challenging the validity of the Emergency Powers Act, 1961 and the measures taken thereunder. The restriction of the appellant's movements in that respect was such that he could not even leave the area where he was restricted to attend the Supreme Court to argue his case. The Court was equally satisfied from the facts of the case, that public order would not be impaired if the applicant was allowed to leave the restricted area to attend the Court at least. Consequently it was held that the applicant cannot be deprived of his right to appear in person and plead his own case before the Court. The restriction was lifted in that regard. The restriction of the applicant "was not based on considerations of public order" as the defendant had earlier intimated to the applicant that he would allow him to attend the Court, but subsequently changed his mind. It was not therefore reasonably justifiable to restrict the applicant under the circumstances.

In another case, *Arzika v Governor, Northern Region*, [219] the applicant an Ex-Native Office Holder sought for an order of *Certiorari* to quash a Removal Order made against him under the Ex-Native Office Holders Removal Ordinance, Cap. 68, and also for an Order of Prohibition restraining the Governor from any further exercise of such removal powers with regard to the applicant. The appeal was dismissed. The court holding that the exercise of the power of removal under the Ordinance was a ministerial not a judicial act and as such not open to review or prohibition. The applicant however contended that his restriction was not reasonably justifiable. But the Court in rejecting that and resting on the presumption of constitutionality of the Governor's act said: "There is a presumption that the Legislature had acted constitutionally and that the laws which they have passed are necessary and reasonably justifiable. The same presumption must also apply where the Governor, acting as he is and was bound to do, upon the advice of his Executive Council, makes a legislative order in exercise of powers conferred upon him by the Legislature."[220a]

It may be observed with great respect that 'presumption of constitutionality' was carried too far in this case, for the learned judge relied solely on it in dismissing the contention that the order by the Governor was not reasonably justifiable. The mere fact that the Ordinance

---

218 See *Williams v Majekodunmi No. 2 1962 1 All N.L.R. 328.*

219 (1961) 1 All N.L.R. 379.

220a ibid. at p.382.

test laid down in the Constitution did not therefore mean that all the executive acts deriving from the Ordinance automatically passed the test and became unimpeachable. It is submitted that each case must be examined according to its facts and must stand or fall on them. Hence despite the fact that the Emergency Powers, Act 1961 was declared constitutional by the Federal Supreme Court, yet the Court held in *Williams v Majekodunmi No. 11 (supra)* that an order restricting the applicant's movements was not justifiable under the circumstances.[220b] Freedom of movement, as we pointed out earlier is very essential; so the courts should very carefully examine any measure restricting it whether they emanated from a legislation or an executive act. Nothing prevents a court in our country where it has jurisdiction, from declaring a measure unconstitutional. It does not matter that such a measure is an executive act.[221]

(I) *Freedom from Discrimination*

The Constitution [222] provides that a citizen of Nigeria of a particular community, tribe, place of origin, religion or political opinion shall not by reason only that he is such a person be subjected either expressly by, or in the practical application of, any law in force in Nigeria or any executive or administrative action of the Government of the Federation or the Government of a Region to disabilities or restrictions to which citizens of Nigeria of other communities, tribes, places of origin, religion or political opinions are not made subject or be accorded either expressly by, or in the practical application of, any law in force in Nigeria or any such executive or administrative action any privilege or advantage that is not conferred on citizens of Nigeria of other communities, tribes, places of origin, religious or political opinions. It is equally provided *inter alia*, that a law shall not be invalidated by reason only that it imposes restrictions with respect to the acquisition or use by any person of land or other property; or imposes any disability or restriction or accords any privilege or advantage that, having regard to its nature and to special circumstances pertaining to the persons to whom it applies, is reasonably justifiable in a democratic society. It may be observed that the exceptions provided in this section are so wide that they leave great loop-holes through which discrimination might be perpetrated. It will be worse if our courts allow themselves to be unduly swerved by the

---

220b See equally *Williams v Majekodunmi (No. 3) 1962* 1 All N.L.R. 413.

221 *Cf. Oliver v Buttigieg 1966 2 All E.R. 459 (supra)*; a case from Malta where a circular passed by a member of the Executive was held by the Privy Council to be unconstitutional. In a South African case of *Sachs v Donges N.O. 1950 (2) S.A. 265*, it was held that where a subject has been granted a passport by the Crown he cannot be deprived of it by an Executive revocation of the grant; and if it is so revoked, the revocation may be questioned in a court of law.

222 Section 39, *ibid.*

so-called presumption of constitutionality of every legislation or every executive or administrative act. Discrimination, although inherent in human nature and forming part of human frailty, must be fought and vanquished if harmony amongst different sections of the country could be built up and preserved.

(J) *Compulsory Acquisition of Property: Right to Property*

The Constitution[223] guarantees that no property, movable or immovable, shall be taken possession of compulsorily and no right or interest in any such property shall be acquired compulsorily in any part of Nigeria except by or under the provisions of a law that requires the payment of adequate compensation therefore and gives to any person claiming such compensation a right of access for the determination of his interest in the property and the amount of compensation, to the High Court having jurisdiction in that part of Nigeria. It is further provided that nothing in this section shall affect the operation of any law in force on the 31st day of March, 1958, or any law made after that date that amends or replaces any such law and does not, add to the kinds of property that may be taken possession of or the rights over and interest in property; that may be acquired or make the conditions governing entitlement to any compensation or the amount thereof less favourable to any person owning or interested in the property or deprive any person of such rights as access to the High Court for the determination of the amount payable in respect of the person's interest in the property.

The section went on to provide that nothing in the section shall be construed as affecting any general law, for the imposition or enforcement of any tax, rate or due; for the imposition of penalties or forfeitures for breach of the law, whether under civil process or after conviction of an offence or relating to losses, tenancies, mortgages, charges, bills of sale or any other rights or obligations arising out of contract; or relating to the vesting and administration of the property of persons adjudged or otherwise declared bankrupt or insolvent, of persons of unsound mind, of deceased persons and of companies, other bodies corporated and un-incorporate societies in the course of being wound up; or relating to enemy property or to trusts and trustees or relating to the limitation of actions; or to property vested in bodies corporate directly established by any law in force in Nigeria or relating to the temporary taking of possession of property for the purposes of any examination, investigation or enquiry, or providing for the carrying out of work on land for the purpose of soil-conservation.

The word"property" has very wide meaning, that is to say, it can be used in various sense. In one sense it is synonymous with ownership, or

---

223 S.40, *ibid.*

dominium, to use the Roman Law term. Thus a person may be said to have "property" in a piece of land or a vehicle or an ornament. Property is generally divided into *'real'* and *'personal.'* Thus Blackstone says: "Things *real* are such as are permanent, fixed and immovable, which cannot be carried out of their place, as lands and tenements; things *personal* are goods money, and all other moveables which may attend the owner's person wherever he thinks proper to go."[224] From this point of view, it may be said the description of property which appears in the Constitution will cover land, chattels, choses in action and all types of proprietary interests, real or personal, tangible or intangible, present, future or contingent. The terms 'taken possession of' and 'acquired compulsorily' appear to involve the removal of possession or ownership or any interest in moveable or immovable property from one person and the consequent transfer of the right involved to another. In this respect the State is regarded as a legal person,[225] compulsion, of course, presupposes that the deal did not emanate from the volition of the owner of the right concerned.

One of the most jealously guarded rights is the right of a person to retain any property which he has acquired out of his labour and sweat. Where therefore it becomes inevitable for the State to acquire such property, justice demands that fair and adequate compensation should be paid for the loss.

At common law, a person may be deprived of his property for some purposes relating to the defence of the realm or State in time of war or other great emergencies. Some conflicting pronouncements were made by eminent Judges[226] on the issue of payment of compensation. The Crown had always paid compensation when the property of the subject was requisitioned. Even in the *Saltpetre Case*,[227] when the saltpetre was taken under right of purveyance, payment was made to the dispossessed. But the important question was whether a right to compensation existed. The doubt cast on the law with regard to compensation was admirably cleared in the case of *Attorney-General v De Keyster's Royal Hotel Ltd.*[228] In that case the Crown took possession of a London hotel for use as headquarters of the Royal Flying Corps during the war. It was held that the Crown was not entitled as of right either by virtue of its prerogative or under any statute, to take possession of the land or building or any other property of the subject

---

224 Blackstone; Commentaries, Book II Ch. 2 16.

225 For a more detailed examination of the concepts of 'property' and 'acquisition' see Basu op.cit pp.726-731; Gledhill, Fundamental Rights in India, pp. 67-69.

226 In the case of The Zamora 1919 2 A.C. 77, 100 Lord Parker said: "The municipal law of this country does not give compensation to a subject whose land or goods are requisitioned by the Crown." The same view appeared to be taken in In re a Petition of Right (1915) 3 K.B. 649.

227 (1606) 12 Cop. Rep. 12.

228 (1920) A.C. 508.

without paying compensation for the use or occupation of the property in question. Swinfen Eady M.R. was pertinent on the subject; he said: "... it appears to me to be almost inconceivable that the Crown should claim the right to do such things as prostrate fences, take possession of the great industrial works mentioned, or cause any building to be destroyed, without being bound at law to compensate the owners thereof."[229]

The dust on the law on the subject was more appositely cleared by Atkin L.J. in *Commercial and Estates Co. of Egypt v Board of Trade.*[230] He said:

> ... municipal law of England by a series of statutes, if not by the common law, provides for compensation either in full or with some restrictions when the subject's property is taken for the defence of the realm. Lord Parker's dictum to the contrary in *The Zamora (1919) 2 A.C. 77, 100,* delivered after the decision in *In Re Petition of Right (1915) 3 K.B. 649* and before the decision in *Att. Gen. v De Keyser's Royal Hotel (1920) A.C 508* is no longer justified by the authorities.

It follows therefore that even at common law where the property of the subject is requisitioned for the defence of the State, he is entitled to compensation. In *Burmah Oil Co. Ltd. v Lord Advocate*[231a] the House of Lords held that the appellants, whose installations were destroyed on the order of the General Officer Commanding in Burma to avoid such installations falling into the hands of the advancing Japanese army, were entitled to compensation. Lord Reid re-stated the law as follows: "First, there is nothing novel in the idea that prerogative right to take property carries with it an obligation to pay compensation. That has apparently always been recognised with regard to the prerogative rights of purveyance and angary.[231b] Secondly, it is well established that taking or destroying property in course of fighting the enemy did not give rise to any claim for compensation, whether that was done by the armed forces of the Crown or by the enemy."

---

229 ibid, at p.544.

230 (1925) 1 K.B. 271. In that case it was held that compensation was payable under the Indemnity Act, 1920 (10 & 11 Geo. 5 C.48) for the requisition of timber under royal prerogative.

231a (1965) A.C. 75.

231b *The Right of Angary* in the modern sense is that of a State at war, for military purposes, to requisition neutral property found within the limits of its authority, either for use or, if need be, for destruction. It is generally recognised under international law that there is a duty to pay adequate compensation to the owners of such property. See Lauterpacht H., *'Angary and Requisition of Neutral Property,' (1950) 27 British Year Book of International Law pp. 455-459.* The learned author stated: "There is a consensus of views and practice that in the case of angary, as distinguished from requisition full compensation is the rule." See also Bullock C.Ll. *'Angary' (1922-23) 3 B.Y.I.L. pp.99-129; and Oppenheim's International Law Vol. II 7th ed. p.759 et seq.* It is legitimate under international law for a State, where public interests demand, to acquire alien property provided always that fair, reasonable, prompt and effective compensation is paid to the owner or owners.

It follows that where property was destroyed in course of actual fighting, no compensation is payable. Such destruction may be said to have done under *force majeure*. But is is different where the property was deliberately destroyed to prevent it from falling into the hands of the enemy. In such a case on the authority of the *Burmah Oil Co's case*, compensation is recoverable.

As we have seen above, the Constitutional provisions do not affect the law in force on the 31st day of March, 1958. But it may be observed that even under the existing law of Nigeria, provisions were always made for payment of compensation whenever property was acquired for public purpose. The law on the subject is now governed generally by the Public Lands Acquisition Act.[232] Under the Act,[233] where any lands are required for a public purpose[234] either of the Federation or of a Region the President in the former case or the Governor of the Region concerned in respect of any lands within the Region in the latter may acquire such lands for an estate in fee simple or for a term of years as he may think proper, paying such consideration or compensation as may be agreed upon or determined by the High Court within whose area of jurisdiction the land is situate.

The Courts have been entrusted with the onerous duty not only of determining title to the land but also to calculate and decide the amount to be paid as compensation. This is the case not only under the present enactment[235] but also under the earlier ones. Thus in *Administrator of the Colony v Thomas & Another*,[236] the Government acquired land under Public Lands Acquisition Ordinance, Cap. 88. A standard rate was followed in payment of compensation to various holders. This satisfied the majority but the two defendants objected to the standard rate and furnished proof that they had genuinely purchased their holdings some seven years previously at a higher price than the compensation offered by the Government. The Court found as a fact that the defendants had purchased the property in question for £40 but the Government assessed the compensation at £22.18.1d. Barkeley Ag. C.J. held that the measure of

---

232 Cap. 167, Laws of Fed. of Nigeria, 1958, Vol. V. p.3118.

233 S.3 ibid. For the Western and Mid-Western Regions, see the Public Lands Acquisition Law, Cap. 105, Laws of Western Nigeria 1959 Vol. V. See equally Land Tenure Law, 1962 Cap. 59, Law of Northern Nigerian 1963 Vol. II.

234 The acquisition must be for public purpose. In *Chief Commissioner v Ononye & Ors 1944 15 N.L.R. 142*, Waddinton J. held that the acquisition of land for the purpose of granting a lease to a commercial company was not a public purpose within a commercial company was not a public purpose within the Public Acquisition Ordinance, Cap. 88. Consequently certificate of title was refused by the Court.

235 S.10, Cap. 167.

236 (1930) 10 N.L.R. 71.

compensation payable should accord with the amount genuinely expended by the defendants in acquiring their hold. Consequently in holding the Government offer inadequate he decided that the sum of £40 was recoverable with costs. In another case, *Commissioner of Lands v Adeleye*,[237] the court was called upon under the Public Lands Acquisition Ordinance, Cap. 88, to determine the amount of the compensation payable in respect of land in Lagos together with buildings on it acquired by the Government under the Ordinance. The court determined the amount payable accordingly. Butler Lloyd. J. laid down what he considered to be the cardinal principles in respect of acquisition of land with buildings on it. He said: 'The first of these principles is that in the case of a building some years old the fact that the cost of erection was at the time higher or lower than the present cost of erecting similar building is entirely irrelevant to an enquiry as to its present value. If the former figure was higher the owner is so much worse off, if lower he is the gainer by so much. The second principle is that the present value of a building some years old is necessarily less than the cost of erecting a similar building today by whatever amount it is proper to allow for depreciation in respect of its actual age.' The learned Judge then concluded on the evidence before him: 'I do not propose to go in detail into the elaborate calculations as to cubic contents and prices on which these various estimates were based but will content myself by saying that upon the whole of the evidence before me I have come to the conclusion that a fair estimate of the present value of the buildings included in the acquisition is in the neighbourhood of £500 and that the Government's offer was in this case also adequate.[238] The Court however award compensation at £720. It may be observed that in handling this technical issue, the key word which should oscillate before the Judge or Judges should be fairness. A balance[239] should be held between the owners of the property in question on one hand and the public on the other. The compensation must be prompt, adequate, fair and effective. It follows therefore that the individual should,not be subjected to any hardship as a result of the acquisition.

(K) *Derogation from Fundamental Rights & Freedoms:- Period of Emergency.*

The interesting thing is that the Constitution lists those sections of the guaranteed rights and freedoms which could be derogated from during the period of emergency. Thus it is provided that 'an Act of Parliament shall

---

237 (1938) 14 N.L.R. 109.

238 *ibid*, at pp. 112-3

239 See *The Chairman Lagos Executive Development Board v Joye & Anor (1939) 15 N. L. R. 50 Chief Secretary to the Government v George & Others (1942) 16 N. L. R. 88*

not be invalid by reason only that it provides for taking, during periods of emergency, of measures that derogate from the provisions of Sections 18, 21, 22 or 28 [240] of this Constitution, but no such measure shall be taken in pursuance of any such Act during any period of emergency save to the extent that those measures are reasonably justifiable for the purpose of dealing with the situation.[241]

The section went further to provide a check as follows 'Provided that nothing in this section shall authorise any derogation from the provisions of section 18 of this Constitution (dealing with right to life) except in respect of deaths resulting from acts of war or any derogation from the provisions of Sub-section (7) of section 22[242] of this Constitution. 'Period of emergency' has been defined as 'any period during which:'

(a) the Federation is at war
(b) there is in force a resolution passed by each House of Parliament declaring that a state of public emergency exists, or
(c) there is in force a resolution passed by each House of Parliament supported by the votes of not less than two-thirds of all the members of the House declaring that democratic institutions in Nigeria are threatened by subversion.

Such a resolution remains in force for twelve months. As far as the declaration of state of emergency is concerned, the Constitution makes it abundantly clear.that it is the responsibility of Parliament. The representative of the people should be in a position to decide when a state of public emergency exists. Thus Lord Parker of Waddington said in the case of the Zamora:[243] "Those who are responsible for the national security must be the sole judges of what national security requires. It would be obviously undesirable that such matters should be made the subject of evidence in a Court of law or otherwise discussed in public. Although this judicial pronouncement went a bit too far, it demonstrated the wide scope left to the executive and Parliament to determine issues of national security. Identical view was expressed by Ademola C. J. F. in *Adegbenro v Attorney-General*

---

240 These sections deal with deprivation of life, deprivation of personal liberty, determination of rights, and freedom from discrimination. It may be said that as the derogation is confined to specified sections, the principle of: *expressio unius est execlusio alterius* would apply.

241 S. 41 of the Constitution.

242 This prohibits conviction of a person in respect of a criminal offence on account that such act or omission did not, at the time it took place, constitute such an offence. Equally no penalty shall be imposed for any criminai offence heavier than the penalty in force at the time the offence was committed.

243 (1916) 2 A. C. 77 at p. 107

of the Federation and Ors.[244] when he stated: ... it is not for this Court to go outside the provisions of section 65 (3) now 70 (3) of the Constitution defining emergency.

It may be observed that although Parliament should have sole power to declare state of emergency, the Courts should have the power to determine the constitutionality of the measure taken during the period of the emergency, especially with regard to the fundamental rights and freedoms. Thus in *Williams v Majekodunmi (No 3)* [245] the Federal Supreme Court set aside a restriction Order made against the plaintiff during the period state of emergency was declared in the Western Region of Nigeria. After hearing evidence about the part played by the plaintiff in reconciling the two warring factions of the Action Group and other peaceful steps taken by the plaintiff to arrest the crises in the party, the Court held that his restriction only on the ground that he was the legal adviser of that party was not reasonably justifiable. But where the Court is satisfied that 'the steps which have been taken are reasonably justifiable as a preventive measure to attain peace and order.[246] it will uphold the restriction or detention.[247] It follows that as the sentinel of liberty, the Courts have extra duty during the period of emergency to protect the individual against any excesses of the executive.

5. *Value of the Constitutional Guarantees of the Fundamental Rights and Freedoms*

The fundamental rights and freedoms provisions have more particularly spelt out those ideal rights and freedoms in our legal system and not only codified them but elevated and enshrined them in such a way that an infringement of any of those rights and freedoms will amount to the infringement of the Constitution itself—the organic law of the land. As we have seen from decided cases and earlier statutes, the provisions introduced

---

244 (1962) 1 All N. L. R. 338 at p. 340. In *The State (Walsh & Others) v Lennon & Others 1942 I. R. 112*, Provisions for Summary trial by military officers of person acting in contravention of emergency order were held valid, since the legislation was of a temporary nature and it was for Parliament to determine what measures were necessary.

245 (1962) 1 All N. L. R. 413 see also *Williams v Majekodunmi (No 1) (ante).*

246 Per Taylor, F. J. in *Adegbenro v Att-Gen of the Federation & Ors (1962) 1 All N. L. R. 431 Cap. 439.*

247 Where security of the State makes detention of dangerous persons necessary during emergency the Courts would uphold the measure: *R. V. Halliday 1917 A. C. 260; R. v Secretary of state for Home Affairs Ex. parte Lees 1941 1 KB 72, see also Liversidge v Anderson 1924 A. C. 206.* After the military revolt in Nigeria on the 15th of January, 1966 and the consequent military rule, several politicians whom the Military Government thought would cause some trouble that might lead to break-down of law and order, were put in detention and the fundamental rights and freedoms in respect to them were suspended. See state security (Detention of Persons) Decree, Nos 3, 8, 10, and 18 of 1966. Those detained have however since been released.

little new in our legal system. It is difficult to criticise them without criticising the very foundation of rule of law in our society. This does not however mean that the provisions are completely perfect. The exceptions provided are too wide that they nearly emptied the rights and freedoms so enshrined or their efficacy. Any Government that decides to part company with democratic ideals could easily find a loophole by passing laws which it could claim to be 'reasonably justifiable in the interest of defence, public safety, public order, public morality or public health. This is of course where the Government is sure of a large majority. But from what one has experienced in Nigerian politics, it is just easy to pass such laws as there were little or no oppositions in our Parliament and the respective Regional Legislatures. So the whole burden of checking the excesses will fall on the judiciary with the co-operation of the public.

If the executive therefore wants to push its way through the path that might erode the fundamental rights and freedoms, it is the duty of the courts to check that just as it is the duty of the public to bring such cases before the courts where their rights and freedoms have been infringed. The British Constitutional Committee in turning down a proposal to embody a set of fundamental rights in the Indian Constitution in 1934 stated: "either the declaration of rights is so abstract in nature that it has no legal effect of any kind, or its legal effects will be to impose an embarrassing restriction on the powers of the legislature and to create a grave risk that a large number of laws may be declared invalid by the Courts.[248] While there may be some truism in the statement, experience in Nigeria has shown that the pessimism could not be justified. The provisions are valuable. They provide set of standards by which legislative and administrative actions can be judged. Being part of the Constitution, they serve as bulwark against any gradual erosion of the fundamental rights of the individual. Having been so spelt out, those in power will easily know those areas that are out of bounds in their legislative processes. Any law which contravenes any of the fundamental rights provisions will be declared ultra vires, and consequently void by the Courts,[249] equally the Courts have not allowed any denial of the guaranteed rights and freedoms[250] to stand.

The Minorities Commission in Nigeria expressed apposite view on the subject as follows: Provisions of this kind in the constitution are difficult to interprete. Nevertheless we think they should be inserted. Their presence defines beliefs widespread among democratic countries and provides a standard to which appeal may be made by those whose rights are infringed. A government determined to abandon democratic courses will find ways of

---

248 Report of the Joint Parliamentary Committee on Indian Constitutional Reform (H.L. 6 and H. C. 5 1933-34)

249 *Doherty v Balewa (1961) 1 All N. L. R. 604; Williams v Majekodunmi (No.3) ante*

250 *Gokpe v Inspector-Gen of Police (ante); Aoko v Fagbemi (ante).*

violating them. But they are of great value in preventing a steady deterioration in standards of freedom and the unobtrusive encroachment of a government on individual rights.[251]

It is our suggestion that these fundamental rights and freedoms provisions should be transplanted into any future Constitution which Nigeria might choose to adopt for the provisions are vital in any society where rule of law[252] prevails.

---

251 Cmnd. 505 (1958) 97.

252 The International Congress of Jurists in their 1959 Declaration of Delhi recognised the Rule of law as dynamic concept for the expansion and fulfilment of which jurists are primarily responsible and which should be employed not only to safeguard and advance the civil and political rights of the individual in a free society, but also establish social, economic and educational and cultural conditions under which his legitimate aspirations and dignity may be realised. See *'The Rule of Law in Press Society'* (a Report on the International Congress of Jurists, New Delhi, India, 1959 ed. Norman S. Marsh) p. 3.

Chapter 8

The Courts and Social and Economic Laws

As we have seen, the fundamental rights and freedom provisions in the constitution serve as apposite codification of those important rights and freedoms already known to our legal system. There are, however, many other equally important rights which by their nature could not be incorporated into a written Constitution in such a way that they could broadly speaking, be justiciable *vis-a-vis* the individual and the State. Our Courts have therefore played a very important part in protecting and upholding these rights, their absence in the written Constitution notwithstanding. Most of the rights emanate from the social and economic activities of the community, and handling issues arising therefrom the Courts are guided by relevant enactments and other laws regulating these activities.

In this respect the United Nations Universal Declaration of Human Rights of 1948 has gone further than most constitutions in spelling out certain social and economic rights which the individual should have as a member of the society. Thus, Article 22 provides that 'Everyone, as a member of society, has the right to social security and is entitled to realisation, through national effort and international co-operation and in accordance with the organisation and resources of each State, of the economic, social and cultural rights indispensable for his dignity and the free development of his personality.' Article 16 was more fully devoted to one of the most important aspects of the social life of the community — marital relation. It provides that; 'Men and women of full age, without any limitations due to race, nationality or religion, have the right to marry and to found a family. They are entitled to equal rights as to marriage, during marriage and at its dissolution.' It went on to provide that 'Marriage shall be entered into only with the free and full consent of the intending spouses.' The article then concludes, 'the family is the natural and fundamental group unit of society and is entitled to protection by society and the State.' In another article the Declaration provides that 'Everyone has the right to work, to free choice of employment, to just and favourable conditions of work, and to protection against unemployment'[1]

---

[1] Article 23, The Universal Declaration of Human Rights Proclaimed by the General Assembly of the United Nations on 10th Dec. 1948.

It may be observed that although these rights mentioned in the Declaration may not be enforced by the individual against the State — as such in the absence of a specific contract, yet they help to spell out those important rights, which generally arise out of contracts between individuals in the society. In this modern industrial age, in which the State through its organs engage in activities hitherto reserved to the individual, the individual can successfully enforce any right arising out of a contract between him and the organ of the State concerned. The Courts are of course guided by the laws enacted by the legislatures of the State and as we shall see in this part of our study, very important enactments directed to the protection of the members of the community in our rapidly developing society. The most glaring of these enactments which have been subject of many judicial decisions, in some cases conflicting, are: The Illiterates Protection Act, The Moneylenders' Act, and the corresponding Regional enactments; and the Workmen's Compensation Act. We shall equally, presently be seeing how the Courts have been dealing with many delicate social questions arising from marital relations; and finally we shall be dealing with the adjudication of issues arising from commercial transaction as well as judicial construction of the enactments relating to them.

1. Judicial Construction of the Illiterate Protection Act [2]

It is a notorious fact that in Nigeria, there still exists a large number of people who may be classified as 'illiterate persons.' In this modern age where most of the important transactions are conducted in writing, it had been thought to be expedient to tackle the social problem of protecting this large section of the population from exploitation by fraudulent people. Thus section 3 of the Illiterates Protection Act provides that 'Any person who shall write any letter or document at the request, on behalf, or in the name of any illiterate person shall also write on such letter or other document his own name as the writer thereof and his address; and his so doing shall be equivalent to a statement:- (a) that he was instructed to write such a letter or document by the person for whom it purports to have been written and that the letter or document fully and correctly represents his instructions; and (b) if the letter or document purports to be signed with the signature or mark of the illiterate person, that prior to its being so signed it was read over and explained to the illiterate, and that the signature or mark was made by such

---

[2] Cap. 88; Laws of Nigeria, 1948 p. 276; this enactment was formally known as the Illiterates Protection Ordinance, now see Designation Act, 1961, laws of the Federation of Nigeria, p. A 395. See equally Illiterate Protection Law, Cap. 51 (N.R) Laws of Northern Nigeria, 1963 Vol. 2; for Western States, see Cap. 47, Laws of W. Nigeria, 1959, and for Lagos see Cap. 83 Law of the Federation of Nigeria and Lagos, 1958. Cap. 88 is still the Law on the subject in the Eastern States. The Act does not apply to documents prepared by or at the direction of a Barrister or Solicitor in the course of his business, S. 4. *ibid.*

person.' The Act then goes on to provide for a penalty to be incurred in the event of a writer of a document or letter not complying with the provisions of the Act. It is provided that 'if the writer of any such letter or document shall fail to write thereon his name and address, or if, having done so, any statement which under the last preceding section is in consequence implied shall be found to be untrue, the writer shall be liable to a fine of one hundred Naira or in default of payment to imprisonment for six months.[3]

An Important question which has received conflicting judicial treatment is, what is the legal position of a document which fails to comply with the relevant provisions of the Act? In *Eke v Odolofin* [4] Madarikan, J., was of the view that non-compliance with the provisions of the Ordinance rendered the document in question void, and consequently inadmissible. In that case, the plaintiff, who was a building contractor, claimed £660 damages for an alleged breach of contract by the defendant for whom he had erected a building. The defendant was an illiterate person. Evidence was adduced to the fact that after the parties had agreed, in 1955 on the amount for the erection of the building, the defendant had brought to the plaintiff a draft document which was not prepared in accordance with the Illiterates Protection Act. The plaintiff alleged that after the completion of the building in 1957, the defendant failed to pay the agreed sum of £660. The case for the plaintiff was erected on the vital document which failed to comply with the provisions of the said Act. Madarikan, J., held that the document was inadmissible.

In arriving at this decision the learned Judge not only rejected but also attacked another decision to the contrary. Thus he said: 'The decision in *Akohwere of Okan v Emayobor and another, in 1959 W. R N. L. R. 83*, would appear to be inconsistent with the general stream of authorities. In that case it was held that a writ of summons which did not comply with the Illiterates Protection Law was not for that reason alone void and of no effect.[5]

In *Akohwere of Okan v Emayobar et al;* Duffus, J., in rejecting the submission that the action should be struck out on the ground that the writ offended against the provisions of sections 3 and 6 of the Illiterates Protection Law, 1956;[6] said as follows

> The Illiterates Protection Law is, as the title itself states, a law to protect and not to penalise illiterates and the fact that the writer did not carry out all the provisions of

---

[3] S. 4, *ibid*,

[4] (1961) I All N. L. R. 404 see equally *Niiashagwo v Amodu and Another (1959) W. R. N. L. R. 273*

[5] *ibid* at p. 405

[6] These sections of the Western Region Illiterates Protection Law correspond with S. S. 3 and 8 respectively, of Cap, 88 (supra).

that law, cannot in my view mean that the document prepared is for that reason alone void and of no effect.[7]

It may be observed that in construing an enactment of this kind, the Courts should endeavour to find out, from the wording of the Act, the true intention of the legislature. In this case, it is abundantly clear that the object of the Act is to protect the illiterate persons against fraudulent practices, as they could easily be defrauded — being unable to read and write. Suppose in *Eke v Odolofin (supra),* the plaintiff were to be the writer of the rejected document, it follows then that if he had wanted to defraud the other party, he could have benefited from his criminal act. The poor illiterates would have suffered from the criminal act of another person instead of being protected. It is submitted that as the Act is silent on the effect of a non-compliance with the provisions on the document, such non-compliance should render the document voidable not void.

In *U. A. C. v Edems et al,* [8] Smith J., stated: 'The document on the face of it does not comply with the section. The object of the ordinance is to project an illiterate person from possible fraud. Strict compliance therewith is obligatory as regards the writer of the document. If the document creates legal rights and the writer benefits thereunder those benefits are only enforceable by the writer of the document if he complies with the provisions of the Ordinance. If a document which does not comply with the provisions of the Ordinance creates legal rights between the illiterate and a third party, then evidence may be called to prove what happened at the time the document was prepared by the writer and the parties signed it. But the writer himself cannot adduce evidence in his favour to remedy the omission. It follows that if a document which does not comply with the provisions of the Act was prepared for say, A and B who are illiterates by C who of course is literate; evidence would be admitted to explain to the court what transpired between the parties at the time the document was prepared. If on the other hand the writer of the document happened to be the plaintiff in an action, he will not be allowed to enforce his right if the document on which he relies does not comply with the provisions of the

In *S. C. O. A. v Okon* [9] the Federal Supreme Court was called upon to decide whether rights accrued to the benefit of an illiterate could be enforceable if the writer failed to comply with the provisions of the Illiterates Protection Act, Cap. 88. In that case, the appellant company claimed a sum of £200 or N400 from the respondent upon a letter which was signed by the respondent as a surety guaranteeing the repayment of any

---

[7] (1959) W. R. N. L. R. 83 at p. 84

[8] (1958) N. R. N. L. R. 33 at p. 34. See also *Amao v Ajibike and Others* (1956) W. R. N. L. R. 121.

[9] (1960) N.R.N.L.R. 34, see also *Barclays Bank D. C. O. v Hassan* (1961) 1 All N. L. R. 836.

shortages of a third party, who was to be employed by the Company. The amount involved in the surety was N400. The letter in question was written by the appellants' Manager and signed by respondent. The provisions of the Act were not complied with. The respondent was an illiterate person within the meaning of the Act. The letter was not read over to him. There were no explanation[10] of all that were involved. In his evidence the respondent stated that he understood the figure of N400 which he saw on the document and no more. The Federal Supreme Court had no difficulty in upholding the finding that he was an illiterate and as the writer of the document was acting for the company, i.e. the appellants, the document could not be enforced against the illiterate surety as it offended against the provision of the Act.

In another case of *Ezera v Ndukwe*,[11] it was found as a fact that a third party prepared a document under which an illiterate person borrowed money from a certain Union. The document was in a form of promissory note. It did not comply with the provisions of the Illiterates Protection Act. The writer of the document who incidentally was the secretary of the Union concerned, testified to the effect that he drew up the document at the request of the appellant, i.e. the illiterate, and he fully explained the contents of the document to him before he thumb-printed it. There was no dispute as to the amount involved, which was £13. 19. Od. The document was admitted in evidence as to what happened at the time the document was drawn. He satisfied the trial court that he was acting in his personal capacity and not as an agent of the Union when he prepared the document at the request of the illiterate appellant. It was held *inter alia*, that the Illiterate Protection Ordinance' (Act) did not render a document which did not comply with its provisions inadmissible in evidence; that evidence to prove that the contents of the document were explained to the illiterate person prior to his thumb-printing or signing the document in question was not admissible in an action brought by the writer of the document against the illiterate person to enforce rights or benefits derived from the document by the writer. But such evidence could be properly admitted in an action brought against the illiterate person to enforce rights under such document, where it was prepared by a third party at the request of the illiterate person.

In reaching his decision Idigbe, J., observed that the Act did not make a document inadmissible in evidence for want of compliance with its provisions. This point is worth emphasising as it appears to have been over-looked. In fact what the Act did was to create a penalty against its contravention; it may therefore be said that a writer who contravenes the

---

10 In *Halliday v Alapatira* (1881) 1 N. L. R. L. the Full Court held that delivery of a printed circular to an illiterate person without an explanation of its contents did not convey notice of an act of bankruptcy available for adjudication under English law, and therefore payment by the illiterate person to the bankrupt after the receipt of the circular was a valid payment.

11 (1961) All N. L. R. 564

statute will not be heard to say that he is entitled to the assistance of the Court to enforce his right-*ex turpi causa non actio oritur.*

Another important question which requires examination in this very important enactment is: who is an illiterate person? Apparently the Act is silent on this point. But the question is obviously important in view of the type of society predominating in Nigeria. Some regard a person who, cannot write his name as an 'illiterate'. Others think that an illiterate person is one, who cannot read and write 'English.' To be sure, these definitions are defective one way or the other. In Nigeria there are many efficient, prosperous and industrious traders or even workers who can write and add figures in the conduct of their business, yet outside such scope they could not read nor write. The question then is, are such people 'illiterate persons' protected by the Act and the respective Regional Laws on the subject? It is submitted that a Nigerian who cannot read or write with understanding the language used in the preparation of the document (usually English) may be regarded as an illiterate. It must, however, be pointed out that if the document is written say in Igbo, Hausa or Yoruba (the three main languages) and the person concerned happens to belong to one of these ethnic groups and fully understands the language used, he may not be regarded as illiterate within the meaning of the Act or Law.

In *Kantoma v Paterson Zochonis & Co. Ltd.* [12] the vital question was whether a person who could read and write in Arabic was an illiterate within the meaning of the Illiterates Protection Ordinance. In that case, the appellant signed a guarantee indemnifying the respondent company in respect of a third person's indebtedness to the company. The guarantee was typed out by a typist in the employ of the respondent company. There were blank spaces for the appellant's name, the amount and the date of the transaction. The company's manager filled in the blank spaces on behalf and in the name of the appellant. The document would have offended against section 3 of the Illiterate Protection Act. It was held by the Federal Supreme Court that although the appellant could not read English, the language in which the guarantee was prepared, yet he was able to read and write in Arabic. Consequently he was not illiterate in the sense in which the word was to be constructed in the Illiterate Protection Ordinance; he did not therefore come within the provisions of the Ordinance. The case was rightly decided. But it may be observed that the principle established in this case should not be unduly extended otherwise it could be dangerous. It may lead to a situation where a person who could only read and write say in Hausa, Igbo or Yoruba or any of the minor languages of the country is held not to be an illiterate in a case emanating from a document written in English language. Such a decision would obviously defeat the object of the Statute. It is submitted that a person who would only read and write in one of the

---

[12] (1964) N. N. L. R. 54.

indigenous languages and could not read or write in English (if the document is prepared in that language) should be regarded or be deemed to be an illiterate person for the purpose of the enactment. Such a person is entitled to protection under the Statute.

Taylor F. J., dealing specifically on this point referred to the judgment of the learned trial Judge who defined 'an illiterate person' as a ;person who is unable to read the document in question in the language in which it is written, subject to the proviso that the expression includes a person who, though not totally illiterate, is not sufficiently literate to read and understand the contents of the document.'[13] It may be further observed that the Court in *Kantoma v Paterson Zochonis Ltd. (supra)* was greatly influenced by the facts of the case. Referring still to the findings of the learned trial Judge, Taylor, F. J. stated; 'I am satisfied that the defendant said, that he understood the guarantee' and he went on: 'I am satisfied that the defendant raised no objection when the guarantee was read over to him and I conclude that the guarantee correctly represents his instructions.' The Learned Judge in the course of his judgment stated that, 'The Illiterate Protection Ordinance was designed to protect illiterates from being taken advantage of by being made to sign or acknowledge a writing or document which does not bear out their real intention.[14]

The law on the subject of protection of illiterates could have been straightforward but for the conflicting judicial construction [15] of the enactment. However, the dust appeared to be a bit cleared in the case of *Jiboso v Obadina.*[16] In that case an appeal was made from the Abeokuta Grade "A" Customary Court to the High Court of the Western Region. Counsel for the respondent took a preliminary objection to the effect that the appeal was nullity in that the notice of appeal which was thumb-impressed by the appellant (an illiterate person) was not prepared in accordance with S. 3 of the Illiterate Protection Law,.[17] for the argument that the document

---

[13] *ibid.*, at p. 56

[14] *ibid.*, at p. 57. At common law, if a person is fraudulently induced to sign a document the nature of which he does not understand, in absence of negligence, he will be heard to *plea 'non est factum'* that is to say, that the deed is not his. In the case of *Foster v Mackinnon (1868-69 L. R., 4 C. P. 704*, the defendant was induced by fraudulent representation of the prerogative to put his name upon the back of a bill of exchange thinking he was signing a guarantee. In an action against him as endorser at the suit of a *bona fide* holder for value, the jury was directed thus: If the defendant's signature to the document was obtained upon a fraudulent representation that it was a guarantee, and the defendant signed it without knowing that was a bill, and under the belief that it was a guarantee, and if he was not guilty of negligence in so signing the paper, he was entitled to the verdict' - at p. 710. The jury found for the defendant.

[15] See T. A. Aguda on the subject, in (1962) 4 N. B. J. (Nigerian Bar Journal) p, 35.

[16] (1962) W. N. L. R. 303.

[17] Laws of the Western Region of Nigeria, 1959, vol. II p. 551. This section 3 corresponds with S. 3 of Cap. 88. 1984 Laws of Nigeria.

was a nullity, Counsel relied on the decision in *Ntioshagwo v Amodu (ante)* and *Eke v Odolofin (ante)*. Charles, J. held that the document was voidable not void. He was of the view that a document which did not comply with the provisions of the Law was voidable at the instance of the illiterate person.

The Ntiashagwo's case is particularly interesting because Charles, J. in that case stated that a document which did not comply with the provisions of the Ordinance was nullity. His pronouncement was apparently followed by Madarikan, J, who rejected a more correct decision in *Akohwere of Okan v Emayobor (ante)* as being 'against the stream of authority.' In trying to put the record straight, Charles, J, stated as follows: "Madarikan, J., apparently thought, in *Eke v Odolofin (1961) All N. L. R.* that Smith, J. said the word "unenforceable" was synonymous with "void", as he considered that the judgment in *Akohwere of Okan v Amayabor and Another (1959 W. R. N. L. R. 83* as being against the stream of authority as represented by *U. A. C. ltd. v Edem & another (1958) N. R. N. L. R. 33* and *Ntiashagwo v Amodu (1959) W. R. N. L. R. 273*. Actually, the judgment of Madarikan, J. appears to be the first decision that a document which has been prepared for an illiterate and was not signed by the preparer in the prescribed manner, is a nullity, as, in that case, a document which was tendered by the plaintiff against an illiterate defendant was rejected as being inadmissible because the preparer a third person who was not the plaintiff's agent apparently, had not signed the document in the prescribed manner.[18] The learned Judge went further to state that, ';the manifest object of the section is to protect the illiterate from signing a document which he does not understand. It is unnecessary, in order to promote that object, to impute to the legislature an intention to render void, or a nullity, a document signed by an illiterate without the writer having complied with the section: on the contrary such an imputation could defeat the object of the protection and render the intended protection to a trap for an illiterate in many case.[19]

In conclusion he demolished his earlier view as well as that of Madarikan, J., who followed him, by saying that 'my opinion in *Ntiashagwo's case* and with respect, that reasons of Madarikan, J., in *Eke v Odolofin* were wrong.[20]

It follows therefore, that the opinion expressed by Charles, J. in *Ntiashagwo v Amodu et al. (supra)* and the principle established in *Eke v*

---

[18] (1962) W. N. L. R. at p. 305.

[19] ibid. at p. 306. In Barclays Bank D.C.O.v. Hassan [1961] 1 All N.L.R. 836 at p. ¨10 Charles, J. stated: "I am satisfied from further consideration of my remarks in Ntiashagwo v. Another 1959 W.R.N.L.R. 273, that non-compliance with the requirements of the illiterates Protection Ordinance by the preparer of a document renders the document void, were too widely stated and inaccurate on that account".

[20] [1962] W.N.L.R. at p. 307.

Odolofin (supra) and the principle which failed to comply with the provisions of the Illiterate Protection Ordinance was a nullity can no longer be followed as good law. The important aspects of the law on the subject may therefore be, summarised as follows:

(a) A document which is prepared in such a way that it does not comply with the provisions of the Act or Law is not void but voidable at the instance of the illiterate person.
(b) The preparer of such document which does not comply with the provisions of the Statute cannot enforce any of his rights deriving therefrom.
(c) If an illiterate person requests a third party to prepare for him a document, and such document does not comply with the provisions of the Statute; evidence will be admissible to show that the contents of the document were read and explained to the illiterate person before he signed or thumb-printed it. If the Court is satisfied with such evidence the rights emanating thereof may be enforced against the illiterate: *Ezera v. Ndukwe (supra).*
(d) If such a defective document was prepared by a third party on behalf of two illiterate persons, evidence will be admissible to prove what happened at the time the document was prepared...provided such evidence would not conflict with the contents of the document or section 131 of the Act and the evidence should not operate to make the illiterate liable where he denies knowledge of the contents of the document. In case of document touching land, where the illiterate is dead, such document should not be enforceable against his successors in title; in such case the document should be declared void to obviate fraud against the dead and his successors in title.

2. Judicial Handling of Some Important Marital Issues.

Most of the cases handled by our Courts in this respect usually emanate from marriages celebrated under the 'Marriage ordinance'. Issues arising under marriages contracted under the customary law are usually settled by the families of the spouses. Unlike marriages celebrated under the Marriage Act,[21] there need not be the necessity to go to the Courts to obtain a decree for divorce. When any of the parties feels that the marriage has broken down, that person will take the initiative to bring the marriage to an end. In the case of a woman, she will run off from the matrimonial home to the parents and demand the termination of the marriage. The families of the two spouses will then meet to settle the matter. Where no agreement is possible, the parties will then agree on the termination of the marriage. Decision will

[21] Cap. 115, Laws of the Federation of Nigeria, 1958, Vol. IV p. 2349. Now Matrimonial Causes Act No., 18 of 1970.

be made on the return of the bride price i.e. the money or some other property paid or given by the husband to the parents of the woman in question in consideration for giving their daughter to the marriage. Usually some deductions are made, but the return is necessary; for it finally and legally terminates the marriage.

Where the parties disagree on the return of the bride-price, the issue is taken to the Customary Court for determination. Some other marital disputes which cannot be settled by the families of the spouses are taken to the Customary Courts where they are finally decided. However, the Courts do not usually decide whether there should be divorce or otherwise like in marriage contracted under the Marriage Act.[22]

In the case of marriage celebrated under the Marriage Act, our Courts play an important part in deciding questions arising from disagreements between the parties in this important aspect of human relations. It is remarkable that in certain cases where a husband fails to maintain his wife for no just cause, the /courts have upheld the right of such a wife to bring an action seeking the order of the Court to remedy the situation without resorting to divorce petition. Thus in *Ekisola v Ekisola*,[23] Mrs. F. D. Ekisola made an application by way of originating summons and supported that by an affidavit to the effect *inter alia*, that when she was living with the respondent he did not provide enough money for maintaining the family, and that on the 12th May, 1960, the respondent drove the applicant away from the matrimonial home with her child. The Court held that she was entitled to succeed. Maintenance allowance was fixed at £6. per month to be paid by the husband to the wife for herself and the infant child. Leaving ample room for amiable relations to emerge, Coker, J., in conclusion stated: "This Order is with liberty to both sides to apply in case of changed circumstances."

It may be observed that in cases of this nature, the paramount thing to be aimed at should be the smoothening of relations between the spouses. For a marital relation to endure, there must be amity, tolerance, sympathy and understanding. An order of the Court which appears to be too drastic in fixing maintenance allowance may in some cases operate to wreck the marriage altogether. On the other hand the courts are under a duty to uphold

---

22 See Obi S. N. C., *Modern Family Law in Southern Nigeria (1966) p. 363 et seq.*

23 (1961) L. L. R. 8 The action was brought under S. 23 of the Matrimonial Causes Act, 1950, 14 Geo. 6 C.25 which provides that (1) where a husband has been guilty of wilful neglect to provide reasonable maintenance for his wife or the infant children of the marriage, the Court, if it would have jurisdiction to entertain proceedings by the wife for judicial separation, may, on the application of the wife, order the husband to make to her such periodical payments as may be just; and the order may be enforced in the same manner as an order for alimony in proceedings for judicial separation. This enactment is applicable in Nigeria- See High Court of Lagos Act, S. 16 Cap., 80 and Regional Courts (Federal Jurisdiction) Act, S.4., Cap. 177 Laws of the Federation of Nigeria and Lagos, 1958.

an application for maintenance in a clear case of neglect and to make apposite order accordingly.

As is well known, where a party to a marriage celebrated under the Marriage Act, wants to bring the marital union to an end, he may bring a petition to the court to that effect. Under English law and our law on the subject, certain grounds must be proved in a petition for divorce. Prominent among these are cruelty, desertion and adultery. Any of these grounds alleged must be established to the satisfaction of the Court otherwise the petition will fail. Thus in *Johnson v Johnson*,[24] Coker, J., dismissed a wife's petition for the dissolution of her marriage with the respondent on the grounds of cruelty as the evidence given on behalf of both the petitioner and the respondent did not establish the charge and counter-charge of cruelty. On the other hand, where, for instance, cruelty is proved to the satisfaction of the Court, the Court will grant a decree *nisi* for dissolution of the marriage. In *Lewis v Lewis* [25] a wife petitioned for dissolution of her marriage with the husband on the ground of cruelty. In her evidence she stated that the respondent sometime in August 1957 packed away all his belongings and other property from the matrimonial house and had on occasion assailed the woman and inflicted injuries on her and in certain incident inflicted such injury on the wife's eye that she was compelled on medical advice to be wearing glasses. There were two children of the marriage. Coker, J., found all the allegations of cruelty established. He consequently granted a decree *nisi* for the dissolution of the marriage and also awarded the custody of the children to the petitioner.[26] Equally where desertion is proved, our Courts have granted decree *nisi* for the dissolution of marriage. In *Ikpi v Ikpi*, [27] a wife persistently refused to join the husband despite the fact that both of them agreed that the husband should proceed on transfer to another part of the country and the wife to join him later. When all attempts to persuade her to join the husband failed, he then petitioned the Court for divorce on the grounds of desertion and adultery. Adultery was not proved but desertion was established. Ademola, C. J. (as he then was) held that the husband's petition was entitled to succeed. A decree *nisi* was granted to the husband; he was also awarded the custody of the children of the marriage.

---

24 (1961) L. L. R. 11

25 (1960) L. L. R. 215

26 See also *Magbakor v Magbakor* (1950) E. N. L. R. 37; *Nwokedi v Nwokedi* (1958) L. L. R. 94. However, under the Matrimonial causes Act 1970 S. 15, all that is required now is to show that the 'Marriage has broken down irrevocably' for decree *nisi* to issue for dissolution of the marriage.

27 W. R. N. L. R. 59. See also *Ilevbare v Ilevbare (1958) W. R. N. L. R. 46; Tinubu v Tinubu (1959) W. R. N. L. R. 314.*

Our Courts have also granted decree *nisi* for dissolution of marriage where adultery is pleaded and proved.[28] The adultery to be proved to entitled the grant of decree *nisi* must be the particular one pleaded.[29] Our Courts have always maintained that the standard of proof required in cases where adultery is alleged should not be less high than that required in a criminal case. That is to say, the allegation must be proved beyond reasonable doubt. Thus in the case of *Oloko v Oloko*, [30] Irwin, J. after hearing evidence in a cross-petition for divorce on the ground of adultery said: 'On a review of all the material, I conclude that, while there is suspicion, the evidence falls short of that standard which the law requires in a case of adultery.'[31] consequently the learned Judge dismissed the cross-petition and equally the petition as cruelty was not established.

It may be observed that while it is essential to protect the sanctity of marriage and encourage the possible amicable solution of marital disagreements, the Courts should see it as a duty to bury a marital union which is assuredly dead. Thus in the case of *Blunt v Blunt*,[32] Viscount Simon, L. C. called attention to the need for "a true balance between respect for the binding sanctity of marriage and the social considerations which make it contrary to public policy to insist on a union which has utterly broken down."

3. The Courts in the Field of Industrial Relations

It may be stated that the relationship which exists between employer and employee usually arises out of contract. The contract of employment, as it is called, may be written or oral. Our Courts perform an important function in the interpretation of the terms of contract between the parties. The parties, i.e. the employer and the employee are bound by the terms of their contract, so that if the employer terminates the employment of his employee, the latter could sue him for breach of contract. The success and failure of such action would, however, depend on the construction to be given by the Courts to the contract of employment. An action for wrongful dismissal will lie where the appointment of the employee is terminated contrary to the express or implied agreement between the employer and the employee.

Thus in the case of *Akpagu v The Minister of Local Government*, [33] the plaintiff who was employed by the Okigwi County Council was dismissed by the Council without notice and without salary in lieu of notice. The

---

28 *Olugele v Olugele* (1961) E. N. L. R. 35, *Ademola v Ademola* (1957) W. R. N. L. R. 208 ·

29 *Jibunoh v Jibunoh* (1955-56) W. R. N. L. R. 117

30 (1961) W. R. N. L. R. 101 See also *Galler v Galler* (1954) 1 All E.r. 536

31 *ibid.*, at p. 103

32 (1943) A. C. 517 at p. 525.

33 (1959) E. N. L. R. 34

dismissal was approved by the Minister of Local Government. In an action for wrongful dismissal the plaintiff contended that he was dismissed contrary to Standing Rules of the Council having to do with Staff matters; and that being so, his dismissal was void and wrongful. Reynolds, J. held that the dismissal was wrongful and that the plaintiff was entitled to succeed in his claim for damages in respect of pension and gratuity. In another case, *Garabedian v Jamakani*,[34] the plaintiff was employed under a contract which was in writing. A clause provided for dismissal in case of misconduct by the employee. The defendant, who was the employer, had earlier on ordered some catalogues through the plaintiff when he was in Lebanon. The defendant was not prepared to pay for the catalogue despite frequent demands by the plaintiff. On one occasion when the plaintiff requested payment for the said catalogues, the defendant whereupon returned the materials to him and dismissed him from his employment without notice. The defendant pleaded that the plaintiff was dismissed because of 'inefficiency and incompetence.' No sufficient evidence was adduced to establish this. Savage, J., held that the dismissal was wrongful and consequently the plaintiff was entitled to recover damages assessed at £700 and a refund of £20 being the amount wrongfully deducted by the defendant from the plaintiff's salary.

It may be observed that while no person will be forced to employ anybody, once an employer has agreed to employ someone, the law requires him to treat the employee fairly. The mere fact that an employer pleads in an action for wrongful dismissal, that the employee was inefficient and incompetence is not conclusive. The Court will require this plea to be established satisfactorily or the plea fails. Thus in *Garabedian's case (supra)* Savage, J., after hearing evidence on both sides, sated: "I cannot imagine a businessman would increase his employee's salary because the employee's work is unsatisfactory." On this point the learned Judge concluded "I accept the plaintiff's version that the increases were paid to him by the defendant because the defendant was satisfied with his work."[35] where, however, a good case is made for the termination of an employee's appointment the courts will uphold the right of the employer in that regard; provided appropriate notice[36] or salary in lieu of notice is

---

[34] (1961) 1 All N. L. R. 177; see also *Walters v Harrison (1922) 4 N. L. R. 71*. In *Munnik v Costain-Blaneevoort Dredging Ltd. (1960) L. L. R 90*. Dickson, J. held that in an action for wrongful dismissal, if the employer alleged incompetency on the part of the employee, the onus rested on the employer to prove such incompetence. he observed that the whole question should be whether there was justification for the dismissal.

[35] *ibid.*, at pp. 179-80

[36] *Ogunsanmi v Furniture (W.A) Co. Ltd., (1961) 1 All N. l. R. 862*. See also *Ahuronye v The University College Ibadan (1959-61) W.R.N.L. R. 232*. In *Unity v Odukpani Road District Council (1959) E.N.L.R. 28*. Palmer J. upheld the right of the Council to dismiss the plaintiff after a month's notice because of general inefficiency. In *Moeller v Monier Construction (Nigeria) Co Ltd,*

given.[37] Even if the contract is silent on the appropriate notice to be given by either party for the termination of the appointment, the Court will decide on what should be reasonable notice in any particular case.[38]

Another point which has been the subject of judicial pronouncement is the measure of damages in cases of wrongful dismissal. Coleridge, C. J. in the case of *Maw v Jones*,[39] stated that 'a plaintiff is entitled to recover for all damage flowing naturally from the breach, and in considering what that would include the jury may take into account the difficulty a plaintiff would have in given circumstances obtaining employment elsewhere.' Identical view was expressed by Fletcher Moulton, L. J. in *Chaplin v Hicks*, thus: 'There is no other universal principle as to the amount of damages than that it is the aim of the law to ensure that a person whose contract has been broken shall be placed as near as possible in the same position as it it had not.[40] It follows that the amount of damages awarded should be closely related to the remuneration which the employee was receiving and the one which he is likely to receive. Our Courts have not allowed excessive damage to stand.[41]

Death or Personal Injury to a Workman

With regard to employer's liability for compensation in respect of the death or injury of the workman in the course of his employment; section 5 of the

---

Ltd, 1961 All N. L. R. 167, Savage, J., was called upon to interpret a term of a written contract in which the employer was given the right to terminate the employment of the employee 'if he commits any act which in the opinion of the Company is likely to bring the latter into disrepute with any other persons..the plaintiff was in the habit of bringing 'hotel girl' into the flat of the defendant company to the annoyance of other inmates. In dismissing the action for wrongful dismissal against the Company who summarily dismissed him, the learned Judge stated that the conduct of the plaintiff was such that the Company were entitled to form the opinion that it could bring the company into disrepute with 'any other persons' and with the public. The plaintiff was bound by the terms of his contract.

37 *Daniels v Shell -BP Petroleum Development Co. Nigeria Ltd., 1962 1 All N.L.R. 19. Chiozie v U. A. C. Ltd (1956) 1 E. R. N. L. R. 28.*

38 *Daniels v Shell BP. (supra); Ogunsanmi v Furniture (W.A.) Co. Ltd., (supra); Payzu Ltd., v Hannaford (1918) 2 K. B. 348.*

39 (1980) L. R. 25 Q.B.D. 107 at p. 109.

40 (1911) 2 K.B. 786 at p. 794. In a case decided by the East African Court of Appeal: *Witu Rubbe Estates v Parke (1913) 5 E. A. L. R. 17 at p. 21*, Hamilton C. J. said: 'The real test appears to be : What time might reasonably be expected to elapse before the Appellate would in the ordinary course be likely to obtain similar employment to that he had lost by his wrongful dismissal? Having fixed that period he should be given a sufficient sum to reimburse him for the loss he suffered, calculated on the basis of the emoluments he was enjoying at the time of such loss.'

41 See *Gaiser v Cole 1958 L. L. R. 83; Cattanco v Candido da Rocha (1932) 11 N. L. R. 57.*

Workman's Compensation Act [42] provides that 'If in any employment personal injury by accident arising out of and in the course of the employment is caused to a workman, his employer shall, subject as hereinafter mentioned, be liable to pay compensation in accordance with the provisions of this Act.' Then follows an important proviso; 'provided that (a) the employer shall not be liable under this Act in respect of any injury which does not incapacitate the workman for a period of at least five consecutive days from earning full wages at the work at which he was employed; and (b) if it is proved that the injury to a workman is attributable to the serious and wilful misconduct of that workman, any compensation claimed in respect of that injury shall be disallowed.'

It follows that for an injury sustained by a workman in the course of his employment to ground compensation under the Act, it must be a serious injury which incapacitates him for at least five days from earning his full wages at the work at which he is employed. In the case of *United Africa Company (Nigeria) Ltd. v Orekyen*,[43] the Respondent, who was an employee of the Appellants was placed in charge of a petrol station operated by the Appellant. One morning, owing to the unruly behaviour of a stranger, a fight ensued between the stranger and one of the attendants. The respondents, in an attempt to stop the ugly scene, took position between them. Whereupon the stranger struck him in the eye. He lost the sight of that eye. The respondent sued the appellants under the Workmans' Compensation Act. The learned trail magistrate held that he was entitled to succeed. The employer appealed, contending that the injury sustained by the respondent did not arise out of his employment. De Lestang, C. J. held that the injury was sustained by the respondent in the course of his employment. The appeal was dismissed. In the course of his judgment the learned judge observed that 'it was the duty of the respondent to maintain order at the Petrol Station, and too protect his subordinate co-employee from being molested by a stranger.'[44] There is no doubt that this observation stands to reason, for an employee will be failing in his duty if he fails to protect the property under his charge as well as his subordinates in the establishment.

As we pointed out above, the injury, must be a serious one that incapacitates the employee in respect of his employment in such a way as to reduce his earning ability. The test is disability and not the permanency of the injury of the employee. Thus in *Metal Containers (W.A.) Ltd v Iyomifokhai*, [45] a workman was involved in an accident during the course of

---

[42] Cap. 222, Laws of the Federation of Nigeria, 1958, Vol. VI. See equally Ss. 6-9, *ibid.* As regards death of a workman, see ss. 13 -15, ibid.

[43] (1961) 1 All N. L. R. 719

[44] *ibid.*, at p. 721

[45] (1959) L. L. R. 130.

his employment. He lost two teeth. The injury did not prevent him from carrying out his pre-accident work. In an action for compensation the magistrate awarded him £50. The employers appealed. Bellamy. J. allowed the appeal. The learned Judge was of the view that although the injury in question could leave a permanent mark on the workman yet it is only in respect of a reduction of earning capacity either in the employment in which the workman was engaged at the time of the accident or in any other employment which he was capable of undertaking at the time that compensation is payable.'

As we have seen in *Moeller v Monier Construction (Nigeria) Co. Ltd*; [46] where an employee binds himself under a contract of employment not to do an act, he is bound by the terms of his contract and our Courts have held accordingly. The position is not wholly the same in the case of contract between employer and employee in restraint of trade.

Contract in Restraint of Trade:

At common law, contracts in restraint of trade are *prima facie* void. The Courts view with jealousy contracts which operate to restrain the employee from setting up his own trade at will, or serving another employee after leaving the service[47] of the employer. Thus Lord Macnaughton in *Nordenfelt v Maxim Nordenfelt Guns and Ammunition Co.*,[48] said: 'There is obviously more freedom of contract between buyer and seller than between master and servant or between an employer and a person seeking employment.' Lord Atkinson in *Morris v Saxelby* [49] went further "All cases when they come to be examined, seem to establish this principle, that all restraints upon trade are bad as being in violation of public policy, unless they are natural and not unreasonable for the protection of the parties in dealing legally with some subject matter of contract. The principle is this: Public policy requires that every man shall be at liberty to work for himself, and shall not be at liberty to deprive himself or the State of his labour, skill, or talent, by any contract that he enters into."

Our Courts have always adhered to this great principle of the law. Thus in *Compagnie Francaise de L'Afrique Occidentale (C.F.A.O.) v Leuba*, [50] an employee of a Company in Lagos bound himself "not to take part under any title (Patron, partner, party interested or clerk) in any commercial or

---

[46] (1961) 1 All N. L. R. 167

[47] The doctrine of restraint in trade has no application in covenants dealing solely with the rights of the parties during the employment: *Warner Brother v Nelson (1937) 1 K.B. 209*

[48] (1894) A. C. 535 at p. 566

[49] (1916) 1 A. C. 688 at p. 701; see also Younger, L. J., in *Attwood v Lamont (1920) 3 K. B. 571, 586, 587.*

[50] (1918) N. L. R. 60.

industrial enterprise in West Africa during a period of twelve months from the moment when, for any reason whatever, he ceases to be a member of the staff of the Company." The Full Court, affirming the decision of the Divisional Court held that the restriction was too wide and unreasonable. The covenant was declared void and as being in restraint of trade or employment. Webber, J., in that case observed: 'In all these covenants in restraint of trade the authorities have laid down the general principle of law that all interference with individual liberty of action in trading and all restraints of trade themselves, if there is nothing more are contrary to public policy and therefore void.'[51] In another case of *John Holt & Co. Ltd., v Chalmers* [52] a clause of an agreement between an employer and employee provided that 'on the determination of this Agreement from any cause whatsoever the Employee shall not for a period of three years thereafter in any of the rivers or places in Africa where the Employee may, during his engagement, have served the company trade or carry on business of any description either directly or indirectly on his own..." The Full Court once more upheld the decision of the Divisional Court in holding that the restriction went beyond that which was necessary for the protection of the interests of the covenant. Consequently it was declared unreasonable.

It is for the employer seeking to enforce a covenant in this respect to show that it is reasonable in the interest of the parties and more particularly that such covenant is designed to protect some exceptional proprietary interest owned by the employer. The question of reasonableness in this respect is one of law to be decided by the Court. It follows that evidence of the opinion of persons in the particular trade is inadmissible, since the reasonableness or otherwise of the covenant in question is one of construction and legal effect and is therefore for the Court alone.[53] It must be pointed out, however that an employer is entitled to impose any restrictions in protection of his trade or industry, provided always that such restrictions are reasonable.[54]

4. Judicial Handling of Issues Arising from Major Financial and Commercial Transactions.

In this section we shall be dealing with the adjudication of issues arising from, *money lending* (under the Money-Lenders' Act [55] and the respective

---

[51] *ibid.* at p. 66-7: See also *Commercial Plastics Ltd. v Vincent (1964) 3 W. L. R. 820.*

[52] (1981) N. L.R. 69; See also *Mason v Provident Clothing and Supply Co. Ltd. (1913) A. C. 724*

[53] *Haynes v Doman (1899) 2 Ch. 13*

[54] See *ibid*

[55] Cap. 136, Laws of Nigeria (1948) Vol. IV. In the Eastern Region, this enactment has been amended by the Money-Lenders' Ordinance (Amendment) Law, 1964 No. 5 of 1964, Laws of Eastern Nigeria, 1864 p. A. 41

States enactments [56] on the subject), *banking* and hire purchase. We shall equally be examining how the Courts have been dealing with issues emanating from *designs*, *patents* and *trade marks*.

Money-Lending

Under the Moneylenders' Act, a moneylender can only enforce his rights for any money lent if he complies with the provisions of the Act. The Act therefore renders unenforceable but not void, any contract entered into by the moneylender and the borrower if the provisions of the Act are not complied with.[57] Section 23, however, preserves the rights and interest of a *bona fide* purchaser for value without notice of any defect in the contract between the moneylender and the borrower due to the operation of the Act.

Our Courts have rigorously interpreted the respective enactments on this subject of money lending and an analysis of the decisions show that the preponderance has always been against the moneylender. In *Baba-Egbe v Kasumu and others*,[58] a moneylender advanced a sum of money to B. Property at 55 Great Bridge Street, Lagos was mortgaged in consideration of this. Contrary to the provisions of section 19 of the Act, no book was kept for the transaction. The West African Court of Appeal held that the mortgage transaction was unenforceable. The Court ordered the recovery of possession of the premises in question which involved 'the cancellation and delivery up of the deed of mortgage.' It follows that in the event of non-compliance with the provisions of the Statute, the entire money lent will be lost. Appeal to equitable remedy will be of no avail. In another case, *Nwankwo v Orji*, [59] the plaintiff, a licensed moneylender alleged that he lent to the defendant, a sum of £500. The defendant signed documents relating to the transactions. In Nov. 1960, a sum of £10. was repaid but the plaintiff neither sent a receipt for that nor did he enter the repayment in his account book. That was contrary to section 19 of the moneylenders' Act. The plaintiff contended that in equity the Court ought not to deprive him of £500 to which he was entitled simply because he neglected to give a receipt for

---

[56] For Lagos, see Cap. 124 Laws of the Federation of Nigeria and Lagos, (1958) Vol. IV; see equally Money-Lenders' (Amendment) Act, 1960, Laws of the Federation of Nigeria and Lagos, 1960. For the Northern Region see Money-Lenders Law, Cap. 74. laws of Northern Nigeria, (1963) Vol. VII; and for the West and Mid-West, see Money lenders' Law Cap. 78, Laws of the Western Region of Nigeria (1959) Vol IV On the whole, the Regional enactments on the subject are complete adaptation of the Money-lenders' Act, Cap. 136. So there is uniformity in this respect.

[57] See ss. 12, 19(4); S.14 makes it an offence punishable by a fine of £50. to lend money at a rate of interest higher than that authorised under the Act. An offence committed contrary to S. 26 renders a contract, subject to s. 26, void.

[58] (1954) 14 W. A. C. A. 444.

[59] *Suit No. E/94/60, decided at Enugu High Court* of Eastern Nigeria on 15th Jan. (1964) (Unreported yet). See also *Eldridge and Morris v Taylor* (1931) 2 K. B. D. 416.

£10 and to enter the payment in his book. Palmer J., found as a fact that the plaintiff was only careless and had not dishonest intent in the regard. The learned Judge, however, held that the transaction was unenforceable as the provisions of the Act had not been complied with. Consequently the defendant kept the remainder of the money lent. The learned Judge recognised that the decision was "harsh" on the plaintiff whose appeal to equitable jurisdiction of the Court was rejected.[60] We shall return to this case later.

As was observed above, the proviso to section 23 of the Act protects the rights and interest of a *bona fide* purchaser for value without notice of a non-compliance with the provisions of the Act. This lends weight to the view that such contracts or transactions which are entered into, are not rendered void but unenforceable by the non-compliance with the provisions of the Act. In *Sanusi v Daniel & Another*, [61] the appellant mortgaged his house to D, the 1st respondent as security for loans received. D. Exercised his right of sale under the mortgage deed. The property was sold by public auction and conveyed to C. The appellant by this action asked the Court to set aside the sale on the ground that the mortgage deed was defective because of the non-compliance with the provisions of the Money-lenders'Act. At the trial it was found as a fact that C, the second respondent, was a *bona fide* purchaser for value without notice. It was held by the Federal Supreme Court that C, the second respondent, obtained valid title notwithstanding any defects due to the operation of the Money-lenders' Act. In another case *Balogun v Obisanya & Another*, [62] a moneylender in a mortgage transaction failed to comply with the provisions of section 12 (1) of the Act in that he failed to sign the mortgage deed, nor did he furnish the appellant with a copy of the deed. The Federal Supreme Court held that the second respondent being a *bona fide* purchaser for value without notice acquired a valid title following a sale conducted by the money-lender. Jibowu, F. J. observed: 'It is quite clear, therefore that the mortgage deed in question is not void or illegal but unenforceable. The rights of the transferees of securities taken by the moneylenders are protected.[63]

This observation of the learned Judge is very important and illuminating, for as we pointed out earlier, the object of the Act is not to render void such contracts. They are merely unenforceable. In *Re Chetwynd's Estate, Dunn Trust, Ltd. m. v Brown*, Sir Wilfrid Green, M. R. dealing with section 6 of the (U.K.) Moneylenders' Act, 1927 stated:

---

[60] See equally *Kadiri v Oluso-ga* (1956) F. S. C. R. 56; and *Abesin v Iyaegbe* (1958) W. R. N. L. R. 67

[61] (1956) F. S. C. R. 93.

[62] (1956) F. S. C. R. 22; see also *Efuwabe and Ors. v Dr. Afodu & Ors.* (1960) L. L. R. 238.

[63] *ibid.*, at p. 24 See also In re Robinson, 1911) 1 Ch. 230.

"The section does not have the result that there is no contract it merely makes the contract unenforceable."[64]

It may be observed that although the Act was intended to protect the borrowers from likely exploitation by the moneylenders, yet justice equally demands that the moneylenders should not be exposed to exploitation by seemingly clever borrowers who would rush to the Court to obtain an order to set aside the entire transaction merely because the moneylender by an honest error failed to furnish the borrower with a copy of a memorandum within a stipulated period of seven days; or negligently, without any dishonest intent, failed to forward a receipt to a borrower. In *Nwankwo v Orji (supra)*, Palmer, J., said: 'It is no doubt harsh that a moneylender should be deprived of £500 because he has neglected, without any dishonest intent, to give a receipt for £10 and to make an entry in his account book. But that, so far as I can see, is what the Statute says. From the moneylender's point of view it is a harsh Statute, and I do not see that I can refuse to enforce it. With some reluctance, therefore, I feel constrained to hold that the claim cannot be enforced."

This passage demonstrates vividly the frustration in which many Judges find themselves when called upon to construe this "harsh" enactment. While we recognise that there are many 'Shylocks' around the corner, this should not lead us to the conclusion that moneylenders are not in fact doing a good service to the community. They in fact, in a large measure, help some members of the public out of their pressing financial troubles. It is therefore suggested that the law on the subject of money lending needs to be reformed or amended; there could be a provision authorising the Courts to do what is just in the interest of the parties, where it appears to the Court concerned that no fraud or dishonest practice or deliberate act to flout the provisions of the Statute was contemplated by the moneylender.

The Banker and the Customer

With regard to issues arising from the relationship between the Banker and his customer, our courts, in handling such issues have very closely followed English decisions on the subject. That is to say, they have not only interpreted the contract between the parties but also implied certain terms which would naturally follow 'the course of business.' Thus in the case of British and *French Bank v Opaleye*, [65] the Respondent had two accounts with the Appellant Bank. One was in his own name and the other in which he transacted his business under the name of "Fekemo Brothers."

---

[64] (1937) 3 All E. R. 530 at p. 531; see also Tucker, J., in Cohen v Leicester Ltd., 1938 4 All E. R. 181 at p. 191

[65] (1962) 1 All N. L. R.. 26

He was the sole account holder of the latter account. At one time the private account stood at credit balance but the business account was overdrawn to the extent of £500. A cheque for £350 was paid into the private account; the bank thereupon without notice to or the consent of the Respondent transferred the credit in the personal account to the business account to reduce the overdraft in that account. The Respondent was consequently informed that he could not draw on his personal or private account.

The Federal Supreme Court held that in the absence of an express agreement to the contrary, there was an implied term in the contract between the parties that the accounts were to be kept distinct and separate. The Court further held that the banker had no right to combine two distinct and separate accounts or to transfer assets or liabilities from one account to another where by agreement, express or implied, the accounts were to be kept separate.

The decision accords with the judicial pronouncement of Swift, J., in *Greenhalgh v. Union Bank of Manchester.*[66] He said: 'If a banker agrees with his customer to open two or more accounts, he has not, in my opinion, without the assent of the customer, any right to move either assets or liabilities from the one account to the other; the very basis of his agreement with his customer is that the two accounts shall be kept separate, and, if the customer pays bills drawn upon him not into his general account, where they will be dis-counted and he will receive the benefit of being able to draw against them, but into an account in which they will only be used either to pay bills accepted by the bank or bill drawn by the customer which they are specifically to meet, I do not think a banker, any more than any other individual, can change them from the one account into the other without the customer's assent'. The learned Judge further stated that the overriding factor in this regard should be what the parties agreed. Where therefore there is an agreement to open two distinct accounts and money is paid into one of them, the banker or any other individual, in the absence of the consent of the customer expressed or implied, is precluded from transferring money from one account to the other.

It must be pointed out however, that the case of British and French *Bank. v. Opaleye* dealt specifically with transfer from one distinct and separate account to another. There were in fact two different names used,[67] as we have seen. Where therefore a person opens two accounts under the same name, it is for the courts to determine from the circumstances of the case whether the parties intended that in the course of business, the accounts should be run separately and that there should be no transfer without the notice and consent of the customer. Although in *Garnett v.*

---

66 [1924] 2 K.B. 153 at p.164.

67 One account was in the name of "Opeleye, Rafin Afolabi Bellow" while the other was named, "Fekemo Brothers."

M'Kewan [68] it was held that the bank was entitled any time to combine any separate accounts maintained by a person under his name in different branches of the bank; Mathew, J.in *Buckingham and Co. v. The London and Midland Bank Ltd.*,[69] held that where a customer had a loan account and a current account the bank could not without reasonable notice to the customer transfer money from one account to the other. It may therefore be said that smooth running of business, good faith and implied term in agreement between a banker and his customer demand that where a customer opens two accounts, the banker should not in absence of an express agreement to the contrary, transfer money from one account to the other without the consent of the customer or at least, without a reasonable notice to that effect.

Guarantor's Liability

The principle of adherence to the terms of agreement between the banker and his customers extends to the guarantors of the customers. The Courts have held that where a person guarantees the account of another, both the banker and his customer, in the course of business, are precluded from altering the terms of the agreement without the consent of the guarantor; if however, such alteration is effected without the said consent, the guarantor is discharged from liability; thus in *Awolesi v. The National Bank of Nigeria Ltd.*,[70] The Federal Supreme Court held that a guarantor of a current account which stood at £10,096. 16. 9d. was discharged from liability because the bank, without the consent of the guarantor, insulated the said account and opened a new one in the name of the same debtor whose account was guaranteed. The Court was of the view that the liberty to open a new account did not come into being until after the guaranty ceased to be binding as a continuing security on the guarantor or his estate.

It follows that the guarantor is bound as long as the parties confine themselves within the ambit of the agreement; 'beyond the proper interpretation of that engagement you have no hold upon him. He receives no benefit and no consideration. He is bound, therefore, merely according to the proper meaning and effect of the written engagement that he has entered into'.[71]

---

68 (1972), L.R. 8 Ex, 10

69 (1895), 12 T.L.R. 70.

70 [1962] W.N.L.R. 102; see also Cotton L.J. in Re Sherry, London and County banking v. Terry, (1884) 25 Ch. D. 692. Mutton v. Peat [1900] 2 Ch. D. 79; Clayton's Case,Devaynes v. Noble (1816) 1 Mer. 572

71 Per Lord Westbury, L.C. in Blest v. Brown (1862) De G. F. & J. 367, 365, 45 E.R. 1225 at p. 1229.

Hire-Purchase

As we have seen, the Courts in handling issues emanating from financial or commercial transactions invariably have great regard to the terms of agreement between the parties. This attitude of the Courts is more manifested in deciding cases arising from hire-purchase agreements. A hire-purchase agreement involves a transaction which passes the possession and not the ownership of the goods concerned to the hirer. It follows that until purchase price (which is usually paid by instalments) is wholly paid, ownership does not pass; with the result that the owner can resume possession of the goods if there is default in the instalmental payments. Such right is usually reserved by the owner in the agreement between the parties.

If the hirer purports to sell the property, such transaction is void and the transferee acquires no title from such purported sale. Thus in *Gladys Olametan v C.F.A.O. (Compagnie Francaise de L'Afrique Occidentale)* [72] the defendant company let out a lorry on hire-purchase to one O. O fraudulently and without the defendants' authority removed the lorry from Ghana to Nigeria and disposed of it to the plaintiff. The defendants' agent in Nigeria acting on the instructions of the owners of the lorry in Ghana seized it from the plaintiff, who claimed to have purchased it from O. In an action against the defendants for damages from conversion of the lorry, Coker, J., held that the plaintiff was not entitled to succeed. The learned Judge was of the view that the hirer of an article on hire purchase agreement acquired no proprietary interests in the article other than those conferred by the hire-purchase agreement; consequently if he sold it without the authority of the owners the sale was void and the purchaser acquired no title to the property concerned.[73]

Where an owner of an article which is subject of a hire-purchase agreement exercises his right to re-take possession of the property in the event of a default by the hirer, an action for wrongful seizure will not lie. This was so held by Irwin, J., in *Atere v. Dada and Another.*[74] In such a case equity will not release the hirer from the effect of his default.[75] It may be equally pointed out that where one confers upon another the right to seize a chattel and the licence is properly exercised no action lies in trespass.[76]

---

72 [1959] L.L.R. 42.

73 See a similar decision by McNair, J., in United Dominions Trust (Commercial), Ltd. v. Parkway Motors Ltd. [1955] 2 All E.r. 5571 see equally Butterworth v. Kingsway Motors Ltd. [1954] 2 All E.r. 694.

74 [1957] W.R.N.L.R. 176.

75 Animashawun V. C.F.A.O. 1960 L.L.R. 151

76 Se Delor v. Foll (1952) 14 W.A.C.A. 54 and Akuff v. Asante [1953] AW.A.C.A. 275.

To obviate possible abuse and hardship, the Hire purchase Act, 1965 was passed. The act restricts recovery of goods otherwise than by order of a court of competent jurisdiction, in case of motor vehicles three-fifths, and in other cases, one-half of the purchase price had been paid by the hirer.[77a] This Act, which fills an obvious gap in the law on the subject, applies only to Lagos. We may therefore suggest that other legislatures in the country should effect apposite enactments on the subject.

Trade Mark, Design or Patent, Copyright[77b]

The task of the Courts is less onerous when they are called upon to interpret agreements dealing with hire-purchase than when called upon to decide whether a certain name or trade mark, design or patent so closely resembles any one already in existence to be likely to cause confusion in the minds of the people and mislead them. The usual question which the Courts pose and answer is whether such a name or trade mark or design is 'calculated to deceive'? In answering such a question, the Courts in most cases appear to regard the intention of the offending party as not very relevant;[78a] once it is established that the name or design[78b] in question is likely to deceive the public, injunction will be granted restraining the defendant from using such name or design. Thus Lord Cozens-Hardy, M.R., said: 'I know no authority, and I can see no principle which withholds us from preventing injury to the plaintiff in his business as a trade by a confusion which will lead people to conclude that the defendants are really connected in some way with the plaintiff or are carrying on a branch of the plaintiff's business'[79]

In *Niger Chemists Ltd., v. Nigerian Chemists and another*,[80] the plaintiff company had carried on business as chemists and druggists for some years in Onitsha and several branches in Eastern Nigeria. The firm adopted the name 'Niger Chemists' and this was registered under Registration of Business Names or Ordinance, Chapter 195. The second defendant and his partners founded a firm carrying on exactly the same business in Onitsha under the name of "Nigeria Chemists". The plaintiff Company unsuccessfully appealed to the defendants to change the name.

[77a] S.9 Hire-Purchase Act, 1965.

[77b] Copyright is now protected by Copyright Decree No. 17 of 1988.

[78a] In Ewing v. Buttercup Margarine Co. [1917] 2 Ch. 1, it was established as principle that the Court has jurisdiction to restrain a person from using 'a trade name colourably resembling that of the plaintiff, if the defendant's trade name, though innocently adopted, is calculated to deceive' Vide also Beecham group Ltd. V. EFP. Ltd (1985) 3 NWLR(pt-11) 112

[78b] Designs are registrable under the Trade Marks Act, 1965.

[79] ibid., at p. 11; See also s.13 of the Trade Marks Act, 217.

[80] [1961] 1 All N.L.R. 171.

Whereupon he brought proceedings for an injunction to restrain them from using the name and style: "Nigeria chemists." Palmer J., in holding that the plaintiff was entitled to succeed was of the view that in an action of this kind 'it is not necessary to prove that there was any intention to deceive'.[81] All the plaintiff need do is to prove that the name used by the defendant is so similar to his own as to deceive people who are likely to deal with him. In a place like Nigeria where some members of the community are not literate, trade marks and designs play a great part in distinguishing the goods of one firm from another. The goods are usually given local names deriving from the design on them. It follows therefore that any imitation of such popularly known design could be given the same name as the old and mistaken for the accustomed one. In *W.B. McIver Co. Ltd. v. C.F.A.O.*[82] Rose J. said, 'In a highly intelligent and civilised community I should have no hesitation in saying that likelihood of confusing the two marks is so very negligible that no one could reasonably say that the respondents' mark is calculated to deceive; however; I cannot but feel in coming to a decision in this case, that attention must be paid to surrounding circumstances and local conditions'. In holding that a design whose main distinctive feature was a puncheon was calculated to deceive; he further observed: 'Both marks would be known to the natives by a description of the essential point in both marks, i.e. by the cask - they would both be referred to the firm by which the goods represented are sold or to the surrounding details in the marks'.

In *De Facto Works Ltd., v. Odumotun Trading Co.* [83] Coker J. Found as a fact that the plaintiff's bread had come to be known and recognised by the public as *breadi Oniyelo* because of the design of the paper with which it was wrapped. The paper was laid out in yellow and brown. In that case the learned Judge held that a similar design by the defendant was calculated to deceive, and granted an injunction restraining the defendant from using the wrappers and also awarded general damages fixed at £200 or N400.00 to the plaintiff.

While the Courts are, in handling these cases, placed in a very delicate situation of protecting the rights which people have by their hard work acquired, great care must be taken to avoid placing dangerous clogs in the field of commercial competition. It is for the Judge in each case to decide for himself whether a certain name, trade mark or design is calculated to deceive. Warrington, J. in 1905 said: 'It seems to me that each of these cases must be looked at by itself, and the Judge, looking at the label or the get-up device, whatever it may be that is complained of, with such

---

81 ibid, at p. 173.

82 (1917) 3 N.L.R. 16 at p. 19, See also Tew, j. in Distillerderij En Alcoholfabriek v. Netherlands Distilleries (1982) 8 N.L.R. 48 at p. 51.

83 (1917) L.L.R. 33. see equally U.K Tobacco Co. Ltd., v. Carreres Ltd. v. (1931) 16 N.L.R. 1: and G. Gotts Chalch & Co. Ltd v. Spruce Manufacturing Co. Ltd. [1956] F.S.C.R. 42.

assistance as to the practice in the trade as he can get from the witnesses must decide for himself whether the article complained of is calculated to deceive or not.'[84] Lord Macnaghten in 1900 was more emphatic: 'The Judge, looking at the exhibits before him, and also paying attention to the evidence adduced, must not surrender his own independent judgment to any witness whatever.'[85] The need for independent judgment of the Judge cannot be over-emphasised for witnesses appearing in such cases are obviously interested parties usually subject to be influenced by pressure groups. Their evidence must be handled with great care.

Under the Trade Marks Act,[86] 'It shall not be lawful to register as a trade mark or part of a trade mark any matter the use of which would, by reason of its being calculated to deceive or otherwise, be disentitled to protection in a Court of Justice, or would be contrary to law or morality, or any scandalous design'. It is equally provided that except by order of the Court or in case of trade marks in use before 30th March, 1901, no trade mark shall be registered in respect of any goods or description of goods which is identical with one belonging to a different proprietor which is already on the register with respect to such goods or description of goods, or so nearly resembling such a trade mark as to be calculated to deceive.[87]

A person can oppose any registered trade mark which is similar to his own already registered;[88] and if it is established to the satisfaction of the Court that the design in question was calculated to deceive, the Court will make an order for the expunging of the entry form the Register of Trade Marks.[89]

---

84 Schweppes Ltd. v. Gibben [1905] R.P.C. (Report of Patent Case) 113 at p.119.

85 Payton & Co. v. Snelling, Lampard & Co. Ltd., 1901 A.C. 308 at p. 311.

86 Cap. 217, Laws of Nigeria, (1948) Vol. IV; this was a consolidated 'ordinance' meant to operate from 31st Dec. 1914.

87 SS. 13, 25, ibid.

88 S.42, 18, ibid; see also Ferries George v. John Malkden & Co. Ltd., (1926) 7 N.L.R. 64.

89 S. 42, ibid; see equally In re The Welsh Tinplale and Metal stamping Co. Ltd. and Enamelware Factory Co. Ltd., 1951 L.L.R. 33.

Chapter 9

The Role of The Courts in The Political Arena

In this chapter we shall be dealing with election petitions and issues arising thereunder, before going into that, however, we shall try to show how electoral laws under which those elections were conducted developed. It will be interesting to see how the Courts have maintained the independence and integrity of the judiciary despite obvious political pressures under the circumstances. Also we shall examine how the Courts have handled questions touching and concerning Members of Parliament as well as adjudication of political offences; and finally we shall deal with the judicial determination of the constitutional crises in Western Nigeria in 1962.

1. Electoral Laws and Election Petitions:

(a) Electoral Laws:

(i) Historical Developments from 1922 to 1958:

It has always been the traditional British practice to lead the dependant territories gradually and stage by stage until they are eventually considered ready for full nationhood by attainment of independence. Thus it was not until 1922 that franchise was first granted in Nigeria.

Under the 1922 Constitution, there were to be four elected members[1] for Lagos and Calabar in a legislature with a maximum membership of forty-six.[2] The people who were entitled to vote under the Order were adult males (i.e. those who were up to 21 years or upwards); they were also to be British subjects or natives of the Protectorate with a residence qualification of twelve months and a gross income of £100 per annum.[3] Anyone who had been found guilty and sentenced by a British Court having jurisdiction to do so, for a crime punishable by death, hard labour or more than one year's imprisonment or who was of unsound mind was disqualified from voting.[4] Any registered elector was qualified to be elected to the Legislative

---

[1] Article 6 of the Nigeria (Legislative Council) Order in Council, 1922. There were three members for Lagos, and one for Calabar.

[2] Art. 4, *ibid.*

[3] Art. 20, *ibid*; the income qualification as reduced to £50 per annum under the 1946 Constitution, *post.*

[4] Art. 21, *ibid.*

Council provided that he was not an undischarged bankrupt, had not within five years before the date appointed for the election received charitable relief in Nigeria from any public source or was not receiving a salary being paid out of the public revenue of the country.[5] It may be pointed out that the 1922 Constitution made no provision for the franchise to be extended to women and consequently they were excluded. This non-enfranchisement of women provoked serious agitation and led to a resolution being passed in 1946 by the Igbo federation in favour of the enfranchisement of women.[6] Even in respect of men, the qualifying conditions were such that many people in Lagos and Calabar were not eligible to vote. By the year 1943 Dr. Nnamdi Azikiwe had conceived the idea of universal adult suffrage and urged its adoption in Nigeria.[7] But events showed that that was a bit too early for the country.

In 1946 a Constitution (popularly known as Richards Constitution) was introduced. Section 56 which dealt with elections provided as follows:

> Provisions may be made by any law enacted under this Order regarding the election of Elected Members including (without prejudice to the generality of the foregoing power) the following matters, that is to say:
>
> (a) the qualification of voters for election of such members;
> (b) the registration of voters;
> (c) the ascertainment of the qualification of voters and candidates;
> (d) the holding of elections of such Members;
> (e) offences in relation to such elections, including the trial and punishment thereof; and
> (f) the disposal of election petitions, and determination of questions otherwise arising regarding membership of the legislative Council.

(2) Until other provision has been made as aforesaid,

(a) the Governor may by Proclamation make provision for the purpose aforesaid and may thereby add to, amend or revoke the Nigeria (Legislative Council) (Registration of Electors) Regulations and the Nigeria (Legislative Council) Registration of Electors Regulations (Amendment) Ordinance, 1941 (Ordinance No. 24 of 1941); and

(b) Subject to any such proclamation, the said Regulations and Ordinance shall apply in relation to the matters aforesaid, reference therein to the Legislative Council being construed as references to the Legislative Council constituted by this Order."[8]

---

[5] Art. 15, *ibid.*

[6] See *Daily Comet 30th March, 1946.*

[7] See Azikiwe N.: *Political Blueprint of Nigeria, Lagos 1945.*

[8] The Nigeria (Legislative Council) Order in council, 1946, S.I. No. 1370, 1946.

The regulations referred to above were made under the 1922 Constitution for elections to the Legislative Council constituted thereunder. The number of elected members under the Constitution of 1946 remained four - three Members for Lagos and one Member for Calabar.[9]

As we have seen in Chapter Three, the 1946 Constitution laid the foundation of the Nigeria Federal system. Provisions were made for the establishment in the Northern, Eastern and Western Provinces of Regional Houses of Assembly.[10] For the Northern Provinces it was provided that the Regional Council was to consist of the House of Chiefs and a House of Assembly. One would have thought that the expansion of the Legislative Council and the establishment of Regional Houses of Assembly would have accelerated the expansion of franchise. Rather, the 1946 Constitution provided as follows:

> The Provincial Members shall be selected by such Native Authorities in the Northern, Western or Eastern Provinces (as the case may be) from among their own Members, or where a Native Authority consists of a sole Chief or other person, from among the Members of his Advisory Council, and in such manner, as the Governor may from time to time direct in writing.[11]

It follows that the franchise in this respect was not extended to individuals as such but to the native authorities as corporate entities.

The years following the Constitution of 1946 saw a wave of vigorous agitation for introduction of universal adult suffrage or at least the expansion of the franchise. Most of the agitation was headed by the National Council of Nigeria and the Cameroon (later called National Convention of the Nigerian Citizens - the N.C.N.C). This prime political party had submitted their criticisms and the recommendations in a form of a memorandum to the Governor [12] on learning of the Constitutional proposals. This led to modifications in the Constitutional proposals; for instance, the franchise qualification for voters in the Calabar and Lagos elections was reduced from £100 to £50.[13]

There were no significant developments in the electoral system of the country until 1951. This year saw the materialisation of federalism in Nigeria. The Northern House of Assembly had a total of ninety elected Members, the Western House of Assembly, eighty elected Members and the Eastern House of Assembly equally had eighty elected Members. Each of the Houses of Assembly had Official and Special Members as well.[14]

---

9 *Ibid*, S.9.

10 *Ibid.*, ss..33, 34, 35.

11 *Ibid.*, s.37

12 See Memorandum on the New Constitution of Nigeria, 27th March, 1945, Lagos.

13 See 416 House of Common Debates, 5s, 166.

14 The Nigerian (Constitution) Order in Council, 1951, S.I No. 1172, SS.19, 30, 36.

Anyone who by virtue of his own act was under the acknowledgement of allegiance, obedience or adherence to any foreign State or was an undischarged bankrupt, or had been sentenced by a Court of law in any part of the British Dominions to death or imprisonment for a term exceeding six months and had not suffered the punishment to which he was sentenced or granted a free pardon; or held an office of emolument under the Crown or was under any law in force in Nigeria found to be of unsound mind or adjudged to be a lunatic was disqualified from being elected to the Regional House of Assembly,[15]

As Regionalisation had by then become a *fait accompli*, the 1951 Constitution refrained from making a uniform electoral system for the whole country obligatory. It only provided a skeleton on which the electoral laws of different Regions could be erected. Thus section 63 of the Constitution provided:-

(1) Subject to the provisions of this Order, the Governor may by regulation, make provision for the election of members to the Northern, Western and Eastern House of Assembly including (without prejudice to the generality of the foregoing power) the following matters, that is to say:-

(a) the qualification and disqualification of electors;

(b) the registration of electors in any Region or part of a Region;

(c) the ascertainment of the qualification of persons who submit themselves for election;

(d) the holding of elections direct or indirect;

(e) the establishment of electoral districts (by whatever name called) for the purpose of returning members of a House of Assembly; and the allocation to any electoral district of seats in such House;

(f) the division of any such electoral district for any purpose connected with elections;

(g) the determination of any question which may arise as to the right of any person to be or remain an elected Member of a House of Assembly or to take part in any election;

(h) the qualification of any person for membership of a House of Assembly by reason of his holding, or acting in, any office the functions of which involve:-

(i) any responsibility for, or in connection with, the conduct of any election; or

(ii) any responsibility for the compilation or revision of any electoral register; and

(iii) the definition and trial of offences relating to elections and the imposition of penalties therefore, including disqualification for membership of a House of Assembly or for registration as an

---

[15] *Ibid.*, S.42.

elector, or for voting at elections, of any person concerned in such offence.

Having been so empowered to make regulations for elections to the Regional Houses of Assembly, the Governor delegated this power to the Lieutenant - Governors of the respective Regions. In drafting the regulations, the Lieutenant-Governors took account of the recommendations of the respective Regional Legislatures and due regard was had in each case to recommendations of the Ibadan Conference on the review of the Constitution.[16] It must be pointed out that the elections to the Regional Houses of Assembly under the 1951 Constitution were by electoral college system.

Although section 63 of the 1951 Constitution provided a guide for the formulation of these electoral regulations; the mere fact that uniformity was not obligatory, the regulations made, in the final analysis, provided glaring differences. For instance in the Northern Region, the Native Authorities were under the electoral Regulations given the power to add to the final college ten per cent of the total membership of that body from among their members.[17] This provision could lead to the Native Authorities pushing certain people into the legislature who in fact had suffered defeat in primary or intermediate stages of the election, thus making a mockery of the electoral system. On the other hand, there were many provisions in the electoral Regulations of the Regions which were similar, thus making for uniformity of some sort. With regard to qualifications entitling an individual to be registered as an elector, it was provided that the person should be a British subject or a British protected person of the age of twenty-one or upwards and if in the North must be a male. He must have during the period of twelve months immediately preceding the qualifying date, paid tax anywhere in Nigeria or been exempted during that period.[18] A person was disqualified from being an elector if by virtue of his own act he was under the acknowledgement of allegiance, obedience or adherence to a foreign Power or State or had been sentenced by a competent British Court to death or imprisonment for a term exceeding six months and had not either suffered the punishment to which he was sentenced or received a free pardon; or had since five years been convicted of an offence under regulation 139 - (i.e. voting when not qualified to do so, or inducing or procuring any person so to do or falsely publishing a statement about the

---

16 For Northern House of Assembly (Elected Members) Electoral Regulations, 1951 See Nigeria Gazette No. 50 of 1951 in Laws of Nigeria 1951 p.400; for Western House, see No. 45 of 1951 in Laws of Nigeria p.340; for Eastern House, see Nigeria Gazette No. 25 of 17th May, 1951.

17 For details of the procedure of the electoral college. See C.R. Niven, *Elections in Northern Nigeria, Corona*, London, May, 1952.

18 See Regulation 21 of the Northern House Electoral Regulations 1951; Regulation 1 of the Western House Electoral Regulation; and Rep. 9 of the Eastern House Electoral Regulation, 1951.

withdrawal of a candidate); or had been under any law in Nigeria declared to be of insane mind or adjudged to be a lunatic.[19]

One of the most important provisions in these regulations was the one which invalidated the election if an elected person was found guilty of corrupt practice. The expression "corrupt practice" was defined to include any of these - personation, treating, undue influence bribery and aiding, abetting, counseling or procuring the commission of personation.[20] Under the regulations, it was not necessary that the corrupt practice should be committed by the candidate, it was sufficient if it was committed with his knowledge and consent, or with the knowledge and consent of a person who was acting under the or special authority of the candidate. It follows that the candidate was vicariously liable for the corrupt practice of his agents.

The acts enumerated under the definition of "corrupt practice" have always been offences known to the common law. In the *Bradford case No. 2.* [21] Martin B. said in respect of treating:

> If it could be proved that there was treating in all directions on purpose to influence voters, that houses were thrown open where people could get drink without paying for it, - by common law such election would be void.

It follows that if people are given entertainments of whatever description which could operate to influence their voting in an election that is a corrupt practice which can avoid an election.

Undue influence is also a common law offence. This could be in the form of intimidation; for instance, to administer an oath on an elector and threaten him with some calamity to influence his voting constitutes an offence which can avoid an election. To use violence or a threat of it on a voter can also operate to avoid an election. In order to avoid an election on the ground of undue influence, it must be shown that the violence was instigated by the candidate or his agents for whom he is responsible or it must otherwise be shown that it was of such magnitude as to prevent the election from being fair and free.[22]

Bribery at common law not only avoids an election but also is punishable by indictment. In the *Bridgwater Case,* [23] it was established that bribery prevented a fair and open election. The Court held that the election was void.

---

[19] *Ibid.*, Regulations 22, 13 and 10 respectively

[20] *Ibid.*, Regulations 131, 152 and Part VII respectively; c.f. SS. 99 to 101 of the United Kingdom's Representation of the Peoples Act 1949; for Personation see S.47 of the Act.

[21] (1869) 1 O'M. & H. 35 at p.41.

[22] Staleybridge Case (1869) 1 O'M. & H. 66.

[23] (1869) 1 O'M. & H. 122.

Under the respective Regional Electoral Regulations, the Supreme Court was vested with the power to entertain elections petitions.[24] The election of a member of the House of Assembly could be questioned in an election petition on the grounds that the final electoral college was avoided by corrupt practices or offences against the electoral regulations or that the successful candidate, at the time of the election was not qualified or was disqualified, from being elected as a member of the House of Assembly or that he was not duly elected by a majority of lawful votes at the election by the final electoral college. The election petition was to be presented by a member of the final electoral college concerned or by any member of the electoral college for the electoral area concerned. The petition was to be presented to the Supreme Court in its civil jurisdiction within a month from the publication of the result of the election.

The arrangement whereby each Region, was left to make regulations for the elections to the Regional legislature appeared to have met the wishes of the politicians; for the 1953 Constitutional Conference expressly stated that there was no need for uniformity. For the purpose of the 1951 elections each province in the Northern Region formed an Electoral District returning at least two members to the Northern House of Assembly. The number of people to be returned by each Province must not fall below this number otherwise that would be contrary to the 1951 Constitution.[25] An electoral Area was sub-divided into Intermediate Electoral Areas, which were further divided into Intermediate sub-Areas, each of these being again sub-divided into Primary Electoral Areas.[26]

In the Western Region each Division was to be represented in the Western House of Assembly by at least two Elected Members.[27] For the purpose of the 1951 election the Western Region was therefore divided into 25 Electoral Districts. Each Electoral District was sub-divided into Intermediate Electoral Areas which were further sub-divided into Primary Electoral Areas.[28]

The 1951 Nigerian Constitution provided that each Division in the Eastern Region was to be represented in the Eastern House of Assembly by at least two Elected Members.[29] Each Division in the Region formed an

---

24 See Regulations 121, 171 of the Northern and Western Regional Electoral Regulations 1951 as well as that f the Eastern Region, 1951.

25 See S.64 (a) of the Nigeria (Constitution) Order in Council, 1951, No. 1172.

26 See Northern House of Assembly (E[illegible]d Members) Electoral Regulations, 1951, Public Notice No. 50.

27 See S.64(5) of the 1951 Constitution

28 See Western House of Assembly (Elected Members) Electoral Regulations, 1951, Public Notice No. 48, Reg. 4.

29 See S.64(c) of the 1951 Nigerian Constitution.

Electoral District, and this in turn was divided into Electoral Units.[30] The method of election in the Eastern Region was the least complicated of the Regions. The voters in each Electoral Unit created within a District elected representatives to an Electoral Meeting of the District. This Electoral Meeting therefore elected from its members the actual members who would represent the District in the Eastern House of Assembly.

It follows that there were in fact two stages only, the primary and the secondary as opposed to the Northern Electoral system with many complicated sub-divisions and the Western Electoral system with the intermediate electoral sub-division. These differences manifested the weakness of not having a uniform mandatory electoral system throughout the country.

As we have seen, the 1953 Constitutional Conference favoured having different electoral systems in the Regions, consequently, the 1954 Constitution made no provision for uniform electoral regulations for election to the House of Representative. However, there was a section like Section 63 of the 1951 constitution which provided a guide of some sort. This was Section 8 of the 1954 Constitution which provided as follows:

(1) Subject to the provisions of this Order, the Governor-General may by regulation make provision for the election of persons as Representative Members of the House of Representatives, including (without prejudice to the generality of the foregoing power) the following matters:-

(a) the qualifications and disqualifications of electors;
(b) the registration of electors in Nigeria or any part thereof;
(c) the ascertainment of the qualifications of persons who submit themselves for election;
(d) the holding of elections direct and indirect;
(e) the establishment of electoral districts (by whatever name called) for the purpose of returning Representative Members to the House of Representatives and the allocation to any such electoral district of seats in that House;
(f) the division of any such electoral district for any purpose connected with elections. And any regulations made under this sub-section may provide for different methods of election in respect of different parts of Nigeria."[31]

Thus the last clause in the above quoted section made it clear that the regulations to be made by the Governor-General should provide for different electoral system in different parts of the country. Although that was not mandatory on the Governor-General but the provision took account

30 See Eastern House of Assembly (Elected Members) Reg. 1951, Public Notice No. 37 Every adult male was eligible to vote.

31 The Nigeria (Constitution) Order in Council, 1954. S.1. No. 1146.

of the different electoral systems already existing in different parts of Nigeria. But it may be observed that there should have been uniform electoral regulations throughout the country for elections to the Federal House of Representatives.

What resulted from the absence of uniformity in the electoral system was different electoral systems for election to the same Federal House of Representatives - the Northern Region had the indirect electoral college system, the Western Region had tax suffrage in which only adult males who paid tax were eligible to vote by secret ballot; the Eastern Region had universal adult suffrage (i.e. citizens of both sexes of 21 years and upwards were entitled to vote by secret ballot). Under these electoral systems elections to the Federal House of Representatives were held on November 10th and 11th, 1954 in the Eastern and Western Regions. The results [32] of these were promptly declared but in the Northern Region the election to the same Federal House lasted from October to December, 1954 and the results were not known until the end of December, 1954. The view is generally held that it was because of this complicated and easily manipulated nature of the indirect electoral system the N.P.C. encountered no difficulty in capturing all the seats allocated to the Northern Region in the Federal House of Representatives, at the expense of the main Opposition Party, the Northern Elements Progressive Union (N.E.P.U.) which despite the large support it had in the North won not even one seat in the elections.[33] What emerged therefore from the Federal Elections was that the N.C.N.C. was in control of the whole of Southern Nigeria while the N.P.C. controlled the whole of the North. After some political overtures, the two parties inevitably agreed to form a coalition government at the Centre.

At the 1957 Constitutional Conference, the N.C.N.C having been obviously embittered by the fate of its ally, the N.E.P.U.in the North, during the Federal Elections, vigorously agitated for a change in the electoral system so as to remove the indirect electoral system in the Northern Region. The Conference therefore set up a Committee, under the chairmanship of the Governor-General, consisting of delegates from all political parties represented at the Conference and including the United Kingdom representatives. This Committee was charged with exploring avenues for the establishment of an electoral law for the Federation of Nigeria.[34] The Committee therefore recommended as follows:

---

[32] The N.C.N.C. defeated the Action Group in the Western Region and thus won the Federal Elections; in the Eastern Region the same N.C.N.C. won a landslide victory thus controlling the whole of Southern Nigeria in the Federal House of Representatives. The North easily fell in to the N.P.C. (i.e. the Northern Peoples' Congress).

[33] See Kalu Ezera: *Constitutional Developments in Nigeria*, 1960, p.21.

[34] See Report on the Nigeria Constitutional Conference Cmnd. 207, 1957. p.16.

(a) that ad hoc Delimitation Commission should be appointed by the Governor-General acting in his discretion for the division of the whole Federation of Nigeria into single member electoral districts;
(b) that the Delimitation Commission should be instructed to divide the Federation into 320 electoral districts of approximately equal population. The Commission was to be enjoined to ensure that no electoral district should be partly in one Region and partly in another;
(c) that the recommendations of the Commission should be submitted to the Governor-General who, acting in his discretion should amend them as he deemed necessary and these should be embodied in a Proclamation determining the electoral districts for the purposes of the ensuing election;
(d) that there should be constitutional provision for the establishment of a permanent Electoral Commission;
(e) that the Electoral Commission should be responsible for supervision and direction of the preparation of the Federal Electoral Register and for the conduct of all elections to the House of Representatives in accordance with regulations made by the Governor-General; the constituency boundaries were to be reviewed after each census;
(f) that electoral regulations should include provision for the appointment of a Registration Officer and Electoral Officer for each constituency by the Electoral Commission.
(g) that the Committee was to re-assemble in Lagos for the continuation of its work which should include *inter alia* the qualification of candidates, the residential and registration requirement for voters, the functions of Registration and Electoral Officers and drafting of electoral regulations for the Federation.

These recommendations were far-reaching and were responsible for the adoption of a uniform electoral system for the whole of the Federation of Nigeria in 1958. But the recommendation which provided that the electoral districts which were to be established should be such that none of these 'should be partly in one Region and partly in another' tended to bring about the water-tight compartments which emerged and flourished in our body politic. It resulted in a situation which tended to foster Regional instead of National consciousness. The division of the country into electoral districts should have been such that involved division into single-member constituencies according to the number of seats in the House of Representatives and not having regard to Regional divisions. If this method was adopted the unhealthy rivalries between political parties which entrenched themselves in the Regions in such a way as to threaten the very existence of the Federation would have been averted. The House of Representatives which could be regarded as an essential symbol of national unity should have been seen to sail above Regional boundaries.

(ii) The Electoral Regulations of 1958

As we have seen, the 1954 Constitution by its Section 8 gave the Governor-General the power to make regulations for election of persons to the House of Representatives. Following this and having regard to the recommendations of the 1957 Constitutional Conference, the Governor-General after consultation with the Council of Ministers made the 1958 Electoral Regulations [35] for elections to the House of Representatives. For the first time universal adult suffrage was adopted for the whole of Nigeria. Thus regulation 4 provided that every person should be entitled to be registered as an elector and when registered should be eligible to vote at an election; provided that he was ordinarily resident in Nigeria and a British subject or British protected person of the age of 21 or upwards and if ordinarily resident in the Northern Region and was a male. It is most surprising to notice that the women of the Northern Region were denied the right to vote. The political party in power in the Northern Region (before the Army take-over) argued that it was not consistent with the Moslem religion to allow women to vote.[36] But this argument could convince nobody, for in the Western Region where there are many muslim women, these women vote in all elections including local government elections. In Pakistan which is predominantly muslim there is universal adult suffrage and women are not excepted.[37] There is no reason therefore why every Nigerian citizen irrespective of sex, religion or region should not be entitled to vote.

The 1958 Electoral Regulations basically covered all the electoral regulations which were previously made and based in the Regions; as we have already examined them, we could then only deal with some glaring aspects of the 1958 Regulations. Any person who by virtue of his own act was under any acknowledgement of allegiance, obedience or adherence to any foreign power or State or sentenced by a British Court to death or to imprisonment for a term exceeding six months and had not suffered the punishment to which he was sentenced, or such other punishment as a competent authority might have substituted or received a free pardon was disqualified from voting under the Regulations. Equally a person who was under any law in force in any part of Nigeria declared to be of unsound mind or adjudged to be a lunatic or was found guilty of corrupt practice at elections was disqualified.[38] A person should not be entitled to be registered

[35] See Nigeria (Electoral Provisions) Order in Council, 1958, Laws of Nigeria, 1958 p. B. 315; Nigeria Gazette No. 49 Vol. 45, 24th July, 1958.

[36] See Eme Awa: (Federal Government in Nigeria, California, 91946) p. 122.

[37] See Art. 157 of the Constitution of the Republic of Pakistan 1962; see also Syed Anwer Ali; *Election Laws in Pakistan*, p.14 and S.8 of the Pakistan Electoral College Act, 1964.

[38] Regulation 5 of the Nigeria (Electoral Provisions) Order in Council, 1958.

as an elector in more than one constituency or to vote more than once in any election.[39] To the Electoral Commission was vested the general supervision of the preparation of a Register of Electors and conduct of the elections.[40] This provision which is highly commendable was an adaptation of the recommendation of the 1957 Constitutional Conference,[41] which saw the need to insulate the conduct of elections from political influences.

Under the electoral regime set up in 1958, the 1959 Federal Elections were held. This election was particularly remarkable, for it witnessed the first move in the introduction of a uniform electoral law throughout Nigeria. There was direct election by secret ballot throughout the country and as we have seen earlier, the supervision of the registration of voters and the election itself were entrusted to the Electoral Commission, an independent body in which all the Regions of the Federation were represented.

The 1958 Electoral Regulations endured well after 1960 when Nigeria became an Independent Country. To accord with the new order, the Electoral (Transitional Provisions) Act 1961 was passed.[42] This Act was described as "An Act to make Temporary Provisions for Election of Members of the House of Representatives." The Governor-General in Council was empowered to make regulations under the Act 'for any purpose for which regulations for conduct of elections are necessary or expedient.'[43] The Act then incorporated the Elections (House of Representatives) Regulations, 1958 by reference 'to the extent to which they, have not been amended or revoked.' It followed that on the passing of the Act those rules should be deemed to have been under the 1961 enactment.[44] It was stated that the Act should 'continue in operation until the 31st day of December, 1962 and if no sooner replaced or extended shall then expire.'[45]

It must be pointed out that while the 1958 Electoral Regulations achieved the establishment of uniform electoral law throughout the country,, for the elections to the House of Representatives, each Regional Government was left to frame Electoral Regulations for its Regional elections. This was in consonant with the recommendations of the 1958

---

39 *Ibid.*, reg. 6.

40 *Ibid.*, reg. 7.

41 In 1958 and *ad hoc* Constitutional Conference met in Lagos to draft Electoral Regulations. This Conference found its genesis from the Committee which was set up in 1957 Conference and which agreed to resume work at Lagos; see Cmnd. 207, 1957, p.16. For the Lagos Conference, see Cmnd. 569, 1958, pp.34-35.

42 See Laws of Nigeria, 1961, p. A.61.

43 See Laws of Nigeria, 1961 S.3(1).

44 *Ibid.*, S.3(2) (a)

45 *Ibid.*, S.5.

constitutional Conference held in Lagos.[46] While empowered to formulate their electoral regulations, the Regions were urged to follow, as far as possible, the Federal Legislations on the subject. It may be observed that the 1958 arrangement introduced nothing new with regard to making Regional elections dependent on Regional electoral regulations. Since the introduction of the Federal System, these Regions had always formulated their own electoral laws. After 1960 the Houses of Assembly in these Regions passed laws regulating elections to the legislatures.[47] A close examination of these laws and the regulations made under them shows that these Regional Elecıoral Laws had been made to follow, as expected, the Regulations made for elections to the House of Representatives. For instance, the Northern Nigeria Electoral Law, 1963 in its section, described as "Interpretation," defined "register of electors," as 'the register of electors for any constituency prepared in accordance Elections (Houses of Representatives) Regulations 1958, or if such register is replaced, by a register, prepared under the Electoral Act, 1962.' It may therefore be said that the pattern set up under the 1958 Electoral Regulations operated to provide a fairly uniform electoral law throughout the country both on Federal and regional plains. The Nigerian System improves on that of the United States of America in respect of federal elections. For in the United State, Federal elections are the responsibility of the individual States. Article I section 2 of the Constitution of the United States of America provides that the Members of the House of Representatives should be 'chosen every Second Year by the People of the several States, and the Electors of each State shall have the qualifications requisite for Electors of the most numerous Branch of the State Legislature.'[48]

(iii) The Electoral Act of 1962

As has been indicated, the Electoral Act of 1961 was described as 'Transitional,' consequently, in 1962 the Nigerian Parliament passed the Electoral Act, designed to operate permanently for elections to the House of Representatives. This was described as 'An Act to consolidate and amend

---

[46] See Report on the Conference Cmnd. 569 pp. 34-35.

[47] See Electoral Law, 1963, (Northern Region), Laws of Northern Nigeria 1963, Vol. II (Cap. 37) p. 681; see also Elections (Northern House of Assembly) Regulations, 1960, made under Nigerian Constitution 1954-60; and The Elections (House of Assembly Law, 1961 (Eastern Region), laws of Eastern Nigeria 1961 Vol. I p.A.83; see also the Elections (House of Assembly) Regulations 1961, Laws of Eastern Nigeria 1961 p. B.131 and House of Assembly (Disputed seats) Regulations 1961; see equally Parliamentary Electoral Regulations 1960 made under Nigeria Constitution 1954-60 (Western Region); see Legislation Western Region, 1960, p. B.317.

[48] See the Constitution of the United States of America - which came into force on 4th march, 1789. The authority of the States in making regulations for the elections is however restricted by the Fifteenth and Nineteenth Amendments to the Constitution which forbid limitations of suffrage based on race, colour, previous condition of servitude or sex.

the law as to the conduct of Parliamentary Elections and other purposes connected therewith.'[49] Those who were entitled to be registered and vote under the Act are citizens of Nigeria of the age of twenty-one years or upwards who were not under what was described in the Act as 'legal incapacity.' This incapacity includes:

(a) The acknowledgement of allegiance, obedience or adherence by the personal act of an elector to any foreign power or State;
(b) the imposition of sentence of death or imprisonment for a term exceeding six months or other punishment as may lawfully be substituted and the elector had not at the date of election suffered punishment or received a free pardon;
(c) disqualification for corrupt practices and other electoral offences at elections as provided in the Act;
(d) with regard to Northern Nigeria, being a female person.[50]

We have already expressed disapproval of the disfranchisement of women in the Northern part of the country as the theory of this being in conformity with the Moslem religion has exploded - judging from the practice of countries which are predominantly Muslim.

The general supervision of the registration of voters and the conduct of elections were vested in the Electoral Commission.[51] Most of the procedural provisions contained in the 1959 Electoral Regulations were repeated in the Act: display of preliminary list for each constituency, issuing of writs for parliamentary elections, nomination of candidates, payment of deposits, appointment of electoral officers, preparation of ballot boxes, method of recording one's vote.[52] To prevent unruly behaviour at the elections, section 58 spelt out without equivocation the consequences of such act; it reads as follows:-

> (1) If any person misconducts himself at a polling station or fails to obey any lawful order of the Presiding Officer, the Presiding Officer may order the removal from the polling station of the person so misconducting himself or failing to obey a lawful order; and such person may be dealt with as for an offence for which he may be arrested without warrant, and may be removed accordingly.
> (2) No person so removed shall without the permission of the Presiding Officer again enter the polling station during the day of the election;

---

49 See Laws of Nigeria, 1962 p.329.

50 Electoral Act 1962, S.1.

51 *Ibid.*, S.4; see S.50 of the 1963 Constitution. This section however was suspended by Decree No. 1 of 1966 to which we referred in Chap. IV

52 See *ibid.* SS.7 to 49.

> but nothing in this section shall be construed so as to prohibit a voter from recording his vote.

This section was particularly important in view of the fact that certain trouble makers deliberately, for political motives try to cause trouble during elections. But where they succeed in interrupting or obstructing proceedings at any polling station by riot or open violence, the Presiding Officer is empowered to adjourn the proceedings until later in the day or until the following day. Necessary precautions should be taken to safeguard the ballot boxes and ballot papers and other election materials. The electoral officer is under a duty to inform the Electoral Commission of the incident.[53] Where polling was conducted without interruption, the Act made provisions for the procedure to follow. When the time for ending polling was reached, the Electoral officer should not allow any person other than those already inside and those in the immediate vicinity waiting to vote into the polling station. After this the ballot boxes were to be collected and counting of votes should commence as soon as practicable; where necessary, it was provided that there should be a recount.[54] Where there was a tie between any candidates the issue is to be decided by lot conducted by the Returning Officer,[55]

Part III of the Act made provisions to ensure that elections were free and fair. This part of the Act deals with electoral offences. Section 72 provides:- "Any person who -

(a) without proper authority destroys, mutilates, defaces or removes or makes any alteration in any notice or document required for the purposes of registration under this Act; or
(b) knowingly gives false information or makes a false statement with reference to any objection to the retention of the name of a person on the register of electors; or
(c) procures himself to be, or does any act whereby he is by what name or description soever, included in the register of electors for more than one constituency or more than once in the register of electors for a constituency in which he is entitled to be registered; or
(d) publishes a statement, rumour or report which he knows to be false or does not believe to be true so as to prevent persons who are qualified to register from registering as electors; or
(e) makes in any record, register or document which he is required to prepare, publish or keep for the purpose of registration any entry or statement which he knows to be false or does not believe to be true

---

[53] *Ibid.*, S.59.

[54] *Ibid.*, SS.60 to 67.

[55] *Ibid.*, S.68.

- shall be guilty of an offence and liable on conviction to a fine of one hundred pounds or to imprisonment for a term of twelve months or to both."

This section covered generally irregularities which at the early stages of the formulation of electoral regulations would have been overlooked or thought to involve administrative matters of which could not be questioned in a court of law.[56] But with the rapid growth of party politics coupled with the intrigues which inevitably follow political rancour the need for a provision such as this becomes manifest. Section 73 of the 1962 Act dealt with offences in respect of nomination of candidates, such as forging of any nomination paper or defacing or destroying same. It also made it an offence to forge any ballot paper or official mark on any ballot paper or any certificate or return or the wilful destruction of any of these. On conviction for any of these a person shall be liable to a fine of two hundred pounds or to imprisonment for a term of two years or to both.

An attempt to commit any offence under the section was punishment in the manner in which the completed act was punishable.[57] Section 74 deals with an offence which until the glaring mal-practices which predominated the elections to the Western House of Assembly in 1965, would not have attracted public attention. The section reads:-

> Any officer appointed for the purposes of this Act, who without lawful excuse is guilty of any act or omission in breach of his official duty commits an offence against this Act and shall be liable on conviction to a fine of one hundred pounds or to imprisonment for a term of twelve months or to both.

During the time for nomination of candidates for elections to the Western House of Assembly, there were flagrant allegations of Electoral Officers having disappeared after receiving the nomination paper of a candidate belonging to a certain political party, which the officers, one way or the other favoured. The result was confusion and frustration by the candidates belonging to the other political party who could not find the officers anywhere in order to hand in their nomination papers. The days rolled by until the last nomination date was over [58] and the Electoral Officers appeared

---

[56] See for instance, reg. 99 of the Northern House of Assembly (Elected Members) Electoral Regulations, 1951 which provided that "Nothing done by a Chief Electoral officer or Electoral Officer under Part II or Part III or by a Registration Officer under Part IV shall be questioned in any Court." The Part III of the regulations above mentioned dealt *inter alia* with registration of electors; so where any of these Officers did anything even contrary to his duty, such could not be questioned in any court of law. A provision like this could command itself to no one.

[57] S.73(2) of the Electoral Act, 1962.

[58] The United Progressive Grand Alliance (UPGA), an Opposition party comprising the N.C.N.C. and the Action Group called for a three-day extension of the eight-day nomination period, "because it had been physically impossible to file nomination papers of some of their candidates, particularly in Ogbomosho and Ife, home towns of the outgoing Premier, Chief Akintola and Deputy Premier,

only to announce that the other candidates had been returned unopposed.[59] Allegations were made of a certain Electoral Officer who was spotted by the supporters of a certain political party while this officer was in fact running away from his electoral district after receiving the nomination paper of a candidate which happened to belong the political party which he favoured. It was reported that this officer's photograph was published in the Nigerian national paper.[60]

While exaggerated allegations are not usually uncommon when political tension is high; the circumstances leading to the declaration of more than fifteen candidates returned unopposed in a situation where it was a notorious fact that all the political parties were contesting all the seats leave ample room for suspicion. Electoral officers must not only be impartial but must be seen to be impartial. They must maintain what amounts to judicial impartiality when carrying out their official duties especially *vis-a-vis* the political parties contesting the elections.

There is little doubt that the circumstances leading to the collapse of civil administration and the consequent Army takeover throughout the country were accelerated by events surrounding the elections to the Western House of Assembly in 1965. This shows that certain acts or omissions which taken in isolation would not have meant much, could in certain cases combine with explosive issues and lead to grave consequences. It may be said that what happened during [61] and after [62] the elections to the Western House of Assembly in 1965 should not be allowed to repeat themselves in any part of Nigeria in future.

Chief Fani-Kayode, respectively." The extension was refused. See *West Africa* October 2, 1965, p. 1102.

59 Before the election day, over fifteen candidates of the ruling Nigeria National Democratic Party (NNDP) were officially declared returned unopposed. See *West Africa October 2, 1965 p. 1102*

60 The Electoral Officer alleged to have been intercepted was once said to have been caught by the Police at Ikorodu, not far from Lagos, and his photograph was published in *West African Pilot*. See *West Africa* October 2, 1965 p.1102. It was reported that all attempts to locate him at Ile-Ife had failed.

61 There were astonishing reports of seemingly dishonest practices directed at "rigging" the election. One of these reports reads: - "I have been able to verify to my own satisfaction that a "pregnant" woman was discovered on examination to have ballot papers inside her robes." See *West Africa,* October 16th, 1965, p. 1151. This means that this woman, one way or the other, got ballot papers in such magnitude and packed them under her cloths and appeared to be pregnant. This sort of act is a challenge to rule of law and our judicial authorities should in such case impose maximum sentence which would deter others.

62 Discontent about the conduct of the election found expression in violence. A report reads: - "... This brings the total number of deaths in Ondo Province in the past two weeks to an estimated total of 46 and the number of deaths from the political violence in the Region since the controversial Regional elections on October 11th to a figure which some estimates say is well over seventy." See *West Africa,* November 13, 1965, p. 1283. This figure was reported to be increasing daily until the Army takeover in January 1966, and steps were immediately taken to restore law and order.

Corrupt Practices.

The 1962 Act, like the Electoral Regulations of 1958 makes provisions prohibiting corrupt practices during elections. Section 78 reads.[62a]

(1) If at an election, a candidate commits or is deemed under this Act to have committed any offence whereby he is guilty of any corrupt practice, and that candidate is elected, his election shall be invalid.
(2) For the purposes of this section, a candidate is deemed to have committed corrupt practice, if it was committed with his knowledge and consent, or with the knowledge and consent of any person acting under the general or special authority of the candidate with reference to the election.
(3) Every corrupt practice shall be an offence under this Act.

It follows that the corrupt practice of a candidate or of any person acting with his knowledge and consent will operate to avoid the election of the candidate. The knowledge and consent of the agent of the candidate are imputable to the candidate. The Act did not in a material particular define "corrupt practice"; Willes J. in the *Northarllerton case* said: "I call everything of a corrupt character which has a tendency to influence a man's vote with reference to mere lucre instead of honest considerations.[63] It may be said that corrupt practice is any act which is prohibited by law. Blackburn J. referring to the word, "corruptly" in the United Kingdom Corrupt Practices Prevention Act 1854 said:

> ...corruptly there does not mean wickedly, or immorally, or dishonestly or anything of that sort but with the object and intention of doing that which the Legislature plainly means to forbid. In fact, given meat or drink is treating, when the person who gives it has an intention of treating—no otherwise; and in all cases where there is any evidence to show that meat or drink has been given, it is a question of fact for the Judge whether the intention is made out by the evidence, which in every individual case must stand upon its own grounds; and although each case may be a mere feather's weight by itself, and so small that one would not act upon it, yet if there is a large number of such cases, a large number of slight cases will together make a strong one; and consequently it must always be very important inquiring what was the scale, the amount and the extent to which it was done.[64]

It may be observed that the most salient point in this judicial pronouncement is, to constitute an offence of corrupt practice there must be an intention to

---

[62a] This section was reproduced in S. 103 of the Electoral Act, 1982.

[63] (1869) 1 O'M. & H. 167 at p. 173.

[64] The Bewdley Case (1869) 1 O'M. & H. 16 p. 19. The burden is of course on the person who alleges corrupt practice to prove that. In Chief Jim Ifeayinchukwu Nwobodo v. Chief Christian Chukwuma Onoh (1984) 1 S.C. 1, the Supreme Court held that where fraud or criminal offence is alleged in an election petition, it must be proved beyond reasonable doubt.

do an act which the legislature forbids. This principle applies to the candidate as well as his agent.

The Electoral Act of 1962 in prohibiting corrupt practices during elections improved on the earlier enactments by spelling out more particularly what could constitute the offences of personation,[65] treating,[66] and bribery[67] and influence.[68]

Personation

Any person who at an election applies for a ballot paper or vctes in the name of some other person living or dead or even in the name of a fictitious person is guilty of a corrupt practice and commits the offence of personation under the Act. On conviction such person shall be liable to a fine of fifty pounds or to imprisonment for a term of six months or to both; and for any second or subsequent offence maybe imprisoned for a term of twelve months. He who aids, abets, counsels or procures the commission of the offence of personation is equally guilty of the offence and punishable accordingly. For conviction for the offence of personation under the Act there must be at least evidence of two witnesses to that effect.[69]

---

65 Electoral Act, 1962, S. 79, cf. S. 47, U.K. Representation of the People Act, 1959.

66 *ibid.*, S. 80. now S. 10 of the Electoral Law of 1982

67 *ibid.*, S. 82. now S. 108 of the 1982 Act

68 *ibid.*, S. 81. now 107 *ibid*

69 *ibid.*, S. 79 (3) now S. 104 (3) *ibid.*,

Treating

A person is guilty of corrupt practice and commits the offence of treating if he corruptly by himself or by any other person at any time between the dissolution of Parliament and return of the writs directly or indirectly gives or provides food, drink or entertainment to any voter with a view to influencing his voting. It is equally an offence under the Act to act in such corrupt way to make a person refrain from voting in the elections. An elector who corruptly accepts or takes any such food, drink or entertainment shall be guilty of the offence equally. Any person guilty of the offence shall on conviction be liable to a fine of one hundred pounds or to imprisonment for a term of twelve months or to both.[70]

In *Kubeinje v. Edukagho*,[71] the petitioner who was a defeated candidate in an election held in Warri East Constituency for the Western House of Assembly prayed the Court to declare the election null and void. He alleged that the respondent was guilty of election offences of treating, bribery and undue influence. Onyeama Ag. J. (as he then was) in dismissing the petition said:

> The evidence in support of the charge of treating was given by the petitioner himself and three other witnesses. They spoke of events in Sapele, Warri, Ode-Itsekiri and Orere. The consequences of treating are grave... The heavy penalty attached to the offence in my view, obliges any court called upon to consider the matter to examine the facts with anxious care.[72]

During the trial, the petitioner himself and three of his witnesses gave evidence in support of the charge of treating. They said that on several occasions before the date of the election, the respondent and his agents went from one Ode-Itsekiri village to another and summoned meetings of the voters and unlawfully treated them with drinks and other foodstuffs such as biscuits, sardines and common salt. This entertainment, they maintained, was calculated to induce the voters to vote for the respondent. But the learned Judge was not prepared to accept the evidence. In rejecting it he said: "Charges of this nature are not difficult to fabricate in circumstances where political passions are in evidence and witnesses are partisan.[73] We agree with this judicial statement for as treating not only avoids an election but is also a criminal act, a high degree of proof is required. It is not sufficient to make allegations and get some witnesses to support them. It may be suggested that in cases where people were reported to have been

---

70 *ibid.*, S. 80 (b)

71 (1956) W. R. N. L. R. 142

72 *ibid.*, at pp. 143-144.

73 *ibid.*, at p. 144

entertained, some photographs of such occasions should be tendered in evidence and they should be admissible.

Bribery

As we have seen from the *Bridgwater Case*, bribery nullifies an election at common law. In this case Blackburn J said:

> I believe the law to be ... that if the bribery or corruption was to such an extensive degree... as to show that it was not a fair and open election, but a corrupt election; or if it was shown that corrupt practices of any sort, however small, were committed by an agent of the sitting member; the seat is vacated.[74]

The Electoral Act of 1962 clearly makes provision prohibiting bribery during elections. Thus section 82 provides:

(1) Any person shall be guilty of a corrupt practice and commits the offence of bribery who:-

(a) directly or indirectly by himself or by any other person on his behalf gives, lends or agrees to give or lend or offers, promises, or promises to procure or to endeavour to procure, any money or valuable consideration to or for any elector or to or for any person on behalf of any elector, or to or for any other person in order to induce any elector to vote or refrain from voting, or corruptly does any such act as aforesaid on account of such voter having voted or refrained from voting at any election; or

(b) directly or indirectly, by himself or by any other person on himself gives or procures, or agrees to give or procure, or offers, promises, or promises to procure, any office, place or employment to or for any elector or to or for any person on behalf of any elector, or to or for any other, in order to induce any elector to vote or refrain from voting, or corruptly does any such as aforesaid on account of any elector having voted or refrain from voting at any election; or

(c) directly or indirectly, by himself or by any other person on his behalf, makes any gift, loan, offer, promise procurement or agreement as aforesaid to or for any person, in order to induce such person to procure or to endeavour to procure the return of any person as a member of the House of Representatives or the vote of any elector at any election, or

(d) upon or in consequence of any gift, loan, offer, promise, procurement or agreement as aforesaid, procures or engages, or promises to endeavour to procure, the return of any person as a

---

[74] (1869) 1 O'M. & H. 112 at p. 115

member of the House of Representatives or the vote of any elector at any election;

(e) advances or pays to causes to be paid any money to or for the use of any person, with the intent that such money or any part thereof, shall be expended in bribery at any election or who knowingly, pays or causes to be paid, any money to any person in discharge or repayment of any money wholly or in part expended in bribery at any election, or

(f) after the election, directly or indirectly by himself or by any other person on his behalf receives any money or valuable consideration on account of any person having voted or refrained from voting, or having induced any other person to vote or refrain from voting at any such election.

Sub-section (3) excepts from the above any money paid or agreed to be for or on account of any legal expenses *bona fide* incurred during the election. Any person guilty of bribery under the Act shall be liable on conviction to a fine of one hundred pounds or imprisonment for a term of twelve months, or to both.[75]

In view of the essentiality of eradicating corrupt practices, the chief of which being bribery, in our elections, the Act of 1962 should have contained a clear section setting out the limit of election expenses. This was done in the United Kingdom Representation of the People Act, 1949. Section 64 of the Act reads:-

> (1) No sum shall be paid and no expense shall be incurred by a candidate at any election or his election agent, whether before, during or after an election, on account of or in respect of the conduct or management of the election, in excess of the maximum amount specified in this section and a candidate or election agent knowingly acting in contravention of this sub-section shall be guilty of an illegal practice.

The Act then sets out the maximum amount to be £450 together with an additional two pence for each entry in the register of electors to be used at the elections, for a candidate at parliamentary election in a county constituency in Great Britain.[76]

Undue Influence

A person who directly or indirectly uses violence, force or a threat of any (these or restrains or who inflicts temporal or spiritual injury, damage o harm to any person with a view to inducing or compelling him to vote o

---

75 Electoral Act, 1962 S. 82 (4). Now S. 108 Electoral Act, 1982.

76 Representation of the People Act, 1949 S. 64(2) (a). S.91 of the 1982 Electoral Act stipulates a limit to expenses and penalty in default.

refrain from voting is guilty of the offence of undue influence under the 1982 Act. Equally anyone 'who by abduction, duress or any fraudulent device or contrivance impedes or prevents the free use of the vote by any elector' is guilty of the same offence. It is provided that a person who is convicted under this section shall be liable to a fine of one hundred pounds or to imprisonment for the term of twelve months, or to both.[77]

A person who is convicted of corrupt practice or any other offence under Part III of the 1962 Act is in addition to any other penalty, disqualified during the period of five years following 'from being registered as an elector or voting at any election; or from being elected under this Act or if elected before his conviction, from retaining his seat as a member of the House of Representatives.'[78] The Act imposed a duty on the court in which the conviction took place or where an appeal was heard to notify the Electoral Commission accordingly.[79]

Other important provisions of the Act are those which made it an offence for any person to conduct himself in a disorderly manner or to incite others to do so. This offence carried a fine of fifty pounds or imprisonment for a term of six months, or to both.[80] To avoid any possibility of clash between the parties contesting the elections in such a way as to interrupt polling, section 88 of the 1962 Act prohibited certain acts within the polling station and within a distance of 200 yards of the polling station. These Acts included canvassing for votes or soliciting the vote of any elector or persuading any elector to refrain from voting for any particular candidate or voting at all at the election; or shouting slogans about the election or being in possession of any offensive weapon or appear in any form calculated to intimidate electors; or prohibiting any notice or wearing any symbol or photograph or any party emblem having to do with the election; or using vehicle bearing the emblem of a political party or photograph of a candidate or loitering without lawful excuse after voting or being refused to vote. Any person guilty of an offence under this provision is liable on conviction to a fine of one hundred pounds or imprisonment for a term of one year, or to both.[81]

The 1962 Act repealed [82] the Electoral (Transitional Provisions) Act, 1961 which we saw earlier; the 1962 Act itself was amended by the Electoral Act, 1964. But this could not be regarded as a major amendment;

---

[77] S. 81 Electoral Act, 1962, now S. 107 of the 1982 Act

[78] S. 83 *ibid.*

[79] S. 89 *ibid.*,

[80] S. 87, *ibid.*,

[81] S. 88, *ibid.* Under S. 107 of the 1982 the penalty is N1000.00 fine or 12 months imprisonment or both.

[82] The 1962 Act was replaced by the Electoral Act No. 8 of 1982

it substituted "1963" for "1962" with regard to the record of the census and the compilation of register of electors for each constituency.[83] The amount of deposit payable in section 20 of the principal Act by candidates for the election was increased from £25 to £100.

On the local government level, the electoral laws both in Lagos [84] and the regions [85] broadly followed the pattern set up for elections to the House of Representatives and to the Regional Houses of Assembly. There were of course some inevitable variations brought about to meet local circumstances—such as those requiring that the elector or the candidate must have resided in the locality concerned within a certain period and had paid his tax as required. The measures taken to ensure orderly elections are similar to those taken for elections to the House of Representatives and the Regional House of Assembly as we have seen. Local Government Elections Decree 1987 governs all elections to local Government Councils in the country.

(b) Election Petitions

The power of the Courts to adjudicate on the validity of the election of a member of Parliament could be traced under English Legal System, as far back as 1868. By the Parliamentary Elections Act, 1868[86] Parliament transferred this right to one judge and later by the Parliamentary Elections Corrupt Practices Act, 1879 [87] to two judges. Prior to the transfer of this right, it had been the prerogative of Parliament to determine the validity of a member's election. Under the Grenville Act, 1770 [88] a Select Committee was empowered to entertain all questions concerning the validity of a

---

83 The Act was for the conduct of Presidential, Gubernatorial Elections and those for the Senate and House of Representatives.

84 See Lagos Local Government Acts, 1959 to 1964, Laws of Nigeria 1959 and 1964.

85 See Eastern Region Local Government Law, 1960, Eastern Regional Gazette No. 28, Vol. 9 dated 26th May, 1960, Laws of Eastern Nigeria 1960 Vol. 1 P. A. 81. The detailed electoral laws are usually set out in the Instruments establishing the Local Councils, e.g. E. R. L. N. No. 86 of 1960. See also Local Government Law, Cap. 68, 1957 (Western Nigeria) Laws of Western Region of Nigeria 1959 Vol. III p. 277; S. 18 of this enactment sets out the qualifications of a candidate for elections to councils, which include inter alia payment of tax and being a native of the area of the council and being of the age of 21 or upwards. More detailed electoral laws are usually set out in the Instrument establishing the councils. With regard to Northern Nigeria, see Native Authority Law Cap. 77; Laws of Northern Nigeria 1963 Vol. II p. 1267. Like other regions, electoral regulations are set out in the Instruments establishing the N. A. For example see Zuru N. A. ... Electoral Rules 1963, Laws of Northern Nigeria 1963 Vol. II p. E. 521. Now, the local Government /elections Decree No. 37 of 1987 has provided unified Law for all Local Government Elections throughout the Nigeria.

86 31 & 32 Vict., C. 125

87 42 & 43 Vict., C. 5

88 10. Geo. 3 C. 16.

member's election. The substantial portion of the 1868 Act has been repealed and re-enacted in the Representation of the People Act, 1949.

Under the Nigerian Constitution the High Court of a Region (State) from where a member of the House of Representative was elected or a Senator selected was vested with the power to determine questions regarding the election or selection as the case may be.[89] It follows that in Nigeria like the United Kingdom,[90] a parliamentary election or a return to Parliament could only be questioned by a parliamentary election petition presented in accordance with the procedure laid down in the Constitution and the Electoral Act, 1962. Thus section 90 of the 1962 Act provided:

> No election and no return of the house of Representatives in respect of a constituency shall be questioned except by a petition complaining about the election or the return, presented to the High Court of the Region where the constituency is, not later than twenty-one days after the date of the election.[91]

Election petitions may be presented to the appropriate Court by a person whose name is in the register of electors or a person who claims to have had a right to be elected or to be returned at the election or a person who alleges that he was a candidate at the election concerned. The Electoral Officer in the constituency in question may be joined as a party to the petition.[92] As we have indicated above the right to question and determine the validity of a member's election had been the prerogative of the Parliament, as this right has been transferred, Parliament therefore lays down the conditions under which an election may be questioned. Thus section 92 of the 1962 Act provided:

(1) An election may be questioned on any of the following grounds, that is say,

  (a) that a person whose election is questioned was at the time of the election, not qualified, or was disqualified from being elected as a member of the House of Representatives.

  (b) that the election was invalid by reason of corrupt practices or no-compliance with the provisions of Part II of this Act. [93]

  (c) that the respondent was, at the time of the election, not duly elected by a majority of lawful votes at the election;

---

89 See S. 48 (1) (a) of the 1960 Constitution which is now S. 53 (1) (a) of the 1963 Constitution. This section has now been suspended, see Decree No.. 2, of 1966, Extraordinary Gazette No. 20, Vol. 3, 4th March 1966, p. A. 10, see also Decree No. 8. of 1967. Now see S. 119 Electoral Act, 1982 vesting the power in State High Court.

90 See S. 107 of the Representation of the People Act, 1949.

91 Electoral Act, 1962, Laws of Nigeria 1962 at p. A 356. Now S. 119, 1982 Act.

92 S. 91, *ibid;* S. 121, 1982 Act.

93 This deals with procedures to be followed at the elections. A 356. Now S. 122, 1982 Act.

(d) that the petitioner was validly nominated but was unlawfully excluded from the election.

(i) Election of a person who was disqualified *ab initio*

Where a person who was disqualified from an election *de jure* was in fact elected, the Courts are bound to set aside the election in respect of that person. Where therefore, the fact of the disqualification is known to the voters who despite that knowledge voted for that candidate, the votes are deemed at common law to have been "thrown away," and in such case the person who has the next highest number of votes should be declared elected by the Court. On the other hand, where the disqualification is not known to the electors, the Courts have usually declared the whole election void. In *Folarin v. Davies* [94] the Supreme Court was called upon to nullify the election of the respondent and declare the petitioner duly elected. The petitioner and the respondent were candidates for election to the House of Representatives in the electoral district of Oyo North. At this election held on 11th November, 1954, the respondent obtained a majority of the votes, but he was not qualified to stand for the election. Smith, Ag. J. held that the respondent was not duly elected; that the votes cast for the disqualified candidate could not be said to have been thrown away and that being so, no person could be said to have been duly elected; the election was therefore void.

In arriving at his decision the learned Judge relied on the common law principle. He found as a fact that the disqualification of the respondent was not known to the electors or that the disqualification was not so notorious in such a way that it could be deemed to have been within the knowledge of those who voted for the respondent. This decision accords with that of Kennedy J. in *Hodds v Morley*. [95] In that case, the respondent who obtained the majority of votes and was declared elected was both at the time of his nomination and of the election, however, disqualified. It was held that the disqualification not being apparent on the face of the nomination paper and not shown to have been within the knowledge of the electorate operated to render the election void. The petitioner was not entitled to be declared duly elected by the Court as the facts of the case were not otherwise. In another case *Ameokoja v Eyiow-uawi*,[96] the respondent was disqualified by a law which provides that "no person shall be entitled to be elected as an elected member of a council who has, within a period of ten years immediately before the date of the election, been concerned as an unsuccessful claimant in a dispute relating to the office of a chief in or

---

[94] (1955) 21 N. L. R. 50.

[95] (1904) 1 K. B. 74

[96] (1961) 1 All N. L. R. 805.

associated with, the area of the council and has not obtained the consent of the Governor in Council to stand for election."[97] It was established that the fact of this disqualification was not known to the electors and as such election was void and the petitioner was not entitled to the seat. This case having arisen from a local government election, illustrates that the the law on the subject is the same both for parliamentary and local government elections.

A indicated above, where the fact of the disqualification of a person is known to the electors and notwithstanding that they voted for that candidate, the votes are deemed to be thrown away. Thus in *Re Bristol South East Election* [98] the election Court was prayed to declare the election of Mr. A. N. Wedgwood Benn void and to declare instead that the candidate who had the next highest number of votes was duly elected and ought to have been returned. The facts of this case showed that Mr. Benn was a Member of the U. K. Parliament — i.e. House of Commons. His father was a peer. being an heir male, he petitioned the House of Commons on his father's death in 1960 to renounce the peerage. A select Committee of the House of Commons was required to look into the matter. The House of Commons agreed with the findings of its Committee of Privileges and therefore resolved that Mr, Benn, on succession by operation of the law to the Viscounty on November 17th, 1960 ceased to be a member of the House of Commons and was equally disqualified from membership of that House. Consequently a by-election was ordered. Mr. Benn being a young man who had always cherished being a Member of the House of Commons refused to go to the House of Lords and maintained both in public and in private that he was not a peer. he was nominated by his supporters to stand for the by-election. Before the votes were cast steps were taken by Mr. Benn's opponent to notify all the voters that, whether Mr. Benn like it or not, he was a peer of the United Kingdom on the death of his father and was consequently disqualified from the membership of the Commons. Mr. M. A. J. St. Clair, the opponent of Mr. Benn at the election buttressed his notice to the electorate by pointing out that the Committee of Privileges of the House of Commons had declared that Mr. Benn was a peer and was therefore disqualified from membership. Mr. Benn in counter-notices denied that he was a peer and that he was not disqualified as was alleged.

Notwithstanding all this, on May 4th, 1961, polling took place in the by-election. Mr. Benn won — obtaining 23,275 votes while Mr. St. Clair got 10,231 votes. Gorman and McNair J. J. held that by common law of Parliament Mr. Benn, on the death of his father succeeded to the peerage of the United Kingdom and was disqualified from membership of the House of Commons, that as facts which constituted incapacity or disqualification

---

97 S. 19 (1) (g) of the Western Region Local Government Law, Cap. 68.

98 (1961) 3 W. L. R. 577.

were known to the electorate before their votes were cast and the voters were, as a matter of fact, made aware of the legal consequences of voting for the disqualified candidate, those votes cast for such a candidate were null and void and deemed to have been thrown away. The candidate with the next highest number, which incidentally in this case was the only opponent was declared duly elected.

In arriving at their decision, their Lordships followed the decision in *Beresford-Hope v. Sandhurst.* [99] In this case, a woman was elected to a County Council under the local Government Act, 1888. But it was known to the respondent and those who voted for her that being a woman she was in law disqualified from being elected a member of a country council. In a judgment of the Court of Appeal delivered by Stephen J., it was held that the election of the woman was void and the votes given in her favour thrown away and that the petitioner was duly elected. In the course of his judgment His Lordship quoted from the decision given in *Gosling v Veley* [100] as follows:

> Where the majority of electors vote for a disqualified person in ignorance of the fact of the disqualification, the election may be void or voidable... But, if the disqualification be of a sort whereof notice is to be presumed, none need expressly be given: no one can doubt that, if an elector would nominate and vote for a woman to fill the office of a mayor or burgess in Parliament, his vote would be thrown away: there the fact would be notorious and every man would be presumed to know the law upon that fact[101]

It therefore follows that even if the opposing candidate did not take steps to inform the electorate, as Mr. St Clair did in the Bristol S. E. by-election; once the disqualification is announced say be a committee of the House of Representatives or by the Speaker of that House, where he has power under the law so to do; and such news is published in the newspapers and broadcast say over Radio Nigeria, the electorate are deemed to have knowledge of such disqualification.

(ii) Effect of Corrupt Practices on Election

If an elected person is found guilty of corrupt practice in an election petition, the Court will declare his election void. Corrupt practice *ipso facto*, does not disqualify a person from an election in the sense that the votes cast for him in such election are deemed thrown away. hence Lord Coleridge C. J., in *Drinkwater v Deakin* [102] said:

---

99 (1889) 23 Q. B. D. 79

100 (1847) 7 Q. B. D. 406.

101 (1889) 23 Q. B. D. 79 at pp. 84-85.

102 (1874) L. R. 9. C. P. at p. 637

> The conclusion, therefore, is, that neither apart from the Statutes nor created by the Statutes is there in a candidate from the moment of his bribery and after notice of the fact of his bribing any such disqualification as to prevent him thereupon from being a candidate at the then election, and to make all votes given in his favour after such notice as if they had not been given at all. Invalid, upon proof of his bribery, for the purpose of seating him, they are thrown away, for the purpose of seating his opponent, in my opinion they are not.

Corrupt practice under the Electoral Act, 1962 includes, as we have seen, personation, bribery, treating and undue influence. If a person is elected in an election and is found guilty of any corrupt practice in an election petition the Court will declare his election void and may, therefore declare a person with the next highest number of votes duly elected. In handling these election petitions which are obviously tainted with politics, the Courts have been very careful and have ensured that justice is done on both sides and equally that justice is seen to be done. The impartiality of the judiciary is usually at a great test in cases having political flavour such as election petitions. As corrupt practice not only nullifies one's election but also exposes him to other punishments under the Act, the standard of proof required should be as high as those required in criminal case - beyond reasonable doubt and the burden of proof must rest generally on he who asserts that a corrupt practice has been committed.

In *Kubeinje v Edukugho* [103] allegations of treating, bribery and undue influence were made. During the course of his judgement in which he dismissed the election petition, Onyeama Ag. J. (as he the was) said:

> All the witnesses called for the petitioner are either members of his political party,[104] or supporters of it, and the respondent's witnesses are either members of the Action Group or supporters of it. In this welter of biased evidence it is impossible to find on which side the truth lies. There was in evidence of the treating at Orere some evidence of bribery, for it was said that the respondent offered 10 shillings. to the people assembled, in addition to food and drink. The petitioner's witnesses on this matter of treating were not very impressive. One of them Jemide was a light-hearted youth of the N. C. N. C., the other Eruya Omatseye, believed that he was the victim of persecution by the Olu of Warri, an Action group supporter,[105] and the third was thoroughly discredited. From his own evidence there was strong suspicion that he was suborned...[106] The only evidence that fares were not paid was that of the youthful N. C. N. C. fanatic Jemide whom I mentioned earlier on. On the whole I consider that the evidence led in support of the petition is not conclusive and not sufficiently cogent to warrant interference by the Court. Allegations of corruption and illegal

---

103 (1956) W. R. N. L. R. 142 at p. 144

104 The National Convention of Nigeria Citizens (N. C. N. C.)

105 Against whom particularly allegations of undue influence were made.

106 There was also an allegation in the petition that the respondent and/or his agents conveyed voters by vehicles and vessels to and from the polling stations contrary to election Regulations.

> practices must always be strictly proved and I am of the opinion that in this case they have not been conclusively prove.

Although at the first look it might appear that the learned Judge was too outspoken in this judicial statement, but it illustrates the difficulty which faces a judge when called upon to decide issues of political character. There is little doubt that when a person loses an election to another he could make some fantastic allegations of corruption in order to unseat his opponent. But the function of the Court in the circumstances should be to see that justice predominates. After all allegations have been made, it is the Judge or Judges who should determine whether they are true—judging from all circumstances of the case including the demeanour of each witness.

In another case, *Egbe v. Etchie*,[107] decided by the same Judge, the petitioner who was a n unsuccessful candidate in all election held on the 26th May, 1956 in the Warri West constituency for the Western House of Assembly prayed that Court to nullify the election because of alleged corrupt practices perpetrated by the Olu of Warri and his chiefs. It was adduced in evidence that the Olu of Warri as the paramount and spiritual head of the whole Itsekiri people had used his position to prevail on all the people to vote for the respondent who belonged to the party favoured by the Olu. It was alleged equally that the Olu enjoined these people not to vote for the petitioner. To achieve his objective the Olu was said to have sent out his Chiefs with instructions to invoke the wrath of the Itsekiri gods on any Itsekiri voting for the petitioner alleged that the Chiefs carried out these instructions and the invocation operated in the minds of the electors who in most cases were illiterates and believed in such gods; with the result that they could not exercise their franchise freely according to their choice. The petition was dismissed. The learned Judge in the course of his judgment said:

> ...even if the Olu of Warri had threatened spiritual injury to the Itsekiri electors, the respondent would be guilty of undue influence only if he aided, abetted, counseled or procured the Olu of Warri to threaten the electors, or if the threats were made with his knowledge and consent, or if the Olu was acting under his general or special authority.[108]

The important question in this case should be whether the Olu of Warri (assuming the allegations were true) was an agent of the respondent or whether he assumed the position of an agent and was accepted as such by the respondent. It is submitted that the acceptance need not be express, it could be implied in such a way that the respondent would be estoppel from denying that he had accepted the assumption of the agency by the person in question. It may be that for the purposes of criminal law, there must be a

---

[107] (1956) W. R. N. L. R. 134

[108] *ibid.*, at 135

clear case of aiding, abetting, counseling or procuring but in an election petition the facts may reveal that the respondent accepted the assumption of agency by somebody. It was shown that the respondent "caused to be distributed photographs of the Olu of Warri and himself on which were written words indicating that the Olu and his chiefs and the entire Itsekiri people had chosen the respondent as their candidate for the election." This was admitted by the respondent.[109] The question therefore is whether this admitted act could be viewed together with that alleged so as to hold that the Olu assumed the position of an agent and acted as such and was accepted by the respondent impliedly as an agent. In *Tomline v Tyler* [110] Lush J. said:

> It is not necessary, in order to prove agency, to show that the person was actually appointed by the candidate. If a person not appointed were to assume to act in any department of service as election agent and the candidate accepted his services as such, he would thereby ratify the agency; so that a man may become an agent of another in either of two ways, by actual employment or by recognition and acceptance.

In rejecting that the act of the respondent and Olu of Warri in respect of the circulated photographs with the words written on them the learned Judge said: "I consider that the photographs and the false manifesto were no more than false propaganda designed to win the votes of such Itsekiris as looked on the Olu's words as a command and to discredit the party to which the petitioner belonged. Falsehood and false propaganda are not new in election campaigns, and those proved in this case do not in my view amount to undue influence."[111] He went on to say: "Advertising once again to the Olu of Warri and the allegations against him, I must say that all the evidence is completely hearsay."[112]

As we pointed out earlier, heavier responsibility rests on a judge in cases having political tinge such as election petition; whatever pressure, if any, that might filter from the political arena all the judge has to do is to decide a case on the facts before him with the usual unswerving judicial impartiality. In carrying out this onerous task he will bear in mind what Martin B. in *The Warrington Case, Crozier v Ryland,*[113] said:

> I adhere to what Justice Willes said at Lichfield, that a Judge to upset an election ought to be satisfied beyond all doubt that the election was void, and that the return of a member is a serious matter, and not to be lightly set aside.

---

109 *ibid*, at p. 135

110 (1881) 44 L. T. 187 at p. 189.

111 *Egbe v Etchie* (1956) W. R. N. L R. at p. 135

112 ibid., at p. 136. If the evidence was hearsay, it should not have been admitted in the first place. "It is a general rule that such evidence is not admissible" per Grose J. in *R. v Eriswell* (inhabitants) 1790) 3 T. R. 707; 100 E. R. 815.

113 (1869) 1 O'M. & h. 42 at p. 44; (1869) 16 L. T. 812

(iii) Effect of Non-compliance or Substantial Compliance with Electoral Provisions on Election

It may be stated broadly that to be valid, an election must be conducted according to the provisions set out in the Act or Regulations. Thus in *Ijose v Akinfosile,*[114] the petitioner prayed the Court to invalidate the election of the first respondent on the ground that there were several irregularities and non-compliance with some of the provisions of the Election (House of Representatives) Regulations, 1958. In the election to the House of Representatives which took place on 12 December 1959 in the Okitipupa North Constituency, the petitioner and the first respondent were candidates. The petitioner contested on the platform of the Action Group while the first respondent contested as an N. C. N. C. candidate. The respondent had 6,053 votes cast in his favour and the petitioner 4,324 votes; consequently the Returning Officer who was joined as second respondent declared the first respondent duly elected.

One of the grounds for the election petition was that in a certain Registration Area described as 213/A02A Okeraiye A., the total number of votes counted was more than the total number of registered voters in the Area. The Returning Officer however, testified that the discrepancy emanated from the error in distribution of ballot boxes - that certain boxes meant for one polling station and marked accordingly were carried to another station and used therein. Another complaint was that certain ballot papers unmarked were included in the count. The first respondent admitted that such ballot papers were counted but asserted that it was mostly at the insistence of the petitioner. The second respondent, the Returning Officer equally admitted that unmarked ballot papers were counted but said that "such ballot papers bore such other distinguishing official marks by which the prevention of fraud could be assured, and further that the election was conducted substantially in accordance with the Regulations and that if there was non-compliance with the said Regulations (which is denied) such non-compliance did not affect the result of the election."[115] The Returning Officer confirmed that such ballot papers that did not bear an official mark or seal were counted with the consent of the petitioner.

With regard to the consent, the learned Judge said: ...the parties could not by consent circumvent the regulation in this respect. Regulation 92(2) of the Electoral Provisions, 1958 enacts as follows: "Any ballot paper which does not bear official mark shall not be counted. There can be no doubt that the inclusion of these unmarked ballot papers was manifestly illegal." The Judge was prepared to accept the explanation with regard to the error made in distribution of ballot boxes but expressed fear that there were

---

114 (1960) W. R. N. L. R. 44

115 *ibid*, at p. 47

irregularities. he said that up to the time of hearing the petition, the second respondent had not signed and completed the ballot paper account and verification statement and was still in possession of the ballot papers and records contrary to regulation 100 of the Electoral Provisions, 1958.

Dealing still with non-compliance with electoral regulations the Judge said: "No evidence has been tendered in this Court by either of the respondents as to the official mark on the ballot paper, as envisaged by regulation 6819 of the Regulations of 1958 (Electoral Provisions) and I therefore have no means of identifying it on the ballot papers. The unmarked ballot papers were not extracted and tendered as a separate parcel, for the quantity to be easily determined with certainty."[116] The learned Judge then concluded:

> In the final result and after a review of the whole of the evidence has left me with the settled impression that the election was not conducted substantially in accordance with the Nigeria (Electoral Provisions) Order in Council, 1958 and I am unable to say that the non-compliance did not affect the result of the election... I hereby declare the election null and void for non-compliance with the Election (House of Representatives) Regulations, 1958 as provided for by regulation 6 (1) B of the Federal Legislative House (Disputed Seats) Regulations, 1959.[117]

As clearly emerged from the judgment, the vital question in the petition was the inclusion of ballot papers without the official seal in the count, and the non-extraction of these ballot papers so that their total number might be known. For if the number was known, it would have been easy to determine mathematically if their inclusion, which was a transgression of the law, was such that could affect the result of the election. Regulation 7 of the Federal Legislative Houses (Disputed Seats) Regulations, 1959 provided:

> An election shall not be invalidated by reason of non-compliance with the Election (House of Representatives) Regulations, 1958, if it appears to the Court having cognisance of the question that the election was conducted substantially in accordance with those regulations, and that the nor compliance did not affect the result of the election

This provision agrees with what Kennedy J., in *Medhurst v Lough* [118] said

> ...an election ought not to be held void by reason of transgression of the law by a returning officer or his subordinates where the election was, in substance, conducted in accordance with existing election law and the result, as regards the return of one candidate over the other, was not shown to have been affected by such transgression; but if the transgressions were such that the election was not fairly conducted or if is

116 *ibid*, at p. 48

117 *ibid*, at p. 50

118 (1901) 17 T. L. R. 210.

> open to doubt whether it was so conducted and whether the return of a candidate was affected by them, then the election ought to be declared void.

There is no doubt that in *Ijose v Akinfosile*, the Judge could not determine how many of the unmarked ballot papers were counted. But it is interesting to note what he said about this:. "Counsel for the second respondent has argued that all the ballot papers having been tendered during the trial, the Court could sort them out for itself and establish the facts ... It would therefore serve no useful purpose if I were to proceed to scrutinise thousands of ballot papers..."[119] It may be suggested that in cases of this nature, the Court could afford either to adjourn and sort out those unmarked papers or could allocate time and do that during the hearing of the case. This could be inconvenient but any length could be gone to show that justice has been done.

It follows from the above discussed cases that where it appears to the Court having cognisance of the election petition that the result of the election was affected by the non-compliance with the electoral provisions or that it was an open question whether it did affect the result, then the Court would declare the election void. But where this is otherwise, the Court should not disturb the result of the election. Thus section 93 (1) of the Electoral Act, 1962 provides:

> An election shall not be invalidated by reason of non-compliance with Part II of this Act if it appears to the Court having cognisance of the question that the election was conducted substantially in accordance with the provisions of the said Part II and that the non-compliance did not affect the result of the election.[120]

This provision is a re-enactment of regulation 42 (1) of the Election (House of Representatives) General Provisions) Regulations, 1954. In *Abengowe v Wachuku* [121] an election petition was brought under the 1954 Regulations alleging *inter alia* infringement of the electoral regulations, and calling for annulment of the election of the respondent. This election to the House of Representatives was held in Aba Division on the 10th day of November, 1954. The important facts which emerged from the case were that 36 ballot boxes were broken and that some ballot papers without the official mark stamped on them were included in the count. There was evidence to the fact that ballot papers were found in premises of two of the electoral officers. With regard to the unmarked ballot papers the Electoral Officer agreed that such ballot papers were counted but said that it was a result of an agreement between the candidates and their agents. He pointed out that the number of such ballot papers was known and that the inclusion or non-inclusion could not have affect the result of the election. On this

---

119 (1960) W. R. N. L. E. at pp. 48-49

120 Which deals with procedure to be followed for the purpose of the election. Now S. 123, 1982 Act.

121 (1955) 21 N. L. R. 56.

Mbanefo J. (as he then was) said: "I do not agree that the candidates could by any such agreement circumvent the electoral regulations. The election is meant to be carried out in accordance with the regulations and there can be no contracting out of the regulations."[122] The two electoral officers admitted that they collect some ballot papers from the floor of the rooms or the booths where the ballot boxes were kept during the polling but forget to hand them over. This act was contrary to regulation 28 (2) of the Eastern Region Regulations, 1954.[123]

In dismissing the petition His Lordship concluded as follows:

> It remains to consider whether the cumulative effect of the irregularities which I found above could render the election void. After making the deductions about the invalid votes the majorities for Mr. Wachuku and Mr. Ubani-Ukoma over their nearest challenger were 13,174 and 12,392 respectively. These are considerable and one would have to be satisfied that the irregularities would have the effect of reversing the majorities. I am not satisfied that taken individually or collectively they would have the effect.[124]

In another case *Coker v Oyalowo*,[125] Irwin J. dismissed the election petition as it did not appear to him that the transgressions of the electoral regulations were such as could have affected the result of the election. The petitioner in the case was an unsuccessful candidate in an election to the Western House of Assembly held in Egba Central Constituency on 26th May, 1956. Among the irregularities alleged in the petition were that some voters who were present at the polling stations before the closing time were deprived of their right to vote by the presiding officers and that some of the polling stations were not opened for two hours after the prescribed time for polling to commence. It was also shown that the Electoral Officer for the constituency failed to appoint a polling station in respect of each registration area, for example, at Ibara and Aro. In reaching his decision the learned Judge said:

---

122 *ibid.*, at p. 60

123 See Election (House of Representatives) Eastern Region) Regulations, 1954. In a later case, Adebayo v Jinadu (1956) W. R. L. E., 47, Irwin J. held that ballot papers which did not bear official mark as was required by the regulations were not void and ought to be counted. 17 of such papers were rejected and the rejection had affected the result of the election. In granting the petition, the petitioner was declared duly elected after the inclusion of the 17 votes by the Court. In *Ackers v Howard (1886) 16 O. B. D. 739*, it was held that a ballot paper which was in conformity in other respects with the requirements of the Ballot Act, 1872 was not void merely because it had not on the face of it official mark as required by S. 2 of the Act which provided that the ballot paper should bear the official mark on both sides. This was a liberal interpretation of the Act.

124 *Abengowe v Wachuku* (1955) 21 N. L. R. at p. 62

125 (1956) W. R. N. L. R. 163

> Notwithstanding the transgressions that have been established; it appears to me that the election was conducted substantially in accordance with the principles of the Regulations and that the transgressions did not affect the result.[126]

The above decision accord with the decision of Lord Coleridge C. J., in *Woodward v Sarsons.* [127] The petitioner in that case was an unsuccessful candidate in an election held in a borough in Birmingham on 2nd November, 1874. At a polling station the presiding officer wrongly marked upon the face of the ballot paper the number of the respective voters as appeared on the burgess roll before handing the ballot paper to any of the voters. This he should not have done under the law. The result of this transgression of the law was that such ballot papers numbering 294 were not counted. It was held that this error of the presiding officer, which he admitted, did not affect the result of the election and therefore did not render it void either at common law or under the Ballot Act, 1872.

In the course of his judgment His Lordship restated the common law principle thus: "We are of opinion that the true statement is that an election is to to be declared void by the common law applicable to parliamentary elections, if it was so conducted that the tribunal which is asked to avoid it is satisfied, as a matter of fact, either that there was no real electing at all, or that the election was not really conducted under the subsisting election laws. As to the first, the tribunal should be so satisfied, i.e. that there was no real electing by the constituency at all, if it were proved to its satisfaction that the constituency had not in fact had a fair and real opportunity of electing the candidate which the majority might prefer. This would certainly be so, if a majority of the electors were proved to have been prevented from recording their votes effectively according to their own preference by general corruption or general intimidation or by being prevented from voting by want of the machinery necessary for so voting,[128] as, by polling station being demolished, or not opened or by other of the means of voting according to law not being supplied or supplied with such errors as to render the voting by means of them void or by fraudulent counting of votes or false declaration of numbers by a returning officer or by other such acts or mishaps. And we think the same result should follow if, by reason of any such or similar mishap, the tribunal, without being able to say that the majority had been prevented, should be satisfied that there was reasonable

---

126 *ibid.*, at p. 166. See also *The Drogheda Case* (1844) 2 O'M. & H. 201

127 (1874-5) 10 C. P. 733

128 In the Hackney Case, Gill v Reed and Holms (1874) 2 O'M. R. H. 77. as a result of partial failure of persons who contracted to deliver requisite ballot boxes, papers, stamps and other materials, no poll was taken at two polling stations and in some polling stations,polling was delayed. It was proved that thousands of voters were deprived from voting at the election because of irregularity. Grove J. in declaring the election void said: "If the irregularity was so great as to prevent the election being a true election, that would avoid it at common law" at. 81.

ground to believe that a majority of the electors may have been prevented from electing the candidate they preferred. But if the tribunal should only be satisfied that certain of such mishaps had occurred, but should not be satisfied either that a majority had been or that there was reasonable ground to believe that a majority might have been, prevented from electing the candidate they preferred, then we think that the existence of such mishaps would not entitled the tribunal to declare the election void by the common law of Parliament...As to the second, i.e. that the election was not really conducted under the subsisting election laws at all, we think though there was an election... the question must in like manner be, whether the departure from the prescribed method of the election is so great that the tribunal is satisfied... that the election was not an election under the existing law ... So, now when the election is to be an election by ballot, if either wilfully or erroneously, a whole constituency were to vote, but not by ballot at all... it would not be an election ... under the existing election law. But if in the opinion of the tribunal the election was substantially an election by ballot, then no mistaken misconduct, however great, in the use of machinery of the Ballot Act, could justify the tribunal in declaring the election void by the common law of Parliament.[129]

It follows that an election could only be declared void at common law where it appears to the tribunal entertaining the question that there was no real election *de jure* because of the way in which the election was conducted , i.e. contrary to the principle under which such election should be held, such as depriving the majority of the electors the opportunity of exercising their franchise or preventing a substantial number of voters from voting. On the other hand where it appears to the Court that the result of the election would not have been affected by certain irregularities or mishaps, then the Court would not disturb the result of the election. In *Ojiegbe v. Ubanu* [130] there was a claim in an election petition that between six and seven thousand Seventh Day Adventists were deprived of their voting rights in an election to the House of Representatives held on the 12 the December, 1959 in the Aba Central Constituency. It was adduced in evidence that it would be contrary to the ethics of the religion of this people to do anything or any manner of work on a Saturday which is their Sabbath day. Due to the fear of being excommunicated from their Church they refrained from going to the polls. It was shown that when the polling date was fixed by the Governor-General this religious body protested to the Authorities that it was contrary to their belief to vote on a Saturday - and that the polling day should be changed to Friday 11th December, 1959. This was refused. The Federal Supreme Court held inter alia, that even if all the six to seven thousand Seventh Day Adventists in the constituency had voted in favour of

---

129.*Woodward v Sarson* (1874) 10 C. P. at pp. 743 to 744.

130 (1961) 1 All N. L. R. 277

the defeated candidate, the result of the election would not have been affected as he was defeated by over twenty thousand votes. In other words, the mishap did not affect the result of the election.

Where it appears to the Court that despite the fact that there was substantial compliance with the electoral regulations yet the result of the election was affected owing to mismanagement by the electoral officers resulting in many of the electors not given the opportunity to vote, the election would be declared void. Thus in *Okoro v. Emembolu and others* [131] a petition was filed in Onitsha High Court to nullify an election held for Aguata District Council Evidence given by the petitioners and their witness, that the election date was changed but this was not made known to the electors until the eve of the polling day. On the polling day itself, the petitioners showed that despite the fact that their supporters waited the whole day for the electoral officers, (who arrived very late in the evening) to arrive, they were definitely not given the opportunity to vote. According to the arrangement at the polling station, the voters were called to vote according to their family groupings. It was alleged that the families of those who favoured the third respondent, i.e. the successful candidate, were first called and given adequate opportunity to exercise their franchise. But when it was the turn of the families of those who favoured the petitioner, the polling was declared closed after very few of them had in fact voted and the rest were turned out. It was further adduced, in evidence that the second respondent (the Returning Officer) refused a request to postpone the polling or to extend the hours of polling. Reynolds J. found all the allegations proved and it was established beyond doubt that the first respondent, i.e. the Electoral Officer and the second respondent, the Returning Officer, were in default and that the irregularities led to the third respondent getting 90% of the vote of those known to support him whereas only 20% of the supporters of the petitioner had the opportunity to vote. Consequently the election was declared void.

(iv) The Consequence of Declaring a Wrong Person Elected as a result of an Arithmetical Error in Addition of votes

Where a person is declared elected after all formalities[132] have been observed and subsequently it was discovered that in fact the person was wrongly declared elected because of an error in addition, it is the function of the Court, in an election petition, not that of the Returning Officer to reverse the declaration. In *Okunola v Ogundiran*,[133] owing to an error in the addition of the votes cast in Parliamentary Election a candidate who did not have a

131 (1959) 3 E. N. L. R. 11

132 See for instance, SS. 62 to 69 Electoral Act, 1962.

133 1961 1 All N. L. R. 394

have a majority of the votes cast in his favour was declared elected at first. When the error was discovered, the Returning Officer reversed his former declaration and them declared the candidate who actually got the highest number of votes duly elected. Madarikan J. held that the Returning Officer acted wrongly by reversing his first declaration and subsequently declaring another candidate duly elected after the discovery of the error. Regulation 71 of the Parliamentary Electoral Regulations, 1960[134] provides that a return could only be questioned by an election petition presented to the High Court. The learned Judge then declared Mr. Ogundiran, who had in fact the highest number of votes at the election duly elected; thus upholding his cross-Petition and dismissed that of his opponent.

In arriving at his decision the Judge relied not only on regulation 71 but also on what Schofield said in his book:

> It may happen that subsequent to the despatch of the return of the writ it is discovered that an error has been made in the addition of the ballot papers. This can only be rectified in two ways: first by Election Petition, and secondly by an express order of the House of Commons". [135]

It may be observed that to declare somebody as elected and returned in an election could be distinguished from return as used in regulation 71[136] and even in Schofield as quoted. The latter it is submitted meant return of writs whereas the former is usually a part of an expression used when announcing the result of an election. This distinction may appear hair splitting as the announcement is usually made from a certificate of return prepared after counting of votes and ascertaining the result of the election. But the time factor is materials in this case and there the distinction is relevant.\ For if the result was just declared say to the crowd around, and within a split second or so an error was discovered, — it is submitted that the Returning Officer can reverse his first declaration as a return of the writ of the election had not been made to the Electoral Commission.

2. Question touching and concerning Members of Parliament.

Just as the power to determine the validity of the selection or election of a Senator or Member of House of Representatives, as the case may be, is vested in the High Court; the determination of the questions as to whether or not a Member of the House of Representatives, or House of Assembly or a Senator retains his seat is also vested in the High court. Section 53 (1) (b) of the 1963 Constitution provides that "the competent High Court shall have original jurisdiction to hear and determine any question whether the seat in

---

134 W. R. L. N. 277 of 1960.

135 Schofield, A.N. Parliamentary Elections, London 3rd ed. p. 371.

136 Which is similar to that of SS. 69-70 of the Electoral Act, 1962.

seat in the Senate of a Senator or the seat in the House of Representatives of a member of that House has become vacant".[137] Section 48 (2) of the 1960 Constitution which is now Section 53 (2) of the 1963 Constitution provides that 'Parliament may make provision with respect to the persons who may apply to the competent High Court for the determination of any question under this section; the circumstances and manner in which, and the conditions upon which, any such application may be made; and the powers, practice and procedure of the competent High Court in relation to any such application'.[138] Following the provision it was enacted in S. 94 of the Electoral Act, 1962[139] that any such question should be referred to and decided in accordance with the procedure prescribed for the trial of an election petition. Such a proceeding may be instituted by any person who is qualified as an elector in the constituency which elected the member in question. the decision of the High Court concerned should be certified in writing to the Electoral Commission.

This apparently political question of deciding whether or not a member's seat has become vacant was one of those jealously guarded privileges and prerogatives of Parliament which concerned the internal affairs of it. The Parliament has always claimed that despite any transfer to the Courts, it has not totally divested itself of this right. It may be pointed out that as evidenced in Mr. A.N.W Wedgwood Benn's case the Parliament or to be more direct, any of the Houses of Parliament can still determine whether or not a member's seat has become vacant. In Mr. Benn's case the Committee of Privileges of the House of Committee of Privileges of the House of Commons sat over the question and decided that Mr. Benn's seat in the United Kingdom House of Commons was vacant as he had ceased by operation of law, to be a member of that House after automatic succession to the peerage of the United Kingdom at his father's death. The House of Commons on the recommendation of the Committee of Privileges resolved that Mr. Benn was no longer a Member of that House.

A similar question (but not on the same facts) arose in Nigeria and resulted in the case of *Obi v. Waziri*.[140] this was an action brought against

---

[137] For the provisions in the Regional constitutions see SS. 17, 16 and 16 of the Northern, Eastern and Western Nigeria 1963 constitutions. Similar provisions were made in the 1960 constitutions. See also regulation 113 of the 1958 Electoral Regulations, laws of Nigeria 1958, p. B.346. Before 1958 provisions of this nature appeared in the respective Regional Electoral Regulations; see for instance, regulation 117 of the western Region Parliamentary and Local government Electoral Regulations 1955, Legislation of the western Region of Nigeria 1955, p. B 779.

[138] The "competent High Court" referred to was meant to be the High Court of the Region from where the selection or election, as the case may be was made. Under S.11 of the 1982 it means High Court of a State or Federal Capital Territory.

[139] See laws of Nigeria, 1962, p. 'A 356.

[140] [1961] All N.L.R. 371.

the Speaker of the House of representatives by Dr. Chike Obi, a member of Onitsha Urban Constituency. The Speaker, on the strength of a letter received by him and apparently signed by Dr. Obi that Dr. Obi had resigned his seat in the House ruled that Dr. Obi had vacated his seat. The plaintiff denied he had resigned and in the action sought the Court's declaration that the defendant was not competent to to declare his seat vacant and also an injunction restraining defendant from hindering the exercise of his right to take his seat in the House of representatives. The High of Court of Lagos was confronted with an application filed by the defendant seeking dismissal of the action against him on the grounds that the Court had no jurisdiction to entertain the case. The High Court of Lagos was confronted with an application filed by the defendant seeking dismissal of the action against him on the ground that the Court of Lagos held that on the true construction of the 1960 Constitution it had no jurisdiction to determine the question respecting the membership of Parliament of the plaintiff as such a question was reserved to the High Court of the Region from which the plaintiff was elected - i.e. the High Court of Eastern Nigeria. The action was consequently struck out.

It may be said that there is a difference in this respect between the powers of the House of parliament in the United Kingdom and their counterpart in Nigeria. A High Court of Justice in England, on the decision in *Bradlough v. Gosset.*,[141] may not interfere with cases involving the internal affairs of a House of Parliament such as determination whether or not a member's seat had become vacant, but in Nigeria under the Constitution the High Court has power to overrule the decision of the House of Representatives or its Speaker in matters respecting the decision about the vacancy of a seat of a member. Thus in *Ndiwe v. Wariri and others* [142] the High Court at Onitsha in Eastern Nigeria had before it a petition from the Petitioner alleging that because the first Respondent i.e. the Speaker of the House of Representatives had declared Dr. Chike obi's seat vacant, he the plaintiff, as an elector in Onitsha Urban Constituency, from where Dr. Obi was elected to the House, had been deprived of representation. Before going further with this case, we think it serves to point out that the genesis of it was the same as *Obi v. Waziri* [143] which was struck out by the Lagos High Court for lack of jurisdiction. In the instant

---

141 (1884) 12 Q.B.D. 271. It was held in this case inter alia that a court of law has no right to inquire into the propriety of a resolution of the House of Commons restraining a member from doing within the walls of the House itself something which by the general law of the land he had a right to do and that the High Court had no power to interfere in matters relating to the internal affairs of the House of Commons - such as whether or not a member should be excluded from the House as a result of a controversy involving taking of an Oath.

142 [1963] 1 N.B.J. 37.

143 [1961] 1 All N.L.R. 371.

case, Dr. Obi and the Attorney-General of the Federation were joined as second and third respondents respectively. As emerged from the facts of the case, Dr. Obi won his election to the House of Representatives as an N.C.N.C. candidates. This political party devised a method of ensuring that those who won their elections on its platform adhered to the party-line always both inside and outside the House of Representatives or House of Assembly. What the party did was to make all such candidates sign a resignation paper which was undated. This paper was usually addressed to the Speaker of the House of representatives or the House of Assembly as the case may be. The paper was signed at or before the adoption of the candidate as an N.C.N.C. candidate. This paper Dr. Obi signed undated. The idea behind the whole exercise was to date the resignation paper and forward it to the Speaker of the House concerned as a disciplinary measure whenever the candidate fell out with the party. When therefore, there was disagreement between Dr. Obi and his party, the N.C.N.C., the party dated the signed resignation paper addressed to the speaker of the House of Representatives. Dr. Obi protested vehemently and denied he had resigned. This virile young man in anticipation, wrote a letter to the Speaker of the House of Representatives which reads as follows:

> I repudiate Duplicate Resignation signed undated on the understanding that the N.C.N.C constitution will be interpreted according to the rule of law and Order and fundamental Human rights of fair and just trial before condemnation. I am not resigning from the House and have no intention of doing so before the House is dissolved."

The most interesting thing in the case was that this second Respondent's letter of protest to the Speaker reached him and was received before the said resignation letter was received by the Speaker. Section 151 of the 1960 Constitution which was S. 162 of the 1963 Constitution provided that a Member of any of the House of Parliament might resign by writing under his hand addressed to the President of the Senate or the Speaker of the House of representatives, as the case may be, and that the such resignation should take effect as soon as the letter of resignation was received by the person concerned.

The Court was then to consider the delicate political issues: (a) whether the second Respondent actually "resigned" as stipulated in the Constitution; (b) whether the Speaker could in law declare the second respondent's seat vacant and then exclude him from the House of representatives; (c) the effect of the second respondent's letter to the speaker protesting that he had not resigned and (d) the legality of the resignation paper which the N.C.N.C. made the second Respondent sign undated and was subsequently dated by the party and forwarded to the Speaker of the House of Representatives.

After a careful consideration of the facts Betuel J. held that the practice of a political party extracting letters of resignation from candidates on pains of financial support and enforcing them against such people when ultimately they become Members of Parliament or Houses of Assembly is contrary to public policy. Consequently the letter of resignation forwarded to the Speaker was declared invalid and of no effect. In his judgment the learned Judge said

> In the peculiar circumstances of this case, therefore, I hold that the Speaker should have instituted inquires and if satisfied that the soridisant resignation was contrary to public policy, he should have refuse to accept it.[144]

In arriving at his decision His Lordship referred to Section 23 (1) and 24 (1) if the 1960 Constitution which were Sections 24 (1) and 25 (1) of the 1963 Constitution which provide that every person shall be entitled to freedom of thought, conscience and religion as well as of expression and to hold opinion and receive and impart ideas and information without interference. The Learned Judge then added" "any attempt to curtail these freedoms in respect particularly of a member of Parliament [145] is a clog on freedom of thought and conscience and is likely to lead, at least in some cases, to sycophancy and even downright intellectual dishonesty. If even only one member is likely to be affected thereby it condemns the whole system." Another important judicial statement in this interesting case was, "once a member of Parliament is elected and he has taken his seat, he ceases to be a mere delegate of the party sponsoring him but becomes a representative of the nation. He expressly and impliedly undertakes to serve and represent not only those who voted for him on party ticket but also those who voted against him."[146]

It must be said that this decision represents a classic example of judicial dauntlessness and adds more feathers to the wings of judicial independence. More weight will be given to this eulogy when one remembers that the political party whose prime method of ensuring discipline within its rank and file was nullified as being contrary to public policy was the party in power and absolute control in the Eastern Region at that time and also formed a part of the Federal Government. Yet the learned Judge saw to it that rule of law prevailed. With regard to the merits of the case, there is little doubt that the whole affair between the N.C.N.C. and the second Respondent hinged on contractual relationship and the enforcement therein. The party agreed to sponsor the candidate and he agreed not to depart from the policy of the party. If the position is just straight like this no problem would arise as there would be a simple contract enforceable at common law. But if the express or implied terms of

---

[144] [1963] 1 N.B.J 37 at p. 45

[145] It was a statement which Dr. Obi made in Parliament which led to the disagreement between him and the N.C.N.C.

[146] ibid., at p.44.

party or any member of the party does anything wrong or contrary to national interest he should not be criticised or condemned in Parliament or outside it; then such a contract will be manifestly contrary to public policy and void at common law. Equally if the contract will operate to hinder the exposure of certain things or acts which were done by certain individuals against public interest it will be void. Thus in *Coppock v. Bower* [147] It was held that an agreement for pecuniary consideration not to proceed with an election petition is void at common law, as its effect would deprive the public of the benefit which would result from the investigation which should have followed. At Roman law a contract which infringes Public policy is recognised as absolutely void, hence the maxim: *Memo auditur propriam turpitudinem, allegans*. A contract imposing restriction on personal freedom and liberty will generally be contrary to public policy,[148] and unless circumstances of the case make it an exception, it will be invalid.

Under the Nigerian Constitution, it will be a question of interpretation of the constitution whether or not a contact has infringed any section of the Constitution. In *Ndiwe v. Waziri and Others* the learned Judge was of the opinion that the contract or contractual relationship created by the deal between Dr. Obi and the N.C.N.C. would operate to deprive him of his freedom of expression, conscience and freedom to hold opinions receive and impart ideas which he is entitled to under the constitution and therefore the resignation letter was contrary to the Constitution and invalid. There is no doubt that the decision is a right one. In another case *Kure v. The speaker, Western House Assembly* [149] the type of resignation undated letter as signed by one Mr. Adisa, a member of the Western House of Assembly. The letter was addressed to the Speaker of the House. On facts almost similar to those in Dr. *Obi's case* - i.e. disagreement between the member and certain members of the party, the undated letter was dated by the political party which sponsored Mr. Adisa Candidature and then forwarded it to the speaker of the House of Assembly. On the receipt of the letter the speaker declared Mr. Adisa's seat vacant. Mr Adisa protested and denied he had in fact resigned. In this case the Court was invited to decide whether or not seat had become vacant on the ground that the letter of resignation was dated and despatched without the authority of Mr. Adisa and being contrary

---

147 (1838) 4 M. & W. 369, 51 R.R. 627.

148 [1960] W.R.N.L.R. 21.

149 [1960] W.R.N.L.R. 21.

to public policy[150] it should not be accepted as valid. It was held that any question as to whether or not seat of a member of the House had become vacant should be referred to the High Court by the House itself and consequently the proceedings by the petitioner could not be maintained.

In coming to this decision the Court relied on regulation 117 (1) of the Parliament and local Government Election Regulations, 1955. With every respect, we cannot see how this decision could emerge from a true construction of this legislation. The regulation in question reads:

> 117 (1) Any question as to whether the seat of any elected Member of the House of Assembly has become vacant shall be referred to and decided by the High Court in accordance with the procedure prescribed in this Part for the trial of an election petition, and the decision of the Court shall be final
>
> (2) Proceedings under this regulation may be instituted by any person qualified as an elector in the constituency which the Elected Member concerned represents" [151]

This particular provision was enacted in the 1958 Electoral Regulations [152] and has been re-enacted in the Electoral Act, 1962; [153] in each case the only difference was the dropping of the sentence - 'and the decision of the High Court shall be final' there is no doubt that the legislature contemplated that an action should lie to the High Court by proceedings initiated by an elector in the High Court itself and not in the House of Assembly and from thence to the High Court. The regulation was quite clear and should be interpreted accordingly. A new, right was created under this Regulation giving a voter a right to institute and action in the High Court if the vacancy of the seat of an Elected Member in his constituency is in question.

---

150 Public policy was again mentioned in this case. It may be said that it serves to note that judges themselves have warned against the undue extension of this doctrine. Burrough J. in *Richardson v. Melliah (1824) 2 Bing 220 at 252* said: "I for one protest against arguing too strongly upon public policy; it is a very unruly horse, and when once you get astride it you never know where it will carry you In Printing and Numerical Registering Co. v. Sampson (1875) L.R. 19 Eq. 462 at p.465, Jessel MR. said "It must be not be...forgotten that you are not to extend arbitarily those rules which say that a given contract is void as being against public policy, because if there is one thing which more than another public policy requires it is that men of full age and competent understanding shall have the utmost liberty of contracting, and that their contracts when entered into freely and voluntarily shall be held sacred and shall be enforced by Courts of Justice. Therefore with this freedom of contract". It therefore follows that care must be taken in handling this 'unruly horse'- public policy and undue extension of this doctrine could be dangerous.

151 See Legislation of Western Nigeria, 1955, p. B 779

152 See Reg. 133, Laws of Nigeria 1958, p. 346.

153 See S.94 Electoral Act, 1962, Laws of Nigeria 1962, p. A 3566. Now see S. 124 Electoral Act, 1982.

Our view is buttressed by the Federal Supreme Court decision in *Fajinmi v. The Speaker, Western House of Assembly* [154] and the fact that under similar provisions the proceedings in *Obi v. Waziri and Ndiwe v. Waziri and Others* were instituted by individuals directly and were entertained by the High Courts concerned. In Kure's case, the learned Judge in dismissing the petition relied heavily on the Privy Council's decision in *Patterson v. Solomon* [155] But it is submitted that S. 40 of the Trinidad and Tobago (Constitution) Order in Council, 1950 which was interpreted by the Supreme Court of Trinidad and Tobago, the interpretation of which was upheld by the Privy Council, was quite different from regulation 117 of the Parliamentary and Local Government Electoral regulations, 1955. Section 40 of the Order reads:- "All questions which may arise as to the right of any person to be or remain a Member, shall be determined by the Governor acting in his discretion. (2) All questions which may arise as to the right of any person to be or remain an Elected Member of the Legislative Council shall be referred to and determined by the Supreme Court of the Colony in accordance with the provisions of any law in force in the Colony".[156] It could be seen from regulation quoted earlier that there are vital differences in the two provisions. The regulation specifically stated that the proceedings could be instituted 'by an elector". There was no such provisions in the Order. The regulation provided that the proceeding should be initiated in accordance with the provisions made for instituting proceedings in an election petition. One of these being that the proceedings could be instituted by an elector or a person who claimed to be a candidate in the election in question. Election petitions, a fortiori, are always presented to the election Court or the High Court as the case may be not in the recent times to the Parliament or House of Assembly itself before they are transmitted to the Court concerned. From this point of view, it is submitted that the petition in Kure's case should have been entertained as being properly brought.

In *Fajinmi v. The Speaker, Western House of Assembly* [157] the view which we put forward above was apparently approved by the Federal Supreme Court of Nigeria. In this case the Appellant was an elected member of the Western House of Assembly and had been sworn in as such. In this action he sought a Declaration that "he is entitled to take his seat as a validly elected member of the House of Assembly", or alternatively, that "his seat in the House of Assembly is not vacant". He

---

[154] 1962 1 All N.L.R. 205.

[155] 1960 2 All E.R. 20; the pivot of the Board's decision in this case was that appeal did not lie from the decision of the Supreme Court of Trinidad and Tobago in a decision involving the question whether or not the seat of a Member of Legislature and become vacant.

[156] See The Trinidad and Tobago (Constitution) Order in council 1950 S.I. No. 510 of 1950.

[157] [1962] 1 All N.L.R. 205.

equally sought for an injunction to restrain the Speaker from preventing him form taking his seat. The Respondent on the other hand moved the Court, on Notice, to strike off the action "as not being properly before the Court". The respondent during the hearing of the Motion contended that although S.16 of the Constitution of Western Nigeria provided for the determination by the High Court whether or not a member's seat had become vacant; it was dependent on the manner in which such proceedings could be brought as provided in subsection (2) and that the procedure for bringing such action should be according to the regulations made by the House of Assembly. He contended, as he did before the High Court of Western Nigeria which upheld the contention, that as the regulation made in 1955[158] had ceased to exist in view of sections 23 and 26 of the Nigerian (Constitution) Amendment (No.3) Order in Council, 1959, the Court could not entertain the case.

The Federal Supreme Court in rejecting this contention and allowing the appeal held that notwithstanding that Regulation 117 of the Western Region Parliamentary and local Government Electoral Regulations, 1955 ceased to exist as a result of 1959 Amendment Order in Council; once the Constitution conferred upon the Court the power to hear and determine certain questions, and provided that the legislature may make provision as to the parties who may institute proceedings before the Court; failure on the part of the legislature to provide for practice and procedure to be followed could not deprive the Court of the power to exercise that jurisdiction. The Court further held that where a jurisdiction was conferred on a court and it was also provided that the legislature should provide for the procedure to be followed and it omitted to so provide, the Court would entertain an application brought in the form of an Action, invoking that jurisdiction. As the legislature in the instant case provided no procedure to be followed as required by the constitution, the plaintiff was entitled to bring his application in the usual form of an action and to have it heard.

From the point of view of this Federal Supreme Court's decision, it may be said that *Kure v. The Speaker, ante*, is no longer a good law. It follows therefore that an individual can institute a proceedings in the High Court in matters regarding the vacancy of a Member of Parliament; provided he is an elector in the constituency from where the Member was elected and, as the Supreme Court held, he shall be entitled to have the question determined.[159]

---

[158] The regulation referred to here was regulation 117 of the Parliamentary and Local Government Electoral Regulations, 1955 which we had considered.

[159] See Bairamain F.J. *Fajinmi v. The Speaker. Western Mouse of Assembly 1 All N.L.R. 205.*

3. Judicial Handling of Political Offences.

The Courts in Nigeria have on several occasions been invited to decide criminal cases emanating from seemingly political issues. These range from treasonable felony to sedition and inciting one section of the community to take part in rioting for political purposes. In each case the Courts have apparently shown that they are capable of determining the issues involved purely on evidence before them and not in any way swerved by political considerations. This we think should be the position of judges under the circumstances. Although political offences could in certain cases be inflated by politics and leave the judges in embarrassing situations, but in each case their duty under the law is to uphold justice, relying wholly for their decision on evidence before them and fair construction of the Criminal Code where it falls to construe the Code.

In *R. V. Omisade and 17 Others*,[160] the Supreme Court of Nigeria was called upon to hear an appeal from the High Court of Lagos in a case in which the appellants were charged with treasonable felony contrary to Section 41 (b) of the Criminal Code, conspiracy to commit a felony, contrary to Section 516 of the same Code and Conspiracy to effect an unlawful purpose, contrary to Section 518(b) of the Criminal Code Evidence was adduced by the prosecution to show that the accused persons conspired to overthrow the Government of the Federation and to seize power by force. As was shown, the 27th accused in the case was the Leader of Action group of Nigeria - and he, Chief Obafemi Awolowo was the Leader of the Opposition in the Nigerian Parliament. The core of the case for the prosecution was that the offences emanated from the decision of a committee set up by the Action Group Leader and called "The Tactical Committee" It was shown by the prosecution that the object of the committee was expressed thus: 'that as it had become evident that the Action Group Party could not win the elections to the House of Representatives through the ballot box, another means of capturing power, namely by revolution must be sought!'[161] This view was said to have been expressed by the Leader of the party at a meeting of the Tactical Committee. To attain this objective, said the prosecution, arms were imported into the country and 200 young men were recruited and sent to Ghana for military training. The prosecution equally showed that the whole affair emanated purely from the ambition of the 27th accused who was the Premier of the Western Region of Nigeria and in 1954 resigned his seat from the Western legislature after winning his seat in the House of Representatives. But that was not all he desired; he hoped that his party would win sufficient seats to enable it to control the House so that he might appointed the Prime Minister

---

160 [1964] N.M.L.R. 67.

161 ibid., at p. 74

of Nigeria. The prosecution alleged that his hopes were shattered when his failed to materialise.

A quantity of arms and ammunition were found in the possession of two of the key prosecution witnesses. The prosecution alleged that the arms were imported into the country in furtherance of the plot to capture power by force. It is surprising to note that these two key witnesses were charged with offences connected with the possession of arms and that case was pending in a Magistrate's Court while the trial in the instant case went on. This was disapproved by the Supreme Court. In its decision, the Supreme Court upheld the appeals in respect of three persons and these were discharged and acquitted, the appeal of the 4th accused persons, Simeon Oyeshile was upheld in part and his conviction in respect of Count 3 was affirmed. The appeals of other appellants, namely, Michael Omisade, Gabby Sasore, Samuel Akanbi Onitiri, Sebastian James Umoren, Sunday Ebietoma, Lateef Jakande, Uzodinma Iroegbu Nwaobiala, Samuel Adesanya Otubango and Chief Obafemi Awolowo were dismissed and their convictions affirmed.

In the judgment delivered by Ademola, C.J.N., the main legal issues were whether certain evidence of the prosecution witnesses could be regarded as having been corroborated in material particular and to what extent the trial judge was right in believing the evidence of the prosecution witnesses. The Evidence Act requires two witnesses to at least an overt act in a charge under Sections 40, 41 and 42 of the criminal Code. Section 178 of the Evidence Act reads:-

> '(2) (a) No person charged with treason or with any of the felonies mentioned in Sections 40, 41 and 42 of the Criminal Code can be convicted, except on his own plea of guilty, or on the evidence in open Court of two witnesses at least to one overt act of the kind of treason or felony alleged, or the evidence of one witness to one overt act and one other witness to another overt act of the same kind of treason or felony".[162]

The Supreme Court in disagreeing with the trial judge held that the witnesses for the prosecution, Patrick Dokotri, Henry Oleri, and Anthony Oboh were accomplices but the Court was satisfied that the learned trial Judge adequately warned himself of the danger of convicting on the uncorroborated evidence of the accomplices. For the trial Judge added in his judgment, "I am also satisfied that there are other circumstances like the confessional statements of the accused persons which are corroborative evidence of the two witnesses required".[163] It is submitted that this statement of the trial judge is contradictory to what he said earlier, that the three prosecution witnesses in question were only guilty of silence and that

---

162 Evidence Act, Cap. 62, laws of the Federation of Nigeria and Lagos, 1958, p. 1298

163 [1964] N.M.L.. at p. 77.

did not make them accomplices.[164] We are in agreement with the view of the Supreme Court that they were accomplices, *a fortiori*, as two of them were found in possession of arms and were charged before a Magistrate for that. If the learned trial Judge believed that they were not accomplices, his warning himself of the danger of acting on the uncorroborated evidence of accomplices was therefore unnecessary and uncalled for. Our observation is buttressed by what was said on this point by the Supreme Court:

> "It seems that the larned Judge could not make up his mind on accomplices and corroboration, but ultimately he decided to consider the case in the light of some witnesses to the overt acts being accomplices and requiring corroboration" [165]

The establishment that Oleri, Oboh and Dokotri were accomplices was very vital. This led to the acquittal of, Adeyiga Akinsanya, Ayo Akinsanya and Anomougharan Okotie-Yesin. In an impressive review of each case the Supreme Court found that the evidence against these men was evidence of the accomplices and could not be held to have been corroborated in material particular to sustain the convictions. The gravity of the offence charged and the penalty which follows on conviction require that utmost care should be taken in cases of this nature. One of the Sections of the Criminal Code under which the accused persons were charged carried a maximum punishment of life imprisonment [166]

In dismissing the appeal of Chief Awolowo, the Supreme Court came to the conclusion that the charges against him had all been proved. Mbanefo A.J.S.C. (as he then was) dissented in part and said:

> "I agree that the conviction should be sustained as I am in full agreement with the conclusion reached on overt act 4 on the first Court, which by itself is enough to sustain the conviction on that Court. I am however apprehensive of the way the Learned trial Judge accepted the evidence of Dr. Onabamiro and although it makes no difference whatever to the conviction on the first Court, I feel I must express the view in so far as it affects overt act 1 in Count 1.
>
> On the evidence before the Court, I would regard Dr. Onabamiro as an accomplice or at lest a "tainted witness".... According to Dr. Onabamiro himself the 27th accused told him in Feb. 1961 that the purpose of the Tactical Committee was to seize power at the centre by force but it took him until Nov. 1961 9 months later to make up his mind to withdraw. He said he withdraw at a meeting of the Committee at which he had not been invited and into which he "stumbled and when he withdraw he offered to swear not to reveal what he knew and said nothing afterwards until Sept. 1962."

---

164 *ibid.*

165 *ibid.*, at p. 78.

166 S. 41 (b) of the Criminal Code, laws of the Federation of Nigeria 1958 Vol. II p. 618. This deals with Treasonable Felony now amend by Adaptation of laws (Miscellaneous Provisions) Order. 1964, Laws of the Fed. Republic of Nigeria, 1964 p. B 452

The his Lordship drew attention to Section 40 of the Criminal Code which makes it an offence for any person aware of any person intending to commit treason.and failing to inform the President, Governor of a Region or a Police Officer. The offence carries a punishment of life imprisonment. His Lordship after this observation went on:

> It is said that he[167] did nothing actively to carry out the assignment given to him but his tacit acceptances and the fact that for nine months he did nothing to dissuade the other members of the Tactical committee from pursuing the the path of treason and his offer to swear to secrecy must have encouraged the other members in their design. I think that one the above facts Onabamiro, even if he cannot be regarded as an accomplice in strict sense (although I am of the opinion that he is) is one whose evidence it would be unsafe to act on without corroboration. It is not enough to say that the judge regarded him as truthful and credible...That being so overt act 1 has not in my view been sufficiently proved.[168]

It is difficult to see how a person who testified that he was a member of a committee formed for a design and who took part in the deliberations of that committee could not be held to be an accomplice. If such a person changed his mind and withdrew, he was under a duty to report such activities to the authorities of the State. Apart from Section 40 of the Criminal Code which provides for concealment of treason, it is an offence at common law for a person to have knowledge that a felony is being committed and fails to report same to the authorities. In *Sykes v. Director of Public Prosecutions*[169] the House of Lords upheld a conviction based on misprison of felony. The appellant in that case was charged with the common law offence of misprison of felony in that, knowing that others had received stolen firearms, he unlawfully concealed the commission of the offences. Their Lordships held that misprison of felony is an offence known to the common law; that the mere omission to inform the appropriate authorities of a felony constitutes the offence. Lord Denning gave a concise and apposite definition of this crime thus: "It means that a man knows that a felony has been committed and neglects to disclose it".[170] some[171] thought that the offence of misprison of felony had fallen into desuetude but this decision of the House of Lords has proved otherwise.

An important question which was not directly before the Supreme Court in *R.v. Omisade (ante)* was whether in fact the Leader of the Action Group said that he had lost all confidence in the ballot box and to what

---

[167] Dr. Onabamiro was third witness for the prosecution. He said he was a member of the Tactical Committee but later withdraw from it.

[168] [1964] N.M.L.R. at p.99.

[169] [1961] 3 W.L.R. 373.

[170] ibid., at p. 376

[171] In *R.v. Aberg (1948) 32 Cr. App. R. 144,146*, Lord Goddard, C.J. thought, with every respect, wrongly, that the crime is "generally regarded as nowadays as obsolete or fallen into desuetude".

extent did he believe that democracy had suffered and there was need for a change in our body politic. As we pointed out earlier, the way in which the country was divided before he implementation of Federal System negatived the very concept of federation, in that for a federal system to work, no one of the units of the set-up, should be too big as to dominate the rest. It is a notorious fact that the Northern Region was bigger than the rest of the units of the federation put together. It was not easy for any other political party in the country to go to the North and campaign freely during federal elections. The Southern politicians were regarded almost as foreigners in the North and not given adequate opportunity to establish themselves politically. Chief Awolowo was known to have encountered the bitterest experience when he wanted to push through the apparent barrier. The N.P.C. (Northern Peoples Congress) dominated the Federal Parliament because of the political preponderance the division of the country gave it. There were statements from the leaders of the N.P.C. that the party would 'rule Nigeria forever'. The Opposition party in the centre felt frustrated.

We are not for one moment saying that when one is politically frustrated, he should resort to violence or anything of the sort. All that we are saying is that if the political situation in the Country as a whole is such that equal opportunity is given to all the political parties and there is no question of one party entrenching itself in one region to the exclusion of others there would be little or no trouble or even the idea of plotting to overthrow a government by force. Equally if the country is evenly divided as far as possible to maintain a balance among the units of the country certain dangers which loomed before the Regional elections in the Western region in 1965 and exploded after, could have been reasonably obviated. When the Opposition sees that it is impossible to gain power through election, it will either allow itself to be absorbed by the party in power or resort to violence. This we think, is a deplorable situation and should not be allowed to repeat itself in Nigeria.

In another case *R.v. Enahoro,*[172] the accused, an important member (2nd Vice-President) of the Action Group was charged under the same section of the Criminal Code[173] as those in *R.v. Omisade and Others (ante).* The facts of the two cases have the same origin. The prosecution in the instant case alleged that chief Enahoro between Dec. 1960 and Sept. 1962, in Lagos formed an intention to levy war against the State (the Queen). To achieve this, it was alleged, he solicited, incited and endeavoured to persuade and procure Henry Olearie, Anthony Oboh and others to take part in the levy of war. It was shown that between Nov. 1961 and Sept. 1962

---

172 [1963] L.H.C.R. 91.

173 Treasonable felony contrary to S.41 (1), (11) Conspiracy to commit a felony contrary to S.516, see Laws of the Federation of Nigeria and Lagos 1958 Vol. II pp. 618 and 793, for the amendment, see 1964 Order, Laws of the Ed. Republic of Nigeria 1964, p.b.452,

the accused was concerned with Ayo Akinsanya, Olearie and Oho and others in the unlawful importation of arms and ammunition into Nigeria and the possession of these weapons. The prosecution further alleged that the accused was concerned in the importation and possession of special Mare torches for use by those taking part in the levying of war. Other facts about the formation of the Tactical Committee by the Action Group party, the purpose and is activities follow closely those we have seen in *R.v. Omisade and Others.* One interesting aspect of the facts of the case was what the accused was reported as saying: 'that he was not happy about the set-up of things in Nigeria and that as long as the Constitution of Nigeria continued to exist, the people he described as feudal elements of the North would continue to dominate the country'.[174] It was also alleged that the accused said that 'it was impossible to change things through the ballot box because the arrangements in the north made a fair election impossible', and that under the circumstances the best thing was to overthrow the Government of the Federation. In his evidence the accused denied having told one Mr. Collins, who testified to the effect for the prosecution, any thing about a plot to overthrow the Government by violence. Lambo J. in finding the accused guilty said: "I regret I am not at all impressed by his defence which is a bundle of lies".[175]

Before Chief Enahoro stood trial in Nigeria there was a fairly long legal battle in the United Kingdom as to whether or not he should be returned to Nigeria to answer charges against him there. In *R.v. Government of Brixton Prison Ex parte Enahoro* [176] the Queen's Bench Division of the High Court was called upon to consider an application from Chief Enahoro against an order for his return to Nigeria. The applicant was detained under a magistrate's order made on December 13th, 1962 under Section 5 of the Fugitive Offenders Act 1881 Under the order, he was to be held in custody pending his return to Nigeria. After the applicant had unsuccessfully applied to the Divisional Court for an order of habeas corpus and for relief under Section 10 of the 1881 Act, representation was made on his behalf to the Home Secretary decided on March 14th, 1963, under Section 6 of the Act of 1881, that he was of the opinion that it was just to order the applicant's return to Nigeria. This decision was announced by the Home Secretary in the House of Commons. As there was a desire on the part of Members of Parliament to have debate on the issue, the Home Secretary gave an assurance that he would not under the circumstances order the return of the applicant until Parliament had decided. Only a few

---

174 [1963] L.H.C.R. at p. 110. This alleged assertion buttresses our earlier contention and shows vividly the frustration of a member of the Opposition who felt that unless a dramatic change occurred he would remain in Opposition ad infinitum.

175 ibid., at p. 126

176 [1963] 2 W.L.R. 1260

moments after the decision of Parliament was known, the Home Secretary received a notice of the applicant's intention to make application to the Court to order his discharge under Section 7 of the Fugitive Offenders Act 1881 on the ground that there was no sufficient cause for his detention after March 14th. In a judgment delivered by Lord Parker C.J., the Court held that he application must be dismissed for the Home Secretary had good grounds for detaining the applicant for more than 30 days. The court was of the view that the reference of Parliament of the issue was reasonable under the circumstances.

An interesting thing in this case was that the Court interpreted the word"may" appearing Section 7 as being mandatory, that is to say, it should be construed as "Must". Whereas "may" which appears in section 6 was interpreted as not being mandatory, i.e. it should, be given its natural meaning. The Sections provided as follows:

> S. 6 Upon the expiration of fifteen days after a fugitive has been committed to person to await his return, or if a writ of habeas corpus or other like process is issued with reference to such fugitive by a superior Court, after the final decision of the Court in the case, (1) If the fugitive is so committed in the United Kingdom, a Secretary of State ... may, if the thinks it[177] just, by warrant under his hand order that fugitive to be returned to the part of Her Majesty's dominions from which he is a fugitive[178]...
> "Section 7 If a fugitive who, in pursuance of this part of this Act, has been committed to prison in any part Her Majesty's dominions to await his return is not conveyed out of that part within one month after such committal, a superior court, application by or on behalf of the fugitive, and upon proof that reasonable notice of the intention to make such application has been given, if the said part is the United Kingdom to a Secretary of State... may, unless sufficient cause is shown to the contrary, order the fugitive to be discharged out of custody.

In reaching their decision, their Lordships were of the view that "may" in Section 7 should be construed as "must" because the liberty of the subject was at stake. It follows that Section 6 in this respect differs with Section 7 notwithstanding that the word may was used as they key word in each case; because Section 6 sets a limit of 15 days after the committal of the fugitive, for his return to the part of Her Majesty's Dominion unless application for a writ of habeas corpus was pending in the Court. If such application is dismissed and 15 days had elapsed then the Secretary of State may, if he thinks it just, order the return of the fugitive. On the other hand, under Section 7 after the expiration of one month from the committal to prison of the fugitive and he is not yet returned to that part of Her Majesty's Dominion concerned, then his liberty is assuredly at stake the must be returned or set free. If therefore a application is made to a Superior Court and no reasonable cause is shown by the Secretary of State for the further

---

187 Emphasis supplied.

178 For these sections, see Laws of Nigeria, 1958, Vol.XI p.292.

delay, then the Court will order his discharge and under such circumstances, the Secretary of States must discharge the fugitive.

In Enahoro's case there was sufficient cause for the delay in his return because a decision of Parliament was being awaited. In another case[179] decided earlier, the Court was of the view that "may" in section 7 should be construed as "must".

The unique aspect of the Fugitive Offenders Act 1881 is that extradition is granted under it for political offences. This equally exposes the courts to the delicate situation of deciding in the first instance whether a prisoner should be returned. The case of Chief Enahoro exposed certain anomalies in the Act when compared with Extradition treaties which invariably exclude political offences. The Fugitive Offenders Act 1881 was extended to Nigeria by the West African (Fugitive Offenders) Order in Council, 1923.[180] To remove the anomalies in the Act, on April 26th, 1966, law Officers from almost all the Commonwealth countries attended a conference under the Chairmanship of Lord Gardiner, the Lord Chancellor.[181] An extract from the communique was published in a Foreword of a Command paper dealing with a scheme for the return of fugitive offenders within the Commonwealth, It reads:

> The Meeting considered that Commonwealth extradition arrangements should be based upon reciprocity and substantially uniform legislation incorporating certain features commonly found in extradition treaties, e.g. a list of returnable offences, the establishment of a *prima facie* case before return, and restriction on the return of political offenders.[182]

Under the new Scheme, 'a fugitive will only be returned for a returnable offence'. Such returnable offences are now listed in Annex I of the Command Paper. These are apparently pure criminal offences and exclude political offences.

Seditious Publication

The Nigerian Courts have been called upon to decide whether certain publications directed against the Government were seditious. In *D.P.P.v Obi* [183] . the Federal Supreme Court had to decide whether Section 24 subsection (10 of the 1960 Constitution which provided for freedom of

---

179 In re Shuter [[1960] 1 Q.B. 142 A Kenya fugitive wzs held in prison for more than one month after committal pending his return to Kenya; this was because no escort was then available. It was held that there was reasonable cause for not returning till then

180 see S.I. No. 596, Laws of the Federation of Nigeria, 1958, Vol. XI. p. 308.

181 see West African, April 30th, 1966, p. 498.

182 See Scheme relating tod the Redittion of Fugitive Offences within the Commonwealth, Cmnd. 300.

183 [1961] 1 All N.L.R. 186.

expression, including freedom to hold opinions and to receive and impart ideas, and Section I of the Constitution which provided that any law which was contrary to the Constitution was void; had invalidated Sections 50 and 51 of the Criminal Code. The relevant provision of the Criminal Code makes it an offence for any person person to utter seditious publication. The accused Dr. Chike Obi who was a Member of Parliament printed a pamphlet entitled "The People": Facts that you must know". The accused was charged with sedition contrary to sections 50 and 51 of the Criminal Code. The pamphlet in question contained *inter alia* bitter attack on the Federal Government; a portion of its reads:" "Down with the enemies of the people, the exploiters of the weak and oppressors of the poor'... The days of those who enriched themselves at the expense of the poor are numbered. The common man in Nigeria can today no longer be fooled by sweet talk at election time only to be exploited and treated like dirt after the booty of office has been shared among politicians". The Supreme Court held that the relevant Sections of the Criminal Code were not invalidated by Section 24 (1), of the Constitution; consequently the accused was held to be guilty of sedition. It was submitted for the defence that 'any law which punishes a person for making a statement which brings a government discredit or ridicule, or creates disaffection against the government irrespective of whether the statement is true or false... is not reasonably justifiable in a democratic society'. It is submitted that this was an impressive submission. But the Supreme Court appositely said that 'the Supreme Court must be the arbiter of whether or not any particular law is justified'.[184]

The Court was of the view that it is legitimate and constitutional by any fair argument to discuss and criticise, canvass and censure the acts of a government and the policy of the government, but what is not permitted is to criticise the Government in a malignant manner for such attack could affect public peace. We agree with the Court that there is a limit which one must not exceed, but at the same time freedom of expression enshrined in the Constitution should not be disturbed even if the bitterest criticism is directed against the government.

In another case, the Supreme Court in holding that sections 50, 51 and 59 subsection (1) of the Criminal Code had not been invalidated by Section 24 of the Constitution said" "Suffice it that section 24 of the Constitution of the Federation relating to Fundamental Human Rights guaranteed nothing but ordered freedom and that no section of the Constitution can be used as licence to spread false news likely to cause fear and alarm to the public".[185] It follows that despite the fact that there is freedom of expression the Courts

---

184 *ibid.*, at p.196.

185 *R.v. Amalgamated Press (of Nigeria) Ltd.*, 1961 1 All N.L.R. 199 at pp. 201-202.

will not allow any reckless incitement[186] in the name of liberty of expression; the liberty is liberty according to law.

4. Judicial Determination of the Constitutional Crisis in Western Nigeria in 1962.

As we have seen, the constitutional crisis in Western Nigeria in 1962 stemmed from a split in the Action Group party which formed the government of the Western Region. In Chapter three we saw how the Governor removed Chief Akintola who was the Premier and the Deputy leader of the Action Group from office as the as the Premier of the Region, following a letter he received from 66 members of the House of assembly that Premier no longer commanded the support of the majority of the members of the House. In *Akintola v. Aderemi and Adegbenro*,[187] the political battle which went on in the Action Group with unswerving acridity was moved into the judicial forum. In this case, Chief Akintola sought a declaration from the Court to the effect that his dismissal from office by the Governor and the appointment of the second defendant as the Premier in his place were invalid. As the Governor maintained that he acted under the powers vested in him by the constitution, the Courts found themselves beset with undoubtedly explosive issue to determine. The Action group whose split gave rise to the crisis was the official Opposition party in the Federal Parliament, the Leader of the Action Group Chief Awolowo was the leader of Opposition in the Federal Parliament and of course the Western Region was by then dominated by the same party. As professor de Smith put it: "In an atmosphere [like this] highly charged with political tension the task of the judges may be acutely embarrassing, especially if they are called upon to decide between two claimants to legitimate political power, of whom one commands the effective means of imposing his will and the other is able to marshall equally or more persuasive legal arguments."[188]

The Federal Supreme Court, importing into the written Constitution of the Western Region of Nigeria the convention of the Constitution prevalent in the united Kingdom, held that the removal of Chief Akintola from office was invalid. The Court was of the view that the Governor should not have acted solely on the letter signed by 66 members of the House which he received. The convention which the Supreme Court imported was the one which required that before a Prime Minister is removed from his office there must be a vote of no confidence passed in the legislature itself. In his

---

186 In *Basharu v. Bornu N.A. [1961] 1 All N.L.R. 664*, the accused was convicted for inciting the supporters of his political party in a political speech against another political party and its supporters

187 [1962] 1 All N.L.R. 442.

188 de Smith *op. cit.* p.87.

dissenting opinion Brett, F.J., was of the view that the whole issue revolved on the interpretation of Section 33(10) of the Constitution of Western Nigeria, 1960. This subsection provided that the Governor would only remove the Premier from office if it appeared to him that the Premier no longer commanded the support of the majority of the members of Assembly. The learned Judge held the opinion that on the true interpretation of the Constitution undisturbed by any political exigency emanating from unwritten convention of the Constitution, the Governor validly removed Chief Akintola from office as the Premier of Western Region of Nigeria.

On appeal[189] to the Judicial Committee of the Privy Council, the Board held that on the proper construction of the relevant section of the Constitution of the Western Region of Nigeria, Chief Akintola was validly removed from his office as the Premier of the Western Region by the Governor. The decision of the Federal Supreme Curt was therefore reversed.

By the time the decision was given, Chief Akintola was still acting as the Premier of the Region deriving the strength for so acting mainly from decision of the Federal Supreme Court. The Court had decided that his removal was invalid because there was no vote of no confidence against the Premier passed in the House of Assembly. Also, by the time the Board delivered their judgment, some members of the Action Group had crossed over to Chief Akintola's side and with the support of the members of the N.C.N.C. (National Convention of the Nigerian Citizens), he was able to obtain a vote of confidence when the Western House of Assembly again met. He followed that up by securing the passage of a bill through the House of Assembly and the House of Chiefs and in effect nullified the decision of the Privy Council. The Law [190] thus enacted required that the Premier could only be dismissed by the Governor after a vote of no confidence had been passed in the House of Assembly to the effect that the Premier no longer commanded the support of the Majority of that House. Both the House of Representatives and the Senate resolved by two-thirds majority approving the action taken by the Western House of Assembly. The measures thus taken completely nullified the decision of the Privy Council.

It may be observed that to have decided to annul the decision of the Privy Council by an enactment is unjustifiable. That made mockery of judicial determinations. It will be remembered that it was on the strength of the decision of the Federal Supreme Court that Chief Akintola resumed his office as the Premier of the Western Region. It is, therefore, irreconcilable that it was the same person who saw to the passage of a Law to nullify the decision of the highest Tribunal of the land, simply because the decision did

---

189 See *Adegbenro v Akintola 1963 A.C. 614.*

190 See Constitution of Western Nigeria (Amendment) Law, 1963.

not favour him. It is hoped that such action should not be taken in the future; for nothing should be done to endanger the integrity and independence of the judiciary.

Selected Bibliography

Books

Ali, S.A. — Election Laws in Pakistan, Karachi, 1965.

Allott, A.N., — Essays in African Law, London: Butterworths, 1960

Anderson, J.N.D — Changing Law in Developing Countries, London: Allen & Unwin, 1963.

Archbold. J.F., — Criminal Pleading, Evidence and Practice London: Sweet & Maxwell, 1962.

Austin, J., — Lectures on Jurisprudence or the Philosophy of Positive Law, Vol. 1., London: Murrey, 1885.

Awa, E., — Federal Government of Nigeria, California, 1946.

Azikiwe, N., — Political Blueprint of Nigeria, Lagos, 1945.

Baikie, W.B., — Narrative of an Exploring voyage up the Rivers Kwora and Binue, 1854.

Basu, D.D., — Commentary on the Indian Constitution, Vol. I., Calcutta, 1965.

Bentham, J., — Anarchical Fallacies, Works, Vol. 2.,(ed. Bowring).

Blackstone, Sir William, — Commentaries Vol. III.,Oxford, 1775.

Blackstone, Sir William, — Commentaries Vol. II., Oxford, 1775.

Borchard, E., — Declaratory Judgments, Cleveland, 1941.

Bracton, H., — Treatise, De Legibus et Consuetudinibus Angliae, folio 93E and 247A, London: Flesher & Young, 1640.

Burns, A.C. — History of Nigeria, 3rd Ed., 1942.Lord Bryce: American Commonwealth, Vol. I., 1917 ed.

Chitty, J., — Prerogative of the Crown, London: Butterworths, 1820.

Daniels, W.C.E., — The Common Law in West Africa, London: Butterworths, 1964.

de Smith, S.A., — The New Commonwealth and its Constitutions, London: Stevens, 1964.

de Smith, S.A., — Judicial Review of Administrative Action, London: Stevens, 1959.

Diamond, A.S., — Primitive Law, London: Longmans, 1935.

Dicey, A.V. — Law of the Constitution, London: Macmillan, 1959.

Elias, T.O., — The Nature of African Customary Law, Manchester, 1956.

Elias, T.O., — The Nigerian Legal System, London: Routledge & Kegan Paul, 1963.

Ezera, K. — Constitutional Developments in Nigeria, Cambridge, 1960.

Gledhill, A., — Fundamental Rights in India, London:

Stevens, 1955.

Goodhart, A.L., English Law and the Moral Law, London: Stevens, 1953.

Gould J. and Kolb W.L. A Dictionary of the Social Sciences (U.N.E.S.C.O.), London: Tavistock, 1964.

Gray, J.C., The Nature and Source of the Law, Columbia, 1921.

Green, M.M. Igbo Village Affairs, London: Sidgwick & Jackson, 1948.

Grotius; De Jure Belli ac Pacis, translated by Campbell, A.C.

Hartland, E.S., Primitive Law, London: Methuen, 1924.Lord Hailey, Native Administration in the British African Territories, Port III, London: H.M.S.S.O., 1951.

Hanbury, H.G., Modem Equity, Oxford, 11962.

Hoebel, E.A. The Law of Primitive Men, Cambridge, 1954.

Hertslet, E., Map of Africa by Treaty, Vol. I., 1909.

Holdsworth, W.S. A History of English Law, Vol. I., London: Methuen, 1956.

Holmes, O.W., The Path of the Law, 1897 ed.

Hood Phillips, O.., Constitutional Law, London: Sweet & Maxwell, 1957.

Hutchinson. T.J., The Wandering Among the Ethiopians; London, 1861.

Jain, M.P., Indian Constitutional laws, Bombay, 1962.

Jennings, Sir Ivor, The Law and the Constitution, London, 1959.

Jennings, Sir, Ivor, The Approach to self-Government, Cambridge, 1956.

Jennings, Sir Ivor, Constitutional Problems in Pakistan, Cambridge, 1957.

Kesy, E.A., and Richardson, S.S., The Native and Customary Courts of Nigeria, London: Sweet & Maxwell, 1966.

Keeton, C.W., An Introduction to Equity, London: Pitman, 1960.

Lauterpacht, H., International law and Human Rights, London: Stevens, 1950.

Lloyd, P.C. Yoruba Land Law, Oxford, 1962.

Lloyd, D., Public Policy, London, 1953.

Lloyd, D., Introduction to Jurisprudence, London: Stevens, 1965.

Markose, A.T., Judicial Control of Administrative Action in India, Madras, 1956.

Mayers, L., The American Legal System, New York, 1954.

Maitland, F.W., Constitutional History of England, Cambridge, 1926.

Mcwhinney, E., Judicial Review in the English Speaking World, Toronto, 1960.

Meek, C.K., Law and Authority in a Nigerian Tribe, Oxford, 1937.

Nwabueze, B.O., Machinery of Justice in Nigeria, London: Butterworths, 1963.

Obi, S.N.C., Igbo Law of Property, London: Butterworths, 1963.
Obi, S.N.C., Modern Family Law in Southern Nigeria, London: Sweet & Maxwell, 1966.
Odumosu, C.I., The Nigerian Constitution: History and Development, London: Sweet & Maxwell, 1963.
Oppenheim L., International Law, Vol. I., London: Stevens, 1950.
Oppenheim, L., International Law, Vol. II., London: Stevens, 1950.
Park, A.E.W. The Sources of Nigerian Law, London: Sweet & Maxwell, 1963.
Salmond, Sir J.W., Jurisprudence, London: Sweet & Maxwell, 1966.
Schofield, A.N., Parliamentary Elections, London: Shaw, 1955.
Schwartz, B, American Constitutional Law, Cambridge, 1955.
Schwarzenberger, G., A Manual of International Law, Part I., London: Stevens, 1960.
Schwarzenberger, G., International law as applied by International Courts and tribunals, London: Stevens, 1957.
Stephen, Sir James F., Digest of criminal Law, London; Sweet & Maxwell, 1947.
Stowell, E.C. International law, New York, 1931..
Todd, A., Parliamentary Government in England, Vol. II., London: Longmans, 1987.
Tresolini, R.J., American Constitutional Law, New York: Macmillan, 1959.
Wade, H.W.R., Administrative Law, Oxford, 1961.
Winfield, P.H., Torts, London: Sweet & Maxwell, 1963.
Wheare Joan, The Nigerian Legislative Council, London: Faber & Faber, 1949.
Wheare K.C., Federal Government, Oxford, 1953.
Wheare, K.C. Modern Constitutions, Oxford, 1951.
Webster Encyclopedic Dictionary of English Language 1977, Chicago, U.S.A.
Wynes, W.A., Legislative, Executive and Judicial Powers in Australia, Sydney: Law Book Co.., 1962.

Newspapers and Periodicals

Daily Times
Daily Express (Nigeria)
Daily Comet
West Africa
The Times (London)
The Guardian
The Evening News (London)

Articles and Notes

Aguda, T.A., 'Illiterates Protection Ordinance Examined', (1962) 4 Nigerian Bar Journal, 35.
Bishop, J.W, ' Declaratory Judgments', (1949) 62 Harvard Law Rev., 787.

Bullock, C. Ll. Angary', (1922-23) 3 B.Y.I.L. 99.
Cohen, M., 'Some considerations on the Origin of Habeas Corpus', (1938) 16 Can. Bar. Rev.
Davies, S.G., 'Some Recent Decisions on the (Nigeria) Constitution', (1962) 11 I.C. L.Q. 913,933.
'Defence of Necessity', (1921) 21 Columbia Law Rev. 71.
de smith, B.A., Fundamental Rights in the New Commonwealth', (1961) 10 I.C.L.Q. 83, 215.
Holland, D.C. 'Freedom of the Press in the new Commonwealth' (1956) Current Legal Problems 184.
Holland, D.C., 'Human Rights in Nigeria'. (1962) C.L.P. 145.
Holland, D.C. 'The Law of Courts Martial', (1950) 3 C.L.P. 173.
Holsworth, W.S. 'His Majesty's Judges (1932) 173 Law Times 33-377.
Jenks, E., ' The Story of Habeas Corpus'. (1902), 18 L.Q.R. 64.
Laskin, B., "An Inquiry into the Diefenbaker Bill of Rights', (1959) 37 Can. Bar Rev. 77.
Lauterpacht, H., 'Angary and Requisition of Neutral Property', (1950) 27 B.Y.I.L. 455.
Lauterpacht, H., 'The Universal Declaration of Human Rights', (1948) 25 B.Y.I.L. 354.
Lederman, W.R., 'Independence of the Judiciary', (1956) Can. Bar Rev. 169.
Marsh, N.S., 'The Rule of Law in a Free Society', International Congress of Jurists Report, New Delhi, 1959.
Papastathopoulos, Catherine D., ' Constitutionalism and Communalism, The case of Cyprus', 1965) 16 University of Toronto Law Journal 118.
Rewane, O.N., Contempt of Court in Nigerian Criminal Law. (1957) 3 J. A. L. 172
Singh, C., 'The Republican Constitution of Kenya', (1965) 14 I.C.L.Q. 878, 885.
Williams, G., 'The Defence of Necessity', (1953) C.L.P. 216.

Index

The Courts and Administration of Law in Nigeria

A

B

D

G

H

I

O

Q

R

S

T

U

V

W

www.ingramcontent.com/pod-product-compliance
Lightning Source LLC
Chambersburg PA
CBHW031319230926
51848CB00001B/15